Kinship, Business, and Politics

Latin American Monographs, No. 70
Institute of Latin American Studies
The University of Texas at Austin

KINSHIP, BUSINESS, AND POLITICS
The Martínez del Río Family in Mexico, 1824-1867

By David W. Walker

University of Texas Press, Austin

Library of Congress Cataloging in Publication Data

Walker, David W. (David Wayne), 1948-
  Kinship, business, and politics

  (Latin American monographs/ Institute of Latin American Studies, the University of Texas at Austin; no. 70)
  Bibliography: p.
  Includes index.
    1. Martínez del Río family. 2. Businessmen—Mexico—History. 3. Mexico—Commerce—History—19th century. 4. Industry and state— Mexico—History—19th century. 5. Mexico—Politics and government—1810-   . I. Title.
  II. Series: Latin American monographs (University of Texas at Austin. Institute of Latin American Studies); no. 70.
  HC135.W35   1986   330.972   85-22514

  ISBN 978-1-4773-0649-9

First Edition, 1986
Requests for permission to reproduce material from this work should be sent to:
  Permissions
  University of Texas Press
  P.O. Box 7819
  Austin, Texas 78713-7819
  www.utpress.utexas.edu/index.php/rp-form

First paperback printing, 2015

Contents

Tables

Figures

Money

During its first half century of independent life, Mexico used two money systems simultaneously—the Spanish colonial pesos and reales (1 peso = 8r.) and the official decimal-based pesos and centavos (1 peso =100 centavos). Mexican merchants like those studied here usually kept dual sets of accounts with separate cash boxes for each type of currency. Separate accounts and cash boxes were used for copper currency. Silver pesos (pesos fuertes), the standard currency unit, contained approximately 0.91 ounces of silver. Gold pesos of a similar weight also were minted, but these were used much less in commerce. The ratio of the value of silver to gold in Mexico, as in the rest of the world, was about 16:1. Unless otherwise specified in the text, pesos will refer to the silver currency and onzas to the gold currency. References will appear in the text for both the Mexican peso and the U.S. dollar. The character "$" is used for both types without distinction, as they were roughly equivalent in value (and even interchangeable in circulation) for all of the period of this study. Currency values also are reported in pounds sterling, "£," where appropriate. The ratio of value of the pound to the dollar and the peso remained nearly constant at 1:15. The character "f" is used to indicate the French franc. The ratio of value of the franc to the pound was roughly 25:1.

Orthography

The spelling of proper names used in the text has been standardized as much as possible. As no distinctions were made between the letters *b* and *v*; *i*, *y*, and *ll*; and *s and z*, readers will find some names spelled differently in other sources.

Weights and Measures

1 arroba = 25 pounds
1 caballería = approx. 105 acres
1 carga = 350 pounds = 50 mantas
1 manta = 1 piece of woven cotton cloth; 0.5 vara to 1 vara in width; 30 varas to 38 varas in length
1 quintal = 100 pounds = 4 arrobas
1 tercio = 175 pounds = 7 tercios = 25 mantas
1 vara = 36 inches = 0.8359 meters

1. Introduction

Prologue

In 1823 an aging, well-to-do Creole trader from Panama disembarked at the port of San Blas, Mexico. Business had been bad back home and here he expected to find new and safer investment opportunities while personally collecting the unpaid balance of commercial accounts opened a decade earlier with merchants situated in the nearby cities of Tepic and Guadalajara. Frustrated by the lack of progress in collecting his debts and uncertain about the climate for business in Mexico, the merchant left the country late in 1824, bound for London. But he soon returned to try to salvage what he could from his debts in Mexico. Later, his children joined him there. They brought with them their patrimony—a sizable fortune and a European upbringing—which they hoped to put to good use in their new home. That was the dream. This is their story . . . and Mexico's.

A Troubled Nation: Mexico, 1810-1867

History would record how much easier it was to lose than to make money in early national Mexico, but contemporaries shared great, even unrealistic, expectations about its future. Mexico had been the jewel of Bourbon Spain's American empire, and Mexican and European investors alike believed that once freed from imperial constraints its economy would flower. It was not to be, however. The first fifty years of independence brought not the hoped-for peace and prosperity, but bloody internal divisions and absolute economic prostration.

Significant political dissension was absent in New Spain until after Carlos IV and his son, Ferdinand VII, were obliged by Napoleon's invading armies to abdicate the Spanish throne to Joseph Bonaparte in 1808. The unprecedented collapse of the Bourbon monarchy created in the colony a political vacuum whose effects would be felt long into the nineteenth century.[1] In the absence of the king—the universally accepted source of political legitimacy—who ruled Mexico? Anticipating the variety of conflicts that would plague an independent Mexico, rival social and economic groups connived after 1808 to capture control of the colonial government to protect or advance their respective interests. *Peninsulares*, the privileged native-born Spaniards who occupied the most lucrative positions in the civil and ecclesiastical bureaucracies, insisted that Spanish authorities should govern Mexico in the king's absence. Creoles, being Mexican-born and excluded from sensitive positions in commerce as well as politics, endorsed the concept of home rule. Taking the initiative, Creoles led by Francisco Azcárate, a member of the Cabildo of Mexico City, pressured Viceroy José de Iturrigaray to recognize a Mexican junta. This new ruling body announced plans to give Creoles preference in government employment, to reduce the level of forced remittances to Spain, and to open Mexican ports to neutral shipping. Spanish merchants, anxious to preserve their trading monopoly, reacted to these threatening reforms by organizing a conspiracy of their own. Gabriel Yermo, an officer in the Consulado of Mexico City, ordered the merchants' guild's private militia to arrest Iturrigaray. Leaders of the Creole junta were imprisoned or exiled and a new viceroy loyal to peninsular interests was appointed.

Outnumbered in the capital, disaffected Creoles shifted their attention toward the provinces. The Bajío, a region with a well-developed agroindustrial complex that fed mining centers such as Guanajuato, was a fertile setting for Creole conspiracies, but a poorly organized and prematurely staged revolt begun there in September 1810 failed to win broad support from Creole landowners and militia officers. Instead, the Hidalgo revolt quickly assumed the character of a caste war, and the Creole elite in whose name Hidalgo had proclaimed the revolution repudiated the movement and helped royalists crush the rebels. A more subdued and consciously moderated campaign led by Morelos fared no better. Tactical errors notwithstanding, the aborted movements of Hidalgo and Morelos showed how little practical support existed for social and political change in early nineteenth-century Mexico.[2]

The same forces of reaction that foiled separation from Spain in 1810 afterward conspired to break with Spain. In January 1820 a military revolt in Spain obliged Ferdinand VII to restore the liberal Constitution of 1812. Reforms in the homeland seemed certain to jeopardize traditional institutions in the colony. Consequently, Colonel Agustín Iturbide's Plan de Iguala, a program for Mexican independence that reconciled the interests of Creoles and *peninsulares* while guaranteeing the survival of the old institutional order, won broad support. Independence came easily, bloodlessly, in 1821, but there was a long-term price. Independence enabled Creoles to supplant *peninsulares* in positions of prominence and so it eliminated one source of political friction, but more fundamental social and economic conflicts were left unresolved.

In the half century that followed, Mexico's citizens would expend their energies and resources in many frantic and often futile attempts to give the nation a discernible political form and substance.[3] Out of a myriad of warring camps there emerged two essential political tendencies associated with European ideals: liberalism and conservativism. Although their proponents enthusiastically adopted the rhetoric of European programs, these movements and the circumstances from which they derived were peculiarly Mexican.

Conservatives, those anxious to preserve the social and economic arrangements that had worked so admirably for some in New Spain for three hundred years, were initially the dominant force. Their social base lay in the political order and venerable institutions of the past. Liberals, a more compact group of reformers and ideologues, exploited the impracticality of conservative initiatives, for seemingly the old ways were unworkable in a new age. But, lacking a durable social base, the liberals were no more successful than conservatives in forming stable governments. They failed time after time to cultivate the broad political consensus required to implement fundamental institutional change. As both liberal and conservative governments forcibly seized power or forcibly fell from power, the political stalemate in Mexico intensified, becoming ever more prone to violence and destruction.

Iturbide's grandiose plan for an imperial Mexico, begun with much fanfare in 1822, succumbed to fiscal and political bankruptcy in 1823. The following year a coalition of groups with diverse political interests drafted a new constitution modeled after that of the United States and its system of federalism. In substance, however, the Constitution of 1824 was no mandate for change, only a tenuous and delicate political compromise—promising reform while pledging protection for traditional institutions like the church. With the help of foreign loans, the first president of the Republic of Mexico, Guadalupe Victoria, completed his elected term of office.

By 1828, however, both the national treasury and the liberal-conservative consensus were exhausted. After fending off a coup headed by Victoria's conservative vice-president, General Nicolás Bravo, liberals led by Lorenzo Zavala proceeded to stage their own coup in December 1828 to guarantee the election of a liberal presidential candidate, Vicente Guerrero. When liberal ministers in the new government proposed to sell previously nationalized church properties and to impose an income tax, Anastasio Bustamante, Guerrero's vice-president, revolted. Taking power in December 1829, Bustamante's government acted swiftly to reassure traditional interests. Guerrero's execution in 1831, however, provoked a liberal reaction and a popular uprising.

General Antonio López de Santa Anna, a military commander who had helped to overthrow Iturbide's regime in 1823, joined the revolt and contributed materially to Bustamante's overthrow in December 1832. Elected president in March 1833, Santa Anna soon retired and turned over the government to his liberal vice-president, Valentín Gómez Farías, who proposed an ambitious reform program: abolition of the compulsory tithe on agricultural produce, an end to civil enforcement of monastic vows, the sale of excess church properties, and the elimination of the *fueros* (the special legal privileges that exempted corporations such as the church and the army from the jurisdiction of Mexican courts).[4] Disturbed by the radicalism of his vice-president, Santa Anna defected to the conservatives, dissolved the liberal government and the Constitution of 1824, and created in 1835 a new centralist state governed by a conservative body of law, the Siete Partidas.

Following Santa Anna's military disgrace in Texas in 1836, Bustamante reemerged in the late 1830s as the leader of a moderately conservative government that held power until 1841, when a politically rehabilitated Santa Anna again revolted. Heading an intensely conservative government, Santa Anna retained power until 1844, when, no longer able to pay his troops, he was ousted in a barracks revolt by his own generals. In 1845 and 1846 successive military governments failed and, in the absence of any stabilizing political presence at the national level, liberals and conservatives joined forces to form a coalition government to organize Mexico's defense against the aggressive designs of its powerful neighbor to the North. Santa Anna and Gómez Farías were installed as president and vice-president, respectively, late in 1846. The coalition was short-lived. To raise funds to finance the war effort, Gómez Farías ordered the forced sale of church assets valued at $10 million. Responding to clerical denunciations of those policies, Santa Anna deposed his vice-president and annulled the confiscatory decrees in March 1847. Afterward, his campaigns against the North American armies turned into disastrous routs. The following year, as conservatives were generally discredited by the outcome of the war, liberals successfully formed a new government headed by General Mariano Arista. But this government was no more immune to fiscal and political bankruptcy than were its predecessors. A triumphant conservative revolt in 1853 reinstalled Santa Anna as the head of a government attempting once more to rejuvenate an increasingly moribund old order.

The liberal revolt of 1854, begun as an unpretentious and personal revolt by the caudillo Juan Alvarez, inaugurated an era of profound political change, La Reforma. Promulgation of the liberal Constitution of 1856 set off the most intense episodes of political violence experienced in all of nineteenth-century Mexico. After a conservative military coup in 1858 and a bloody civil war lasting until 1861, liberals emerged as victors only to face new reversals as conservatives invited France to invade Mexico and to install a puppet ruler. In the end, however, the Intervention failed and liberal reforms designed to revitalize the Mexican state and to overhaul the institutional structure of Mexican society were irreversible.

Instability: The Costs

In six years (1810-1816) the violent disorders of the Hidalgo and Morelos revolts caused about $900 million in damages. Much greater was the devastation wrought by the marathon of political violence that gripped Mexico from 1821 through 1867. In the endemic political feuds that too often degenerated into indecisive civil wars, all sides suffered heavy casualties. The burden of maintaining huge armies emptied government treasuries and consumed ever larger portions of Mexico's national income. As early as 1822, Iturbide's government was spending 80 percent of its revenues for military purposes. In a relatively tranquil year, 1825, almost $19 million (90 percent of the budget for Victoria's government) was spent on the army. By way of contrast, the combined expenditures of the colonial government in New Spain seldom amounted to more than $6 million annually. Whereas Spain had ruled its colony with only a handful of regular soldiers, Mexico's standing army in 1855 numbered in excess of ninety thousand.

Judging from the overall level of government expenditures, it is clear that the Mexican state's capacity to extract resources from society did not decline, but rather increased after 1821. Customs duties on imported goods made up approximately three-fourths of the government's ordinary revenues, which also included such diverse sources as head taxes, sales taxes, indirect taxes on real and personal property, and income from government monopolies and licenses. Although government income from these sources did increase, it could not keep pace with increased expenditures. Ordinary revenues annually produced up to $10 million, against government expenditures of more than $25 million. The balance came from irregular sources: confiscations, forced loans, and borrowing. After Mexico defaulted in 1827 on $32 million in loans contracted from Goldschmitt & Company and Barclay & Company in London, foreign banks declined the invitation of successive Mexican governments to provide new loans.

Even without the help of foreign banks, Mexico increased its public indebtedness rapidly in the first fifty years. Domestic providers of voluntary loans to the state ranged from reluctant institutional investors like the church to speculation-minded private moneylenders. As early as 1824 the public debt stood at $76 million (including pre-Independence government debts). With annual government deficits of $15 million commonplace in the 1840s, the domestic portion of the public debt reached $50 million by 1850. Interest charges on the unpaid London loans helped push the foreign portion of the public debt to more than $55 million by 1850. Following the Three Years' War and the French Intervention, Mexico's public debt zoomed to over $455 million.

Aside from economic costs, the endless political discord jeopardized the very existence of the nation. At best, political instability encouraged foreign powers to meddle in Mexican politics: to protect their nationals, to seek commercial or diplomatic advantage, or to press for payment of their share of the public debt. At worst, internal divisions rendered the nation powerless to defeat foreign aggression that threatened Mexico's sovereignty.

Spain fecklessly attempted the reconquest of Mexico in 1829. The worsening persecution of Spanish businessmen provided an excuse for intervention; the struggle for the presidential succession in 1828 accounted for the timing of the invasion.[5] Only grave tactical errors by the invading army saved the Mexicans from themselves. Three thousand Spanish soldiers made an unopposed landing at Tampico in July. Because the port routinely was evacuated in the summers due to the terrible heat, the threat of hurricanes, and the pestilential scourge of yellow fever, the Spanish presence in Tampico posed no threat to authorities in faraway Mexico City. After a short siege, the Spanish army surrendered to Mexican forces commanded by Santa Anna and was hospitalized.

In Texas Santa Anna was less fortunate. Anglo-American immigrants took advantage of the liberal reaction to Santa Anna's centralist coup in 1835 to launch a separatist revolt. Texas was lost to Mexico in April of the following year, when Santa Anna's army was routed in a surprise attack at San Jacinto. A dirty war of sorts continued until 1845, as the Republics of Mexico and Texas fought one another for control of disputed borderlands.

Taking note of Mexico's vulnerability, King Louis Phillipe's government assumed an aggressive posture toward Mexico in April 1838.[6] French emissaries demanded the immediate payment of $600,000 for damages allegedly suffered by its nationals during the political upheavals of the previous decade. When a naval blockade of Mexican ports failed to produce results after six months, French warships shelled Veracruz and landed marines to occupy the port in November 1838. Mexico responded with a declaration of war. (Since the French claims for indemnities included those of a French pastry chef for delectables unlawfully consumed by Mexican combatants in 1828, the affair was dubbed the Pastry War.) Meeting unexpected resistance in Veracruz, the landing party hastily retreated to its ships in early December. The victory (of sorts) soothed Mexico's injured national pride and made possible a quiet capitulation to French demands. With payment of the $600,000 indemnity assured, France tired of the adventure and withdrew its fleet. Having lost his leg to a French cannonball, Santa Anna, known thereafter as "the immortal three-fourths," was proclaimed a national hero by a public eager to forget the humiliation of San Jacinto.

When the United States brushed aside Mexican protests and annexed Texas in March 1845, war between the two nations was inevitable, especially after Mexico indignantly refused President Polk's offer to purchase New Mexico and California.[7] Internal political divisions made effective Mexican resistance to American aggression impossible. As tension reached the breaking point early in 1846, General Mariano Paredes was given command of an army to reinforce the vulnerable northern frontier. Marching instead on the National Palace, Paredes used his troops to overthrow the government headed by General Joaquín Herrera. As General Winfield Scott's forces landed in Veracruz in March 1847, heavy fighting broke out in the capital in reaction, not to the invasion, but to news that Santa Anna had ousted Gómez Farías. Encountering little organized resistance, a small American army with a long and exposed supply train moved virtually unopposed into the interior. Puebla and Mexico City fell easily. Hostilities ended with the forceful annexation by the United States of one-half of Mexico's national territory.

Although Great Britain and Mexico never warred with one another formally, this is not to say that their diplomatic relations were always cordial. From 1827, when Mexico first defaulted on the London loans, through 1867, when liberals returned triumphantly to power (and severed diplomatic relations), one crisis after another tested Anglo-Mexican relations. In the 1830s Great Britain required Mexico to set aside a progressively larger portion of customs duties to service the London debt. In the 1840s and 1850s British ministers like Richard Pakenham and Percy Doyle obliged Mexican presidents like Santa Anna, Arista, and Comonfort to fix additional quotas to repay other debts owed to British nationals. On several occasions between 1858 and 1860, British naval squadrons blockaded Veracruz to force Mexican governments to honor debts owed by British citizens. The confiscation (by a conservative government) in 1860 of $600,000 being held in the British Legation in Mexico City for the benefit of London debt bondholders and the announcement in 1861 (by a liberal government) of a unilateral two-year moratorium on payments on the foreign debt persuaded Great Britain to join France and Spain in a joint occupation of the port of Veracruz in December 1861.

Nominally, the occupation was intended to persuade Mexico to honor its international obligations. After receiving satisfactory assurances from the liberal government in Mexico City, Great Britain and Spain withdrew their forces from Veracruz early in 1862. France did not withdraw, but instead used its base in Veracruz to launch a campaign of conquest. Although a 6,500-man French army was beaten back at Puebla in May 1862, a reinforced French army of 30,000 occupied Mexico City in June 1863. An Austrian prince, Maximillian Hapsburg, arrived the following year to rule Mexico as its emperor. Nearly always victorious in the field, the French army captured most remaining liberal strongholds in 1865. Liberal forces led by Benito Juárez were pushed to the far northern frontier. Forceful diplomatic pressures from the United States, however, persuaded Napoleon II to abandon his colonization schemes for Mexico. Following the French withdrawal in 1866, Maximillian's Mexican army, which was commanded by conservative officers, began to disintegrate, and in June 1867 the emperor was captured and executed. By the narrowest of margins the republic had survived, but at a great cost.

To be sure, it was not only external threats that menaced Mexico before 1867. The Central American states of Guatemala, El Salvador, Honduras, and Nicaragua took advantage of the revolt against Iturbide to break with Mexico in 1823. The Yucatan, like Texas, had little affinity for governments situated in Central Mexico and often was a setting for separatist revolts. Fighting between rival Mexican political factions set off a bloody caste war, which pitted a small white population against a much larger Indian population. A Maya offensive in 1847-1848 almost forced an evacuation of the Creole and mestizo population from the region, and Mexico did not regain complete political control of the Yucatan until after 1900.[8]

The story was much the same in the North. The Yaquis recaptured the fertile Yaqui River valley in Sonora and preserved their homeland against white encroachment until the 1880s.[9] Elsewhere in the North, Apaches, Comanches, and other nomadic tribes raided ranches and towns in Chihuahua, Durango, Nuevo León, and Coahuila, depopulating whole regions. In Central Mexico, a wave of peasant revolts swept the area in the 1840s and 1850s, as villagers took advantage of the weakness of the central government to repossess forcefully lands or other communal resources lost (or presumed lost) to neighboring haciendas.[10] Elsewhere in the republic, regionally based caudillos recruited private armies to rule sizable personal territories.

Given such portents, many observers (both Mexican and foreign) came to expect that the republic was doomed to extinction. Certainly, in a territorial sense the nation was disintegrating. Central America and precious northern territories like California and Texas were lost to separatism or to foreign conquest. The process of decomposition culminated in the 1850s with new and unprecedented developments. To raise money for his government's empty treasury, Santa Anna sold national territory to the United States in the Gadsden Purchase of 1853. The collapse of his government the following year disrupted negotiations for the sale of the Yucatan to the Yankees and Sonora to the French.

The Economic Misadventure, 1821-1867

Stagnation, depression, and decline—these terms best describe Mexico's economic performance in the first fifty years of national life. Mining, the great motor of the colonial economy, was slow to recover from the disruptions caused by the Hidalgo revolt. Estate agriculture, dependent on prosperity in the mines and in the cities, remained consistently unprofitable. Many large estates were abandoned or broken up. Beset by formidable problems with transport, taxes, and markets, commerce was only slightly more lucrative than agriculture. With every sector of the economy blighted except local subsistence economies, Mexico's economic productivity fell sharply after 1821.

Most of the forty-five governments that ruled Mexico in the first fifty years after independence appreciated the severity of the economic crisis. Recognizing that without economic stability there could be no political stability, they made serious attempts to stimulate economic growth. To revive the mining sectors, these governments relied heavily on foreign private investment. British investors alone sank more than $25 million into several great mining enterprises. Other foreign investors put in twice that sum. Nearly all of these mining adventures ended ignominiously in bankruptcy.[11] To finance industrial development, successive Mexican governments encouraged domestic private investment. After 1830 financial subsidies and generous tariff protections enticed investors to begin construction of a modern textile industry.[12] By 1845 nine thousand workers labored in more than fifty mills, using modern machines to turn out cotton yarns and woven cloth for Mexican consumers. Even in a protected market, however, the Mexican products could not compete with cheaper foreign manufactures, and mill after mill went bankrupt before 1867. With most of the $15 million invested in the textile industry lost, this ambitious experiment in national economic development ended a wretched failure.

Table 1 lists estimates of Mexico's national income over the course of the nineteenth century. The nation began with an economy that was roughly half

Table 1
National Income, Mexico, Selected Years

Year	Per Capita Income (1950 U.S. Dollars)	Total Income (Millions of 1950 U.S. Dollars)
1800	73	438
1845	56	420
1860	49	392
1877	62	613
1895	91	1,146
1910	132	2,006

Source: John H. Coatsworth, "Obstacles to Economic Growth in Nineteenth-Century Mexico," AHR 83:1:80-100 (Feb. 1978).

as productive as that of the United States. After independence, the Mexican economy entered a prolonged period of decline. While the national income of its northern neighbor increased at an annual rate of about 1.3 percent, Mexico's income decreased at an annual rate of about minus 0.5 percent. Although it began a slow recovery after 1867, a historic opportunity for development had been lost. Even with growth rates that reached 2.3 percent annually in the 1890s, Mexico never succeeded in closing the gap that now separated it from the richer and more developed nations. The long-term result of its economic misadventure before 1867 was economic dependency lasting well into the twentieth century and perhaps beyond.[13]

The Problem

How to make money in a setting so inauspicious was the dilemma confronting the Panamanian merchant family that chose to do business in early national Mexico. Chapters 4, 5, and 6 reconstruct the structure of Mexican commerce and industry between 1824 and 1867 to emphasize the practical aspects of the many problems facing business in this era. By posing the following sets of questions, this study highlights the grander implications of microeconomic processes for national economic and political development. First, what was it like to do business in early national Mexico? Given the profundity of the economic failure, how was the behavior of Mexican entrepreneurs and other key economic actors *qualitatively* different from that of their counterparts in Western Europe and the United States? Did foreign participation in Mexican commerce and industry contribute to this failure? Second, what other economic, political, and social factors accounted for deteriorating levels of political stability and economic productivity? Why was the institutional modernization so problematic? Did Mexican social and political structures—what Marx would identify as a society's superstructure—influence and alter the meaning of capitalist innovations introduced into Mexico? That is, why, after substantial quantities of capital, technology, and patterns of business organization were imported to develop a modern industry in Mexico, was there no industrial revolution or economic takeoff of the sort that previously had transformed Europe and the United States? Or, stated more simply, what was the nature of the Mexican transition to capitalism in the nineteenth century and what were the results of those institutional changes for Mexico's social and economic organization?

The Historiography

The literature relating to the questions raised above is sparse and often deficient, empirically as well as theoretically. Why that should be so merits discussion. First of all, the early national period (1821-1867) remains absolutely the most unstudied period of Mexican history because relatively fewer source materials exist in comparison with the colonial (1519-1820), the Porfirian (1876-1910), or the revolutionary (1910-1940) eras. Second, the few general histories of this period focus narrowly on events in the political realm, show little understanding of the basic social and economic processes that were at work, and convey the impression that this was an era of meaningless political and economic chaos.[14] Researchers tended to look for and to find the roots of modern Mexico in the Revolution of 1910. Only recently have scholars come to appreciate that the most significant institutional changes in Mexico occurred after separation from Spain in 1821, but before Porfirio Díaz took office in 1876.

Early national Mexico's political misadventures have been casually explained as the consequence of cultural predispositions, political inexperience, or aberrant personalities. More sophisticated analyses suggest that these political conflicts were intellectual and ideological in nature, brought about by the intrusion of inappropriate European ideas. Others emphasize the environmental factors that encouraged internecine strife: the absence of a source of political legitimacy, a pronounced regionalism, sectorial conflict, and ethnic rivalry.[15] The most recent and, easily, the best work on politics in this period is Richard Sinkin's study of the Mexican Reform.[16] Sinkin argues, first, that the liberal reforms were a reaction to the political and economic breakdown that was virtually complete in Mexico by 1855 and, second, that the reforms were a conscious exercise in the modern state-building process, and as such readily comparable to the experiences of other nation states. Because his work concentrates on the purely political aspects of institutional change, it leaves unanswered important questions about the workings of society and economy in early national Mexico. What caused the breakdown? What was the relationship of economic processes to political change? What was the social base of the victorious Liberal party?

The new social and economic histories of Mexico have begun to answer these and other questions. Studies of Mexico's economic downturn in the nineteenth century center around three vaguely defined, separate, and contradictory schools of thought. These might be loosely labeled as theories of dependency and underdevelopment, entrepreneurship, and institutional structure. Popularized in the works of André Gunder Frank, dependency theory attempts to derive meaning from the past by studying the content and context of contemporary relations between developed nations and the Third World.[17] The accumulation of wealth in the developed nations is interpreted as a function of the unjust expropriation of the resources of the purposely underdeveloped nations, rather than as a function of the productivity of the industrialized economies. In Mexico, dependency theory can tap a rich historigraphic vein reaching back to nineteenth-century polemicists such as

Manuel Payno, the liberal politician, pamphleteer, and novelist who denounced the penetration of Mexican commerce by foreign capitalists.

The application of entrepreneurial theory to the analysis of Mexico's economic misfortune is, in contrast, relatively new because traditional scholars doubted for so long the existence of a spirit of enterprise in old Mexico.[18] As an interpretation of the Western European experience, entrepreneurial theory views economic productivity as a measure of the managerial performance of those in charge of a society's productive apparatus.[19] The model entrepreneur employs capital so as to recover the initial investment and to make an additional private profit. This accumulated wealth in turn may be reinvested. As the entrepreneur's income increases, so does that of society as a whole (as reflected in rising levels of national income). For private *and* public incomes to increase simultaneously, there must be a real savings achieved in the production and distribution of goods and services in a society. In this respect, entrepreneurial theory is consistent with the Marxist conception of the progressive role of the bourgeoisie, the class that introduces into society a new productive system that not only reorganizes economic activity, but also transforms the old social and political structures. This was the model transition to capitalism in Western Europe and the United States.[20] There the unprecedented material prosperity of the nineteenth century, reflected in the explosive expansion of industrial plant capacity and rising national incomes, vividly testified to the efficacy of entrepreneurial energies at work.

Theories of institutional structure share many assumptions common to theories of entrepreneurship, but structural theory is less concerned with the individual behavior of economic actors than with the larger institutional framework in which economic activity takes place.[21] Unlike dependency theorists, structuralists are more cognizant of the immediate (as opposed to the long-term) results a given institutional structure will have on economic activity. Implicitly, however, both structuralists and dependency theorists employ similar macromodels of change. They imagine that precapitalist societies are passive mediums that may be transformed through the worldwide diffusion of capitalism, except that, whereas structuralists stress the positive and productive elements of that transformation, dependency theories warn about the inculcation of an exploitative and degenerative process—underdevelopment. Barbara Tenenbaum's study of foreign merchants, the essays of Margarita Urías and her colleagues at the Instituto Nacional de Antropología e Historia (INAH) on the subject of entrepreneurship, and John Coatsworth's ambitious economic history of nineteenth-century Mexico illustrates the best (and worst) aspects of three contrasting interpretations of Mexico's economic performance in the last century.[22]

Theories of Dependency

In an intriguing analysis of the British presence in early national Mexico, Tenenbaum notes that Mexican governments in this period failed to detect substantive differences between the public and private aspects of the application of British foreign policy in Mexico. The beneficiaries of the confusion that surrounded British attitudes toward Mexico were unethical foreign merchants such as Ewen MacKintosh, who used their official positions as consular or diplomatic representatives for personal gain. A disciple of dependency theory, Tenenbaum goes on to indict the British for a multitude of presumed crimes against Mexico. She draws on a Black Legend that originated in the works of Payno and his liberal contemporaries to condemn foreign merchants as accessories to, if not the principal perpetrators of, Mexico's political and economic ruin in the nineteenth century. Their political crimes included a propensity to engage in illegal acts ranging from bribery of public officials to participation in the contraband trade. Their speculation in the public debt bankrupted the nation and caused political chaos. Unfairly using the influence of their home governments, they maliciously encouraged armed intervention or threats of intervention for personal profit.

The range of presumed economic misbehavior is even greater. Foreign merchants had better access to credit and more useful international commercial connections, and tended to form ethnically based trading networks from which Mexican merchants were excluded. They used these unfair nationality-based advantages to crush local competitors and to stifle Mexican commerce. Their preference for investing in extractive industries and public debt speculation rather than in productive enterprise distorted the development of the Mexican economy and crippled its growth. Foreign trade siphoned off Mexico's wealth. The nation became poorer as foreign countries doing business with Mexico grew richer. To preserve their commercial advantages, foreign merchants conspired with the governments of the developed nations to thwart Mexico's industrial development. Tenenbaum sums up the Black Legend by noting in the conclusion of her study of British merchants, "The British in Mexico . . . in the pursuit of riches for themselves, only made Mexico poorer and more powerless."[23]

The Black Legend paints a fascinating portrait of an economy and a polity destabilized by perfidious outside forces, but perhaps it raises as many questions as it answers. What accounts for a pattern of British behavior in Mexico presumably unlike that in Great Britain? Moral judgments aside, were the British and other foreign merchants misbehaving or were they responding rationally to the structure of the Mexican market where they did business?

Smuggling was common in early national Mexico. Up to 40 percent of the nation's foreign trade may have been in contraband. Many foreign merchants engaged in this illicit trade, but common sense suggests that the comparative advantages here lay with Mexican merchants, who were more familiar with local geography and markets and who were better acquainted with the local officials whose connivance was needed if such ventures were to succeed. In contrast, the experience of foreign merchants was based on a predictably structured market with stable institutions and universal standards of acceptable business practices. Although they often acted otherwise, foreign merchants probably preferred the more secure legal trade to the uncertainties of commerce in contraband. Foreign merchants did bribe Mexican officials, but so did Mexican merchants. If foreigners resorted to bribery more often, it suggests their political vulnerability and their lack of access to the decision-making process, not the contrary.

Likewise, foreign businessmen did use their nationality to protect their enterprises in Mexico. But what was the alternative in an anarchic marketplace sometimes without law and often without justice? What were other plausible recourses to illegal confiscations or outright robberies perpetrated by powerful local interests or a predatory military? How else might one resist tax assessments biased against those without political influence or protest blatant violations of the law and of other contractual instruments? Moreover, was foreign government protection (if it could be obtained) effective? How willing and able were foreign governments to protect the interests of their nationals in Mexico? If the deliberate confusion of foreign public and private spheres of influence was so useful a strategy, why did the careers of influential merchants such as MacKintosh end in bankruptcy and personal ruin?

Foreign merchants invested in mining and in the public debt in preference to other, less-profitable endeavors, but so did their Mexican counterparts.[24] In commerce, foreign merchants had more useful ties to overseas trading and manufacturing centers than did Mexican merchants, but often they were woefully ignorant of local market conditions. The provision of international credit seems to have depended less on the nationality of the borrower than on economic conditions prevailing at a given moment in Mexico or in Western Europe and the United States. For every businessman, the most difficult problem was not how to obtain credit, but how to repay it when profits were elusive in a depressed economy. Secure and profitable opportunities for investment were always in shorter supply than capital. With or without the protection of a foreign power, every merchant faced serious problems in commerce. Foreign intervention could do little to solve marketing bottlenecks. It could not increase the purchasing power of Mexican consumers or alter their consumption patterns. It could not lower transport and handling costs nor could it eliminate internal sales taxes or the need to offer bribes.

Contrary to the assumption of dependency theorists, nationality was not a determinant of attitudes favoring or opposing Mexican industrialization. Situated in the ports, import merchants (whether Mexican or foreign) wanted free trade and low tariffs. They opposed government protection for industry. Merchants in the interior with investments in manufacturing, irrespective of their nationalities, shared a common enthusiasm for protectionism. Whereas dependency theorists blame Mexico's industrial failure in the nineteenth century on legal and illegal importations of cheaper manufactures from industrialized nations such as Great Britain, it might be more useful to ask why Mexican industry was not more competitive. It had access to the same machine-based technologies that made Western European and North American textile manufacturers so formidable. Ample supplies of finance capital were available from both domestic and foreign investors in Mexico. Mexico was closer to sources of cheap industrial raw materials such as cotton than was England. Labor costs in Mexico were as low or lower than in the developed countries. Mexican industrialists enjoyed the protection of a sympathetic state that provided their enterprises with indirect subsidies and tariff protection.

Theories of Entrepreneurship

In the same way that recent studies of the rural sector have rehabilitated the image of hacienda managers (for example, showing that they were rational, calculating businesmen), the collection of essays published by the INAH investigators in 1978 has laid to rest the myth that Old Mexico lacked energetic and capable business leaders. Detailed profiles of economic luminaries such as Manuel Escandón, José Antonio Béistegui, and Gergorio Mier y Terán help to kindle an appreciation for the complexities of the Mexican business world between 1830 and 1880. Although they are an invaluable empirical addition to Mexican social and economic history, the essays do suffer serious theoretical deficiencies.[25] Because they fail to place economic activity in its proper social and political context, the essays leave the reader with the impression that these Mexican *empresarios* were model entrepreneurs of the sort described by Schumpeter and Marx, with the same implications for class formation and economic and political development in Mexico as in Western Europe and the United States. That Escandón and his contemporaries put together impressive business enterprises and made themselves extraordinarily wealthy is indisputable. The desire to make a profit from their businesses was the primary motivating factor in their personal economic behavior and they possessed the acumen to manipulate factors in the marketplace so as to maximize their advantages. Knowledgeable, well traveled, and worldly, their personalities differed little from those of their entrepreneurial counterparts in Western Europe and the United States. But, by themselves, the accumulation of private wealth and the emulation of a spirit of enterprise are not synonymous with the entrepreneurial process. That these *empresarios* were not model entrepreneurs is demonstrated by the very different performances of the economies in Mexico and the United States in the nineteenth century. Historically, the Mexican economy experienced record negative growth rates when these *empresarios* were most active.

Theories of Institutional Structure

Structuralism explains that for an economy to grow and to develop private gain must somehow accrue to the benefit of society as a whole. Coatsworth argues that the primary obstacle to economic growth in nineteenth-century Mexico was the lack of a political framework that not only gave the entrepreneur freedom to manipulate factors in the marketplace, but also guaranteed that society shared in profits. Instead, there survived in Mexico an institutional structure that stubbornly resisted modernization and systematically frustrated capitalist development. The country's economic backwardness was rooted in that dubious colonial legacy, a pattern of institutional organization characterized by an interventionist state and a highly politicized economy.[26]

Although structuralist theory does provide a model that explains economic and political behavior at a given moment in ways that are eminently more plausible than dependency or entrepreneurial theory, it cannot address other important issues. Questions such as why institutional change occurs in one society and yet is frustrated in another are not raised because structuralism's theoretical bias is toward unrelieved staticism. Structuralists can describe Mexico's inherited institutional framework, but they cannot specify precisely why it was so impervious to change. Coatsworth's econometric approach to nineteenth-century Mexico cannot measure the social content of the institutional structures he detects. The institutions that govern political and economic activity in a precapitalist setting are not simply an agglomeration of laws, decrees, statutes, or codes that are susceptible to quantifiable verification; rather, they are recurring patterns of human behavior that are infinitely more complex, based as they are on an unwritten, implicitly understood set of social relationships.

Theories of Kinship and Family

The new social history, especially that related to the family, has begun to decode the intricate structure of social behavior in historical Latin America.[27] In family history two broad tendencies have emerged. The first, and the more predominant, includes those works that aim to develop a general theory of family or, at a minimum, provide a new base of empirical data for such a theory. Methodologically, these tend to be quantitative studies of family ecological patterns: fertility and divorce rates, as well as age, marital, sexual, and occupational distributions across time and space. It is in the second category of family history that the present study can be placed. Here there is less interest in developing a theory of family. Instead, family is a conceptual tool to explore more general questions about Latin America's historical experience. The analysis of family is so fruitful because, universally, family remains across large chunks of time and space an essential and nondivisible unit of social organization. Depending on the overall structure of a given society, the family may or may not perform functions beyond the purely social, functions that extend into economic and political spheres.

Family has been in the past and is in the present (albeit to a lesser extent) a central institution governing economic and political behavior in Latin America. Beginning early in colonial times and continuing well into the nineteenth century, family constituted the core element within the larger sociopolitical institutional matrix that defined Spanish-American society. Family functioned to interface polity and economy with society. A social mechanism that helped to make up for institution shortcomings in the organization of the political and economic spheres in premodern Latin America, family may be universally defined as "a group of people who (a) bear a kinship arrangement, either consanguineal or fictive, to one another; (b) perceive that connection on the basis of a mutual and usually exclusive bond; and (c) deal with each other accordingly, engaging in the exchange of various goods (such as affection, esteem, emotional support, material items) as a result of that bond."[28] The essential corporation in a corporatively disposed society, family united otherwise disparate individuals in a common cause against an often hostile and unpredictable environment. Objective criteria such as class and nationality were not yet substantial enough to serve as durable bases around which economic and political behavior could be structured. Indeed, given the tumultuous disorders that followed in the wake of the disintegration of Spain's American empire after 1810, family was for a time the only source of institutional predictability and social stability.

Stephanie Blank's pioneering essay on colonial Spanish-American social organization demonstrates the relevance of kinship to the clientelistic system that integrated and structured political life in the Spanish colonies.[29] Blank concludes that biological and fictive kinship bound together the elite group, which controlled community resources and connected the elite with the rest of the population. In that capacity, family functioned to reinforce and rationalize the social system as a whole. Peter Marzahl reports a similar finding in his research on seventeenth-century Popayán in New Granada. He concludes that "sets of families, rather than institutions, served as the integrating clamps of this society."[30] There is no reason to believe that political independence in the nineteenth century altered the significance of family and kinship. Mary Felstiner's study of kinship in the independence movement shows how family politics left a lasting imprint on developing national institutions in Chile.[31]

In purely economic terms, family was just as important.[32] The works of Susan Socolow and John Kicza on merchants and urban elites in Buenos Aires and Mexico City during the late Bourbon period document the myriad ways in which family and kinship served to structure the economy of colonial Spanish America.[33] In Buenos Aires marriage was a crucial element in commercial success and kin were preferred business partners and agents. In Mexico City most businesses were family enterprises and marriage was a flexible social device that linked the great commercial families into powerful associations that dominated formal institutions like the Consulado.

The dynamism of family enterprise is captured gracefully in Charles Harris's study of the latifundia of the Sánchez Navarro family in Northeastern Mexico.[34] Harris demonstrates convincingly that estate owners in nineteenth-century Mexico displayed many of the traits ordinarily associated with the modern entrepreneur. He is less successful in placing family enterprise in an institutional context, as his primary unit of analysis is the unit of production—the hacienda—instead of the family. His study forms part of a very large body of literature that attempts the historical reconstruction of rural Mexico. These extensive investigations have shown, paradoxically, that this emphasis on the rural sector is misplaced if one is seeking a larger understanding of Mexican society. The hacienda was not a feudal institution of the type often associated with the manor lords of early modern Europe. On the contrary, it was, as Enrique Semo notes in his research on the origins of capitalism in Mexico, an enterprise oriented toward rational profit-taking and surrounded by a society that was not yet modern.[35]

In concentrating their energies on the hacienda, historians overlooked something less tangible, but far more consequential, than rural social relations, that is, the pattern of feudal economic and political organization imposed by the interventionist Spanish crown on its American colony and subsequently inherited by the society of republican Mexico. Coatsworth was the first to point out in a landmark essay that "the social base of Mexico's conservative movement was not determined by the nature of rural social relations but by the pattern of relations between a narrow stratum of the propertied elite—however their fortunes were made—and the central government."[36] It was in the urban centers, above all in Mexico City, where political power remained concentrated and where important political decisions continued to be made. There urban-based elites astutely employed their social and political resources to advance and defend their economic interests. Doris Ladd's study of the Mexican nobility reveals that merchants and miners in New Spain purchased titles of nobility in part because they facilitated access to the decision-making process within the royalist bureaucracy.[37] After independence, when political changes had destroyed their utility, these titles (and the costs of maintaining them) were relinquished eagerly. The political innovations and turnovers that occurred after 1821 took place first in the city. *Then* the effects of those changes were felt in the countryside. John Tutino's work on haciendas in the Chalco region near Mexico City shows how old fortunes were ruined in the independence era as the creation of a new Mexican state was accompanied by new patterns of landownership.[38] Elites in Chalco, who previously had monopolized land and economic opportunities in the region, were partially displaced by outsiders more attuned to the new centers of power.

How did traditionally privileged groups assimilate and accommodate potentially disruptive new elements without making concessions of a kind that might have led to wholesale changes in the social structure? Richard Lindley suggests that family and kinship helped to bridge such gaps in social organization.[39] His study of Guadalajara's elite in late Bourbon Mexico confirms that a social institution, marriage, was used for political and economic ends. It allowed the dominant class of Northwestern Mexico to pool its resources for mutual benefit and to ameliorate potentially explosive conflict between Creole landowners and peninsular merchants.

What happened when these resilient and vital family and kin structures were challenged by modernizing forces, as capitalism and industrialization began to sweep over Latin America in the nineteenth century? The prevalent vision in many studies of the historical evolution of the family has described change as a linear process. For example, in his study of an elite family in São Paulo, Levi Erville concludes that, as European ideas were disseminated and inculcated into successive generations, the Prado family reacted by striving to modernize Brazil.[40] In doing so, the family inadvertently eliminated its own traditional role in society. Seeking to develop a model to explain the historical impact of capitalism on family structures, Francesa Cancián, Peter Smith, and Louis Goodman propose a hypothesis that incorporates ideas implicit in much of the literature on family and modernization. They suggest that "the international economic system . . . is a major determinant of local kinship relations."[41]

But is it? Marx also observes that the relations of production (that is, the economic system) determined a society's superstructure (that is, the social and political systems), but he is describing the outcome of a historical experience specific to Western Europe. Did the Mexican transition to capitalism replicate that experience? Even in Marx's model, the economy, the polity, and society seldom march together in a perfectly orchestrated harmony. Rather, in a given moment they manifest discrete, even contradictory, presences. Such incongruities certainly must abound in those prolonged and ill-defined situations that result when capitalist society encounters the precapitalist. Although the predominance of capitalism may well be established in the long run, an immediate transition to capitalism through the process of diffusion is problematic and likely to be incomplete at the level of the superstructure. As anthropologist Raymond Smith argues, when two distinct social universes collide, the outcome is less transformational than dialectical: "Modern capitalism is extremely powerful and creates the special conditions outlined in dependent theory, but in turn it is acted upon by the societies and cultures which it encounters, so that the peoples of the underdeveloped world are not mere passive recipients; they are active agents in the historical process."[42]

The Methodology

To answer the questions and issues raised in the preceding discussion, the chapters that follow will document the problems of doing business in early national Mexico and analyze the implications of those problems for the nation's subsequent economic and political development. Substantively, these chapters draw on significant aspects of the historical experience of a single family in Mexico from the inauguration of the first federal republic in 1824 through the successful conclusion of the liberal struggle to overcome foreign intervention in 1867. What was for this family an interminable tragedy—a painful and costly lesson in political economy—is for the student of Mexican history a unique opportunity for understanding the complex nuances of everyday life in a largely unexplored era. A record of this family's extraordinary adventure is preserved in public and private documents. These yield an enormous quantity of empirical data that record the origins of economic nationalism, detail the structure of national and international commerce, explain the organization of an industry, and describe operations relating to public and private finance in early national Mexico.

What follows is a case study, but the reader should keep in mind that the subject investigated is not so much the family as it is the environment in which it moved. Here the family is conceptualized as a discrete social unit that owns certain quantities and qualities of resources useful for advancing its interests in society. This collection of resources constitutes a family portfolio composed of various social, political, and economic assets. Taken together, chapters 2 and 3 reconstruct and inventory one such family portfolio. By way of reference, social assets are those norms, values, and patterns of social interaction (including kinship and affective relationships) that define the family and structure its exogenous and endogenous comportment. Political assets are actual or potential inputs into the political system. Economic assets are the material possessions owned collectively or individually by family members. The meaning of these assets, their social significance, and the ways in which they may be employed are not determined by any absolute intrinsic qualities; rather, such properties are arbitrarily (or functionally) assigned by the superstructure of a given society.

This last point is particularly relevant to understanding the representativeness of the subjects of the case study that follows. The Panamanian merchant and his offspring—the Martínez del Río family—were strangers to Mexico. His children, reared in Europe, lacked the social assets (or the foresight to acquire such assets) needed to advance their interests in Mexico. That is not to say that the impressive social assets they owned were defective, only that they were out of place in early national Mexico. As a social corporation, this family was functionally disadvantaged in the Mexican environment. Its portfolio varied considerably from a hypothetical average portfolio owned by a Mexican elite family with extensive ties to other Mexican elites. Instead, the Martínez del Ríos shared many social similarities with the community of foreign merchants resident in Mexico and their economic and political behavior followed a common pattern.

As the Martínez del Ríos would learn, everyone—natives and immigrants alike—faced difficult problems in doing business in Mexico. Collectively, family members concentrated their resources in two companies organized as family enterprises. The first, begun as a partnership with a nonfamily associate, was moderately successful as an importer, wholesaler, and agent for European manufacturers until it was liquidated in 1837. A second company, founded purely as a family enterprise the following year, eventually became the repository for the bulk of the family fortune. Here the capital accumulated by the Panamanian merchant as silver coin and commercial credits during the reign of the last Bourbon kings in Spanish America was transformed into textile manufacturing facilities, mining shares, and government debt issues in early national Mexico. Although the family succeeded in increasing the speculative value of these investments several times over, the final product of its enterprise was bankruptcy. The factors that provoked this business failure were less economic than social and political in nature. The forces that victimized this family were the same ones that devastated (and created) a nation. The discussion that follows briefly describes the institutional context in which the Martínez del Río family was obliged to conduct its business and outlines plausible answers to the questions raised earlier about the larger implications of entrepreneurial activity for political change in early national Mexico.

The Model

The system of political organization imposed by Spain on its colony was a variant of the feudalism usually associated with early modern Europe. Political, social, and economic subordination to the Crown was mediated directly through the state and its bureaucratic appendages rather than through intermediaries such as a rural nobility. The state organized and administered society in New Spain with the assistance of various corporate interest groups: clergy, militia officers, mine owners, communal villagers, artisans, and merchants. The state or its surrogates—the colonial bureaucracy and the corporations—not the individual, took the initiative in the economy. The bureaucrats, the monopolies, the guilds, and the *fueros* left pitifully little institutional space for entrepreneurs to work their miracle. Public and private spheres of interest remained undefined. In this politicized economy, an interventionist state meddled continuously, usually for fiscal ends. Political decisions originating with favoritism, expediency, or even chance distorted the economy, suppressed market forces, and discouraged efficiency and innovation.

Independence did not change this basic organizational scheme. On the contrary, even the mediocre level of colonial productivity declined rapidly in the absence of a strong state to direct, coordinate, and structure economic activity. Because political fiat, not economic criteria, continued to be the principal determinant of profit and loss in nearly every sector of the economy, Mexico's *empresarios* fought among themselves and against other interests to use the resources of an increasingly inept state for personal advantage. In the ensuing political disorder, the ship of state foundered ever deeper and was less able to intervene positively to give needed direction to the economy.

In this same economic climate the *empresarios* sometimes accumulated impressive personal fortunes. In what commodities did they deal? As chapters 4 and 5 show, commerce was generally depressed and fell far short of producing profits commensurate with the risks of the trade. Capital tended to shift into other sectors of the economy that gave better returns. But what were these? One might invest in agriculture, but conditions there were desperate. Manufacturing appeared momentarily attractive, but failed to yield any sustained profits. Instead, as chapter 6 explains, industry required progressively larger cash supplements to keep its operations solvent and, in practical terms, it became a sinkhole for capital.

If commerce, agriculture, and industry were too uncertain for the prudent investor, the practice of lending moeny at high rates of interest, *agiotaje*, promised to be more secure. In theory, lenders sacrificed a share of potential profits, but escaped many of the risks of direct investments. But even in private finance there were structural limitations. How could borrowers consistently repay capital and high interest in an economy with a negative growth rate? Quite simply, they could not. More often than not, they went broke and, under ruinous terms, lenders acquired the valuable properties offered as collateral for loans. With a small supply of cash it was possible for a lender to amass a portfolio of properties with great speculative value. In the short term, however, these were unproductive and could not easily be liquidated with a profit. Without new cash supplements, because debtors regularly defaulted on their loans, the lender inevitably must fall victim to a liquidity crisis—a situation in which one's assets exceeded liabilities by a wide margin, but in which no cash was readily available to satisfy current obligations. To delay bankruptcy, the lender might be forced to become a borrower. A second lender subsequently would acquire the extensive collection of properties offered as collateral. With multiple repetitions and some variations of the cycle, this was the basic mechanism for the accumulation of wealth in early national Mexico, not the genuine income-producing activity of Schumpeter's model entrepreneurs.

But even here there was a paradox. By itself, private sector finance could not offer those with capital a secure and profitable opportunity for investment because *every* lender must at last empty the cash box as a finite supply of cash was converted into an ever-larger inventory of unprofitable properties. To escape this structural constraint on liquidity, lenders needed to replenish regularly their supply of silver coin, the standard medium for the repayment of debts in early national Mexico.

There were only two sources of abundant silver in Mexico: the mines and the state. Mining investments were well regarded. Good fortune in the silver districts might quickly fill empty cash boxes, but mining could not be a general solution to the dilemma that confronted investors. The industry was not immune to the general depression and, as chapters 2 and 5 suggest, overall investments in mining probably exceeded overall returns. For the *empresario* determined to do business in Mexico, that left only the public sector and, as investors discovered, it was often easier to extract silver from the state than from the ground. Although the state could not create new wealth, it might greatly affect the allocation of existing wealth.

Empresarios concentrated their public sector activities in two areas. irst, they directly tapped the state's resource base so as to transfer national properties and government resources into private hands. The primary instrument for this process was speculation in government debt issues. As chapter 7 documents, *agiotistas* appreciated that they might make more profits more securely by lending to the state in preference to the private sector. They also increased individual incomes by expropriating state revenues informally through tax fraud and evasion and by seeking those public offices that promised high salaries and optimum opportunities for corruption. A second method of exploiting the public sector was indirect. *Empresarios* turned the propensity of the state to intervene extensively in the economy to their personal advantage by employing coercive state power to create extensive artificial economies in which otherwise inefficient and unprofitable enterprises might flourish. These ranged from technologically primitive and traditionally organized *de jure* monopolies (like the tobacco companies, which operated under formal state patents) to well-managed and technologically advanced de facto monopolies (like the textile industry, which was sheltered by protectionist trade policies). Because conditions in the free market were chaotic, *empresarios* preferred to invest in a regulated market. There consumers might be more easily coerced to purchase goods at fixed prices. Politically loaded supply-and-demand schedules offered more predictability (and profitability) than the free market. Government supply contracts functioned much like the other economic artifices. They provided businessmen with politically structured markets for commodities ranging from armaments and provisions for the army to meat for the cities.

In summary, *empresarios* used the state as a gigantic engine of income redistribution. Those who could exercise control flourished; those who could not were devoured. Economic activity in the downwardly spiraling economy of early national Mexico was a zero-sum game. No new wealth was created. Rather, old wealth was redistributed and consumed. This interpretation of the microeconomies of the *empresario*, developed in detail in the chapters that follow, best reconciles the burst of entrepreneurial-like activities described in the INAH essys with the macrolevel economic data collated by Coatsworth. To make a fortune, the *empresario* did not rely on income generated from (absent) economic growth. Instead, what marked the successful businessman in early national Mexico was intimate access to the political decision-making process.

The economic disadvantages of an institutional structure that discouraged productivity, innovation, and efficiency and, instead, rewarded political prowess are readily apparent. Less obvious are the high political costs this politicized economy imposed on Mexico. The fierce struggles to manipulate the state for private gain promoted political instability on a grand scale. Every movement of Mexico's politicized economy set off divisive conflicts as contenders from all sectors of the economy battled one another for momentary control of the state. Under such pressures, it is understandable that governments in Mexico collapsed so often. Chapter 8 describes the political fallout from the struggle to corner public debt speculation, but equally serious conflicts divided the tobacco monopoly, the textile industry, and the armaments suppliers, to name only a few.[43] These rivalries fractured the tenuous unity of the dominant class in Mexico and helped to produce the political confrontations that ended in bloody civil wars.

The class split occurred along the lines of two alternative and mutually antagonistic strategies that *empresarios* used to achieve the decisive political influence needed for success in the economic arena. On the one hand, an *empresario* might apply energy and resources to shape domestic politics so as to secure a desired, politically mandated economic outcome.

On the other hand, another *empresario*, who lacked the will or the capacity to influence the decision-making process within Mexico, might rely instead on comparative advantages overseas. Well-placed lobbyists helped this *empresario* mold foreign policy in Great Britain, France, Spain, and the United States so as to apply outside pressure on the Mexican government for the same end. Chapter 8 explains how intense competition between *empresarios* who had invested heavily in the public debt finally degenerated into overt political violence. As the state's resources for servicing its debt were exhausted, creditors with domestic political clout fought creditors with foreign political influence in a zero-sum game for exclusive access to dwindling national revenues. This economic conflict fueled the more extensive political feud between liberals and conservatives that exploded into the savage Three Years' War in 1858. The same public-debt controversies provided a pretext for foreign intervention, which was to have such disastrous consequences in Mexico after 1861.

Given the institutional context in which business was carried out, the Mexican *empresario* could never be an authentic champion of economic liberalism and the laissez-faire state even though he was intimately associated with the physical accoutrements of modern capitalism—new technologies, new machines, new patterns of business organization, and the like. The push for institutional reform and an end to costly state intervention that blocked growth, was not forthcoming from the *empresario* because, however disadvantageous for the whole, individual fortunes were committed to the status quo. The emerging dominant class in Mexico could not perform the revolutionary role played by the bourgeoisie of Western Europe and the United States, who had used the power derived from their economic productivity to capture the state and to transform it irreversibly into an instrument to further their collective interests. Clearly, the idealized laissez-faire state that was their creation was never truly neutral. This system of political organization did imply, however, that the state should rule on an objective basis to advance the *general* interests of the bourgeoisie. It required the state not to act to suit the whims of a favored few, especially when naked bias might jeopardize economic growth or political stability. It forbade the state to subsidize inefficient and unproductive enterprises or to interfere with genuine entrepreneurial activity, the dynamic and creative force in a developing capitalist society. In stark contrast to this ideal model, the *empresarios* and the other groups that made up the emerging dominant class in Mexico ruthlessly manipulated the state for private gain, to the detriment of class interests, economic growth, and political stability.

To understand why self-interest among Mexico's entrepreneurial constituency discouraged institutional change, whereas self-interest in Europe and the United States stimulated change, one must consider not only the workings of the political economy, but also what might best be described as the social economy. The structure of this social economy is analyzed in chapter 3, and its influence is seen in many of the episodes chronicled in this book. The historical predominance of Mexico's social economy derived from a porous social structure's ability to absorb and to mediate divergent economic interests through social mechanisms like kinship and family. Although in a positive sense that social arrangement helped to dampen and defuse incipient political conflict (consider the ease with which Spain governed Mexico for three hundred years), it also discouraged economically productive social differentiation. There never occurred in Mexico a confrontation between traditional and modern sectors over the question of modernization, such as occurred in Europe between a landowning nobility and urban-based merchants and manufacturers. In Mexico, diffuse family enterprises blurred such distinctions. The *empresario* was at the same time a merchant, a miner, an hacendado, an *agiotista*, a politician, and an industrialist, or was related to someone who was. It took a long-term economic decline after independence to defeat those operative social devices. Only after recurring conservative failures to resurrect a political economy that had been functional in the past and only when there was no other alternative to the dissolution of the state and the extinction of Mexican society, did liberals become a relevant force able to implement institutional modernization.

2. Family Life, 1792-1860

The Beginnings

A merchant of Panama, Ventura Martínez, was the great-great-grandson of Juan Martínez Retes, a soldier who came to America in 1683 to command the garrison at Portobello. The hero of many Spanish military campaigns in Europe, Martínez Retes was disgraced when an English squadron captured Portobello, so he retired from the army and moved his family to the city of Panama on the Pacific Coast. In the next hundred years his children and his children's children worked as merchants and served as militia officers and priests in Panama. In 1792 Ventura Martínez married Ana del Río, the daughter of the treasurer of the Cathedral of Panama, Isidrio del Río. From the union of these two well-established Creole families was born the Martínez del Río family. Before her death from an accident in August 1811, Ana del Río gave birth to twelve children. Along with her husband, Ventura, six children survived her: José María, Manuel María, Gregorio José, María Dolores, Ventura de la Cruz, and José Pablo. All were minors in 1811. The youngest, José Pablo, was two years old. Two of Ana's sons and her only daughter would live to old age in Mexico and play leading roles in the drama unfolding there.[1]

Ventura Martínez

The fortune the family brought to Mexico was not old; it was wealth that Ventura Martínez had accumulated in Panama before 1823. Martínez began his career in commerce as a man of relatively modest means; his net worth before his marriage in 1792 was only about $30,000 and his bride's dowry was less than $2,000. Two decades later, his properties were valued at $429,750, a fourteenfold increase in net worth (equivalent to a simple growth rate of about 70 percent annually).[2] How did he make that fortune? Table 2 provides important clues. Real property was insignificant, only 6.4 percent of the total, so speculation in land or buildings played no role in his

Table 2
Property Belonging to Ventura Martínez, 20 October 1812

Assets	Value (Pesos)
Venture with Lino Barrera: Panama-Lima	28,321.0r.
Wax venture with Castro: Trinidad-Portobello-Lima	22,730.3r.
Sale of iron and mules with Lucas Estevan	364.0r.
Seven notes for debts, $33,533.5r.2g. - $5,089	127,247.2r.
Various accounts and debts	18,740.3r.
Houses, furnishings, etc.	27,652.1r.
Orders for payments, drafts, gold, silver	204,695.0r.
Total	429,750.1r.

Source: AN-531-1835:70-85ff, 13 May 1835.

economic success. A relatively small proportion (11.9 percent) of his wealth was invested in direct trading.

More prominent were loans to private persons, 34.0 percent of the total. On the one hand, the presence of many assets in the form of loans may have reflected the implementation of a common strategy for guarding the next generation's inheritance and preserving the future well-being of the family. After 1812 half of his property did belong to his children in their category as heirs to his wife's estate. In such cases, capital ordinarily was withdrawn from direct (and risky) investments in commerce and converted into loans secured by mortgages on real property. On the other hand, the existence of an excessively large supply of cash in the form of negotiable orders for payment (both public and private), silver bars, and silver and gold coins— 47.6 percent of all the property listed—tends to confirm the impression that Martínez worked primarily as a *prestamista* and not as a *comerciante*. The latter—a merchant—would have had most of his capital invested in trading goods; the former—a moneylender—owned an inventory that consisted of an ample supply of silver and the muscle needed to collect debts.

The 1812 inventory shows that as a trader Ventura Martínez was oriented mostly toward Peru and that many of the ventures he participated in were intercolonial (that is, wax from Trinidad shipped to Lima) rather than international (that is, dry goods shipped from Spain to Panama). After 1814 his interest in intercolonial trade shifted away from Peru as the flow of silver from Lima to Panama was interrupted by revolutionary violence in the viceroyalties of New Granada, Peru, and La Plata. Although the Hidalgo and Morelos revolts inflicted severe damage on the Mexican economy as a whole, the consequences for the Panama-Mexico trade were quite different. The disruption of communications between Western Mexico (where silver was mined in great quantities) and Gulf ports like Veracruz (where large shipments of silver were loaded on ships bound for Europe) temporarily altered traditional trading patterns. Silver now moved through Pacific ports like San Blas for reshipment through Panama, the shortest route to Europe. With rebels to fight, colonial authorities had little time to police commerce in remote Western Mexico. A semi-illicit international trade, originating in the factories and warehouses of Great Britain, wormed its way through Jamaica, Panama, San Blas, Tepic, and Guadalajara before finally tapping the wealth of rich silver mining towns like Zacatecas.

Well acquainted with the British, Panamanian, Spanish, and Creole merchants situated in Western Mexico, Ventura Martínez financed the purchase of trading goods bound for Mexico and served as an agent for merchants who needed to move goods through the Isthmus. As Martínez's accounts were credited for the costs of those services, for commissions, and for interest on capital lent, his clients often accumulated sizable debts. By 1820 a British merchant resident in Guadalajara, Daniel O'Ryan, owed $26,819 to the Panamanian agent. Two Spanish merchants situated in the same city, Pedro Juan de Olasgarre and José Prieto, owed nearly $100,000 on their accounts.[3]

The strangulation of the Peru trade and other commercial dislocations, spreading political disorder, and a general climate of uncertainty associated with imminent dissolution of the Spanish-American empire all were felt in Panama as a rash of bankruptcies ravaged the merchant community. Martínez's base in Panama became risky and unprofitable. Adjusting to the new conditions, he removed his children in 1819 to the safety of Jamaica and began to liquidate his holdings in Panama and to collect the large sums owed to him in Peru and Mexico. Recovery of those debts was complicated by the collapse of traditional trading patterns in 1821, as Spain evacuated its last strongholds in Mexico and Peru and as new governments throughout Spanish America opened their ports to a flood of foreign manufactures. The sale of the more expensive inventory acquired prior to independence became impossible without unacceptable losses. In the ensuing confusion, Martínez's trading partners, large and small, were ruined.

It was in these circumstances that Martínez quit Panama permanently in 1823, hired agents in Lima to work on the overdue accounts in Peru, and set out for Mexico to reach a personal understanding with his clients in Guadalajara. To ensure that Olasgarre and Prieto would repay their account in full, Martínez required them to register an *escritura* of debt before a public notary in November 1823. This instrument stipulated that the principal owed was $106,581, that the annual rate of interest was 5 percent, that substantial penalties might be imposed for tardy payments, and that Olasgarre's rural estate, the Hacienda de Atequisa, was mortgaged to Martínez as collateral for the debt. In his dealings with O'Ryan, who had moved his business to Mexico City, Martínez managed to win only the promise of a partial payment.

Leaving matters in Mexico in the hands of his agents, José María Landa and Manuel Moreno de Tejada, Martínez traveled to London in 1825 to visit his children, who had gone on to Europe to continue their education. While visiting London, Martínez laid his grievances against O'Ryan before an English court, which awarded him only a fraction of the sum allegedly owed. Embittered by English justice, he returned to Mexico in 1827 to try his luck in the courts there. While awaiting settlement of his suits, Martínez was determined to put his idle capital to work. Aside from the substantial sums tied up in old debts ($175,000), assigned to his children's inheritance ($122,445), or managed by his sons ($165,677), Martínez had $40,000 to $50,000 free to invest in Mexico. As in Panama, here he invested primarily in private loans earning lucrative interest rates (1 to 2 percent monthly). Wisely, the large sums tied up in old debts and the smaller amounts placed in risky ventures in Mexico were balanced with substantial, relatively secure investments in Europe and the United States. His estimated assets and liabilities for 1832 are listed in table 3. Doing business as a moneylender in Mexico City and in Guadalajara, Martínez was only moderately successful until he formed a partnership in 1829 with a young and ambitious German businessman, Guillermo de Drusina. Together with Martínez's sons, they founded the Mexico City commercial house, Guillermo de Drusina & Gregorio Martínez, which flourished from 1830 until 1837.

Martínez's last years in Mexico were bitter and swollen with mounting personal frustrations—business reverses, family quarrels, a failed marriage, endless litigation—set against the backdrop of a rapidly changing world in which merchant adventurers like him were becoming irrelevant. Now an old man, he could not replicate in Mexico the pattern of business dealings that had made him fabulously wealthy in Panama. He lacked here the intimate knowledge of local affairs a moneylender needed to screen potential borrowers and he missed the clout needed to force repayment or to seize collateral on overdue or defaulted loans. If he chose to work in commerce, the local marketplace also was an alien environment. And in these last years, he was simply unlucky. Investments of $3,000 and $30,990 in Mexico City and London commercial houses were lost in bankruptcies. When the ship *Thetis* sank with a cargo of his trading goods, $10,000 was wasted. Contemplating a return home, Martínez attempted covertly in 1829 to influence business and politics in Panama, but he was forced afterward to regret "the copious losses suffered . . . with a certain ministerial person."[4]

His problems in the courtrooms of Mexico suggest the obstacles that faced investors willing to do business in the new country. As the variety of outcomes that resulted from Martínez's prosecutions of debtors showed, institutional predictability was absent in the legal arena. In a notable case begun in 1828, Martínez sued a former trading associate, the Englishman William Dollar.[5] After several enterprises financed with assistance from

Table 3

Estimated and Reported Assets and Liabilities, Martinez del Río Family, 1832
(Current Pesos)

Category	Ventura	Manuel	Ventura de la Cruz	Pedro A. & Dolores	Gregorio José	José Pablo	Total
Assets							
Old debts	175,000	—	—	—	—	—	175,000
Capital accounts/shares in family businesses	—	—	23,687	—	23,687	23,687	71,061
Other accounts/deposits in family businesses	24,545	—	—	—	—	—	24,545
Intrafamily accounts and loans	199,697	19,173	1,625	100,291	2,800	1,624	325,210
Accounts/stocks/shares/interests in nonfamily businesses	40,000	—	—	3,055	46,671	—	89,726
Stocks/bonds/debt issues/other government paper	—	—	13,200	7,050	103,422	13,200	136,872
Real property	3,000	—	—	18,000	—	—	21,000
Personal property	6,652	500	1,000	4,132	1,000	1,000	14,284
Total gross assets	448,894	19,673	39,512	132,528	177,580	39,511	857,699
Liabilities							
Family	122,445	21,175	10,000	20,913	135,677	15,000	325,210
Nonfamily	30,990	—	—	—	—	—	30,990
Estimated net worth	295,459	3,498	29,512	117,528	41,903	24,511	501,499

Source: CMRFH.

Martínez had failed in Panama in 1822, Dollar fled to Mexico, where he unwisely invested in several mining companies. When Martínez found him, Dollar was living in extreme poverty in a ramshackle house in the capital. In asking Mexican courts for their assistance in collecting $9,425 owed by Dollar, Martínez insisted that his debtor had enormous sums hidden. Martínez prefaced his arguments with a strong appeal to xenophobia: "But are the judges of the republic going to permit this foreigner to keep the fruits of his malignity?"[6] A sympathetic court ordered the embargo of Dollar's property pending a final judgment on the merits of the case. When the embargo failed to produce the desired results, namely, a concession from Dollar, Martínez went back to court to demand Dollar's imprisonment to guarantee payment of the debt. Martínez also requested that an English artisan, the carriage maker George Winterton, be incarcerated as an accomplice, as he had not cooperated in the embargo against Dollar. Although not a Mexican citizen, Martínez reminded the court that he was a fellow Spanish-American being oppressed by Europeans: "The insults that accompanied these infamous schemes, illustrate the degrading concept that these foreigners have of Our Laws, of Our Justice, and of Our Respective Rights . . . the unhappy fate of the Americans, that some impudent Foreigners should be the one to unleash the bitterness against their families; mine cries out eternally for the disgrace he worked."[7] After a week in jail, Dollar agreed to submit the matter to arbitration in exchange for his freedom. To stay out of jail, he surrendered assets (uncollected debts and mining shares) valued at $11,000.[8]

Martínez's unqualified success in squeezing a settlement from his former partner represented an extreme example of the possible outcomes from recourse to the judicial system in early national Mexico. A noncitizen used punitive court action against another noncitizen to collect a debt incurred years before in transactions unrelated to Mexican commerce. The outcome of Martínez's litigation with O'Ryan, who had reestablished himself as a prominent merchant in Mexico City, and with Olasgarre, whose family in Jalisco had powerful friends, was quite different. Although Olasgarre defaulted on the debt owed to Martínez, Martínez was never able to use the mortgage to gain possession of the Hacienda de Atequisa. After years of litigation, the debt still exceeded $100,000, with no prospects for repayment. Similarly, in the courtrooms of Mexico City Martínez failed to beat O'Ryan. After six years as a defendant, O'Ryan turned the tables on his persecutor and countersued Martínez in 1834 for defamation of character. In another instance, Martínez's four-year effort to collect $3,000 from E. J. Grothe, the consul of Holland, ended in a meaningless victory.[9] The embargo came too late, Grothe had left the country, and the value of the possessions that remained to be seized by his creditor was far less than the amount of Martínez's claim. In Mexico City, Guadalajara, Aguas

Calientes, and elsewhere in the republic, Martínez's attorneys directed a seemingly endless series of legal actions without producing conclusive results.[10] Martínez's experiences were not unique. Property rights remained so ill-defined in early national Mexico that many lenders found it expensive, time-consuming, or even impossible to use the mortgages offered as collateral.

After ten unhappy years of residence, Martínez decided to emigrate and escape the vexations and risks of doing business in Mexico. Hopeful of retiring comfortably in Burdeos (as was the custom of many of his colleagues in commerce), he wrote his son José Pablo in the spring of 1835, instructing him to purchase public debt bonds in Europe. In October 1835 his son warned that the outlook overseas was bleak: "There is no way to invest for now, because the funds are at an exorbitant price; neither can one do anything in land, houses, or similar estates; consequently, it seems best to me to wait until some political happening makes the funds fall, leaving the matter until then as it is. The present state of Europe may very well yield the opportunity we want at any time."[11]

Martínez died in Mexico City the following March before the anticipated opportunity in Europe presented itself. To avoid the rapacious attention of the Mexican government, his executors did not make a formal division of his estate and did not prepare and register an inventory of his possessions, as was customary. Two decades later, the surviving heirs submitted a statement that alleged, "An inventory was unnecessary because all the heirs knew perfectly well what his fortune consisted of and how much it was worth . . . they proposed among themselves to divide it fraternally without any formality."[12]

José María

Ventura Martínez's eldest son did not follow his father to Mexico. Trained at his father's side with a practical education in commerce, José María took over what was left of the family's Panama-Peru trade after 1823. Confronted with the reality of a changing international political economy that made the traditional trade route through the Isthmus increasingly irrelevant, José María's Panama-based operations produced staggering losses. Undaunted, he continued after 1825 to ply his trade as a merchant-adventurer based in Kingston. In an unending quest for always elusive profits, he roamed the Caribbean and ranged into the Pacific until 1828, when he was lost at sea in a small boat while making a routine search for a harbor along a remote, fog-shrouded Colombian coast.[13]

Manuel María

Showing little interest in the family business, Manuel María settled in Paris in the early 1820s. Considered dissolute by his more industrious kin,

Manuel María supported himself with allowances from his father and by constant borrowings against his maternal inheritance of $19,000. His sporadic attempts to establish himself as an independent businessman ended disastrously. In an 1833 misadventure, his scheme to trade French perfumes for Cuban cigars ran afoul of customs police in Paris, and the embarrassed entrepreneur was obliged to flee from angry creditors and seek sanctuary in Brussels. In another instance, his younger brother José Pablo lent him f2,500 to finance the shipment of a cargo of cloth to Mexico. Instead of returning a share of the proceeds, Manuel María pocketed all of the receipts and left his brother to pay the bills he had incurred. Scandalized by his son's behavior and fearful that the family's good name in commerce would be besmirched, Ventura Martínez cut off Manuel María's allowance and held up his maternal inheritance. To preserve the family's reputation, José Pablo contacted his brother's creditors and began paying off his debts. When Manuel María was threatened with deportation from Belgium in 1833, José Pablo arranged a solution to his passport problems through a friend in the Belgian legation in Paris. More serious was a complaint brotherly love could not overcome: Manuel María's health began to decline precipitously and irrevocably after 1834.[14]

In the face of such unhappy results, Manuel María attempted to reform his life. He began to study pharmacy, and a portion of his allowance was returned.[15] Two years later, on the eve of his father's death, Manuel María was assigned a portion of the Olasgarre debt as his share of the maternal inheritance. As this was useless to him in Paris, he afterward exchanged it for French public debt bonds owned by his brothers. Interest from those bonds and a modest share of his father's estate (invested somewhat involuntarily in the family's enterprises in Mexico and the United States), provided him with a secure, if limited, income. In 1843 his brothers owed him $18,366, a curious reversal of past relationships. Always refusing to move to Mexico, Manuel María instead married a French woman and began to rear his own family in Paris. When José Pablo inspected Manuel María's children during a visit in 1841, he pronounced them "all very cute and interesting" and boasted that the oldest boy (named after himself) showed promise of great talent.[16] Succumbing after a lengthy illness, Manuel María died in Montpellier, France, in 1844.

Ventura de la Cruz

Like Manuel María, Ventura de la Cruz went to Europe and, opting for a nontraditional profession, he began a course of studies in pharmacy. Unlike his brother, Ventura de la Cruz was a serious and well-behaved son who dutifully answered his father's call to come to Mexico in 1831. Nevertheless, his life was plagued with the same tragic irony that haunted

José María and Manuel María. Like them, Ventura de la Cruz was destined to play only a minor role in the drama unfolding in Mexico. Subordinated first to his father and, afterward, to his brothers, he was denied a management position in the family's commercial house, Martínez del Río Hermanos, which was founded in 1838. That rebuff, a growing dislike for Mexico, and health problems encouraged him to seek solace in Europe; to become, in his brothers' words, "a sleeping partner." Ventura de la Cruz's arrival in Paris in August 1844 marked the beginning of a self-imposed exile in Europe.[17]

When at last invited back to Mexico in 1851 to help manage the family business, Ventura de la Cruz left England ahead of his brother Gregorio José and his nephew José Ansoátegui y Martínez del Río, who remained behind to visit their friends in London and Paris during the December holiday season. Alone, he boarded the Royal Mail steam packet *Amazon* outbound from Southampton, England. On 2 January 1852 the steamer caught fire and went down in the Bay of Biscay. Two days later Ventura de la Cruz was reported among the casualties.[18]

María Dolores and Pedro

Left behind in Jamaica when her brothers went abroad, María Dolores married Pedro Ansoátegui, the offspring of another displaced Panamanian merchant family that had taken refuge in the British Caribbean. Although Pedro was a man of modest means, his family having been ruined in the revolutionary decade, María Dolores was an heiress. Favored by her mother, who awarded her *el tercio y el quinto* in her will, María Dolores inherited one-third ($71,900) and one-fifth ($28,670) of the maternal estate *and* one-sixth ($19,173) of the remaining balance of the estate, which was shared with her five brothers.[19] Consequently, her total assignment was $119,833 compared with just $19,173 for each of her brothers.

After an unhappy residence in Europe from 1828 until 1830, María Dolores and Pedro joined Ventura Martínez in Mexico. They established a home in Mexico City in 1831, and María Dolores gave birth to three children who lived to adulthood: José in 1832; and Ana and Dolores, twin daughters in 1837. Soon after Pedro's arrival in Mexico, he learned that his father-in-law had arranged a partnership for him in a dry goods business in Guadalajara. Pedro refused the opportunity to begin a career in the retail trade: "I frankly make it clear that I do not like this business."[20] He used elaborate calculations to demonstrate the disadvantages of becoming a storekeeper. In this case he supposed that if the store's volume of sales averaged $400 daily, that would produce a gross income of $112,000 over 280 working days per year, equivalent to an annual gross profit of $25,000. To purchase his share of the store's inventory, Pedro would have to put up $40,000. The minimum cost of the use of his own or someone else's money was 6 percent per year ($2,400). Other overhead costs such as rent for the store and salaries for the clerks would amount to at least $6,000 per year, reducing the net profit to $16,600 annually. If that amount were divided with a partner, Pedro would have as his share an income of only $8,300 per year, which he insisted was barely sufficient to allow his family to live with "decency and economy." Nor was there any assurance that the business would be able to maintain the volume of sales necessary for even that paltry profit. Worst of all, Pedro was concerned that if he invested in this store he would have no capital left over to increase his own fortune in the future.

Determined to give guidance to his son-in-law (and to maintain control over his daughter's inheritance), Ventura Martínez proposed in the following year (1832) that Pedro begin speculating in silver or that he invest in a rural estate. In reply to the former, María Dolores's husband conceded, "I consider that very good," but added that it was not right for him, as he would have to leave his wife and family for long intervals to do business in the mining districts.[21] Initially, he was more enthusiastic about a second suggestion—that he invest in the Hacienda de Atequisa, which Martínez still hoped to acquire from the Olasgarre family in Guadalajara. Pedro calculated that one might clear $3,900 and $1,500 per year, respectively, on a modest investment of $2,500 in cattle raising and wheat cultivation. He was especially impressed with the history of the estate:

The Hacienda was developed by Basanry [sic; a wealthy Spanish merchant]; with the revenue from it he made a large house, the Chapel, the bull ring; he purchased the hacienda of Miraflores and I do not remember which other; also he built a house or houses in Guadalajara and kept his family, which was numerous, with the greatest luxury known there. After his death, his children turned their attentions to merriment and instead of caring for it, they destroyed it to the condition in which Olasgarre received it, who because of his foolishness threw much money into it, but without producing the profit it should have made.[22]

When Pedro learned that his father-in-law wished to invest all of María Dolores's dowry in the hacienda and not merely $4,000, which he had free to put into the venture, he refused the plan and suggested that Martínez deliver to him the $100,000 intended for Atequisa:

With this sum in my hands, I am convinced that by going into the streets here [Mexico City], I would earn much more than that indicated in my calculations for Atequisa . . . this way is the most advantageous means to situate myself with security and profit. . . . Here there is more capital than business [opportunity], even so, today the following are available with some regularity: la usura [loans with high interest rates], orders on tobacco with 2-1/2% to 3% discount monthly, some government drafts with good interest, consumer goods in the city (sacrifices by the exigencies of some), and purchases of [silver] bars with some discount; that is, even though here there is not the vast field for a thousand operations as in Europe, nevertheless there are various for those with energy and cash so that one can secure a good interest on his money without the risks that are present there.[23]

Speculation in loans and other kinds of paper in preference to the ownership of real property characterized Pedro's investment strategy over the next three decades (his assets and liabilities in 1832 are listed in table 3). However much Pedro and Ventura Martínez disagreed about how María Dolores's inheritance should be spent, both businessmen were intrigued with speculations in finance and placed much of their available capital in loans. Whereas Martínez's cash went to men of high stature like José Francisco Fagoaga, a Mexico City *empresario* from a noble family, Pedro's more modest resources were destined for less prominent persons. In May 1833 he lent $6,000 to Baltazar Rizo and María de los Angeles Zapata of Veracruz. The *escritura* for the loan noted that the borrowers were in company together and needed funds to finance their businesses. The stipulated rate of interest was 6 percent on the principal for an eight-month term ending January 1834, when Rizo and Zapata were to repay Pedro with $6,240. As was a common practice, the borrowers waived the provisions of the Ordenanzas de Bilbao, which specified that all money received from lenders should be counted in the presence of witnesses. In such circumstances, the actual amount of money received from the lender was less than the nominal amount of the loan, allowing lenders to boost interest rates while avoiding overt conflicts with laws against usury. Lenders stayed within the prescribed boundaries of legitimate business practices sanctioned in the traditional commercial codes and provided themselves with the security of legally recognized instruments such as the *escrituras*, which recorded and registered the transactions. As collateral for this loan, Pedro received mortgages on several properties: an aguardiente factory in Jalapa valued at $8,106, a wine shop in Mexico City valued at $3,941, and a store in Veracruz of undeclared value.[24]

Pedro chose not to invest in Drusina & Martínez, the Mexico City commercial house partly owned by his brother-in-law, but later he did join his wife's family in founding a much larger firm, Martínez del Río Hermanos. His share in the company, $100,000 (later increased to $150,000), consisted primarily of his wife's dowry and other inheritances. His personal worth continued to be modest compared to that of his wife's family, perhaps $12,000 in 1832 and $20,000 in 1838. Although he managed to increase his personal fortune to almost $90,000 by 1857, his personal finances remained tightly linked with the family firm—his only regular source of income was a $7,000 annual allowance from the company and a share of its profits, if any.

His partners' frequent absences from the country, and Pedro's own disposition to travel as little as possible, gave him a leading role in establishing investment policies for the firm, if only by default. He left Mexico only twice. In 1837 he spent an uncomfortable summer in an English boardinghouse in New Orleans while looking after the family's business interests in the United States. He made a second, and more extended tour of the United States and Europe from 1854 through 1856. This trip had several purposes: to find relief from a chronic debilitating illness, to give his daughters (who he complained were nearly illiterate) exposure to a higher level of culture, and to promote family ventures that required foreign financing.[25] None of the objects of the journey were fulfilled. After his return to Mexico, he remained too ill to manage the family business in the critical years after 1856.

Whereas Pedro's daughters had to make do with an improvised education in Mexico, his son, José, was sent to Europe at an early age to be properly educated. After spending almost five years in a grammar school run by Quakers in the London suburb of Clapham Commons, José was bundled off to a commercial school in Germany in 1846. Pedro's brothers-in-law had suggested the appropriateness of a liberal education, but he insisted that his son's training be practical:

I have to work continuously in order to procure my subsistence, his education, and that of his sisters, and even though fate watches over my endeavors, I believe that I will never succeed in earning enough to leave him a fortune so that he can live without working, and that as I am already old . . . I want to see him learn to be able to serve as a father to his sisters and to be a source of consolation to his parents in their old age.[26]

Gregorio José

Like Pedro Ansoátegui, Gregorio José came of age while living in Jamaica, and both young men took out papers to become naturalized citizens of the British Empire. Whereas Pedro detested the thought of residing in England, Gregorio José was delighted at the prospect. After leaving Jamaica in the early 1820s, he spent the next several years in London—studying for a liberal education, then working as an apprentice clerk, and finally investing in ventures associated with prominent commercial houses such as Whitworth & Gilbee. As the decade drew to a close, he played a progressively more important role in the European end of José María and Ventura Martínez's trade with Spanish America. In 1829 he conducted the complex negotiations in Europe that led to the creation of Drusina & Martínez in Mexico. The following year he assumed his father's place in that company. After arriving in Mexico in 1831, Gregorio José assumed responsibility for managing family funds invested in Mexico, the United States, and Europe (table 3 shows Gregorio José's control of the family's finances in 1832).

In personality, Gregorio José was pensive and introverted, the most serious of this first generation. His personal correspondence, and his brothers' assessments of him, suggest a thoughtful, hard-working, conscientious individual who was reserved at work and restrained at play. With the profits from Drusina & Martínez and the extra income earned from management of his father's estate, Gregorio José was able in the late 1830s to finance his capital share in Martínez del Río Hermanos while at the same time beginning ambitious speculations in the United States and in Europe. Table 4 lists his assets and liabilities for selected years from 1831 to 1860.

Like his partners, Gregorio José made extensive use of Martínez del Río Hermanos's resources to facilitate and develop his own economic pursuits. He channeled the buying and selling of most of his properties through private accounts with the company. Although convenient, such practices did have the unfortunate long-term result of making it too easy for him and the other partners to concentrate too much of their wealth in the family firm.[27] In the end, Gregorio José, whose fortune far surpassed Pedro's, found himself no less committed to the singular success of Martínez del Río Hermanos in Mexico.

Except for the acquisition of shares in the New York Bank of Commerce (which he acquired from Martínez del Río Hermanos in the 1840s), Gregorio José showed little interest in investing in nonfamily companies. His disdain for that class of investment reflected the perceived risks they seemed to carry. The $30,990 that Gregorio José had deposited for his father in Holden, Vanhouse & Hanky in London was lost when that house declared bankruptcy in 1833. The $5,000 placed with the American Insurance & Trust Company had to be written off as a total loss in 1844 for the same reason.[28] By way of contrast, a very satisfactory experience with shares of the Bank of the United States owned between 1828 and 1836 persuaded Gregorio José that the best mixture of profit and risk lay in investments in public debt instruments. In 1838 and 1839 he unwisely purchased large quantities of stocks and bonds issued by the states of Indiana and Pennsylvania. Acquired at the beginning of the banking panic that swept the United States after 1837, this paper never increased in value but, instead, depreciated relentlessly.

Now disappointed with the United States, Gregorio José turned his attention to various foreign government debt issues that circulated in the London financial market during the 1840s (table 5 summarizes his speculation in London from 1841 through 1843). Though normally a cautious investor, he was for a time completely mesmerized with the speculative possibilities promised by Spanish-American public debt bonds.

In the bond market, the prices of the Spanish-American government debt issues vacillated wildly.[29] Mexican bonds (representing the debt Mexico contracted with London bankers in the 1820s and unpaid interest) sold at 35 percent of their face value in April 1842. The same paper sold for 42 percent in June 1842 and 29 percent in March 1843. Chilean bonds went from less than 70 percent in February 1842 to 85 percent in November 1842 to 101 percent in September 1843. Venezuelan bonds fell from 40 percent in 1841 to 30 percent in 1843. For speculators, the idea was to buy bonds when they were low, sell them as their price rose, and make a tidy profit without getting stuck with large quantities of worthless paper.

Table 4
Estimated and Reported Assets and Liabilities, Gregorio Martinez del Rio, Selected Years
(Current Pesos)

Category	1831	1833	1834	1835	1836	1841	1842	1843
Assets								
Capital accounts/shares in family businesses	23,138	24,903	26,667	33,365	36,486	150,000	150,000	150,000
Other accounts/deposits in family businesses	—	—	74,336	49,142	10,566	76,601	40,663	5,636
Intrafamily accounts and loans	2,800	2,925	5,970	3,890	3,155	9,425	1,055	—
Accounts/stocks/shares/ interests in nonfamily businesses	17,108	10,785	180	10,879	8,830	16,455	23,665	16,473
Stocks/bonds/debt issues/ other government paper	94,190	99,858	42,798	42,798	44,756	77,385	134,839	175,120
Mining shares	—	—	—	—	—	—	—	—
Real property	—	—	—	—	—	—	—	—
Personal property	1,000	1,000	1,000	1,000	1,000	1,500	1,500	1,500
Total gross assets	138,236	139,471	150,951	141,074	104,793	331,366	351,722	348,729
Liabilities								
Family	96,080	96,388	80,567	67,433	25,969	20,625	24,400	31,920
Nonfamily	14,194	3,050	17,397	395	398	106,225	89,747	69,760
Estimated net worth	27,962	40,033	52,987	73,246	78,426	204,516	237,575	247,049

Category	1844	1853	1854	1856	1858	1859	1860
Assets							
Capital accounts/shares in family businesses	150,000	200,000	200,000	200,000	200,000	200,000	200,000
Other accounts/deposits in family businesses	9,239	27,254	2,099	—	7,948	39,733	—
Intrafamily accounts and loans	—	1,079	—	931	—	—	9,625
Accounts/stocks/shares/ interests in nonfamily businesses	2,425	114,293	114,388	72,762	56,353	55,134	46,387
Stocks/bonds/debt issues/ other government paper	150,914	105,377	104,009	107,245	106,823	93,980	94,034
Mining shares	—	19,690	28,594	53,600	47,486	22,252	16,253
Real property	—	—	14,288	16,288	16,288	31,455	31,455
Personal property	1,500	2,300	2,300	2,300	10,800	10,800	10,800
Total gross assets	314,078	469,993	465,678	453,126	445,698	453,354	408,554
Liabilities							
Family	23,682	—	171	6,183	981	240	—
Nonfamily	17,085	—	3,612	6,307	44,000	53,000	14,000
Estimated net worth	273,311	469,993	461,895	440,636	400,717	400,114	394,554

Source: "Libro de Cuentas, 1828–1836"; "Borrador, 1841–43"; "Balance . . . G.J.M.R.," 1852, 1853, 1855, 1857; "Rough Ledger, 1856– ," CMRFH.

Table 5
Speculation in South American and Mexican Foreign Debt Issues in
London Market, Gregorio Martínez del Río
(£)

Year	Face Value & Type	Cost of Purchase	Dividends	Sales
1840	30,000 Venezuela	8,190	—	—
	33,300 Mexico	5,462	—	—
	2,100 Chile	812	60	—
1841	41,613 Venezuela	2,260	—	—
	50,000 Mexico	1,017	—	—
	400 Chile	228	150	—
1842	52,100 Venezuela	7,145	411	596
	113,300 Mexico	11,028	1,400	18,338
	23,271 Chile	3,141	336	6,192
1843	35,500 Venezuela	1,529	641	1,560
	61,000 Mexico	—	80	27,061
	27,700 Chile	14,508	—	—
	1,000 Peru	221	—	—
Total		55,541	3,078	55,747

Source: "Borrador, 1841-43," CMRFH.

With his knowledge of Spanish America and his many contacts and lines of communication with Mexico and South America, it seemed that Gregorio José should have had a comparative advantage in the London market. That turned out to be a false assumption. Advice from Mexico City or Bogotá produced no better results than random selection in London. He did best with Chilean bonds, where his advantage was minimal, and worst with Mexican and Venezuelan bonds, where his own perceptions and those of his associates came into play. Between 1841 and 1843, he invested a total of $277,704 in Chilean, Mexican, Venezuelan, Colombian, and Peruvian bonds. Adding dividends to income from sales, the total returns on these bonds were $295,550—equivalent to a gross profit of $17,846 over three years. Large cash outlays for these risky speculations produced an annual return of less than 2 percent on the capital invested. The infrequent, but flamboyant, successes of a few of these bonds (like the Chilean) obscured their overall poor performance.[30] In 1860 Gregorio José's Venezuelan bonds, with a face value of £68,000, were virtually worthless, as were $20,000 in Indiana State 5 percent, $20,000 in Indiana Canal Preferred 5 percent, $10,050 in Indiana Special 5 percent, and $1,960 in Indiana Canal Loan stocks.[31]

Before 1850 Gregorio José had little interest in acquiring Mexican mining shares, but the poor performance of government debt issues and his other investments, in contrast to the spectacular successes of the Mexican investors who purchased and began working the Real del Monte mines in Pachuca, encouraged him to discard his old prejudices. Hoping to replicate the good fortunes of acquaintances such as the Béisteguis and the Escandóns, who had struck it rich in mining, Gregorio José worked feverishly to acquire a broad selection of mining shares. Although his friends were lucky, Gregorio José was not. Table 6 summarizes his mining investments and their returns (or lack of returns) from 1856 to 1859.

As was the case with mining, Gregorio José's interest in making investments in real property was slow to develop. Before 1856 the opportunities to purchase urban real estate in Mexico were relatively restricted. The few persons who owned their homes seldom put them up for sale. The many properties belonging to the church and the civil corporations could not be alienated. The disamortization of corporate properties in 1856, however, changed all that. The new law gave Gregorio José a chance to purchase the house he desired, a property belonging to the Oratorio de San Felipe.

Even with the liberal reforms, though, buying a home was not always a straightforward proposition. First, the house located at No. 12 San Agustín

Table 6
Mining Investments and Returns, Gregorio Martínez del Río, 1856-1859
(Current Pesos)

Mine/ Mining Company	Location	Disburse- ments	Divi- dends	Comments
San Rafael	Guanajuato	19,743	0	Write-off in 1859
Villariño	Guanajuato	8,405	0	Total loss
Veta Grande	Zacatecas	14,633	0	Total loss
La Higuera	Guanajuato	933	0	Write-off in 1856
La Magdalena	Temascaltepec	2,998	0	—
San José del Cura	Temascaltepec	3,976	444	—
La Arizona	Guanajuato	2,080	0	Total loss
La Valenciana	Pachuca	353	0	—
El Roble	Guanajuato	688	0	Write-off in 1857
Remedios	Comanja	8,556	0	Write-off in 1857
San Nicolás Nauchititla	Temascaltepec	5,602	0	—
San Felipe Nerí	Tepenene	80	0	—
La Purísima Nauchititla Compan	Guanajuato	2,000	0	—

Source: "Rough Ledger, 1856- ," CMRFH.

Street in Mexico City was adjudicated to Francisco Schiafino, a public official who bought many such properties. Schiafino acquired the house for $8,000; its legitimate valuation was $16,000. Gregorio José purchased it from Schiafino for $12,500 in December 1856. When a conservative government took power in 1858, Gregorio José was obliged to pay Miguel Ycaza, a former tenant in the house, $2,000 for a waiver of his rights as renter. Repairs and improvements cost Gregorio José an additional $4,426. In 1865 the original transaction from 1856 was reaudited by Maximillian's government, and Gregorio José was required to pay the difference between the price Schiafino acquired the house for and the price it should have sold for. Such were the pleasures of owning a home in early national Mexico.[32]

Gregorio José had fewer problems with two houses in Tlalpam on the outskirts of Mexico City, which he purchased from a private owner in 1853. This same year he acquired three parcels of land from developers who were marketing properties belonging to the Parcialidad de San Juan de Tenoxtitlan, a civil corporation. These were sold as *censos enfitéuticos*; that is, the use and usufruct of the property were conveyed to the buyer, but not the whole rights of property (these were devices used before 1856 to evade prohibitions against the sale of corporate lands). For these properties, Gregorio José paid $599 annually—equivalent to 6 percent interest on the capitalized value of $9,966. After disamortization, Gregorio José redeemed that capital and received full title to the lots.[33]

Gregorio José never purchased a rural estate. His attitude toward owning an hacienda stayed true to the feelings he expressed to Pedro in 1840 when his brother-in-law suggested they become rancheros and purchase the Rancho y Molino de Santa Mónica, a wheat-producing and milling operation located a short distance from the capital. He insisted absolutely that he would not participate in the sort of enterprise where he would have to associate with "Bakers—Planters—and other riffraff [*lepería*]."[34]

Living in Mexico imposed on the family many costs that were not purely economic in nature. One of the most visible drawbacks of an extended residence in a backward country was the problem of staying healthy. Seriously ill in November 1836, Gregorio José left the family business in the hands of Pedro and Ventura de la Cruz and bolted to the coast to escape the country and to seek recuperation abroad. He returned to Mexico a year later when those symptoms had subsided. No sooner had he rented a house in Mexico City in 1837 and made preparations for his new business partnership with his brothers than he was forced once more to seek relief abroad. London's cold and humid climate may not have been healthier than Mexico City's, but clearly Gregorio José was more at home there.[35] In part because of business speculations and partly because of social considerations—his quixotic search for a British bride—he extended his stay in England through 1844. Soon after his return to Mexico, he was not displeased when family business required his immediate presence in London in 1845. The war between Mexico and the United States prevented his return before 1848. The following year he found a new excuse to leave Mexico, first to visit the United States to try to make arrangements for family property in Texas, and then on to his beloved England. Returning to Mexico City in 1852, he was destined never to leave Mexico again. He died in 1888.

José Pablo

Fate was kindest to the youngest of the Martínez del Ríos. José Pablo was the most dynamic of Ventura Martínez's children and it was he who eventually took charge as leader of the family after the passing of the patriarch. José Pablo was the only one of his brothers to father children in Mexico—the family's second generation. His personal and professional life was fruitful, though not immune from tragedy.

After receiving his bachelor's degree in Paris in 1828, José Pablo enrolled in medical school. Because of extended holiday excursions to Rome, Geneva, and London, he failed to complete his final examination until July 1834. Then, in a burst of activity, he wrote his thesis for the degree of Doctor of Medicine in ten days. After graduation, he extended his stay in medical school to seek an advanced degree as Doctor of Surgery. José Pablo took care in these early years to publish his work in medical journals, to seek appointments in medical societies in Europe and the Americas, and to establish a reputation as a capable physician. A satisfied client wrote to Ventura Martínez in 1835: "Dr. Martínez has earned the general esteem of all the persons who know him; I am his debtor especially for the cure of my wife, whom he treated for a grave illness. Take these my sincere congratulations for the fortune of having a son who cannot do less than merit the most complete satisfaction possible."[36]

Believing the practice of medicine to be hopelessly backward in France and the prospects for a remunerative career grim—"In France better a beggar than a doctor"—José Pablo moved to London in the spring of 1835 to seek a residency in an English maternity hospital.[37] Although he failed to find the position he sought, his short stay in London did have a very important consequence for the family. Like his brothers, José Pablo used "Martínez" as his surname, but it was not very distinctive. In May 1835 he wrote to his father, "As I have already found various doctors with the same name, I have put Martínez del Río on my card because it is important to avoid any confusion of names: tell me if this is all right and if I should also change my signature."[38]

The last of his family to arrive in Mexico, José Pablo landed in Veracruz in December 1836. The following month he began the practice of medicine in the capital. Catering to the well-to-do families of the city, the young physician had many competitors—English, French, Swiss, German, and Polish doctors already had well-established practices. Epochs of generally good public health must have seemed a conspiracy of sorts. José Pablo complained in the summer of 1839, "This season, which ordinarily is the harvest time for us [doctors], has been so healthy this year that there is almost nothing to do, and if it were not for my new position as birther I would have my arms crossed."[39]

José Pablo specialized in obstetrics and gynecology, areas in which he had above average skills. Once, he boasted, "with the Dunlop birth I had a difficult and complicated time, but happily it went well, and I hope this will preserve my reputation with the English."[40] Even so, the young doctor observed that he could not please all of his clients all of the time: "Mrs. Morphy . . . made afterward a thousand efforts to get me away from her and to put Villete in my place!—I cannot attribute it to anything more than the custom she has of treating her illness as 'pretty' and 'cute'—well, at the same time this is going on I am the general practitioner in the Morphy house in place of Jecker."[41]

Aggravated by the social pretensions of his patients, José Pablo complained loudly in the late 1830s about the "sterility and difficulty" of his practice and the "uselessness of having an intelligent activity" in Mexico that produced neither social recognition nor financial security. He earned only about $1,500 from his practice in 1838 and he gave serious thought to retiring, but his luck in winning a teaching chair in obstetrics at the National School of Medicine in Mexico City ameliorated his disaffection with the profession, at least for a while.[42]

With the pretext of a health problem, the doctor took a leave of absence and returned to Europe in 1841. His real motives were personal, an intent to contract matrimony, and professional, a desire to develop his skill in obstetrics and gynecology.[43] He hoped to break into the European medical establishment in a big way. As he saw the matter, everything depended on finding the right patron, so he planned to secure an appointment as physician to the Rothschild family. He persuaded Gregorio José to exert his influence to get him a letter of recommendation to the famous financier. The doctor saw Rothschild, but the meeting was an absolute failure. Nor was José Pablo able to obtain a residency in an English hospital. Instead, he was obliged to work in a maternity hospital in Paris. When not working or studying, the young physician used his free time to woo his young and attractive sweetheart, Angela Pedemonte, whom he married in May 1842. Within a year their first child was born. Faced with growing responsibilities (and expenses), José Pablo returned with his new family to Mexico in 1844. With his added expertise from the extra training in Europe, he anticipated a more productive practice. By 1845 he had increased his income from the practice of medicine to about $7,000 a year. Although not a large sum, it was equivalent to his yearly allowance as a partner in Martínez del Río Hermanos (representing an investment of $150,000).

The next few years were times of difficulty, hardship, and danger. Political violence in Mexico reached epidemic proportions. The doctor was nearly killed in March 1847 while treating wounded soldiers in a Mexico City hospital. His assailants were not invading American troops, but partisans in the street fighting that had broken out in the capital after Santa Anna had expelled the liberals from his government. To escape the fighting expected when the Americans began their assault on Mexico City in the autumn of 1847, José Pablo moved his family outside the capital to a textile mill, Miraflores, located near Chalco at the base of the snow-covered volcanoes that ringed the eastern side of the Valley of Mexico. There the refugees were discovered by a detachment of American soldiers, who asked the doctor to treat a seriously wounded officer. José Pablo described the fortuitous results of the incident:

The coincidence of having treated Scott's aide, whom they brought to Miraflores unconscious, but fortunately alive, put me in a good position with that General; later I met other generals on a casual basis so that I have somewhat friendly relations with them, and also with Mr. Trist, the Plenipotentiary. This circumstance has made it possible for me to know the direction of their policy, which has varied with events.[44]

Because of his many contacts on both the Mexican and the American sides, the doctor was drafted as an intermediary to arrange a cease-fire. The peace treaty subsequently negotiated by Trist was signed in Guillermo Drusina's house in Mexico City.

With the war finally over, José Pablo returned his attention and energy to his practice and to his classes in the School of Medicine, but the old dissatisfaction with his career remained. After Ventura de la Cruz's death in 1852, José Pablo dropped his practice to manage the family business and to launch new private business ventures of his own. His first chance to exercise his entrepreneurial talents came in 1850 when a friend, Felipe Nerí del Barrio, invited him to join his nephew Luis Flores in forming a company to operate the Hacienda Apapasco in Huejotcingo, Puebla.[45] Both partners contributed an equal share of capital to the enterprise, which rented the hacienda for a fixed five-year term from the Augustinian Order for $5,000. Apapasco's principal activities were intended to be mule breeding and tallow rendering, but because the property contained a good supply of timber, the sale of wood to the nearby city of Puebla became a lucrative source of income. Grain and forage were the principal crops: corn for the workers, alfalfa for the livestock, and wheat for urban markets.

The enterprise overcame serious obstacles and returned steady, if modest, profits for its investors.[46] Provisions of the rental contract that forbade commercial exploitation of the hacienda's timberlands were easy to evade.

But when the new management denied residents of nearby villages their traditional free access to the hacienda's forests, a controversy erupted, and the managers were forced to back down when local officials sided with the villagers. A more difficult problem was an acute shortage of workers. A cholera epidemic had depopulated the countryside. Other laborers fled to escape the debts accumulated in their accounts with the hacienda. Many more had left because the hacienda had failed to pay their wages. Despite the offer of higher than normal wages (up to three reales daily), the hacienda could not recruit a full complement of workers in the summer of 1850. When Flores attempted to attract peons by offering to pay off their debts to other haciendas, he encountered stiff resistance from local hacendados. Flores reported their foreman's encounter with Juan Rondero, a well-known Mexico City businessman who owned the Hacienda de Cuatlapanga in Puebla:

Rondero made it clear that these peons were obligated to him for a year, which will not expire until Holy Week [in April] and since he had not entered into the new arrangement to make accounts in August he was not in any way obligated to cede them. . . . Even though we are the ones it costs because we lack these laborers, justice and good harmony between neighbors comes first, and there was no solution except to give in.[47]

Even without the extra help, the hacienda produced record crops of corn and alfalfa in 1850. Although a bumper crop of wheat was damaged by a hailstorm the following year, other growers were more affected and, with the subsequent shortage of wheat in the area, Apapasco turned a better-than-average profit. Each new year brought fewer problems and new profits. But like other agricultural operators who leased instead of owned their estates, they could be victimized by their success. When the two partners sought to renew their lease in 1855, they were outbid and they lost the enterprise they had worked so diligently to develop.

Because his family owned Miraflores, one of the largest and most modern textile factories in Mexico, because he was acquainted with the problems and prospects of the textile industry, and because (more important) he was blessed with friends occupying high offices in Santa Anna's goverment, José Pablo secured an appointment as agent for the Consejo de la Industria Fabril, a quasi-corporate organization of Mexican textile factory owners. His accounts with Martínez del Río Hermanos showed he received a total of $9,500 in 1854 for salary and expenses paid by the Mexican government.[48]

Losing this job because of the change of governments in 1855, José Pablo became a moneylender. In October 1855 he lent José María Cervantes the nominal sum of $30,000, to be repaid with 6 percent interest in two equal installments on the last days of 1856 and 1857. Three months later he granted Cervantes a second loan for $7,000, "to attend to his businesses."

In April 1856 Felipe Neri del Barrio sold José Pablo his house at No. 5 San Francisco Street in Mexico City. The bill of sale contained a clause that allowed Barrio to repurchase the house for the same price within a fixed period of time. Such repurchase agreements frequently were disguised loans. By transferring title to property when receiving a loan, borrowers provided lenders with collateral free from the risks and costs of litigation associated with mortgages.[49]

Although foreign debt issues remained an insignificant part of his investment portfolio, José Pablo began as early as 1849 to invest heavily in Mexican mining shares. Except for his purchase of shares in the Real del Monte mining company, which paid lavish dividends to its shareholders in the 1850s, José Pablo's mining investments produced no more for him than for the rest of the family.

José Pablo's overall investment strategy was characterized by his concern to provide a secure inheritance for his children. That and his early decision to make a permanent home in Mexico and, later, the good fortune of having surplus income to invest, encouraged him to buy much more real property than anyone else in the family. Table 7 compares his assets and liabilities with those of Pedro and Gregorio José in 1857.

Table 7
Estimated and Reported Assets and Liabilities, Martínez del Río Family, 1857
(Current Pesos)

Category	Pedro A. & Dolores	Gregorio José	José Pablo	Total
Assets				
Capital accounts/shares in family businesses	150,000	200,000	200,000	550,000
Other accounts/deposits in family businesses	—	—	—	
Intrafamily accounts and loans	—	3,700	—	3,700
Accounts/stocks/shares/interests in nonfamily businesses	—	54,483	37,000	91,483
Stocks/bonds/debt issues/other government paper	—	106,131	26,072	132,203
Mining shares	10,189	40,384	40,292	90,865
Real property	38,000	16,288	146,000	200,288
Personal property	10,632	2,300	14,733	27,665
Total gross assets	208,821	423,286	464,097	1,096,204
Liabilities				
Family	—	—	3,700	3,700
Nonfamily	15,000	28,262	54,000	97,262
Estimated net worth	193,821	395,024	406,397	995,242

Source: CMRFH.

When he made up his mind to marry in 1841, José Pablo gave orders to Ventura de la Cruz to find him a house in Mexico City. Although his instructions contained the single admonition that the house should be located on the sunny side of a street, the search produced only two potential residences. First, there was the house belonging to Barrio's partner, Francisco Fagoaga, who had gone off to Europe terminally ill. But, as was often the case, relatives got the first opportunity to buy the house. There was also the house at No. 12 Bethlemitas Street, the residence of the British minister in Mexico, Richard Pakenham. Ventura de la Cruz made a deal with Pakenham, who was being recalled to Great Britain in 1842, to take possession of the house and its furnishings for $13,733.[50] Because Pakenham did not own the house, which was the property of a religious order, only his rights as renter were conveyed to José Pablo. As to acquiring full property rights to the house, José Pablo was not bound by traditional values, but there were other problems, as he explained to Ventura de la Cruz: "About the goods of the *manos muertos* [the *capellanías*], I will tell you that I continue to hold the same ideas, but you know well enough that right now I do not have the power; to apply these ideas it would be essential that a real bargain present itself, and that there be hard cash; that does not seem very probable."[51]

José Pablo was dismayed, however, to learn in May 1844 that his agreement with Pakenham had given him only the rights to six more years on the rental contract originally negotiated with the Convento de Encarnación in 1832. He feared that when the contract expired he would be at the mercy of the convent's mayordomo, "an old scoundrel," more obnoxious even than Gregorio José's previous landlady, the former countess Cortina.[52] Since his brother had paid $2,500 annually to rent a house of lesser quality, the increase in rent from the $1,000 a year figure established by the 1832 contract was likely to be dramatic.

The economic advantage that José Pablo looked for so that he could acquire his house presented itself in 1847, when Santa Anna's government forced a $1.5 million loan from the church to finance the war effort. The loan was financed by promissory notes, *libranzas*, drawn on the principal church agencies and religious orders in Mexico. With $20,000 in cash, José Pablo acquired six $5,000 promissory notes drawn on the Dominican Order. In June 1847 he proposed to the *vicario capitular* in Mexico City that La Encarnación sell him his house in exchange for these notes. By cultivating friendly relations with the vicar, José Pablo hoped to win speedy approval for his scheme. He went as far as to donate £200 for the vicar's use when he traveled to Rome seeking confirmation as the new archbishop of Mexico.[53] The plan went awry when José María Covarubias, the *promotor fiscal* representing the government agency that supervised such transactions, informed the vicar that as the promissory notes were not drawn on La

Encarnación their value was questionable. In March 1848 José Pablo made a new proposition to the vicar, offering $12,000 in cash and a $14,000 mortgage on the house. Citing the urgent need for funds and the vicar's recommendation that the offer be accepted, the government's Junta de Préstamos approved the transaction the following month.[54]

As a homeowner, José Pablo became eligible for inexpensive loans from church agencies. In October 1850 he borrowed $6,000 from the Archicofradía del Sacramento, repayable in six years with 6 percent annual interest. Three months later the same agency increased the loan to $10,000 after José Pablo submitted proof that the actual value of his home was $59,314. In 1857, after his wife and children had left for Europe, José Pablo sold the Bethlemitas house to Manuel Escandón for a share in the Real del Monte mining company.[55] At about this same time, José Pablo sold a second house, located in Tacubaya, a prestigious suburb west of Mexico City, to Alejandro María Aranjo y Escandón, Manuel Escandón's nephew and proxy attorney in Mexico. José Pablo had acquired this house, known locally as the House of Arazam, from Lina Fagoaga, the widow of Joaquín Escandón, in 1853. Subsequently, he had leased Arazam to the British minister in Mexico, George Lettson.[56] The sale of these properties in 1857 was a consequence of several circumstances, but most compelling was the fact that the properties had become superfluous. José Pablo had developed a property to take the place of both houses.

In January 1853 he purchased a tract of land located near Tacubaya and the old military fort on the heights of Chapultepec. The property, known "vulgarly" as the Molina del Rey, extended over an area totaling 179,350 square varas. By combining that land with separate piecemeal acquisitions, the doctor acquired a sizable rustic estate quite cheaply. In contrast to nearby Chapultepec (the Nahuatl word for grasshopper), this area was called La Hormiga (the ant). To straighten its boundaries and to validate his title to the land, José Pablo donated $100 to the Ayuntamiento of Tacubaya in December 1855. In exchange, the corporation ceded to him a portion of its land contiguous to La Hormiga, and José Pablo began building a fine house on the ruins of the old Molina del Rey. It was then that his ownership of the land was contested in three separate lawsuits. Litigation continued until he managed to secure releases from the offended parties in 1859.[57] His experience was not unusual. Property rights in early national Mexico were so confused that many investors were reluctant to invest in land.

José Pablo's enthusiasm for investments in land, to the point of ignoring the predictable risks of such purchases, was apparent again in his determination to acquire a rural estate. Along with Pedro, he had tried to persuade Gregorio José to join them in purchasing an hacienda in 1840. His admiration of Barrio's sugar hacienda, Temisco, provided a further stimulus in that direction. The problem with rural estates was that money put there was money wasted—or so many investors had come to believe. Barrio sank more than $400,000 in Temisco, but the enterprise never produced profits commensurate with the scale of investment. The depressed condition of the rural sector made investments in estates generally unattractive, but José Pablo possessed a grander vision. He was familiar with the experience of Texas land in the 1830s. Prior to 1835 the area was undeveloped and land was cheap. After secession from Mexico in 1836 and, especially, after annexation to the United States in 1845, Texas land prices skyrocketed. José Pablo shared the view of many of his contemporaries (which neither he nor they necessarily were pleased about) that Mexico would be progressively dismembered by its aggressive northern neighbor. When the United States invaded Mexico in 1846, he sketched out a plan to take advantage of the inevitable: "I persist in my dreams of buying estates in the towns that the Yankees found or develop now and also land in the provinces that they are usurping; I believe this kind of investment, being well done, would become in time a 'Duchy.' "[58]

The generalized agricultural depression after 1810 had ruined the large, formerly prosperous great estates of the colonial era. Without a strong government to ward off incursions of barbarous Indians (or to buy them off), to subsidize and promote the general development of remote regions, and to ensure unbroken communications with markets thousands of miles away, extensive estate agriculture in the North was especially vulnerable. *Mayorazgos*, juridical devices engineered by the founders of prestigious families in New Spain to guarantee the well-being of future generations, failed to function properly when the latifundia stopped producing income. The estates declined and so did the families.

Consequently, in the postindependence era legal codes were amended to permit disentailment of these properties, and, as family fortunes dwindled, sales of these estates became increasingly common. In a typical occurrence, Concepción Cosío de Romero was persuaded to sell one of the Cosío family's estates, the hacienda of San Juan de Encinillas y Anexas. This estate sprawled across six million acres of land in Northern Chihuahua, just south of Paso del Norte (present-day El Paso) along the border with Texas. After lengthy negotiations, José Pablo and Cosío's attorney agreed to terms for the sale of Encinillas in August 1854. The price for the estate, $60,000, was payable as $6,000 in cash delivered immediately and one share in the Real del Monte mining company (valued at $18,000) to be delivered after Cosío's mother's estate had formally adjudicated the property to Cosío and the sale was made final. The balance, earning 3 percent annual interest, was payable in three annual $10,000 installments beginning in 1859.[59]

To ensure that the government would recognize his property rights, José Pablo negotiated with Santa Anna's regime to gain title to the public lands lying between the various properties he owned. Latifundia like Encinillas were a conglomeration of separate ranches, haciendas, and land grants acquired from private persons and from the state over the course of two centuries. Their boundaries were not contiguous. Strips and parcels of public land constituted a substantial part of the total area encompassed by the poorly defined, unsurveyed outer boundaries. A *composición de tierras* was arranged with Santa Anna, but that, along with all the other acts of his government, was thrown out by the Revolution of Ayutla and the liberal Congress that succeeded it. José Pablo had to start the process (and possibly the bribes) all over again. Finally, in June 1855 he registered a new agreement with the minister of hacienda, Miguel Lerdo de Tejada. For $2,000 José Pablo acquired all public lands lying within the described boundaries of Encinillas. The document noted that a precise survey to verify the actual amount of land conveyed to the buyer was impossible because of the Indian threat.[60]

Buying Encinillas was one thing; taking possession was another. Two days before the sale of the property in August 1854 José Pablo received a letter from General Angel Frías of Chihuahua warning him not to sign a contract with Cosío that "afterward might result ruinous, and perhaps null."[61] Frías argued that because he had rented Encinillas since 1843 he enjoyed *tanto*, the traditional preferential right of purchase. Furthermore, he claimed that his $20,000 investment in improvements to Encinillas would have to be paid for before he would allow anyone to occupy the property. At this time Frías was the governor and commanding general of the Department of Chihuahua. Although ousted after the liberal Revolution of 1855, he continued to be a strong man in the region. José Pablo's agents in Chihuahua, themselves prominent liberals in the state government, were powerless to evict Frías, and José Pablo was forced to accept a compromise in 1857, paying the general $11,900 for his rights as a tenant.[62]

With Frías out of the way, that left only the problem of *how* to take possession of Encinillas. The Indian threat was so serious that even bringing out a judge to witness the act of possession was a large and costly production. In August 1857 José Pablo's agent in Chihuahua prepared to lead an expedition from the state capital, Chihuahua City, to the *casco* of Encinillas, located about twenty-five leagues to the north. A well-armed fifteen-man escort was a necessary precaution. Just before the caravan left for Encinillas, Indians attacked a stagecoach and killed two passengers on the road that passed through the hacienda. After a thorough inspection, accomplished without incident, José Pablo's representative described the estate as "magnificent," with abundant pastures, woodlands, and springs. Sections such as Carrizal, Ojo Caliente, Peñalito, and El Saúz looked especially promising, although the actual condition of the hacienda's installations was dismal: "All the buildings . . . are of adobe and as they are in complete ruin they present a very sad spectacle."[63] Aside from a few plots of corn, beans, and wheat, nothing was cultivated on the entire latifundium. All of its livestock had long since been carried off by bandits and Indians.

Rather than risking his own capital in such an uncertain enterprise, José Pablo hoped to promote a colonization company to develop Encinillas. Having witnessed in 1853 the sale of a 30,000 square mile tract of land adjacent to Encinillas (the Mesilla territory), he expected that his land would be annexed by the United States in a similar transaction. While awaiting those developments, José Pablo was content to rent out the *casco* of Encinillas at a low price, $600 per year in five-year leases beginning in 1858 and 1862.

Escalating political violence nearer home forced the physician-turned-businessman to choose between remaining in Mexico to look after his investments or moving with his wife and children to safety in Europe. With the nation on the brink of civil war in 1856, José Pablo sent Angela and the children out of the country. He stayed behind to finish personal and family business matters. Not until June 1859 did he finally free himself for a joyful reunion with his family in Europe. Already, events in Mexico had begun to undermine his finances. Soon after his arrival in Milan he was struck by personal tragedy as well. In September 1859 his oldest and favorite son died suddenly of appendicitis. Of the six sons he had fathered, only three still lived: Manuel, Nicolás, and Pablo, the youngest, born in Milan in 1856 while José Pablo was still in Mexico. In the cold and dampness of that fall and winter in Milan, Nicolás and Pablo and their sisters, Dolores and Angela, contracted serious respiratory infections. José Pablo worried also about the condition of his wife, whom he described as "thin, discolored, and so worn out I fear a new misfortune."[64] To escape the cold in Northern Italy, José Pablo moved his family south. They passed the final days of December 1859 in Florence.

Family Structure

A complex system of extralegal social expectations tied together the interests of family members and created from the many individual properties described in the biographical sketches a larger and more functional family economy. For individuals, this family economy might work to one's advantage or disadvantage, depending on the outcomes of intrafamily politics, since intrafamily exchanges distorted formal, legally prescribed property distributions. Contrast María Dolores's limited access to her large maternal inheritance and Ventura de la Cruz's powerlessness in Martínez del Río Hermanos with Gregorio José's control of family wealth in the 1830s and José Pablo's dominant role in the family firm after 1838. For the group as a whole, however, family organization of individual economies had distinct benefits. It enhanced economic coordination and reduced opportunity and transaction costs. Where modern economic and political infrastructures were absent, family brought individuals together and guaranteed correct and predictable behavior. At the same time, when few individuals by themselves had sufficient resources to create large enterprises and when outside financing was costly and difficult to obtain, family organization provided a means of combining assets for a common goal and redistributing enterprise risks among a larger, more resilient group.

The economic life of the first generation of the Martínez del Río family was structured around these truisms.[65] By combining all of their assets in a single enterprise, Martínez del Río Hermanos, the family founded one of the best-capitalized commercial houses of the era in Mexico. Its size alone gave it considerable advantages over competitors. Rationalizing otherwise diverse interests into a coherent network, the family economy of the Martínez del Ríos grew to encompass public and private finance, commerce, textile manufacturing, ranching, real estate speculation, and mining in Mexico, Colombia, Great Britain, Germany, France, and the United States. (The operations of Drusina & Martínez and Martínez del Río Hermanos, within which most of the family's collective economic activity took place, are analyzed in chapters 4 and 5.) It is worth noting that, apart from the Martínez del Ríos, none of the important native entrepreneurs of early nineteenth-century Mexico operated outside the bases of family enterprise.[66]

Before 1836 the unquestioned patriarch of the family was Ventura Martínez. By design, he should have been succeeded by Gregorio José. His father had marked him for that role as early as 1830, and after Martínez's death his brothers assumed that he would take charge. Pedro advised Gregorio José in 1837: "Do not think solely of yourself; consider that today you are the Father of the family and that whatever indisposition in you will cause great prejudice to all."[67] Unfortunately, knowing what decisions should be made is not the same as *making* decisions. Gregorio José neither wanted to replace nor was he capable of replacing his father.

A process of elimination left the job of family leader to Martínez's youngest son. Manuel María and Ventura de la Cruz were excluded and both died prematurely. The latter had hoped to have a say in setting economic policies, but his other brothers generally concurred with Pedro's assessment in 1839: "Ventura likewise seems not to be right for business."[68] Gradually, Ventura de la Cruz became resigned to a passive role, confessing in 1849, "I am useless or nearly so for business."[69] Pedro, an aggressive and strong-willed individual, made fateful decisions for the family business, especially in the early 1840s, but he was *not* a Martínez del Río and his leadership of the family was neither solicited nor tolerated. That left only José Pablo, who seems always to have played a dominant role in family politics. Even in the 1820s and 1830s his correspondence with his father and brothers was punctuated with judgments of his siblings and *his* recommendations as to how a particular matter should be handled. Like Pedro, José Pablo seems to have preferred the excitement of risky speculations in Mexico to more secure, but less lucrative, investments elsewhere.

The domineering manner in which José Pablo and Pedro conspired to fix family business policy was illustrated in the decision-making process that led to Martínez del Río Hermanos's participation in Miraflores. They both wanted to buy into the project in 1841. Ventura de la Cruz wanted no part of the factory. Gregorio José was not consulted. Instead, José Pablo insisted, "I answer for Pepe [Gregorio José]"—and with Pedro's cooperation he quietly arranged the deal with Barrio.[70] Ventura de la Cruz's death, Pedro's declining health, and Gregorio José's continuing reluctance to lead confirmed José Pablo's preeminence in the family. That state of affairs was reflected in Pedro's aside to José Pablo in 1854: "You know the character of Pepe [Gregorio José] and you know very well that he is not the right man for our situation. . . . Your relations, disposition, etc., I consider indispensable for our salvation."[71]

Conclusion

Ventura Martínez's good fortune as a moneylender and merchant in colonial Panama provided the material foundations for the family's life in early national Mexico. Prosperity in Panama was a function of the political economy of Bourbon Spanish America, which assigned to Panama a favored role in intercolonial and international commerce. This role enabled merchants such as Martínez to profit as intermediaries between European manufacturers and Spanish-American consumers. The family's ties to Mexico were at first only incidental, arising from Martínez's interests in the short-lived boom in the Panama-Mexico trade between 1811 and 1821. The culmination of the independence movement in Spanish America had a profound impact on the family economy, as it destroyed or made irrelevant the once-lucrative colonial trade patterns.

With traditional ways of doing business defunct, Martínez and his children faced the dilemma of how best to cope with the new facts of life that had been spelled out for most of Spanish America by 1821. The decision to relocate in Mexico was one way to adjust, although in this case the family's residence was not so much planned as it was an accidental outcome of Martínez's attempt to liquidate the old debts that had accumulated there.

The family also adjusted to the new circumstances of the nineteenth century by educating and socializing its children abroad. Born as they were in an era of transition, the dissolution of traditional bonds made possible a fascinating experiment in self-guided social development and occupational differentiation. Intead of militia officers, merchant-adventurers, and priests, the family now featured liberally educated businessmen, doctors, and pharmacists trained in London and Paris. Anomie, the absence of established norms and values to guide personal behavior, had a darker side as well, as reflected in Manuel María's experience in Paris. The disappearance of José María, the drowning of Ventura de la Cruz, and the premature deaths of María Dolores's and José Pablo's children testify vividly to the other cruel hazards of the day. The less tangible, but very real, menace that quietly stalked the family was the risk of losing all its patrimony in this Mexican adventure. Martínez, a third-generation Creole, had an instinctive knowledge of the institutional medium in which he worked and he shared with his Mexican counterparts the molding experience of colonial commerce. Even so, his lack of a personal acquaintance with the intricacies of the Mexican marketplace resulted in formidable reverses. More foreboding, his children, born Panamanians but educated and socialized as Europeans, were less prepared in their formative years to make the necessary adjustments to the problems of family, business, and politics in Mexico.

As was documented in the preceding biographical sketches, Martínez's children transformed the patrimony they inherited. That transformation reflected developing trends in the international economy as well as the personal proclivities and prejudices of individual family members. The Martínez del Ríos worked in a more modern era than had their father and, consequently, their economic activity was structured around durable, well-organized, general-purpose enterprises like Drusina & Martínez and Martínez del Río Hermanos. Absent were the highly individualized, short-lived, single-purpose *compañías* that their father and, before him, untold generations of traders in Spanish America had found so useful.

What the Martínez del Ríos did or did not invest in was determined also by the limited possibilities of the Mexican economy. The few opportunities for profit tended to be speculative, like those in public and private finance described by Pedro in 1832. Institutional obstacles discouraged other types of investment. As Ventura Martínez's experiences showed, property rights remained vaguely defined. The Mexican court system was a poor arbiter of conflict. Its judgments were arbitrary at best. At worst, it was inconclusive, and litigation could continue unresolved indefinitely. Commercial activities were regulated by traditional codes such as the Ordenanzas del Bilbao. Church and civil corporation ownership of real property restricted the development of a market for urban and rural land. As José Pablo's experience with La Hormiga and Encinillas showed, the abuses of local strongmen and politicians might jeopardize the few opportunities that were available.

At first glance it would appear that the family did exceptionally well in Mexico, even with all these dangers and inconveniences. The era of the

Wars of Independence and the emergence of new nations in Spanish America, 1812 to 1832, was a period of slow growth, or perhaps of decline, if the immediate cash value of the various types of assets is considered. That era was even less attractive if compared with the years 1792 to 1812, when Ventura Martínez managed rapid growth rates averaging 70 percent annually. The performance between 1832 and 1857 would seem more impressive, but here the figures are deceptive. In 1812 family property was constituted as cash, silver, gold, jewels, and readily negotiable paper. In 1832 it was situated in varied, productive, and reasonably secure investments—Drusina & Martínez in Mexico and government stocks and bonds in the United States. In 1857 the family may have had the consolation that old debts no longer made up the largest share of assets, as in 1832, or that the listed value of assets was double that of 1832, but in 1857 its mining shares and government paper were worth only a fraction of their nominal value. Martínez del Río Hermanos accounted for more than 50 percent of the family's $1 million net worth in 1857, and it was on the verge of bankruptcy.

Symptomatic of this family economy's hidden instability was its poor performance as an income producer. Table 8 shows estimates of Gregorio José's income for selected years. He relied heavily on fixed returns for Martínez del Río Hermanos (whether or not the company actually produced annual profits). His government bonds and mining properties failed to generate sustained revenues. Investments in nonfamily enterprises, which were more lucrative, like the shares of stock in the Bank of Commerce of New York, were sacrificed to keep the family firm solvent a while longer. Table 9 compares his average income against net worth for selected years between 1831 and 1858. These figures suggest a steady deterioration of income (profit) in comparison to net worth (capital). Deletion of the high income ingeniously reported in 1857 as a share of surplus profits in Martínez del Río Hermanos would sharpen the trend toward declining profits. As chapter 5 will demonstrate, Martínez del Río Hermanos seldom made a profit. The $10,000 extracted annually by Gregorio José as an allowance (and the $17,000 taken out by Pedro and José Pablo) actually represented a progressive decapitalization of the company.

In a general sense, then, the Martínez del Ríos' family economy was a failure. It did not produce adequate income to support the family and it exposed the whole family fortune to the risk of catastrophic ruin, jeopardizing the material well-being of future generations. What saved the second generation were the family's few, almost incidental, investments in land. The value of the family's assets in real property increased nearly five times over in the quarter of a century after 1832. Although these properties produced little income, they were among the very few investments that retained or increased their value over time. They were for succeeding

Table 8
Income Sources, Gregorio Martinez del Rio, Selected Years
(Current Pesos)

Income Source	1841 (%)	1842 (%)	1843 (%)	1856 (%)	1857 (%)	1858 (%)	Average (%)
Martinez del Rio Hermanos allowance	7,000 (44.1)	7,000 (71.2)	7,000 (25.5)	10,000 (52.0)	10,000 (58.2)	10,000 (18.0)	8,500 (35.1)
Martinez del Rio Hermanos excess capital interest	2,400 (15.1)	2,400 (24.4)	2,400 (8.7)	3,000 (15.6)	3,000 (17.5)	3,000 (5.4)	2,700 (11.2)
Martinez del Rio Hermanos profit share/other income	4,200 (26.5)	—	—	—	—	35,000 (62.9)	6,533 (27.0)
Stocks and bonds	2,135 (13.5)	364 (3.7)	18,045 (65.7)	5,778 (30.1)	4,179 (24.3)	7,603 (13.7)	6,351 (26.3)
Mining dividends	—	—	—	444 (2.3)	—	—	74 (0.3)
Other	125 (0.8)	65 (0.7)	24 (0.1)	—	—	—	36 (0.1)
Total	15,860 (100.0)	9,829 (100.0)	27,469 (100.0)	19,222 (100.0)	17,179 (100.0)	55,603 (100.0)	24,194 (100.0)

Source: CMRFH.

Table 9
Income as Percentage of Net Worth, Gregorio Martínez del Río, Selected Years
(Current Pesos)

	Average Annual Income	Average Annual Net Worth	Income as % of Net Worth
1831-33	7,634	39,899	19.2
1841-43	17,386	230,524	7.6
1856-58	30,771	411,892	7.5

Source: CMRFH.

generations of the Martínez del Río family a lasting patrimony.

What accounts for the family's failure in Mexico in this early period? It was not a lack of interest or technical ability. As the preceding sketches demonstrate, the Martínez del Ríos were well trained in commerce and they actively promoted an array of economic endeavors. In designing their enterprises, they were rational and calculating and motivated by the incentive for profit. They had an abundance of capital at their disposal. Others who began with fewer economic assets succeeded in enriching themselves even in the dismal conditions of the time. What occurred, then, was not purely a business failure. Chapter 3 records the social dimensions of the family's misadventure.

3. The Martínez del Río Family in Mexico, 1830-1860

Marriage and Kinship in Mexico

Marriage, an institution that helps to define the family, also provides in most societies a mechanism by which broader group alliances can be constructed for more general or specific social, economic, and political objectives. In early national Mexico, marital alliances were especially important. Consider the frequent marriages between foreign merchants and Mexican families in this era. These were appealing to the merchants because in many cases the host families controlled extensive economic enterprises or had access to those who did. Marriage made available as well the many useful social and political resources owned by established families.

Mexican families had their own motives for welcoming alliances with outsiders. There were compelling historical precedents: peninsular merchants commonly married into the Creole families of New Spain. The rationale for such unions did not change after independence. With their overseas connections, foreigners gave Mexican families a chance to employ their capital more effectively by expanding the range of available economic opportunities. Grooms often brought with them large sums of cash needed by Mexican families who, wealthy as they might be, suffered from a chronic lack of liquidity. Finally, these marriages helped to revitalize the old families by bringing in ambitious people with new ways of doing things. In a culture where family longevity was esteemed, marital alliances were a proven way to help ensure a family's adjustment to changing times.[1]

Many important figures in the foreign merchant community in Mexico City took Mexican brides. Daniel O'Ryan married into a prominent family based in Guadalajara. Edward P. Wilson, a shareholder in the large private company formed to administer the tobacco monopoly in 1830, married María Ignacia Agreda, the daughter of the Conde de Agreda. Ewen MacKintosh, the British consul in Mexico in the 1840s, married Tercia Villanueva. Guillermo Drusina, a Protestant, obtained a papal dispensation to marry María de la Cruz Noriega y Vicario, the daughter of the late

Sergeant Major Juan de Noriega and María Luisa Vicario (who was also the widow of Antonio Vivanco). María Noriega's sister, Ana, was the wife of Charles O'Gorman, the British consul-general in Mexico in the 1830s. Felipe Nerí del Barrio, the Guatemalan consul and an active *empresario* in Mexico City in the 1830s, took for his wife Rafaela Rengel y Fagoaga.[2]

A complex network of kinship and shared interests linked the Noriega, Morán, Vivanco, and Moreno families into a clan alliance. In these social groupings based on kinship, families tended to work together in economic and political ventures—all benefited from the combination of resources. Marriage permitted foreigners such as Drusina and O'Gorman to join these larger groups. Drusina's mother-in-law, María Luisa Vicario, was an active entrepreneur whose properties included the Hacienda de San Antonio located in Tlalpam, just south of Mexico City. Her daughter from her first marriage, Loreto Vivanco, the marquesa de Vivanco, married General José Morán, the minister of war and president of the Council of State in the 1830s. Like her mother, Loreto Vivanco was active in business. María Luisa Vicario's sister, Leona Vicario, was the wife of Colonel Santiago Moreno, another prominent military officer from a noble family.

A look at two enterprises involving the extended clan in which Drusina and his business partner, Gregorio José Martínez del Río, took part helps to illustrate the convenience of family-structured activity. Political connections enabled General Morán to take a sizable interest in various land titles granted by the governor of Coahuila and Texas under the Colonization Law. Subsequently, María Luisa Vicario, General Morán, and Drusina and his wife formed a company to develop this Texas land. The venture was characteristic of enterprises well adapted to the politicized economy of the day. A soldier-politician provided the government concession and other political requirements. A patriarchal figure (this time it was the matriarch Vicario) symbolized the family medium around which the company to exploit the concession was structured. The foreign element in the family (Drusina) used his resources and contacts in the merchant community to assemble the venture capital needed to underwrite the project. As with the Texas lands, Drusina invited his partner, Gregorio José, to join him in another company formed to develop the Rosario mine in Chihuahua. The other shareholders in this company included Colonel Moreno, María Luisa Vicario, General Morán, and Loreto Vivanco.[3]

Felipe Nerí del Barrio, José Pablo and Pedro's close friend, belonged to a separate clan formed by the Fagoaga-Flores-Campero-Echeverría families. His wife, Rafaela, the condesa de Alcaraz, was the daughter of José Antonio Rengel and María Josefa Fagoaga. The Fagoagas, a titled noble family in Bourbon New Spain, had made their fortune in mining. After independence, they remained politically influential, even if not as wealthy as before. Soon after his marriage, Barrio joined his wife's uncle, José

Francisco Fagoaga, the marqués de Apartado, in founding one of the more prominent Mexican commercial houses of the 1830s. Fagoaga & Barrio enjoyed remarkable prosperity, partially because of its successes in acquiring properties from church and state agencies. Like most of the old families, the Fagoagas were assigned places in the directing bodies that managed the properties and the investment funds belonging to various religious associations based in Mexico City. On the secular front, Francisco Fagoaga, José Francisco's brother, was the vice-president and managing director of the Banco de Amortización, a government-owned bank. The bank's president, Pedro José Echeverría, was the brother of Javier Echeverría, the minister of hacienda in 1839. Legislation assigned to this bank various national properties (*bienes nacionales*) to be used to redeem the debased copper currency (the scourge of Mexican commerce in the 1830s). In practice, most of the income from the sale of the bank's properties was diverted into the national treasury to pay the government's many creditors, including the Fagoagas, who owned large amounts of old and new government debt issues.

In managing its various enterprises in Mexico, the Fagoaga family generally worked in unison with the Flores, Campero, and Echeverría families. Although there were great profits derived from this union, the workings of such pacts could sometimes exert negative influences on the individuals involved. For example, José Francisco Fagoaga fell victim to a terminal illness in 1841. To protect family honor (and to ensure that his properties did not end up in the wrong hands), Fagoaga ordered a general liquidation of his assets and arranged a settlement with all of his creditors before his death. The backwash from this, especially the untimely dissolution of Barrio & Fagoaga, nearly bankrupted Barrio. Although the Guatemalan's worth far exceeded his liabilities, he lacked cash to pay off his creditors. Fortunately, family considerations prevailed. Barrio received a friendly, low-interest loan from the Echeverrías, which staved off the liquidity crisis and prevented creditors from seizing his mortgaged properties.[4]

Distinct institutional biases smoothed the way for family-oriented economies in early national Mexico. The main body of Spanish law and customary practices, carried over unchanged from colonial times to the national period, gave extraordinary protection to a family's property. Nowhere is the Spanish preoccupation for social stability so well revealed as in its concern for the conservation of the family, the social organ that faithfully reproduced in the present the order of the past. Individuals could and often did go bankrupt, but their wives and children and the larger family more often did not. All property acquired during a marriage belonged jointly to both spouses. Neither could enter into contracts that risked this joint property without explicit permission or license from the other. Contracts requiring a husband's permission for his wife to engage in business transactions have been interpreted to suggest that the institutional framework was rigged to restrict women's participation in business. Although in a general sense that was probably true, a husband also had to get his wife's permission to enter into certain kinds of transactions. If he did not, creditors might not be able to seize the wife's share of property offered as collateral. Wives enjoyed a special status as preferential creditors of their husbands in regards to property such as the dowries that they introduced into a marriage. They could and did sue their spouses to get control of assets after a business disaster. To take advantage of this institutional shelter, *empresarios* sometimes deliberately assigned property to their family to keep it safe from creditors. Specific legislation existed to protect children's property, not only from creditors, but even from parents who had second thoughts. Property transfers to minors were simple matters; property transfers away from minors required a lengthy and complicated court procedure.[5]

The Martínez del Río Family

After Ventura Martínez decided to make a permanent home in Mexico in the 1820s, one of his priorities was to find a spouse. A marriage, if well conceived, would give his family a place in the social order. Looking out for *all* of Martínez's investments in Mexico City, Guillermo Drusina advised his partner to make a speedy return from Guadalajara in July 1829: "I have seen in the papers the arrival of a certain French Lieutenant Colonel Jaureguiberry, who previously was reputed to be a suitor of a young lady very dear to you if I am not mistaken about a certain seven letters. Careful. Do not let this rival corsair steal from you a good catch, that is, if you intend to continue the hunt."[6] The "certain seven letters" referred to Manuela, the twenty-seven-year-old daughter of Colonel Juan Francisco de Azcárate, a Military Supreme Court justice and a former regidor of Mexico. Through the marriage of Manuela's sister, María, to Manuel de Rul y Obregón (the conde de Rul), the Azcárates were linked to the Rul-Pérez Galvez-Villavicencio families, a powerful combination. Marriage with Manuela would incorporate Martínez and his children into that clan and provide them a high-level entry into Mexican society, which they might use to make even more advantageous marriages in the future. For the senior Azcárate, the marriage offered the prospect of providing his family with much-needed income. Social prominence, even considerable political power, however much they facilitated the accumulation of wealth, provided no lasting guarantees. Colonel Azcárate owed large debts coming due in 1830 and 1831. Conversely, Martínez had money, but he lacked the connections to employ it most advantageously.

What Martínez failed to anticipate was that Azcárate might use his daughter's marriage to extort money directly. Two days before the wedding was scheduled, Manuela's father brought up the matter of a dowry. Somewhat disingenuously, Martínez pleaded poverty, citing old losses and recent business reverses in Mexico. Azcárate was not satisfied and became enraged with his prospective son-in-law. That evening, when the aging merchant was comfortably seated beside his fiancée in a sitting room at the Azcárate house, the colonel, accompanied by his nephew Francisco Madariaga, a well-known public notary, burst into the room and demanded that Martínez sign a document drawn up by the notary. This was an *escritura* that pledged Manuela's husband to donate to his bride a dowry equal in value to one-tenth of all his belongings, up to a maximum of $30,000. It stipulated that if Martínez failed to deliver the dowry when requested or that if the marriage did not last, he was obligated to pay an additional $15,000 penalty.[7] Under duress, Martínez signed the *escritura* and the wedding went on as planned. Immediately after the ceremony on 28 January 1830, the bride's father demanded the dowry. The elderly groom could not, or would not, comply and Azcárate imposed the penalty clause.

A dowry was one problem; the fact that the newlyweds were incompatible was a second, more serious problem. After eleven months, Manuela left her husband, moved back into her father's house, and contracted a lawyer to file a petition for an ecclesiastical divorce (permanent separation) on the grounds of "severe and bad treatment." A brief and disastrous attempt at reconciliation ended in violent arguments and mutual recriminations. The church granted the divorce in August 1832 without naming a guilty party.[8] Afterward, Martínez's wife continued to harass her husband with legal action intended to force him to pay her the $45,000 dowry. Martínez countersued and threatened to withhold her monthly support payments while he attempted to have the *escritura* voided. Whenever one side secured a favorable ruling from one court, the other side had the case transferred to another court or began new litigation in the ecclesiastical court system to undo the judgments of the civil courts, or vice versa. Finally, both sides agreed to submit their differences to informal, but binding, arbitration by Supreme Court justice Manuel Peña y Peña. As ordered, Ventura Martínez delivered $9,000 to his wife in December 1835. The dowry was considered fully paid, all support payments were ended, and his wife could not take further legal action against him. Several years later, after Martínez's death, Manuela married Fernando de Agreda, the son of the conde de Agreda. In a written prenuptial contract, both parties declared the other to be their sole beneficiary and executor.[9]

Martínez's attempt to engineer new social connections for his family nded in a personal fiasco that had a profound impact on his children's future. It meant that they would lack organic ties to Mexican society in the years to come. Useful friends and acquaintances they would have, but

Martínez's children would remain outsiders, more comfortable in London or Paris than in Mexico City and more at home with the foreign colony than with Mexican society. Whether because of the unhappy experience of their father or because of their own predispositions, they did not try immediately to resolve this critical social deficiency. None of them, in fact, took a Mexican spouse before 1855.

An accomplice in Manuel María's commercial misadventures in the early 1830s, Nicolás Pedemonte, was an Italian pensioner of good family and bad fortune who had settled in Paris. Like Manuel María, he was eventually obliged to flee to Brussels to escape imprisonment. Neither Manuel María nor Greogrio José had much positive to say about the Italian and they were puzzled by José Pablo's willingness to lend money to Pedemonte and to attempt to arrange for him a settlement with his creditors. In February 1840 an exasperated Gregorio José warned his little brother: "Mr. Pedemonte is abusing infamously your kindness, and it is essential that you open your eyes. . . . the way in which he acts makes me see that Manuel María is right in the opinion he has of this *Saintly* man, and I repeat, open your eyes!"[10] In fact, José Pablo had eyes only for eighteen-year-old Angela Pedemonte, whom he described as "a creature filled with merit and of true Angelic character."[11] After making elaborate plans to slip the bride's father into Paris to witness the ceremony, José Pablo married his sweetheart in May 1842.[12]

Like his younger brother, Gregorio José was anxious to marry, but with conditions. He confided to José Pablo in June 1840, "As I believe a woman from there [Mexico] would not be right for me, and as those from here [England] go better with my disposition and natural character, I will tell you frankly this is why I have extended my stay here." The problem arose, he explained because, "here it is so difficult to introduce yourself into society."[13] Nevertheless, the hunt was on. He recruited his brothers and their many friends and relatives in Europe to help out. José Pablo's mother-in-law presented Gregorio José with a crowded roster of eligible women. Mary Anne Collins, the sister of a long-time friend, seems to have been a leading candidate, but she died suddenly and tragically, and Gregorio José never found his ideal English mate. As a much older man, he married thirty-three-year-old Josefa Leno de Rascón, the daughter of Joaquín Leno and Josefa Rascón of Jalapa, Veracruz.[14] The marriage took place in January 1856, too late to have an effect on a number of events reaching their conclusion as their era came to a close.

These marriages and the family's relations in its ancestral home, Panama, constituted the basis for a kinship network, but it was one that did little to advance the Martínez del Ríos' interests in Mexico. In no sense was the Martínez del Río-Martínez-Retes-Ansoátegui-Dorè-Pedemonte clan equivalent to the Mexican groups previously described. Although the family had relations scattered around the world—in Mexico, in Panama, New Granada, France, and Italy—they were misplaced, nonfunctional, and provided no access to Mexican opportunities. Although family ties seem to be a precondition for construction of clan alliances, and although these family ties function to structure the workings of such alliances, these social conglomerations are only as durable and effective as the economic exchanges they are organized around.

Consider the changing patterns of relations maintained between the Martínez del Ríos and their Mexican cousins, the Martínez Reteses. Ventura Martínez's uncle Ignacio Martínez de Retes, married in Panama in 1791, but afterward moved his wife and eleven children to the west coast of Mexico. He established a business in Tepic, on the trade route between the port of San Blas and Guadalajara. In the colonial period, Martínez Retes seems to have maintained a close working relationship with Martínez's Panama trade. After independence, Martínez used the Martínez Retes home in Tepic as his base in searching out debtors in 1823 and 1824. Ignacio died in 1826 and his son, José Pablo Martínez Retes, assumed his role as Martínez's *apoderado* in Western Mexico. Building on that relationship, Drusina & Martínez employed Martínez Retes as its agent for moving money and collecting accounts in the region. As a deputy in the Jalisco legislature and as the *jefe político* of Tepic, Martínez Retes was a useful kinsman, especially as his own twelve children had married into local families, giving him contacts in Tepic, Culiacán, and Rosario.

Serious problems arose, however, which undermined the compatibility of these intrafamily exchanges. With his personal finances in complete disarray in the mid-1830s, Martínez Retes failed to honor drafts against his account by Drusina & Martínez. His inability to maintain positive economic exchanges might not have been so problematic had his social and political connections in remote Western Mexico been more relevant to the Martínez del Ríos, whose interests were centered around Mexico City. Although their economic differences were settled amicably in 1840 without recourse to the courts, no interaction based on family identification took place afterward between the two groups.[15]

The relationship of the Martínez del Río family with the Ansoáteguis was more complex. Delineating family boundaries to define who was entitled to what share of family goods and services was a particularly vexing probelm when one family's finances were derelict. María Dolores's husband, Pedro, was the son of Juan Ansoátegui, a Panamanian merchant contemporary with Ventura Martínez. Pedro's brother Manuel managed a business in Panama in partnership with his brother-in-law, Julián Sosa. Pedro's other brothers included Miguel, who ran a store in Guayaquil; Domingo, who emigrated to Mexico in 1839; and Juan, who took over José María's trade route—Jamaica-Panama-Peru—in the 1830s.

After José María's accident at sea, Pedro suggested to his in-laws that his brother Juan would be an excellent choice as successor because Juan had extensive trading experience in the area and because, as a relative, he could be trusted to look out for the family's interests. Materially, Juan Ansoátegui was ill-equipped for such a task. He operated with little capital and with tiny profit margins. The Peru trade never recovered from the shock of independence, and small-scale operators like Pedro's brother were the most affected. First Pedro, then Pedro's in-laws were required to subsidize his business. In 1830 Pedro assisted his brother with £1,500 in credit drawn against Gregorio José's private accounts with London commercial houses. Despite periodic injections of new operating capital, Juan's business soured and he was obliged to leave Jamaica and return home to Panama in 1838.

It was a dismal homecoming. His father was too old to work and needed constant care. Manuel owed $10,000 to creditors after his business with Sosa went bankrupt. Again, Pedro borrowed from his wife's family and persuaded Gregorio José to open a new line of credit for Juan. Three years later, Juan's business in Panama was embargoed and he found it impossible to secure outside financing to keep his company open. After much discussion with his in-laws, Pedro offered Juan a line of credit with Martínez del Río Hermanos in 1841. Conditions in Panama continued to worsen. When the family firm closed Juan Ansoátegui's account in 1846 because of repeated overdrafts, Pedro's brother had accumulated a large debt, which was still outstanding when he died in 1850.

Domingo Ansoátegui joined Pedro in Mexico in 1839. His brothers' businesses had fizzled out and Domingo, who had worked for them in Jamaica, Panama, and Guayaquil, had nowhere else to go. Ignoring his partners' objections, Pedro assigned to his brother the responsibility for managing the 10 Percent Fund. Acting as the representatives for the owners of these Mexican government debt issues (discussed in chapters 7 and 8), Domingo collected and combined the piecemeal payments made by the government and divided the proceeds proportionally among the creditors of the fund. As the agent for the fund, he received a 1 percent commission on the dividends aid out. The Martínez del Río brothers felt these monies should have gone into the cash box of the family business, as would have been the case if Pedro, as a partner in the firm, actually did the work; however, Pedro's brothers-in-law adamantly refused suggestions that Domingo be admitted as a partner—contributing instead of capital (he had none) his "head, activity, and devotion."[16] Instead, Domingo worked as an unsalaried employee of the company until 1845, when he was granted an annual salary of $2,000, most of which was applied toward reducing the size of Juan Ansoátegui's account with Martínez del Río Hermanos. When Domingo returned to Panama in 1851 to settle Juan's estate there, he assumed the balance of his brother's account as his own. Family ethics mandated that a sacred trust should not be abused. At the same time, however, Domingo asked for and received new favors from his brother's kin. He traded nearly worthless credits against the Mexican government to Martínez del Río Hermanos in exchange for negotiable drafts drawn against the family firm and he secured a promise of reemployment. When he returned in 1854, Pedro's illness and a shortage of managerial talent made it necessary for him to assume an active role in the day-to-day direction of Martínez del Río Hermanos in the critical years to come.[17]

José Ansoátegui y Sosa, the son of Julián Sosa of Panama, emigrated to Mexico with his uncle Domingo in 1854. He established himself in Cuernavaca as a merchant dealing in dry goods, mostly consignments from Miraflores. Domingo had trusted Ansoátegui y Sosa enough to name him as his *apoderado* in Panama during the 1840s, but Pedro mistrusted his nephew, suggesting his lack of "morality" might result in new debts for Martínez del Río Hermanos. In the end, Domingo's assessment proved the more accurate, as José Ansoátegui y Sosa's store in Cuernavaca became an important outlet for Miraflores's textiles in the late 1850s.[18]

Pedro seems also to have had little confidence in his son José, who at twenty-two years of age in 1854, was—according to his father—"still like a child."[19] In this instance, Pedro was upset that José spent his time at Miraflores rather than concentrating on his apprenticeship with Blasbach & Company in Mexico City. Even with such failings, by 1858 José had advanced to a position as clerk with Martínez del Río Hermanos and, ironically, in the next two decades he would be the only member of the extended family to enjoy any measure of financial security.

What could the Ansoáteguis do for the Martínez del Ríos? As Ventura Martínez's *apoderados*, they cared for his property in Panama while he was in Mexico. After his death they continued to serve his estate in a similar capacity. From stations in Jamaica, Panama, and Peru, they provided their kin in Mexico and Europe with sometimes valuable news about commercial and political conditions in South America. Juan Ansoátegui even helped out with such incidental errands as securing a copy of José Pablo's baptismal certificate, needed for his marriage in 1842. And of course, Pedro, Domingo, and José managed the family's accounts in Mexico as reliable partners and employees in Martínez del Río Hermanos. Even so, the Martínez del Ríos came to feel that the Ansoáteguis asked too much and gave too little in return. When compared with the Dorès and the Pedemontes, Manuel María's and José Pablo's in-laws, however, Pedro's kin maintained the more useful, if limited, interfamily exchanges.

When Manuel María died in 1844, his brothers feared his widow, Stephanie Dorè, might remove his deposits from the family firm at a time when Martínez del Río Hermanos was hard-pressed to pay its current obligations. Concern about the fiscal management of Manuel María's estate was linked to a more serious disagreement with Stephanie. Manuel María had died without leaving a will, which might have named his brothers as executors of his estate and guardians of his children. After contemplating legal action to assure the children of "their patrimony," Manuel María's brothers were forced to concede the loss of these children to the family in Mexico.[20] His widow did agree to keep Manuel María's funds deposited in Martínez del Río Hermanos as a trust for the children.

José Pablo knew that when he married Angela Pedemonte he was marrying her family as well: "You know that the family for a long time has faced great adversity: consequently, in addition to the usual obligations of matrimony, I take on a heavy responsibility because, if as a friend I have helped them before, now as a member of the family I will be in the future their only support."[21] After the wedding in Paris, José Pablo was required to pay the costs of moving his in-laws back to their ancestral home in Milan. To lighten the burden of maintaining them, he hoped to rehabilitate Angela's younger brother, Amadeo. Using Gregorio José's contacts in Liverpool, José Pablo placed his brother-in-law as an apprentice with Watson Brothers & Company. The firm had branches in Zacatecas and Mexico City and José Pablo believed the apprenticeship would provide excellent opportunities, for Martínez del Río Hermanos and for the Pedemontes. Unfortunately, Nicolás Pedemonte's son—brought up for a life of gentlemanly leisure—could not bear the regimented, monastic existence required of an apprentice clerk. Frustrated and embarrassed by the failure of his project, José Pablo vowed in 1846, "It is convenient to avoid forever any relationship with that man that is not simply the cordial manner that corresponds to kinship . . . my responsibility has ended."[22]

Friends and Family

The Martínez del Ríos were not ignorant of the implications of their social isolation—their lack of family ties—for the family business in Mexico. To compensate for the absence of useful kin, Gregorio José proposed in 1841, "As in this country one cannot do anything by the straight road, I believe that the only way that remains for us to make a good House is to find ourselves some good Compadre or Padrino, as the others do."[23] José Pablo concurred: "You know that in Mexico the best arbiter for everything is personal influence."[24] They hoped that friends like Felipe Nerí del Barrio might take the place of family.

Well respected in Mexico City business and political circles, Barrio's own family connections were superb. A prosperous businessman in the 1830s, his interests were not limited to Barrio & Fagoaga. Beginning in 1837, he joined the Flores brothers and other *empresarios* in founding a company to administer the tobacco monopoly under contracts let by the Banco de

Amortización. His kinsmen and business associates Francisco Fagoaga and José Echeverría managed the bank. With the profits from these and other enterprises, Barrio acquired and began refurbishing the rich sugar hacienda of Temisco, near Cuernavaca. His investments there exceeded a half million pesos. At about this same time, Barrio purchased the Rancho de Miraflores to use as a site for building an iron foundry and a textile factory. With many projects to manage, Barrio was dangerously overextended and he invited José Pablo and Pedro to bring in Martínez del Río Hermanos as a partner in the textile factory. Teetering on the verge of bankruptcy, Barrio was unable to deliver his alloted share of finance capital. When Miraflores failed to produce the easy profits Barrio forecast, Martínez del Río Hermanos was required to commit additional funds to keep the factory running. Friendship compromised the Martínez del Ríos' freedom of action, as they were not eager to impose on this partner the penalties that might have won them outright ownership of Miraflores. Ventura de la Cruz summed up the problems created when friendship and business were confused: "Pedro, without consulting me, got in so deep with the friend Barrio that who knows how we will be able to collect afterward—how well you know about this, above all when there are relations of friendship in between."[25] As for getting an indemnity from Barrio, José Pablo warned that even if they went to court, there was bound to be a problem: "It is not easy to make a clean slate of this matter because of the illegality of so-called usury."[26] Nor was it feasible to collect an extra share of Miraflores's meager profits, because Barrio, without his partner's consent, mortgaged his share in the factory to the Echeverrías to cover his other debts. But the main difficulty was Barrio, the friend, who "never says yes or no and is content to leave it to our judgment, so that the business goes on eternally."[27]

Disagreements between Barrio and the Martínez del Ríos nearly led to a bitter confrontation in the courts when their partnership was dissolved in 1849 and Barrio fixed a high price for selling his share in Miraflores to his friends. But on that occasion, as in many others, a sense of compromise prevailed and their friendship survived.[28] José Pablo and Pedro continued to believe Barrio's personal qualities more than compensated for the inconvenience of his insolvency: "It is true that the businesses in which we have entered with [Barrio] until now have been fatal for us; but in this you cannot blame him; for one in his situation it seems that all is conspiring to slow him down . . . but by this I do not fail to consider him a good friend, on whom in other circumstances we could better depend than on those who now toast to our friendship."[29]

Privy to the inner circles of wealth and power, Barrio furnished intelligence useful to the Martínez del Ríos in their constant struggle to stay one step ahead of rapacious tax collectors. For example, in November 1846 Barrio gave the family advance warning of new forced loans. This enabled

Pedro, who was most affected, to take effective countermeasures.[30] At other times, Barrio let his friends know what the ministers in government had planned, who the effective influence peddlers of the moment were, how relations and business deals between important *empresarios* were shaping up, and when the family firm or its partners might best take advantage of passing opportunities.

Barrio steered the Martínez del Ríos into assorted business ventures. A few gave good results; many, like Miraflores, did not. Martínez del Río Hermanos bought shares in the Veta Grande mining company and suffered heavy losses. Ventura de la Cruz complained bitterly in 1851 that minority interests were sacrificed in this company because its director, Francisco Fagoaga, put his family's interests and those of Barrio and Flores first.[31]

At best, Barrio was a mixed blessing as business counselor. His direction in the social sphere, however, was unchallenged—the Barrios were the center of a broader circle of the family's Mexican friends. The Flores and Campero families, part of the larger group to which Barrio belonged, enjoyed particularly close and cordial relations with the Martínez del Ríos. Compadrazgo helped the Martínez del Ríos to reinforce their friendship with Barrio and to give it new meanings.[32] With compadrazgo, individuals incur ritual obligations to guard the well-being of each other's children. Consequently, fictive ties of kinship are created. This pseudokinship may be as close and as durable as more conventional family ties, although there are limitations, variations, and gradations within the system. Compadres, persons of equal status, exchange goods and services in addition to the obvious child-rearing responsibilities. Barrio supplied José Pablo with the favors described above; his compadre responded by facilitating his access to the economic resources controlled by the Martínez del Río family. As an added bonus, José Pablo was always on call as a physician. Indeed, Barrio's nickname for his compadre was *doctorcito* (little doctor), a term of endearment and an obvious reference to José Pablo's short stature.

If the Martínez del Ríos' experience can be judged as typical, several observations can be made about compadrazgo systems in the context of their function linking families together as pseudokin. First, compadres cement their relationships with considerable social interaction. José Pablo and his family spent much of their free time in the 1840s as guests of the Barrio family at Temisco. There they passed leisurely holidays and found refuge from the capital's cold winters and its seasonal epidemics of cholera, plague, and political violence. Second, although a person may have several compadres, not all of the relationships are of the same intensity; some are more consequential than others. For José Pablo, references to the compadre meant his friend Barrio. Finally, the institution is no more durable than the bonds of reciprocity that bind the two parties together. As the 1840s progressed, Barrio spent more and more time at Temisco. He was less often present in Mexico City to maintain intimate social relations with José Pablo and his family and, because of his deteriorating financial situation, it became difficult to relate to this compadre as a peer. As José Pablo extended his stay in Mexico, he became less dependent on Barrio's social connections and, after acquiring and developing a country retreat of his own near Tacubaya, in an area where the Mexico City elite relaxed for short holidays, the doctor had little interest in making the tiresome, time-consuming trip to Temisco. As the rationale for the compadres' relationship faded, the nature of their relationship was also transformed.

Eclipsing Barrio as José Pablo's compadre in the 1850s was Manuel Escandón, certainly the single most remarkable businessman of this era. Escandón had a well-deserved reputation for profiting from adversity, especially from his partners' misfortunes. That Escandón and José Pablo should become compadres was especially ironic, given their past conflicts of interest and the doctor's strident denunciations of the *empresario*. Manuel Escandón, like his brothers, Joaquín and Vicente, and other members of the Escandón and Amore families, traveled frequently to Europe. The Escandóns and the Martínez del Ríos knew each other through the Mexican and Latin American colonies in Europe within which both families mingled. José Pablo's initial disparagement of the Escandóns seems to have been the result of jealousy—the suspicion that the Escandóns perceived his family as social inferiors. When the Escandóns left Paris in the fall of 1842 without saying their farewell, José Pablo concluded, "These people have too much egotism and too little shame."[33] To make matters worse, Escandón soon became involved in a scheme to consolidate Mexico's foreign debt and his intrigues jeopardized the economic interests of the Martínez del Río family. On learning of Escandón's departure for Europe in 1846, José Pablo warned Gregorio José in London, "No doubt Don Manuelito, like an old and impudent fox, will use all his tricks to find you out and trick you."[34] When the family's plans went awry after 1846, José Pablo believed his worst suspicions of the *empresario* were confirmed. He scolded Gregorio José:

It is truly and very lamentably sad to find ourselves sold out to our enemies . . . and to enemies as perfidious as E . . . and in spite of the warnings and advice that I gave you, and that you yourself know well. I shudder to think that a single moment of carelessness on your part can be enough for his shrewd victory over your good faith, and when you opened your eyes it was already too late!—Mark well that man is already versed in hypocrisy, and he is so skilled in trickery and intrigue that falseness in his hand takes on visions of truth and innocence.[35]

Despite such recriminations, Escandón and the Martínez del Ríos began to work in unison in the same matter that once separated them, and the years after 1848 witnessed increasing collaboration in other ventures as well. The economic reconciliation fostered a dramatic social reconciliation. Escandón became godfather to one of José Pablo's daughters and regularly addressed José Pablo as "Doctorcito" and as "My Dearest Compadre." The relationship with Escandón helped Martínez del Río Hermanos's and José Pablo's private business dealings to prosper in the early 1850s. When the family firm entered a period of profound crisis beginning in 1856, the compadre tried to help José Pablo and his family with loans and other economic assistance.

When fortune altogether abandoned the family, however, the simple fact of friendship, even with the rich and powerful like Escandón, was no guarantee for safe passage through those economically troubled years. Pedro assessed Escandón's priorities in light of the family's plight: "Even though he professes a great friendship, all prefer security."[36] Illustrative of how their life lines had once more diverged, the Martínez del Ríos had begun an inexorable plunge toward bankruptcy in 1856. That same year Escandón was more prosperous than ever. While their friend went on holiday in Europe to visit St. Petersburg and Moscow and to witness the coronation of the czar, the Martínez del Ríos remained in Mexico frantically looking for an escape from the darkening cloud gathering on the political horizon.

The family's friendship with Manuel Olasgarre, the son of Pedro Juan de Olasgarre, was as unlikely as that with Escandón. As Ventura Martínez's heirs, the Martínez del Ríos held a mortgage on Atequisa, but they were never able to take possession, owing to Manuel Olasgarre's determination to retain the only piece of property he had inherited. When Olasgarre sold the hacienda on his terms in 1838, he negotiated a settlement whereby the original *escritura* signed in 1823 was canceled in return for payment of his father's debt to Martínez's estate, minus a $4,000 discount.

With the principal debts of his father settled, Olasgarre began work on his own fortune. In 1844 he constructed the first modern textile factory in Jalisco. For a 70 percent share in Olasgarre's company, Manuel Escandón provided the financing. Olasgarre furnished the Hacienda Magdalena near Guadalajara as a site for the factory and gave his time and attention as its manager. Within a decade he had established a reputation as one of the region's foremost businessmen. And like many *empresarios* he mixed his business with politics. His political career culminated with an appointment as Santa Anna's minister of hacienda in 1854.

The friendship that developed between Olasgarre and the Martínez del Ríos paid handsome dividends for both parties. As fellow textile mill owners, they had much in common. Olasgarre made frequent visits to Miraflores, sometimes to make suggestions for improvements, sometimes to copy innovations. Their businesses were far enough apart that there was little competition for markets. A frequent houseguest of the Martínez del Ríos when he visited the capital, Olasgarre looked out for his friends after he became minister of hacienda. When Santa Anna's government was overthrown in 1855, José Pablo put up his money and his person as a bond for Olasgarre's release from prison.[37]

As this discussion has shown, the Martínez del Río family was not without Mexican friends. It would be an exaggeration to suggest, however, that they matched the social resources of the native families. Befitting the family's foreign character, many of their friends were not citizens of Mexico or, if they were citizens, they were individuals who spent more time in Europe than in Mexico.

Ventura Martínez's associates in colonial commerce and their children constituted the largest part of the family's Spanish and French friends. Like José María Sancho and Ignacio Ybarrondo, many were merchants who remained in Mexico throughout the 1820s and well into the 1830s. Curiously enough, it was not political persecutions such as the decreed expulsion of Spaniards in the late 1820s that persuaded them to give up on Mexico and retire to Southern Spain after 1840; rather, it was the generally bad returns they earned on investments in Mexico. Sancho's son chose to spend his $1 million inheritance in Spain, but Ybarrando's son returned to Mexico in the 1850s and joined the Martínez del Ríos in several mining and land speculations. Other Spanish friends of the family, like Francisco Vallejo and Hermengildo Viya, were more recent acquaintances. Vallejo, while a resident in Mexico City in the early 1830s, struck up a lasting friendship with the Panamanians who lived near his house. Leaving the capital in the mid-1830s, he married into a Mexican family and established a permanent residence and business in the tobacco town of Orizaba. In the early 1840s, he relied on José Pablo and Gregorio José to arrange the education of his son, Manuel, who was a classmate of José Ansoátegui in the Clapham Commons school near London in the early 1840s, and entrusted their family's firm with up to $40,000 deposited in interest-bearing accounts. Like Vallejo, Viya worked in a partnership with a brother. Viya Hermanos, their import-export house in Veracruz, served as Martínez del Río Hermanos's principal agent in the port city.

The Martínez del Ríos' French connections were José Marco de Pont and Justo Víctor Lubervieille and his brother, Juan Bautista. Pont was acquainted with Ventura Martínez and José María in the Peru trade and acted as their agent in Lima throughout the 1820s and 1830s. When Pont retired to Europe in 1840, Gregorio José, already disenchanted with Martínez del Río Hermanos, hoped to become his partner: "I *believe* he has insinuated as much (even though with much delicacy) but mercantile marriages are very delicate things. . . . I have not given any understanding nor have I thought about it."[38] The partnership never materialized (because Gergorio José could never free himself from Martínez del Río Hermanos), but Pont continued to serve as the family's agent and adviser in Europe.

Justo Víctor Lubervieille, like Pont, was invited to witness José Pablo's wedding in Paris in 1842. His association with the family began more than a decade earlier when he won Ventura Martínez's favor by testifying on his behalf during divorce proceedings in 1832. Martínez's children had mixed feelings about this friend, who had a well-deserved reputation as a gossip. Gregorio José was infuriated to learn in November 1836 that Lubervieille had discussed publicly the terms of a loan received from the family and, in retaliation, he refused to renew the loan. But the friendship survived, and Lubervieille was the first to relay rumors in the spring of 1843 that Santa Anna planned to consolidate the public debt by breaking past agreements and promises to creditors and forcibly merging the many separate public debt funds. Lubervieille got his information from another Frenchman, Delumeau, who reputedly was courting simultaneously two sisters of Manuel Gorostiza, an especially venal public official and one of Santa Anna's principal henchmen.[39] After Justo Víctor retired to France, Juan Bautista continued the Lubervieille tradition in Mexico. His son married into the Amor family, important merchants and tobacco growers in the state of Veracruz. Since the Amors were allied by marriage and economic interests with the Escandóns, young Lubervieille's bride was Manuel Escandón's goddaughter.

The family had many English acquaintances. These included J. L. Lemmè and Frederick Huth, senior partners in two London commercial houses that handled most of Martínez del Río Hermanos's European accounts. Huth's relationship with the family originated in the old Peru trade and commerce between Jamaica, Panama, and Lima. Despite these close business ties, English merchants (in contrast to Spanish or French merchants) did not play an important role as friends. Only the Whitehead brothers, who were managers for Watson Brothers & Company in Zacatecas and Tampico, seem to have had an intimate relationship based as much on friendship as on business. Jacob H. Robertson, the Scot who managed the Miraflores factory for three decades after 1840, never managed to cultivate a close friendship with his employers. Edward J. Perry, who was brought to Mexico in August 1841 as a clerk for Martínez del Río Hermanos, was another long-time associate who seems to have had little importance as a friend.

The competitive nature of their business probably fostered as much rivalry as togetherness among the community of foreign merchants. Martínez del Río Hermanos was nominally a British firm. Its fiercest rival in Mexico was another British company, Manning & Marshall (later Manning & MacKintosh). The animosity these firms exhibited for one another in the 1840s had antecedents reaching back to 1829, when Drusina had warned Ventura Martínez that their commission and consignment business would face strong competition from Robert Manning, who had begun making extensive purchases in Europe with the backing of the House of Baring. Feelings engendered by the economic rivalry carried over into the social arena, and the Martínez del Ríos intensely disliked Manning. Before he returned to London in the late 1830s, Manning established a partnership with Ewen MacKintosh, the new British consul in Mexico City. The family discovered that this newcomer was even more disagreeable than their old nemesis. As far as their interests were concerned, MacKintosh was the single most dangerous man in Mexico, given the consul's influence in setting British foreign policy for Mexico.

The best English friends of the family were Stephen and Julie Williams, the Quakers who ran the school at Clapham Commons. José Pablo's and Pedro's sons, and the children of many family friends from Mexico, were educated by the Williamses. Gregorio José and José Pablo were frequent houseguests and when in London they always had Christmas dinner with the Williamses. Aside from a friendship valued in its own right, Stephen Williams offered the Martínez del Ríos business and political connections, which were used to further the family's interests in Mexico.

Midway through the decade of the 1840s, it was apparent that the well-being of the family's economic interests would be tied to its success in influencing British foreign policy toward Mexico. The family's rivalries with other British concerns made shaping that policy a difficult proposition. One way the family perceived that it might thwart MacKintosh was to develop its own network of affective relationships within the British diplomatic community in Mexico. The family had no success with Richard Pakenham, the British minister from 1832 to 1844, and only mixed results with Percival Doyle, chief officer in the British Legation from the mid-1840s until the mid-1850s. In 1854 Pedro aptly described the family's feelings toward Doyle: "That Irishman is perverse."[40]

The Martínez del Ríos had more luck with impressionable young men like Edward Thornton, who was attached to the Legation in 1845. José Pablo took special care to win Thornton's esteem, helping him around Mexico City, introducing him into the social circles there, and inviting him on excursions to Temisco. Thornton returned the favors by providing detailed intelligence on the internal affairs of the Legation, including sometimes accurate assessments of the British foreign minister's current attitude regarding the family's claims against the Mexican government. Even if they could not always counter MacKintosh's intrigues, at least they knew what he was up to. To neutralize the "evil cabal" in Mexico City, José Pablo urged Gregorio José to cultivate personal relations with high officials of the Foreign Office in London. He pointed out that, although bribes would not work in Great Britain as they did in Mexico, friendship might serve the same purpose:

I know of the difficulties there are in that country [Great Britain] for developing relations with a certain class of people, and the perhaps greater difficulty of exerting influence over them, above all by the means that here [Mexico] one is accustomed to. Nevertheless, I repeat to you that the heart, a brother everywhere, is the same and that more flies are caught with honey than without honey. Well you know that a kindness done in time and with delicacy mesmerizes people, without offending anyone, however scrupulous they may be.[41]

Thomas Worrall first came to the family's attention in 1839 when, as a representative for the London debt bondholders, he was involved in a mission to renegotiate Mexico's debt to Great Britain. The Martínez del Ríos expected that he might be named the British minister to Mexico in 1846. They were mistaken, but even without official status Worrall preserved his reputation as a fixer—a person with special influence in the Foreign Office. In 1856 Martínez del Río Hermanos commissioned him as a special agent to plead its cause directly to Lord Clarendon, the minister for foreign relations. Although effective in London, Worral's talents were misplaced in Mexico. He was expelled from the country when he refused to pay the Forced Contributions of May 1859.[42]

The family failed to win the hearts of Pakenham and Doyle, but they did very well with their successors, George Lettson and Frederick Glennie. Lettson, the British minister in Mexico after 1855, was José Pablo's tenant in his Tacubaya mission. In marked contrast to his predecessors, Lettson's relations with the Martínez del Río family were amicable and sympathetic. Frederick Glennie, the British consul in Mexico City in the late 1850s had an even more intimate friendship with the family. As children the Glennies and the Martínez del Ríos were educated together in Geneva. Frederick Glennie's brother, Arthur, had been Gregorio José's closest friend in London in the 1820s. Frederick Glennie rekindled that friendship when he arrived in Mexico in 1849 to establish a business in Guanajuato. He also served as the British consul in that mining center. By coincidence, Glennie was traveling with Ventura de la Cruz on the ill-fated voyage of the *Amazon* in 1852 and witnessed his death. When Glennie returned to Mexico, he married into an important Mexican family, the Trigüeros. As a compadre, Gregorio José was godfather to Glennie's children and was named in Glennie's will as their guardian.[43]

The family's friendships in the United States manifested the same political flavorings that characterized its British relations. Its single most important American friend was General Schuyler Hamilton, whose life José Pablo saved in 1847 when Hamilton was Scott's aide during the invasion of Mexico.[44] After the war, Hamilton gave the Martínez del Ríos fabulous contacts—a whole generation of army officer cronies from the Mexican War who became powerful public figures in the United States in the 1850s and 1860s.[45]

The Latin American colony in Europe was the setting for friendships that would have lasting consequences. José Bacilio Guerra, Ventura Martínez's attorney in Mexico City in the 1820s, spent most of his life as an emigré in the company of Antonio Gutiérrez Estrada, the head of an archconservative, promonarchist group of conspirators who eventually succeeded in offering the throne of Mexico to Maximillian. Gutiérrez Estrada's sister, Manuela, was married to Felipe Nerí del Barrio y Rengel, the son of José Pablo's compadre. Ventura de la Cruz and José Pablo frequently socialized with Guerra and Gutiérrez during their jaunts through Italy in the 1830s and 1840s. These acquaintances were fatefully renewed when José Pablo went to live in Italy in 1859. In the beginning the attraction of these conservatives was purely social, not ideological, as evidenced by José Pablo's friendship with José María Mora, a liberal. When Mora was the Mexican consul in Paris in the 1840s, José Pablo named him as the executor of his estate and attempted to use him (without much success) as a tool to combat Escandón's and MacKintosh's intrigues with the Mexican foreign debt. Colonel José Ignacio Tato, a friend of the family since the 1820s, seems to have been apolitical. As the Mexican consul in the busy port of Liverpool from 1843 through 1866, he served the Martínez del Ríos as a compendium of economic and political intelligence relating to Mexico and Great Britain.

As might be expected, Martínez's children did conserve ties to their homeland, New Granada, but ironically the best relationships with families from the old country did not originate in Panama or in Bogotá, but in London and Paris, where other families from New Granada sent their children to be educated. The head of a prominent family of merchants and politicians, General Tomás Ciprano de Mosquera, was the moderate conservative president of New Granada in the late 1840s. For the next several decades, he (and his kin) continued to wield power in that country. Throughout this era, 1830 to 1860, General Mosquera and his family made frequent trips to Europe to visit their children.[46] The Martínez del Ríos regularly consulted Mosquera on a variety of matters. Using this influence, Pedro secured an appointment in 1847 as New Granada's consul to Mexico. This enabled him to escape the forced loans and other abuses heaped on the unprotected in Mexico. In the following decade, the Martínez del Ríos used their friendship with Mosquera to advance more ambitious designs.

Like José Pablo, many of the foreign physicians working in Mexico preferred business to medicine. Few were as visible in business circles as the Swiss doctor, Jecker, a partner in one of the largest commercial houses in Mexico, an *agiotista*, and a dabbler in politics. More common were José Pablo's physician friends like the Pole Dr. Severino Galenzowski, and the Englishman Dr. John Park Macartney, who earned large salaries by attending the foreign personnel of the large German and British mining companies or by treating Mexico City's domestic and foreign elites. Like physicians from time immemorial, they looked for opportunities to invest their surplus earnings. Both deposited large sums with Martínez del Río

Hermanos. Galenzowski's initial deposit of $20,000 in 1841 grew to $140,000 in the late 1850s. Other physician friends were valuable for their contacts. Dr. Adolfo Hegewich, at José Pablo's request, provided Gregorio José with a letter of introduction to his brother-in-law (Mr. Addington), an official in the Foreign Office in London.[47]

As this survey of friends and acquaintances has shown, the family's ties to Mexico were restricted. Its informal network of affective relationships linked it more to Europe or the United States—especially in a political sense—than to Mexico. Formal institutional arrangements in Mexico, which helped to ease the family's isolation there, tended to show the same imbalance. Male members of the Martínez del Río family participated in professional and social associations of Mexico City business leaders such as the Sociedad de Comercio and the Lonja de México. The latter, an exclusive social club, limited its membership to the most prestigious businessmen. Although native luminaries were welcome in the Lonja, many members were foreigners and its flavor was unmistakably cosmpolitan. Membership was first of all a sign of high economic and social status, but for the Martínez del Ríos it was also a practical necessity. In its lounges one might overhear gossip, speculation, and privileged information pertaining to business and politics. It was here that Pedro, who was always intrigued with the idea of doing business with the government, listened to almost up-to-date advice on a wide variety of subjects—from how best to send correspondence to Europe to whether or not the government would issue new licenses to import cotton.[48] But in no way was second-hand news in the Lonja comparable to the information routinely available to those blessed with more intimate political or social connections. As the chapters that follow will reveal, the family's business blunders derived partially from erroneous information and inaccurate perceptions about the economic and political facts of life in Mexico.

Family and Nationality

The Martínez del Ríos' social isolation in Mexico was mirrored in their ambivalent and often hostile attitudes toward their new home, in their many tentative attempts to leave Mexico permanently, and in their use of foreign nationality as a compensating device to rectify their distressed condition in Mexico. Complicating the many difficulties endemic to Mexico was a problem peculiar to this family. The Martínez del Ríos were Latin American-born, but they were European bred. They were at home nowhere. Gregorio José explained the quandary they faced: "We were very Panamanian to live in Europe, and very European to live in America."[49] Their residence in Mexico resulted from simple accident—Ventura Martínez's prolonged attempt to collect old debts—not from conscious design. The only reason for continuing to stay in Mexico would be if it promised higher returns on time and money invested than did comparable locales. This generation wanted to live well while earning the highest returns on its inheritance. It was committed to the ideal of bequeathing to the next generation an even greater patrimony. Incessant political violence, an irregular economy, and unhealthy living conditions raised serious questions as to the plausibility of reconciling those ideals with the reality of life in Mexico. Ventura de la Cruz outlined the more disagreeable aspects of doing business there: "The state of uncertainty in which everything is here, exposed always to such calamities and extortions and at the mercy of so many Mandarins, rogues, reprobates, capable of whatever thing to rob and enrich themselves."[50]

Whether or not the family should live in such a place was the subject of a constant debate. More than once a simple majority within the family resolved to leave. Ventura Martínez hoped to retire to Bordeaux in 1835. Displeased with the family firm, Gregorio José urged his brothers to dissolve Martínez del Río Hermanos in 1840 and to relocate in England. Ventura de la Cruz pointed out in 1847 that Southern Spain offered more advantages for the family—a low cost of living, access to secure investments in England and France, and an agreeable geographic and cultural climate. He argued that the family should make good its escape from Mexico, even if that meant accepting heavy losses. That way they might at last enjoy "tranquillity, security, and rid [themselves] of dealing with bastards."[51]

The family member most committed to staying in Mexico was Pedro Ansoátegui. He was the first to elaborate the theory that Mexico was the most suitable place for quick enrichment, but that was not his only motive for wanting to stay there. Unlike his wife's brothers, Pedro was reared as a Spanish American and was at home in that culture. He hated the climate in England, was uncomfortable with the language, and dreaded the retirement to a passive role in family business that necessarily would befall him if the family moved its operations to Europe. In part because of his disappointing experience in Europe in the early 1840s, José Pablo came to share a similar point of view: "The more I think about and observe these countries [England and France], the more I am convinced that it better serves me to live in Mexico."[52] When Gregorio José and Ventura de la Cruz began forcefully to insist on the move to Europe, they discovered that Pedro and José Pablo had irrevocably committed most of the family's capital to investments that could not be liquidated without prohibitive losses. In January 1844 José Pablo congratulated Gregorio José on his decision to terminate the family business in Mexico and to start a separate business of his own in England, but reminded him that "the great obstacle to a speedy liquidation is the factory."[53] First, Miraflores and, later, speculations in government debt issues shackled the family to Mexico.

The family's problem of adapting to Mexico was best illustrated by its mixed nationality. Ventura Martínez's children were born in Panama and were citizens of New Granada. Most of them grew up and were educated in Jamaica, a British colony, and in Great Britain, France, and Switzerland. Their extended residences abroad nurtured, and their frequent return visits to Europe reinforced, self-identification as citizens of the metropolis, not of the hinterlands in Latin America. The experience made some of them eligible for formal citizenship. Gregorio José obtained naturalization as a British citizen in June 1840. That single act had tremendous consequences for the family and its economic interests in Mexico. It was a way to escape the disadvantages of not having the connections needed to make the fixes that produced profits in Mexico. As a British citizen, Gregorio José could, in theory, call down the wrath of the British Empire on Mexico if it wronged him or Martínez del Río Hermanos. In practice, the strategy was only sometimes successful. Ultimately, its limitations proved to be the family's undoing.

José Pablo and Ventura de la Cruz tried but failed to obtain formal status as British citizens. Misled by the idle boasts of his shipboard companions, José Pablo stopped over at Kingston in 1843 in an attempt to secure naturalization as a British citizen. He discovered it was no longer a casual matter. The "accursed lawyers" collected fees, but accomplished nothing.[54] In London, Gregorio José worked to win citizenship for Ventura de la Cruz, but reforms in naturalization law defeated his plans. The British government had begun to demand proof of intended permanent residency in Great Britain as part of the naturalization process. When they investigated the United States as an alternative, the family discovered that, although the naturalization process was simpler, five years of residence were required before protection abroad would be extended.

José Pablo often pretended to be a British subject—to win protection, if not in fact, then by association. In 1838 his signature appeared on a memorial addressed by British citizens resident in Mexico City to the British minister in Mexico. In 1855, when negotiating with the Mexican government for special rights to Encinillas, he again claimed to be British. In that transaction and with others involving mining properties, José Pablo was careful to secure waivers of certain restrictions that applied to the categories of properties foreigners might own in Mexico.

Fictitious nationality may have been of dubious utility, but if José Pablo was not British he was even less Mexican.[55] In 1859, as this era came to a close, José Pablo assessed the problem of nationality as it applied to him and to his family: "As I see it, to be Granadan is less than nothing, and not by naturalizing myself elsewhere would I lose it; I intend to do it in England as soon as I am there; even the protection of that . . . Government is better than nothing, and I also consider thereby the English character of our House would be better perfected; that we must conserve with care, we have it so well established that nobody challenges it now."[56]

Conclusion

As was reflected in the ambiguity in their nationality, the Martínez del Ríos remained far removed from the inner, influential circles of Mexican society. For the first generation at least, nationality was a commodity sought to the extent that it could further individual or group purposes. Apart from its utilitarian value, nationality had little or no relevance to individual, family, or class concerns until the very end of the period studied. It remained irrelevant not only to the Martínez del Ríos, but to most citizens of Mexico as well. More significant and highly treasured were less-encompassing, infinitely more specific qualities based on ethnic, regional, occupational, class, or kinship criteria. Of all these, kinship, whether biological or ritual, was the most important. The debacle of Martínez's marriage to Manuela Azcárate and the unwillingness of his children to seek Mexican spouses kept the Martínez del Ríos out of a functional alliance with a clan group. Thus the family was even more isolated than its counterparts in the community of foreign merchants in Mexico (who usually married in). Without access to the *best* economic and political opportunities and isolated in an environment characterized by a paucity of profitable alternatives, the Martínez del Ríos continued to be disadvantaged in their dealings with better-placed competitors. That the family was wealthy in its own right was largely immaterial, as access to the best opportunities could only be acquired through the judicious use of social assets that the Martínez del Ríos had failed to acquire. Ritual, fictional kinship helped to compensate in part for the dearth of marital relations, but it was not a satisfactory substitute. Fictional kin ties quickly eroded in situations of economic stress. There was no family structure to sanction and to guarantee proper behavior; pseudokinship relations were never stronger than the goodwill of the parties involved.

The Martínez del Ríos' social problem was not that they lacked an extended kinship network, but that their network, based as it was in Panama and in Europe, was irrelevant to the family's needs in Mexico. In terms of cost-effectiveness, its kin relations cost the family more than the benefits it received. The family's network of affective social relations—nonkin friendships—showed similar deficiencies. It was not without Mexican friends, but the usefulness of such friends outside the boundaries of family politics was limited at best, even counterproductive in some respects. When treating non-Mexican friendship, the family chose more wisely, and there are indications that pragmatism was a dominant consideration. Contrast, for example, the absence of rival British merchants as friends with the many

British acquaintances who were situated so as to affect the application of British policy toward Mexico.

As was demonstrated in chapter 2, the family's individual and collective outlooks were nontraditional and non-Hispanic in character and thoroughly modern and Western European in inspiration. In the management of their personal affairs, they seemed to be guided by the model of an efficient English enterprise. Certainly, there were no Weberian obstacles (in the sociopsychological sense) to the productive employment of family capital. As the chapters that follow will show, there were indeed many obstacles to the profitable use of the family patrimony, many of which were social in nature, but these had little to do with any presumed deficiency in the spirit of enterprise. Rather, the tragedy was that the family's social characteristics matched so imperfectly the demands of the Mexican environment.

4. Commerce in Mexico: Drusina & Martínez, 1828-1837

The Partnership

Well schooled in commerce and knowledgeable in the peculiar ways of doing business in Mexico, Ventura Martínez's partner, Guillermo Drusina, had worked in Mexico City since 1824 as a clerk in the commercial house of Ruperti, Hartley & Green. Like his employer, Justo Ruperti, Drusina was a native of Hamburg. Before Ruperti returned to Germany in 1828, he arranged for Drusina and Martínez to form a company in Mexico. In a private contract, Ruperti committed himself to act as the company's purchasing agent and, additionally, to secure consignments of goods directly from manufacturers in Europe and the United States. As compensation, he was to receive a one-third share of all profits in transactions involving his services. The agreement stipulated that Drusina and Martínez must restrict their activities to consignment and commission sales—lessening the chance of bankruptcy by reducing their involvement in risky ventures. In theory, that would make their company more attractive to manufacturers who consigned merchandise to Mexico. On Martínez's orders, Gregorio José (who resided in London), delivered to Ruperti £8,000 in letters of credit drawn against various English commercial houses. With those funds, their agent began making purchases and arranging consignments. In a printed circular published on 1 July 1829 in Hamburg, Ruperti publicized the advantages for German commerce that the new company promised.[1]

Often absent from Mexico City, Martínez left management of the enterprise to Drusina, who directed a variety of speculations both inside and outside the realm of activities prescribed by Ruperti. Trade in imported textiles and other manufactures was sanctioned; dealings with government debt issues and public and private paper were not. A closer examination of Drusina and Martínez's business affairs will show, however, that commerce in mundane items like striped cloth from Germany was necessarily a part of flamboyant and risky speculations involving the Mexican government. In related activities, nearly every merchant, no matter what his or her specialization, dealt in silver exchange and in commercial drafts and private orders for payment.

Fearful that his partner might abandon him to proceed against recalcitrant debtors in Guadalajara, Drusina became anxious in 1829 to formalize their company by registering a contract to govern their partnership and by energetically publicizing their business in Mexico and Europe. Drusina insisted, "It is absolutely essential that we present a fixed establishment open to the face of the world," pointing out that this was an absolute requirement for receiving future consignments from Europe.[2] As for the Panamanian's obsession with collections, Drusina argued that if their company was fully operative his partner easily could make "more money than you are looking for in lawsuits" and pleaded, "Do not be deaf any longer to my calls—believe me, I know what we've got in our hands."[3] In reply to his partner's suggestion that they shift their base of operations to the north, Drusina warned Martínez that, although $40,000 invested in Mexico City would turn a $20,000 profit in six months, in Guadalajara he would lose "patience, time, health, and perhaps the money."[4] Vexed by his associate's resolute passivity, Drusina exclaimed in November 1829, "Even though you may be rich enough so that it matters little to you to receive several thousand more or less of profit, it is not the same with me, and I must work to advance."[5] Martínez remained nonchalant, replying to Drusina's query about a preference for naming their company: "You put the name as it suits you, Drusina Martínez & Company or Drusina & Company."[6]

After much bickering, Drusina persuaded his reluctant associate to register their partnership and the rules under which their company would operate. On 4 January 1830 they appeared before Colonel Azcárate's nephew, the public notary Francisco Madariaga, to draw up and sign the necesary documents.[7] Martínez disguised his participation in the company by naming Gregorio José as Drusina's partner. Their enterprise was christened "Guillermo de Drusina & Gregorio Martínez." They agreed the firm's center of operations would be Mexico City, that the company would last for a minimum of four years (with a one-year notice to dissolve the partnership), that the company would engage in consignment, commission, and finance, and would not engage in mining, mineral processing, urban or rural land purchases, or public debt speculation, and that the partners were not to participate in commercial activities independent of the firm nor were they to compromise the fiscal integrity of the firm in any manner without mutual consent.

The contract defined contrasting and unequal roles for each of the partners. Gregorio José contributed $60,000 in capital and left the company's routine management to Drusina, whose capital share was initially $30,000. Profits and losses were divided equally. In this case, the energies of an adroit trader like Drusina, the *socio industrial*, made up for the excess of capital put into the company by Gregorio José, the *socio capitalista*. Each partner earned 6 percent annual interest on his capital shares plus annual allowances of $6,000 as compensation for personal expenses incurred as managers of the company. The contract included instructions for the routine management of the company as well as for the management of potential crisis situations. All records were to be kept in Spanish in the "regular business manner" and annual accounts prepared to keep both partners fully informed of the company's financial condition. The partners were obliged to seek third-party arbitration of disagreements and were specifically forbidden to seek redress in the courts. Also spelled out were procedures for liquidating the company in the event one of the partners died prematurely. Since Gregorio José was still in London, the contract named Ventura Martínez to represent his son's interest in the company until his arrival in Mexico.

In November 1833 Gregorio José and Drusina registered a new company contract to become effective on 1 January 1834.[8] This agreement renewed their partnership for four more years. Except for an increased capital participation by both partners and the inclusion of a statement by Gregorio José that noted that his share of capital in the company was owned jointly with his brothers, the provisions of the 1833 contract were identical with that of 1830. By 1834, however, it was obvious that the company's activities were no longer confined to the areas prescribed by its contract. The restrictive 1833 contract was canceled and, thereafter, speculations involving government debt issues, mining, and land (always a part of the firm's business) were formally recognized. After 1836 the composition of the company's capital accounts changed and Ludulfo Petersen, a German clerk in the company, was admitted as a participating partner. (Table 10 lists the company's assets and liabilities for 1830 to 1837; table 11 shows the distribution of capital shares in the company for 1830 to 1837.)

The Dry Goods Trade

In the beginning, Drusina & Martínez engaged primarily in temporary, single-purpose commercial operations called "ship ventures," which they financed themselves or in partnership with other merchants in Mexico. With Ruperti as their agent, they purchased assorted dry goods cheaply from European suppliers and shipped this merchandise to Mexico in specially chartered vessels. There they sold the goods according to the dictates of the market, sometimes making excellent profits.[9] Wildly fluctuating market conditions made the trade in dry goods an uncertain business, however. Consistent profits depended on prices; erratic and unpredictable supply-and-demand factors determined prices. In March 1829 the sale of cheap

Table 10
Reported Assets and Liabilities, Drusina & Martinez
(Current Pesos)

Assets and Liabilities	1830	1831	1832	1833	1834	1835	1836	1837
Assets								
Cash on hand	1,967	42,907	13,109	3,233	4,170	8,450	952	11,561
Private loans/negotiable paper	170	2,000	9,587	15,488	16,775	11,712	35,024	22,666
Current accounts	171,086	205,297	152,867	328,864	430,750	429,296	386,256	246,444
Past due accounts	—	—	—	—	—	—	—	—
Mining property	—	—	—	—	—	—	—	—
Industrial/manufacturing	—	—	—	—	—	—	—	—
Shares/participation in nonpublic enterprises	—	45,720	31,412	80,820	31,448	5,962	10,726	5,994
Real property	—	—	—	—	—	—	—	—
Mexican public debt issues	—	—	18,361	25,339	15,079	3,587	29,016	20,593
Non-Mexican public debt issues	—	—	—	—	—	—	—	—
Total	173,223	295,924	225,336	453,744	498,222	459,007	461,974	307,258
Liabilities								
Current accounts	64,392	159,258	105,922	214,982	278,886	236,275	248,700	135,090
Finance accounts	—	24,545	—	76,336	49,145	21,067	—	—
Capital accounts	90,000	108,830	112,122	119,416	130,000	170,190	191,668	164,573
Profit/loss accounts	18,831	3,291	7,292	43,010	40,191	31,475	21,606	7,595
Total	173,223	295,924	225,336	453,744	498,222	459,007	461,974	307,258

Source: Drusina & Martinez accounts, CMRFH.
Note: For 1830-36, reporting date is 31 December; for 1837, 31 July.

Table 11
Capital Accounts, Drusina & Martinez

Account	1830	1831	1832	1833	1834	1835	1836	1837
G. Drusina	30,000	39,415	41,061	44,708	50,000	570,095	79,759	89,482
(% share)	(33.3)	(36.2)	(36.6)	(37.6)	(38.5)	(41.2)	(41.6)	(42.0)
G. Martinez	60,000	69,415	71,061	74,061	80,000	100,095	109,759	119,482
(% share)	(66.7)	(63.8)	(63.4)	(62.4)	(61.5)	(58.8)	(57.3)	(56.0)
L. Petersen	—	—	—	—	—	—	2,148	4,309
(% share)							(1.1)	(2.0)

Source: Drusina & Martinez accounts, CMRFH.

cotton cloth (*mantas*) to Agustín Garay in Guanajuato for $6,000 gave the new partners a 30 percent return on their investment. The following month Drusina sold their stock of coarse linens (*liensos*) for $13,600, assuring their company a tidy $2,000 profit (a 15 percent return). Also in April 1829, Drusina purchased 540 pieces of Silesian linen (*platilla*) at $13.6r. per piece from Gustavo Schneider. Knowing the market for this product in Mexico City, Drusina expected to resell these goods easily for $14.4r. per piece, making an easy 5 percent profit. Yet four days later he hurriedly sold the lot to the merchant Valdez for $7,550, making a net of only $70 (1 percent) from the transaction. Nearly 4,000 pieces of *platilla* had appeared suddenly in the local market; only quick thinking by Drusina saved an actual loss as prices for these goods plummeted. Two months later Drusina complained that their shipments from Europe had been delayed at a time when prices for many goods were high. Fine linens sold in Mexico City at $5 per piece over the invoice price in Germany. Coarse linens were out of stock in Veracruz and *platilla* costing $14 per piece after delivery sold in the port city for $18. Wax selling at $50 in Veracruz would cost them only $18 delivered.

Among the demand factors that affected price structure was the unpredictable purchasing power of Mexican consumers. This was partially a function of the perceived (or actual) condition of the mining industry. Most of the silver that was extracted from the mines was minted, so money supply was a function of silver production levels. Bonanzas or rumors of new strikes increased the volume of currency in circulation or, at least, made retailers more optimistic, thereby influencing the tempo of consumer purchases and wholesale orders. As mining production was erratic for this whole period, so was the money supply, and so was the multiplier effect that the industry had on the economy as a whole. Tariffs, or rumors of tariffs, and import prohibitions affected demand schedules by raising the prices consumers paid for goods and affected supply schedules by making certain classes of goods unavailable. These regulations sometimes produced consequences for merchants that legislators did not anticipate. In 1829 Drusina confidently predicted that shipments of coarse linen from Germany would turn an excellent profit because of a new law prohibiting future imports of cheap cotton cloth. He reasoned that prices for cotton cloth would increase due to the legislated scarcity of supply. As consumers turned to less-expensive linens, the price for linen would increase in line with the growing demand.

Merchants had no more control over conditions of political instability in Mexico than they did over consumer buying power or tariff policy. This instability affected both supply and demand schedules—crippling internal communications and altering the political economy. Commenting on the overnight changes that could undo even the most well-planned commercial initiatives, Drusina complained in 1829, "These people work in such a manner that the devil himself cannot say with certainty what they will be doing here in one or two years."[10]

As if the aggravations of local politics were not enough, foreign political interference might also disrupt commerce. The Spanish blockade of Veracruz in 1829 temporarily caused prices to rise in Mexico, not because it interrupted deliveries, but because the demand schedule was altered as merchants who anticipated a lengthy siege frantically sought to increase their inventories. Setting a precedent for his own affairs in the years to come, Drusina reassured his nervous partner that their goods from Hamburg would arrive in Mexico on a ship flying the British flag—guaranteeing safe passage through the blockade and "complete security" for their property.

Although Martínez felt more comfortable with traditional forms of trade such as the ship ventures, these transient operations did have serious disadvantages in a market as unstructured and unpredictable as that of early national Mexico. Direct trading tied up capital in an inventory that might or might not be turned over quickly and profitably. Drusina preferred a role in commerce that was more indirect and that shifted the burdens of finance and risk taking away from Drusina & Martínez.

Commission-Consignment

Despite the diversification in activities that became especially pronounced after the company contract was revised in 1834, Drusina & Martínez continued to concentrate its resources in the lucrative commission-consignment business that Drusina had been so anxious to begin in 1829. To reassure his skeptical partner, Drusina tried to explain to Martínez the nature of this new business: "This kind can be reduced to inspiring confidence in the manufacturers and merchants in Europe, as much in the persons entrusted with their goods as in the political relations and in the prices and other circumstances of the place to where they send their consignments."[11]

Although the company's circumspect behavior in Mexico and the reassurances of its European agent did play a role in shaping the attitudes of consigners, as Drusina suggested, world market conditions and the problems of the industrializing economies probably did more to encourage manufacturers to offer more generous terms of trade. For example, in July 1829 Ruperti reported great difficulties in securing consignments and cheap purchases of linens for Drusina & Martínez because large sales of textiles to Colombia, the United States, and the Pacific had combined with the losses from destructive floods in Silesia to create a shortage of trade goods in Hamburg. Two months later German commerce again was in a "miserable state." With the intervention of his father-in-law, Senator H. J. Mercke, a resident of Hamburg and the senior partner in H. J. Mercke & Company,

Ruperti won promises of consignments from the following manufacturers: Mutzen—coarse linen; Beche—coarse linen; Prelle—coarse linen; Ludendorf—fine linen and striped cloth (*listados*); Linck—silk handkerchiefs and wax. No matter how distressed Mexico might be, the continued problems of the German textile industry in its struggle to compete with the British ensured German willingness to extend credit and to entrust consignments to overseas merchants like Drusina & Martínez.

Figure 1 shows the geographical distribution of Drusina & Martínez accounts. As the nexus between manufacturers in Germany, Great Britain, and France and retailers in Mexico, Drusina & Martínez combined isolated factors—Ruperti's European connections, the Martínez del Ríos' supply of venture capital, and Drusina's commercial acumen (and his kin in Mexico)—with a Mexican market remarkable for its disaggregation. For the *empresarios* the result was a profitable enterprise (table 12 lists the firm's reported profits for 1830 to 1837). As intermediaries, Drusina & Martínez shifted many of the risks of doing business in Mexico to their foreign suppliers. The company's risk was limited to the provision of short-term finance for Mexican retailers who purchased their dry goods. Commission-consignment and its satellite operations—finance, exchange, and customs duties evasion—accounted for $242,109 (53.9 percent) of $448,699 in gross income earned by Drusina & Martínez between 1829 and 1837 (table 13 summarizes the firm's annual profit and loss accounts).

Exchange and Finance

Besides yielding additional profits in the form of interest (usually 1 percent to 2 percent monthly) charged on credit, the finance of sales of dry goods to Mexican retailers made possible more and larger transactions, thus increasing the volume of the firm's commissions on sales. To manage its extensive network of customers in Mexico and to keep its accounts with suppliers current, Drusina & Martínez necessarily engaged in a wide range of operations associated with the flow of silver and paper inside and outside Mexico. The firm was well situated to share in the profits that might be extracted in the eastward movement of silver and paper. For a charge, its surplus exchange capacity was available to handle the banking needs of those unable to make such exchanges.

Silver and paper exchanges structured the commerce in ordinary imported manufactures. Often the actual profits or losses produced by sales of dry goods depended precisely on the terms of payment. Silver cost less in mining centers such as Guanajuato than in Mexico City. It was worth more in the Mexican ports and much more in New Orleans, New York, or London. Even in the mining centers the price of silver was not constant. Its value increased immediately before the departure of the *conducta*, a scheduled

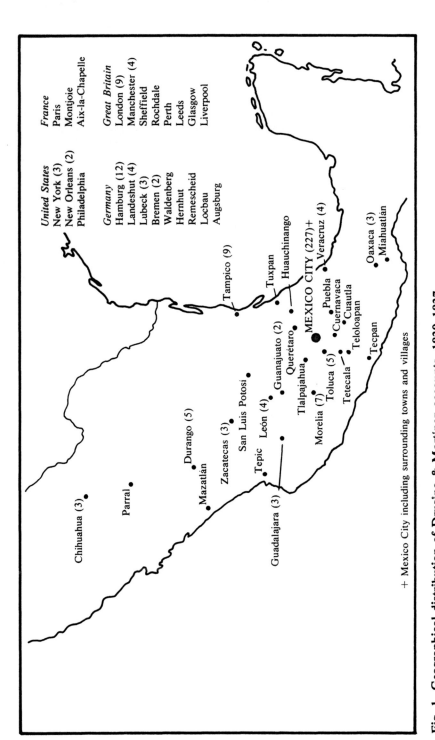

Fig. 1. Geographical distribution of Drusina & Martinez accounts, 1830–1837

France
Paris
Montjoie
Aix-la-Chapelle

Great Britain
London (9)
Manchester (4)
Sheffield
Rochdale
Perth
Leeds
Glasgow
Liverpool

United States
New York (3)
New Orleans (2)
Philadelphia

Germany
Hamburg (12)
Landeshut (4)
Lubeck (3)
Bremen (2)
Waldenberg
Hernhut
Remescheid
Locbau
Augsburg

Tampico (9)

Tuxpan

Huauchinango

MEXICO CITY (227)+

Veracruz (4)

Oaxaca (3)

Miahuatlán

Puebla

Cuernavaca

Cuautla

Teloloapan

Tecpan

Guanajuato (2)

Querétaro

Tlalpajahua

Morelia (7)

Toluca (5)

Tetecala

San Luis Potosi

León (4)

Zacatecas (3)

Tepic

Durango (5)

Mazatlán

Chihuahua (3)

Parral

Guadalajara (3)

+ Mexico City including surrounding towns and villages

Table 12
Profits, Drusina & Martinez

	1830	1831	1832	1833	1834	1835	1836	1837
Profit	18,831	3,292	7,295	43,010	31,475	21,606	7,595	164,573
Capital	90,000	108,830	112,122	119,416	130,000	170,190	191,668	
Profit as % of capital	20.9	3.1	6.5	36.1	30.9	18.5	11.3	4.7

Source: Drusina & Martinez accounts, CMRFH.

Table 13
Profit and Loss Accounts, Drusina & Martinez
(Current Pesos)

Accounts	1830	1831	1832	1833	1834	1835	1836	1837
Credits								
Collection accounts	—	—	—	—	8,210	1,746	19,673	4,352
Commission accounts	19,413	18,598	8,314	31,895	22,539	23,572	18,387	3,594
Customs duties	—	651	917	13,050	596	10,589	—	—
Draft accounts	—	3,567	3,555	4,075	12,471	191	579	898
Government credits	3,906	—	3,735	18,590	12,642	13,880	10,202	—
Guaranty accounts	2,382	2,155	1,451	3,274	8,252	10,586	9,609	2,018
Special ventures	6,550	4,862	2,704	14,122	14,029	10,026	6,230	1,216
Premium accounts	6,804	5,694	13,171	6,604	851	2,532	9,002	—
Warehouse accounts	2,141	366	—	1,089	2,469	2,285	1,506	19
Other	—	254	56	—	—	3	—	—
Total	41,196	36,147	33,903	92,699	82,059	75,410	75,188	12,097
Debits								
General costs	22,365	26,663	24,553	25,136	28,741	29,080	27,708	1,378
Accounts owed	—	6,192	2,058	24,553	13,127	9,146	25,874	3,124
Write-offs	—	—	—	—	—	14,855	—	—
Net Profit	18,831	3,292	7,292	43,010	40,191	31,475	21,606	7,595

Source: Drusina & Martinez accounts, CMRFH.
Note: For 1830-36, reporting date is 31 December; for 1837, 31 July.

convoy that transported precious metals to Mexico City and to the ports.[12] Minted silver always cost more than silver bullion. Drafts, orders, bills of exchange, or promissory notes, generally referred to as *letras* or *libranzas*, were the mediums of exchange more commonly used between merchants, not silver, which was costly to transport and subject to theft. To make payment, a merchant commonly wrote out a *libranza* to be paid by another merchant situated in an appropriate locale with whom he had accrued a positive balance in their accounts or with whom he had negotiated a line of credit. To repay disbursements made by this second merchant, the first merchant might agree to pay *libranzas* drawn by the second merchant on his account. Alternatively, a debtor of the first merchant might pay the *libranzas* drawn by the second merchant, and so on. *Libranzas* always indicated who had accepted them (that is, who would pay), where they were payable, and when payment in what form was due (usually gold or silver in a set number of months). They might or might not earn interest. *Libranzas* circulated at face value or with discounts or premiums depending on whom they were drawn and the terms of payment. Frequently going through successive endorsements, *libranzas* circulated in the place of currency. Less bulky than silver and free for the most part from the threat of permanent loss at the hands of the bandits who kept a close watch over trade routes, the bills had the singular disadvantage that their owners could never know with absolute certainty they would be paid. Consequently, face value and market value might differ considerably. Orders drawn on accounts payable in New York, London, or even Havana usually sold at a premium in Mexico City, Veracruz, or Tampico. Orders circulating abroad but payable in Mexico invariably suffered discounts.[13]

In a hypothetical exchange operation, Drusina & Martínez might sell a quantity of linens to a Guanajuato merchant for $2,000 in silver coin delivered immediately, with the balance to be paid in silver bars placed in Guanajuato two months later. Drusina & Martínez might convert that silver into *libranzas* or other paper credits in Guanajuato or elsewhere or it might ship the silver all the way to New York or London. As it moved eastward, the silver steadily accrued in value. If the costs of handling and transport did not exceed its increased value, an additional profit over the original transaction was made. In Europe or the United States, Drusina & Martínez could sell the silver to a commercial house or have the house act as its broker to convert the silver into paper. In a normal sequence of events, the silver ultimately appeared as a credit in the firm's account with a foreign commercial house. Afterward (or before, if arrangements had been made), Drusina & Martínez could write *libranzas* against this overseas account, avoiding discounts on its own paper and earning substantial premiums for its services from other merchants. And, of course, these accounts provided the means to make future purchases of goods destined for the Mexico trade.

Two examples from Drusina & Martínez's actual experiences demonstrate the opportunities (and the problems) that exchange operations presented to businessmen in Mexico. In March 1829 Drusina complained that the terms of payment in the sale of cloth to Antonio Garay ($2,000 in silver coin; $4,000 in *libranzas*) reduced Drusina & Martínez's net profit in the sale from 50 percent to 30 percent. This same month Drusina refused to draw up a *letra* on his Havana account when he could not get an offer of more than a 14 percent premium. Three months later, persuaded by the continued strong demand in Veracruz for *letras* to Havana, he drew $5,700 against his account with the merchant Morales in Havana. Drusina's agent in Veracruz subsequently exchanged his *letra* for a cargo of linen and aguardiente offered at a low price in the port.[14]

Public Debt Speculation

Drusina's calculations of the probable returns from an expected shipment of dry goods from Hamburg in 1829 illustrate why merchants were attracted to speculation in government debt issues. Drusina expected that his company's purchases in this shipment would be about $40,000 and that the shipment would include consignments of approximately equal value. Altogether the shipment, valued at $80,000, would be assessed duties totaling $40,000. If these goods sold at the normal prices, the company could expect a return of $10,000 on investments totaling $80,000 ($40,000 for its purchases, nothing for the consignment, plus $40,000 for duties), a 12.5 percent return *if prices did not fall.* By reducing the real price paid for duties, the company (or any other importer) could make a larger, surer profit and lessen the possibility of suffering a loss. Drusina bragged to Martínez that he could arrange payment of their duties "in a manner you and I know, without failing to make a $20,000 profit."[15] Later, he confirmed he could get government orders (promissory notes) to pay the duties at only 40 percent of their nominal value, but warned, "Be careful you say nothing to anyone; I know how to do it, but it must remain a secret!"[16]

A delay in the arrival of the ship from Hamburg (insured for a $6,000 profit) produced momentary anxiety that the 110-ton *Heinrich Aldrich* been lost at sea. But in November 1829 the ship docked in Veracruz carrying trade goods for Drusina & Martínez valued at $37,685 and consignments worth about half that much. The assessed duties for the merchandise totaled $27,000. Though the shipment was smaller than expected, Drusina remained enthusiastic about the prospects of a good profit from the venture: "I hope to arrange it in such a manner as to make $12,000 in the [customs] payments, if nothing unexpected occurs in the Ministry [of Hacienda]."[17] From import duties evasion, it was but a short step to other deals with the government, which produced profits free from the risks and bothers of commerce.

Voluntary and involuntary, direct and indirect—speculation in Mexican government debt issues was the second most profitable activity for Drusina & Martínez. Aside from import duty manipulations, the forced loans and contributions imposed by rapacious governments obliged merchants, whatever their inclination, to deal in the public debt. Few *empresarios* could resist the bizarre combination of blandishments and brute force that characterized this business. When assessed $1,000 by the decree of 16 July 1836 as its share of a $2 million forced loan intended to cover the costs of reconquering Texas, Drusina & Martínez joined other commercial houses in seeking the assistance of the British Legation to overturn the decree.[18]

With sufficient pecuniary encouragement, however, the firm displayed no reticence in helping to finance the government. The frequent changes in government sometimes jeopardized these speculations, but many companies routinely bought and sold large quantities of public debt issues. Drusina complained in 1829, "Congress has authorized him [the minister of hacienda, Lorenzo Zavala] to complete the $4 million loan, but he only wants to accept credits of higher preference, which are worth 25 to 40 percent [of face value] for which reason one cannot do business with him like with González [the former minister of hacienda]."[19] When it borrowed from private lenders, the *agiotistas*, the government usually received only a fraction of the nominal amount of a loan in cash. The balance consisted of credits against the public treasury (orders for payment, debt issues, promissory notes, and the like). The government repaid its loans with cash or with negotiable orders drawn on the maritime customs houses. Like other companies in the merchant community, Drusina & Martínez bought paper credits for inclusion in loans contracted with the government. By preference the firm usually acted indirectly as a partner in larger deals arranged by other *agiotistas*. Along with Antonio Garay, James P. Penney & Company, and McCalmont Geaves & Company, Drusina & Martínez signed a contract in July 1833 to guarantee that Juan Vitalba would deliver to the government $62,500 in post-independence credits such as pension and salary vouchers.[20] Three months later the firm joined Garay, Anselmo Zurutura, and Francisco Gámez as *fiadores* for Vitalba's contract to deliver a $300,000 loan to the Treasury. This loan ($103,448 in cash, $93,103 in preindependence credits, and $103,449 in postindependence credits) was repayable in orders on the maritime customs houses.[21] Profits related to speculations in the public debt accounted for nearly one-fourth of the gross profits earned by Drusina & Martínez.

The Tobacco Trade

Not all of Drusina & Martínez's business derived from international trade, although most of it was somehow connected to intrigues with the state.

In the summer of 1829 the company took up a one-eighth share ($6,000) in an enterprise formed to buy tobacco from planters in Córdova, Veracruz.[22] Legislative changes had freed the planters to sell to private contractors after the national tobacco monopoly went bankrupt and was unable to pay them. Desperate for income, the planters sold their tobacco to private dealers at prices much lower than those formerly charged the government. Certain state governments continued to administer their own monopolies, but lacked the capacity to purchase directly from the planters. Drusina & Martínez and their partners intended to capture a share of the profits to be made as middlemen between the tobacco villas in Veracruz and mining centers in Guanajuato, Jalisco, and Zacatecas. They purchased tobacco at 1.25r. per pound with the expectation of reselling it at up to 3.5r. per pound to state monopolies, which would retail it at $1 per pound. Besides excellent returns of 50 percent to 75 percent on their investment, the venture promised to be secure, as the investors would retain a mortgage on the tobacco until they received full repayment from the states.

The organization of a new and larger company by a rival group of *empresarios* who wanted to purchase all of the national government's huge inventory of tobacco (to administer the monopoly nationwide) upset Drusina's plans. He feared (rightly) that the new group would win the special concessions it demanded of the national government: "The Minister [of Hacienda] is undecided because the contractors are asking some very favorable conditions, but the need for money will oblige him to give in."[23] Anxious to dispose of their tobacco before new legislation granted their rivals exclusive monopoly rights, Drusina wrote Martínez in Guadalajara to warn him of these developments and to urge him to sell their tobacco to the state government there as quickly as possible. If necessary, Martínez was authorized to promise officials in Jalisco "un par de talegas" (bribes) to close the deal.[24]

Land Speculation

Drusina's kin made it possible for Drusina & Martínez to acquire Texas land easily and cheaply. Compared with the firm's other interests, these investments were relatively insignificant and produced neither great profits nor serious losses. Although marginal to the firm, land speculation associated with the Texas colonization companies was a factor in the separatist movement that blossomed into rebellion in the mid-1830s.

On 30 January 1832 Guillermo Drusina and his wife, his mother-in-law, and his father-in-law appeared before the notary Francisco Madariaga to register a document naming John C. Beales of the United States as their agent to purchase land in Texas under the provisions of the colonization law.[25] John Beales was the brother of Henry Beales, the owner of a store in

Cuernavaca and a favored client of Drusina & Martínez. In August 1832 Drusina persuaded his partner, Gregorio José, and another Mexico City commercial house, Cotesworth, Cullen & Company, to join his in-laws and Beales in founding a colonization company to develop Texas lands acquired with the help of Drusina's in-laws in the Mexican army.[26] This grant encompassed four million acres between the San Antonio and Guadalupe rivers in the Department of Béxar. Drusina & Martínez and Cotesworth, Cullen & Company were to provide the $14,000 Beales needed to purchase additional land, make necessary improvements, and transport forty families of colonists to Texas. Beales bought up the rights to neighboring land grants, but failed to make progress toward colonizing the land. By November of the following year Cotesworth, Cullen & Company wanted out and the colonization company was dissolved. It was succeeded by a second company, consisting of the remaining partners—Drusina & Martínez, General Morán, and María Luisa Vicario—who were obligated to furnish Beales with $8,000 to develop the Texas lands.[27] Soon after the creation of this second company in Mexico, Beales surrendered its properties (held under the name of the Río Bravo Association) for a three-eighths participation (300 of 800 shares) in the Río Grande & Texas Land Company. In April 1836, after the sale or trade of 132 of these new shares, Beales reported total receipts of $23,767 against $8,500 in expenses. Only $9,666 were cash receipts; the balance was in the form of 5,000 acres in Georgia and 28 town lots in Utica, New York.[28]

While Santa Anna campaigned recklessly in the winter of 1836 to defeat the rebels in Texas, Drusina & Martínez were acquiring title to more Texas land. As compensation for "the many benefits and favors they have provided," Víctor Blanco donated to the firm eight *sitios* located along the Trinity River near the old port of Atascosita, fifty miles northeast of present-day Houston, Texas.[29] (It was in Atascosita where the first uprising of Texas settlers had taken place in 1835.) In a second acquisition, in 1837, Bernardo González Angulo repaid his debt to Drusina & Martínez by ceding to the firm his rights in an enterprise formed in partnership with General Vicente Filisola and Juan Vitalba in 1835. This company had a Mexican government contract to colonize twenty leagues of land in Northeast Texas along with the United States border. Drusina & Martínez, together with the French merchant Victor Massieu (who purchased Filisola's share), owned two-thirds of the company. They authorized Vitalba to continue developing those lands in Texas.[30] In the end, however, neither this nor any of the other colonization companies owned by Drusina & Martínez realized their objects. Texas's independence converted their claims to land in the new republic to so much worthless paper.

Liquidation

Gregorio José gave notice in July 1836 to Drusina that he intended to dissolve their partnership the following July in accordance with the provisions of the company contract. He wished to end the company to concentrate his attention on the family's growing business interests in Mexico. At first, Drusina strongly resisted the planned termination. After arranging to found a new company of his own, he abruptly changed his mind and attempted to persuade his partner to agree to an early liquidation of their contract, on 1 January 1837. From Havana, Gregorio José replied testily to Drusina's overtures with the observation that the matter should be handled "according to contract."[31]

Anxious to begin his new enterprise, Drusina circumvented the contract by informally beginning the liquidation of Drusina & Martínez in December 1836. To guard against the erosion of established commercial relations, his new partners distributed circulars announcing the opening of Guillermo Drusina & Company on 1 January 1837. The capital of the new company was fixed at $100,000. Drusina put up half that sum and his new associates, Edward Landgoothy and Ludulfo Petersen, supplied the remainder. Since Drusina had begun prematurely to refuse new business and to collect sums owed to existing accounts, the liquidation of Drusina & Martínez was nearly completed in July 1837.

Table 14
Liquidation of Gregorio Martínez del Río's Capital Account, Drusina & Martínez, November 1837

Assets Assigned	Value (Current Pesos)
Cash	37,940
Drafts accepted by Drusina & Co.	46,000
Share in losses written off	14,111
Share in accounts difficult to collect	1,911
Share in enterprise with Beales in Texas	2,219
"Créditos antiguos" owed by Mexican government	5,301
Debt owed by Juan Vitalba	270
Various drafts payable to Drusina & Martínez and endorsed to Gregorio Martínez del Río	5,303
Pending	140
Total amount of capital share	113,195

Source: "Convenio . . . en liquidación de Gm. de Drusina y G. J. Martínez," Mexico City, 24 Nov. 1837, CMRFH.

The last of the company's assets were divided between the partners in November 1837 (table 14 shows how Gregorio José's share in Drusina & Martínez was paid out).[32] Drusina assumed ownership of the company's active accounts, paying off his partner's share in cash. Liquidation on Drusina's terms shut the Martínez del Ríos out of the safe and profitable niche in Mexican commerce that Drusina & Martínez had occupied. Besides a long list of Mexican customers, Drusina transferred to his new company the splendid German connections that made the consignment-commission trade so convenient. His Mexican kin relations and political resources likewise were invested in the new firm. Drusina no longer had access to the Martínez del Ríos' cash box and to their overseas banking facilities, but these factors could be replaced easily enough. As a leading consignment-commission house in Mexico in the 1840s, Drusina & Company acted as a representative for (and enjoyed the financial support of) the Rothschilds in a variety of projects.

5. Banking on Mexico: Martínez del Río Hermanos, 1838-1864

Finding a Place

To finance its exchange and commission operations, Drusina & Martínez drew extensively on Ventura Martínez's and Gregorio José's private accounts with banks and commercial houses in London, Paris, and New York. The Martínez del Ríos were reimbursed directly in Mexico City for those overseas charges. As a consequence, the family's cash supply in Mexico (excluding capital invested in Drusina & Martínez) increased from about $40,000 in 1832 to more than $100,000 in 1835. To move these funds back overseas quickly was a costly proposition. Drusina & Martínez's international operations had been so profitable because, unwittingly, the family had subsidized the company by lowering its exchange and finance costs. By way of compensation, the Martínez del Ríos' association with Drusina & Martínez gave the family access to a wide range of subsidiary finance operations in Mexico. As the volume of Drusina & Martínez's sales to retailers continued to grow after 1835, the family's excess funds were diverted to help Mexican buyers finance their purchases from the firm.

The dissolution of Drusina & Martínez in 1837 eliminated these profitable investment outlets. Cut out of the import trade, the family's next best choice lay in offering to the commercial community of Mexico the many banking services it was capable of providing—finance and national and international exchange. As early as 1835, Gregorio José, Ventura de la Cruz, and Pedro had begun working toward that end by transforming Ventura Martínez's unordered activity as a moneylender into a routinized and well-administered enterprise. The termination of the partnership with Drusina freed them to conduct this business as a formally established banking house. On 1 January 1838 their new company opened its doors to customers under the name Martínez del Río Hermanos. As all of the partners were members of the family, a contract regulating the firm was not immediately registered, but instead was ratified in a private family covenant.[1] Like most company contracts, the covenant for the family enterprise provided general rules for administering the company and for structuring relationships between partners. The firm's specialty was banking (*giros de cambios y descuentos*), but its partners agreed that it could engage "in whatever enterprise is considered profitable," including merchandising. Its capital was set initially at $490,000.

Banking

Martínez del Río Hermanos functioned as a clearinghouse for Mexican and international commerce. The public at large also might use its services. The firm accepted funds (in a variety of forms) payable to third parties in the principal Mexican cities and in international trading centers such as London and New York. Exchange constituted the single largest category of monies moving through the firm's cash boxes. For its services, the firm charged fees that were nominal in relation to the costs involved. The dispensation of these services did not in itself generate a great deal of income, but it did create, with minimal investment, a large reserve of liquid assets. For Mexican commerce as a whole, the system of exchange acted as a buffer, cushioning against sharp income fluctuations, and it ameliorated the worst features of an antiquated credit setup.

The firm dealt in spatial and in temporal exchanges. In the case of the former, the direction of exchange helped to determine costs. Premiums were charged as paper moved eastward (that is, the cost of a *letra* exceeded its face value when payable in London or New York). Paper moving westward sold at a discount (that is, the cost of a *letra* was less than its face value when payable in Guadalajara or Zacatecas). For temporal exchanges, Martínez del Río Hermanos accepted, at discounts averaging 0.5 percent to 1.5 percent, *libranzas* and other paper payable in Mexico or elsewhere at future dates (usually in one to three months). The firm charged a commission when it acted as a broker for payments of cash or paper to third parties.

Speculations in government orders drawn on the customs houses in port cities like Veracruz and Tampico and the marketing of textiles from Miraflores in interior cities like Cuernavaca, Guanajuato, and Zacatecas facilitated the firm's national exchanges. At the international level, the structure of exchange was more complex. A basic requirement was the ability to draw on accounts previously established with overseas commercial houses. The Martínez del Ríos' long-time association with international trade, dating back to Ventura Martínez's ventures in Panama, gave them access to houses in New York, New Orleans, London, and Paris. The examples that follow illustrate how the process worked. In 1839 Schmidt & Werner of New Orleans accepted Martínez del Río Hermanos's paper under certain conditions.[2] It paid the firm's *libranzas* originating in Mexico for up to $20,000. Afterward, these were to be covered with shipments of specie, silver bars, paper, or merchandise. For this service, Schmidt & Werner charged a 1 percent commission, 1.5 percent if the *libranzas* were not covered by remittances when due. For negotiating foreign *libranzas* the commission was set at 1.25 percent. The agent collected 2 percent on sales and purchases of merchandise on behalf of Martínez del Río Hermanos, 2.5 percent if Schmidt & Werner was required to put up guarantees. It charged no commission for silver coin remitted to cover accounts. *Libranzas* to cover accounts paid a 0.25 percent brokerage fee.

Terms of exchange varied between commercial houses. In 1846 J. L. Lemmè & Company informed Martínez del Río Hermanos that

your G. J. M. del Río, our valued friend, has acquainted us that you would probably avail yourself of our firm, and give us the preference in entrusting to us—some large banking operations. We shall be happy and thankful to receive your commands and at the desire of said friend we merely mention that 1/2% Bank Com.s (if you cover in bill or in Dollars or silver to sell for you a-c [account] or in any way you return the amount to us) we say 1/2% will be our only charge and interest at 5% p/a [per annum].[3]

This occasion marked the opening of the second of two accounts (£20,000 each) with Lemmè.

Once terms and credits were established, there remained the problem of how best to service the accounts from Mexico. Remittances of silver and cochineal were the preferred mediums. Paper was a costly option for the same purpose. In a representative transaction in October 1849, Martínez del Río Hermanos purchased with an 8 percent premium a *libranza* drawn on Hargous Brothers of New York for $2,936. This the firm remitted to cover its account with a New York correspondent, J. W. Schmidt & Company.[4] For accounts in Great Britain, *libranzas* payable in pounds sterling in London sold at variable rates in Mexico. In November 1838 a common exchange was 43.5 pence to the peso.[5] In February 1843 Martínez del Río Hermanos sold at 45.46 its *libranzas* drawn on J. L. Lemmè & Company. To cover its account with Lemmè in May 1843, the firm purchased a £1,130 *libranza* from Tiburcio Gómez de la Madrid payable in London. As this *libranza* was acquired at 45.13, Martínez del Río Hermanos managed to make a small profit with those exchanges, an exception rather than the rule for paper transactions.

The use of silver as an international medium of exchange, though more profitable than paper, was a cumbersome and possibly costly procedure. The most common (legal) means to move silver within and out of Mexico was to place it physically in the *conductas* (table 15 lists the costs associated with the shipment of $62,000 in silver and gold from Mexico City and Puebla for embarkation at Veracruz). Institutionally, the *conductas* were a holdover from colonial times, during which they functioned partly as a fiscal

Table 15
Costs Associated with Shipment and Embarkation of Silver and Gold from
Mexico City and Puebla to Veracruz, June 1837

Expenses Reported	Amount Paid Out (Current Pesos)
Cost of transport, Mexico City and Puebla to Veracruz	608.0
Cost of escort and packaging, Mexico City and Puebla to Veracruz	145.0
Duties: *derechos de circulación* at 2% (internal tax)	1,240.0
Duties: *derechos de exportación* at 3.5% (export tax)	2,170.0
Brokerage and weighing fees at Veracruz	20.0
Packaging for 25 boxes	22.6r.
Use of launch to load aboard ship	8.4r.
Miscellaneous costs	25.0
Total costs for $62,000 (6.9%)	4,239.0r.

Source: CMRFH.

device to monitor compliance with the royal *quinto*, a tax assessed on silver production. Although independence relieved mine owners of the burden of the *quinto*, the *conductas* continued to serve useful revenue purposes. Evasion of export duties on silver was complicated, as all legal internal transport was by *conducta* or special license. Among the direct taxes assessed on the transport of silver within Mexico were the *derechos de circulación*, a 2 percent charge on the value of shipments. Practical consideration also encouraged utilization of the *conductas*. In bandit-ridden Mexico, they offered the best hope that a cargo might pass unmolested. But as Pedro recounted to Gregorio José in September 1838, even *conductas* guarded by well-armed escorts were not immune from danger:

The *conducta* that left Guadalajara at the beginning of this month was to be robbed, and the escort had agreed with the thieves to shoot into the air when they were attacked; fortunately, the plot was discovered before departure; they took several conspirators prisoner and reinforced the *conducta* with rancheros; it has already arrived in Guanajuato and today it should leave for San Luis [Potosí]; in it we have $1,894 that Luna remitted for Llano's account.[6]

An alternative to placing silver physically in the *conductas* was to purchase *conocimientos de conductas*, paper redeemable in silver at ports such as Tampico. In February 1835 the Martínez del Ríos paid $6,995 for a $7,000 *conocimiento* on the Guanajuato-Tampico *conducta*. In Tampico the *conocimiento* was redeemable at a 2.5 percent discount for $6,825 in silver. Between September 1836 and July 1837, the Martínez del Ríos paid out a total of $64,403 for *conocimientos* in Tampico with discounts averaging 2 percent on nominal value.

The costs of remitting silver to Europe increased in the late 1830s, precisely at a time when the Martínez del Ríos had a large cash supply in Mexico. The export of bullion was prohibited and only minted silver could be exported legally. This new legislation, combined with increases in internal transport and export taxes, worked to raise the overhead costs of shipping silver abroad. Typical of Martínez del Río Hermanos's experiences in this period was an enterprise it formed in collaboration with Geaves & Company of Mexico City and Schneider & Company of Germany. In December 1839 Pedro reacted angrily to complaints from their European partner:

If Mr. Schneider is not content with our company it is because the Rogues that manage his and ours do not give him all the profits they take from us, so that after we pay 2 percent monthly, payment is effected in silver marks at seven pesos, these being valued at 10-11 pesos, and with the gold making the same or greater proportion; to this is added that our company transports his silver to the mint and his pesos are returned to the mining site without any cost, in order for this same operation to begin again; such it is that the *conductas* account only cost $40,000 for the past year!!! I repeat, that if this is not sufficient to satisfy this Gentleman then he has more greed than Croesus: I am keeping an eye on this business and certainly will dispose of it if a favorable occasion presents itself.[7]

The intervention of the British government in silver exchanges at the Mexican ports also had a detrimental effect. Beginning in the late 1830s (probably at the time of the French blockade in 1838), a *comisario inglés* stationed in the ports bought up Mexican silver with *libranzas* payable in London with pounds sterling. In November 1838 Pedro complained, "So long as the English try to get the money they need for their colonies there will never be the exchange you knew here before."[8] In March 1839, Pedro again lamented, "As long as the English Commissary is here, we will encounter few favorable moments for speculation in shipments of metal there [Great Britain]."[9]

In the United States, Mexican silver pesos circulated as legal tender until the early 1870s. Consequently, there were occasional opportunities to take advantage of fluctuating exchange rates there. In the summer of 1837, during his stay in New Orleans, Pedro encountered a rare moment in which pesos could be exchanged for dollars at premiums of up 24 percent. Rumors that the Bank of the United States would redeem its bills in silver fueled a brief epidemic of speculation in Mexican silver during June and July of 1837. The arrival of large shipments of silver from Mexico and fears of a general banking collapse in the United States burst the bubble. Premiums fell quickly to 15 percent and then to less than 9 percent. Pedro, who had bought $15,000 in pesos with a 20 percent premium was among the victims when the exchange rate plummeted.[10]

Because of continuing problems with silver, Pedro reported that exchange operations in 1839 were profitable only if funneled through the cochineal trade. But even that alternative proved unworkable by August 1840. In 1845 the constraints on silver exchange relaxed temporarily, and the following year Martínez del Río Hermanos began to use its accounts with Lemmè and other London houses to speculate in silver shipments from the interior of Mexico. Even so, silver never again became an especially profitable means with which to maintain positive balances in overseas accounts.[11]

Finance

Initially, lending was the single most productive area of the Martínez del Río Hermanos banking operations. This activity evolved from Ventura Martínez's role as a casual moneylender in the late 1820s and early 1830s. It increased in importance after 1835, as the family was obliged to look for new opportunities to invest its expanding cash inventory in Mexico. Between 1835 and 1837 the quantity of the family's funds placed in loans vacillated between a low of $40,000 in February 1835 to a high of $126,193 in July 1836 (table 20 will show the relative importance of loans and other negotiable paper in the firm's portfolio of properties after 1838). For Martínez del Río Hermanos the highest level of outstanding loans occurred in December 1839—$347,977.

Table 16 lists a random sample of one-fourth of all loans dispensed by the Martínez del Ríos between February 1835 and August 1837. Interest rates on these loans varied from 1 percent to 2.5 percent monthly, the most common rates being 1.25 percent and 1.5 percent monthly (15 percent to 18 percent annually). Borrowers can be classified into two general categories. First, there was a large number of small borrowers who secured loans of less than $5,000 to finance purchases of merchandise from Drusina & Martínez. Second, a few borrowers obtained large loans for a variety of entrepreneurial projects. Some, like Benito Maqua, Antonio Garay, Manuel Escandón, and Agüero, González & Company, needed funds for tobacco companies they organized after 1835. Morphy & Morzán sought financing for armament deals being arranged with the government. Manning & MacKintosh required short-term financing in 1837 for its mining and exchange ventures. Others, like the Conde de Regla, needed cash just to stay solvent. The interest rates charged to borrowers reflected conditions in the money market as well as less tangible factors such as the identity and presumed reliability of borrowers. In December 1836, after hearing that Ventura de la Cruz was making loans to certain individuals at 1.25 percent monthly, Gregorio José scolded his brother: "By what you tell me about the

Table 16
Selected Loans Disbursed by Martinez del Rio Family

Date of Loan	Amount (Current Pesos)	Term (Months)	Monthly Interest Rate (%)	Borrower	Amount Repaid (Current Pesos)	Date Repaid
14 Feb. 1835	20,000	6	1.25	Faeber, Sillem & Co.	21,500	14 Aug. 1835
13 Apr. 1835	5,000	3	1.00	B. Maqua	5,225	13 July 1835
17 June 1835	7,000	4	1.25	A. Garay	7,350	15 Oct. 1835
3 Mar. 1836	2,000	4	2.00	C. Gens	2,160	3 July 1836
3 Apr. 1836	4,000	4	1.25	A. Algara	4,240	1 Aug. 1836
21 Apr. 1836	2,000	2	2.00	P. Torrin	2,080	20 June 1836
3/16 May 1836	23,999	5	1.25	D. P. Penny & Co.	25,380	17 Aug./17 Oct. 1836
28 May 1836	8,000	6	1.50	M. Martinez del Campo	8,660	28 Nov. 1836
20 July 1836	5,000	3	1.50	L. Ramirez	5,250	21/29 Oct. 1836
9 Aug. 1836	6,000	2	1.50	A. Meyer & Co.	6,180	9 Oct. 1836
7 Sep. 1836	4,500	5	1.50	M. Equia	4,837	7 Feb. 1837
20 Sep. 1836	4,500	4	1.50	J. Ycaza	—	—
8 Dec. 1836	12,000	5	1.50	Faeber, Sillem & Co.	12,900	31 May 1837
31 Jan. 1837	2,000	2	1.50	J. Vitalba	2,060	31 Mar 1837
14 Feb. 1837	5,000	3	1.25	Manning & Marshall	5,187	14 May 1837
1 May 1837	3,342	3	1.25	Fort & Serment	3,500	1 June 1837
7 Apr. 1837	2,000	4	2.00	D. Noriega	2,160	7 Aug. 1837
15 June 1837	14,000	4	1.50	Manning & Marshall	14,840	10 Oct. 1837
31 July 1837	3,000	5	2.00	Manning & Marshall	3,300	31 Dec. 1837
4 Aug. 1837	1,000	4	2.50	C. Gens	1,100	26 Dec. 1837

Source: CMRFH.

discounts you made I see that either money is very abundant or that some have taken advantage of your inexperience. Fagoaga & Barrio always have paid *at least* 1-1/2 and I have never wished to give money to Vinet at less than 1-1/2 or discounts of letters at 1-1/4."[12]

In 1838, when Martínez del Río Hermanos was formally organized and Drusina & Martínez finally liquidated, the family's lending practices were revised. Without a multitude of small loans to service, the general rule became the disbursement of progressively larger loans to fewer individuals. As of early 1840, when lending had reached record levels, the perils of the new policy had not yet been appreciated. Instead, optimistic partners like Pedro believed their favorable assessments of Mexico's commercial advantages were confirmed by the large amount of interest income earned between 1838 and 1840: "Here one finds as much or more security for business than in any other part of the world and you can be sure of that, since there is no one here with whom we deal who does not know his business well."[13] In May 1840, at a time when commerce was more or less paralyzed and when international exchange continued to be unprofitable, Pedro gloated, "Money is abundant . . . but we have all ours placed at 1-1/2 percent a month."[14] What Pedro and his partners only tardily realized was that by eliminating many small loans in favor of the convenience of a few large loans they had increased the risks of lending. Delayed payments or default on a single large loan could inflict grievous losses. The prominent persons who received these loans *were* better risks because of the extensive properties they owned and because their privileged political status enabled them to make extraordinary profits from their business dealings, but these same qualities could make the speedy recovery of their debts quite impossible.

The dealings of Martínez del Río Hermanos with Morphy & Morzán illustrate how disconcerting the collection of an overdue loan could be, even when the final outcome was satisfactory.[15] As of January 1839 Morphy & Morzán owed the firm $50,604. Security for the debt included two Fresnillo mining shares, which had been deposited with the lender until the loan was repaid. The loan was already overdue because the firm's senior partner, Francisco Morphy, had not received payment from the government for the ships delivered to it in Veracruz. In October 1840 Morphy was still trying to collect from the government. As the armaments deal had been made with Santa Anna and as Morphy had no influence with Anastasio Bustamante, favorable Supreme Court decisions were useless. In July 1841 the status of the loan remained unchanged, except that Morphy—who had made two recent trips to Santa Anna's estate in Veracruz—was leaving for a "tour" of the interior and many observers believed he was acting as the general's agent in plotting revolution. Two months later Santa Anna pronounced against Bustamante and the reverberations of a dramatic shift in political economy were quickly felt in Mexico City. Morphy assured his creditors he would soon be able to settle his debts. As the intermediary between Santa Anna and *empresarios* anxious to return the tobacco monopoly to the government for a profit, Morphy earned a fat commission in November 1841. Still, he did not repay Martínez del Río Hermanos until July 1842, when Santa Anna allocated to him a share of customs duties to pay his armaments deal of 1838. By September 1842 Martínez del Río Hermanos had received full payment of its loan. Soon afterward, Morphy moved with his family to occupy a consular post in London. Rumors claimed that he carried in his luggage $250,000 taken from the National Treasury. Pedro bitterly observed that for Morphy to carry off so much, one could imagine "how much it will cost the poor Mexican nation."[16] In February 1843 the value of Morphy's assets had increased to over $400,000 at a time when the National Treasury once more was on the verge of bankruptcy.

The key to Morphy's success was his influence with Santa Anna. All big government deals went through Morphy, who was, according to observers, the "only one who does business with *el Cojo* [Santa Anna]."[17] For Pedro the lesson to be learned from this was obvious: Why should Martínez del Río Hermanos put up its money and take risks for individuals like Morphy who afterward would walk away with most of the profits? Consequently, after 1841 funds previously earmarked for private loans went directly into speculations with government debt issues (this activity is explored in chapters 7 and 8).

Similar considerations helped to transform Martínez del Río Hermanos from a moneylender furnishing Felipe Nerí del Barrio large sums to buy cotton and machinery for Miraflores in 1839 and 1840 into a participating partner by 1841. As Barrio's creditor for $112,821 in February 1840, the firm held excellent securities, including a mortgage on one of his shares in the Empresa del Tabaco, and it had custody of drafts from the Empresa totaling $289,450. As Barrio's partner, Martínez del Río Hermanos gave up these mortgages. The demand for capital to finance the textile factory required the company to divert its remaining funds away from interest-bearing loans and into direct and, ultimately, unprofitable investments in production (that transformation and the firm's problems in textile manufacturing are the subject of chapter 6).[18]

Exports

Two general considerations governed the participation of Martínez del Río Hermanos in ventures to export Mexican commodities. First, exports were essential for exchange purposes, and so profits more modest than the 15 percent rate of return expected from other investments would not cause the firm to disengage from this activity. The firm recognized that there were few Mexican goods that could be sold advantageously overseas. Second, the firm's involvement in the export trade was restricted to an indirect, financial role.

Precious metals export, especially silver, was discussed in the preceding section on exchange. After silver, cochineal was the next best product for export. Highly esteemed as a dye for European textiles from its discovery in the sixteenth century until the development of artificial aniline dyes in the mid-nineteenth century, cochineal possessed the added attractiveness of a high ratio of value to weight, making it economical to transport and store. The fact that Mexican production was limited to Oaxaca had both positive and negative implications. On the one hand, attention could be focused on a single region, so production was not scattered and diffused in many isolated locales, as was the case in mining. On the other hand, Oaxaca was remote, backward, and inconveniently located.

To purchase and ship cochineal from Oaxaca to London in 1839, Martínez del Río Hermanos and Cotesworth, Pryor & Company formed a special company. In February 1839 Martínez del Río Hermanos remitted $12,000 to Oaxaca as the first installment of up to $50,000 to be placed there for the purchase of *grana* (cochineal). In Oaxaca, Cotesworth, Pryor & Company supervised the purchases and prepared and packed the cochineal for shipment. The normal cycle of trade, from the placement of funds in Oaxaca to the arrival of cochineal in Veracruz, required four months. By early June 1839 the first shipments were en route to Veracruz. The following month fifty-six sacks of cochineal were placed aboard the *Ann Eliza* bound for New York. There the cochineal was reshipped to London. At the end of July another five hundred sacks were marketed in Veracruz for prices ranging from $34 to $36, depending on the quality of the product.

Whereas this partnership was typical of the several cochineal ventures Martínez del Río Hermanos helped to finance in the late 1830s, the pecularities of this 1839 venture included the fact that even as prices in London were falling, those in Veracruz were rising because of a scarcity of cochineal in Oaxaca. This anomaly was a by-product of the 1838 French blockade, an act that many wrongly assumed would obstruct the cochineal trade. When the British minister in Mexico encouraged the shipment of cochineal, vanilla, and silver in British packets and men-of-war, the blockade was neutralized. More cochineal probably left Mexico during the blockade than before. That contributed to an oversupply in London and caused prices to fall in 1839, when normal trade was restored. For Martínez del Río Hermanos, the net result was that its profit for the 1839 venture was less than 4 percent on capital invested, compared to the 16 percent earned by the 1838 venture. When the 1841-1842 ventures produced losses of $6,540 for Martínez del Río Hermanos, the firm politely declined Cotesworth, Powell & Pryor's invitation to try again the following year. Despite the risks and the poor prospects for a profit, the great pressure to secure exchange income obliged the firm to enter into a new venture with Hoffman and d'Oleire in the summer of 1845. Even though prices in Veracruz had fallen to $31 and $32 per sack, Pedro predicted this venture would return a minimum 4 percent profit.[19]

After silver and cochineal, there were few goods that could be exported with the promise of a profit. Agricultural products like tobacco, sugarcane spirits (aguardiente), and cotton not only were too expensive to export, but were protected against competition from cheaper foreign imports. Vanilla had a market in Europe, but Gregorio José refused in no uncertain terms an invitation to deal in vanilla in 1842. The comparative advantage in this trade lay with firms located in Veracruz or Jalapa, which were closer to the collection areas in the coastal jungles. At the request of F. W. Schmidt & Company, Martínez del Río Hermanos shipped fifty barrels of whale oil to New York in 1841, but neither whale oil nor vanilla ever developed into an important trade item for the firm. The failure to develop new export alternatives, combined with declining profitability in traditional exports, had long-term consequences for the firm's ability to continue conducting international exchange.[20]

Foreign Investments

In theory, foreign investments were to be a vital part of Martínez del Río Hermanos's portfolio of properties because they would generate income to cover the firm's exchange accounts with overseas commercial houses. In that role they would ease the difficulties created when exchange earnings from Mexican exports were insufficient to balance their overseas demands for new purchases and credit and exchange operations. The results of investments in New Orleans, New York, and London were uniformly disappointing. At best, large amounts of the firm's capital were tied up in unproductive activities with little or no profit. At worst, the investments were complete or nearly complete losses.

Martínez del Río Hermanos's investment in the New Orleans area originated in the visits of Gregorio José and Pedro to the city in the late 1830s. Its properties there were managed by Schmidt & Werner, a trading partner and a primary source for *libranzas* payable in the United States. Bank stock and real estate mortgages constituted the largest part of Martínez del Río Hermanos's properties in New Orleans. These included one hundred shares in the Carrollton Bank, which Schmidt & Werner had purchased for its client in the summer of 1838. The following January, in the midst of a banking panic, Schmidt & Werner bought $3,000 in notes issued by the Brandon Bank. Its agent assured Martínez del Río Hermanos that these bank stocks and notes were bound to rise to par within the year.

Instead, both banks became insolvent, resulting in the loss of three-quarters of the original investments. Nor were the company's loans to citizens in the New Orleans area any more secure. Beginning in 1839 borrowers began defaulting on loans received in 1837. These and other setbacks, along with the firm's pressing cash shortage in Mexico, persuaded the firm to liquidate its interests in New Orleans.[21]

Some of the funds kept in New Orleans were shifted to New York in 1840 and 1841 and placed under the care of F. W. Schmidt & Company. These monies were situated in state stocks and bonds and in bank shares, but the pattern established in New Orleans prevailed. New York, Pennsylvania, and Ohio bond issues costing $113,659 produced a 6 percent return in 1840, but beginning in April 1841 the state of Pennsylvania defaulted on interest payments and within a year the market value of these bonds had fallen to 50 percent of face value. Domingo Ansoátegui commented in 1846 on newspaper reports that these bonds had begun to rise in value: "It will be a miracle to escape the clutches of these Saintly Quakers without a scratch."[22] Shares in the Bank of Commerce of New York yielded slightly better results, producing annual returns of 3.5 percent in the early 1840s.[23] The firm's London properties consisted mostly of South American public debt issues purchased by Gregorio José in the early 1840s. The income from these bonds was assigned to Frederick Huth & Company and J. L. Lemmè & Company to cover Martínez del Río Hermanos's accounts. These bonds failed to produce consistent dividends, but, by way of comparison, investments in the Royal Mail Steamship Company gave even more dismal results. Most of $5,236 invested in stocks was lost after the company went bankrupt in the mid-1840s.[24]

These foreign mishaps seemed to be conclusive evidence that Mexico, after all, was the most propitious locale for investment. Pedro was quick to point out in October 1842, "If I were a millionaire I would employ with more confidence a part of my wealth in the funds of this country than in those of England."[25] For Martínez del Río Hermanos this assessment of comparative advantage would become in time a fatal proposition.

Mining

The manner in which Mexican mines were financed changed little in the first half-century after independence.[26] There continued to be no personal ownership of subsoil mineral rights. To own a mine one had to work it. By traditional practice, a mine being worked was divided into twenty-four equal shares called *barras*. These belonged to the persons to whom the mine was adjudicated by special tribunals in the mining districts. From these twenty-four *barras*, mine owners set aside for investors a fixed number of *barras aviadoras*. To raise money to work the mine, each investor as a member of the *compañía aviadora* subscribed to pay a fixed number of assessments on the *barras aviadoras* that they owned. The *barras* kept separately by the mine owners (*barras aviadas*) paid no assessments, but the first income from the mine always was assigned to pay off disbursements made by the *aviadora* company. Afterward, profits were divided equally among the owners of the twenty-four *barras* without distinction as to their class.

For investors, this antiquated system had several drawbacks. A frequent complaint was that not all the owners of the *barras aviadoras* paid their subscriptions on time. Under the *ordenanzas* of the ancient code that governed mining, these persons were supposed to forfeit their shares, but in the courts of early national Mexico it was difficult to enforce such forfeitures. Even if investors in default freely surrendered their shares, the remaining shareholders who assumed their subscriptions were obliged to accept new financial compromises. Work on a mine with excellent prospects might cease because not enough subscribers remained to finance its development. When work in the mine was interrupted, the mine might be denounced to authorities and the whole process could begin again. Ordinarily, the market price of a *barra aviadora* was a function of how much had been paid in, how much was owing, and what prospects there were for the mine to be productive—except in those cases where *tanto* was invoked. *Tanto* was a traditional practice that gave other members of the *compañía aviadora* the first option to buy out those who wished to sell their shares; thus, it discouraged the creation of a free market where mining shares might be sold more easily and with more profit.

For those who were reluctant to gamble with mining shares, there was an alternative enterprise—the mint—which promised to reward investors with ample returns of silver coin. In 1838 Martínez del Río Hermanos joined the owners of the Rosario Mine in Guadalupe, Chihuahua, in founding the Casa de Moneda de Guadalupe y Calvo. The venture was not immediately profitable, and five years later its shareholders agreed to combine with the owners of the mint in Culiacán to form a new enterprise, which could monopolize all silver-minting operations in Northwestern Mexico. Before this new company reached the dividend-paying stage, the war between Mexico and the United States broke out, ruining its operations.[27]

By way of contrast, Martínez del Río Hermanos's investments in the Fresnillo Mines of Zacatecas turned out much better. The Mexican government had acquired these mines in the early 1830s after the foreign company that had made heavy investments there fell victim to labor troubles. To finance new operations, the government invited private investors to form a *compañía aviadora*. The government reserved for itself twelve *barras aviadas* and assigned the other twelve to the investors. Each *barra aviadora* was divided into ten shares of $10,000 each. In 1838 Martínez del Río Hermanos acquired 1.25 of the *aviadora* shares. Despite the aggravations of the French blockade, which enhanced the scarcity of the high-priced mercury used to process silver ores, and despite engineering problems in the mines, which necessitated the purchase of expensive new machinery, the Fresnillo mines were soon operating profitably. As early as August 1838, each share received $800 in dividends. By October 1841 the costs of the shares had been fully recovered and profit taking began. Between 1842 and 1847 the shares paid $400 to $600 in dividends four to six times annually (that is, $2,400 to $3,600 annual returns on a $10,000 investment). After 1847 the mines declined and produced few profits. In regards to Fresnillo, Martínez del Río Hermanos's misfortune was that it invested so little in the 1830s when it had so much capital available. Instead those funds went into other ventures, where the capital was squandered.[28]

Martínez del Río Hermanos invested most often in mines situated in Guanajuato, a famous silver-mining area since the seventeenth century. Physically, it was convenient for the firm to invest there because deliveries of textiles from Miraflores could be repaid in mining shares.[29] Receipts from the sale of textiles were spent to rehabilitate mines that had been abandoned since 1810. Belatedly, investors learned that many of these mines had been neglected not because of damage inflicted by the Hidalgo revolt, but because they were played out. For Martínez del Río Hermanos, none of these mines produced enough silver to pay off expensive investments in labor and machinery.

Martínez del Río Hermanos invested less often, but more intensively, in mines located in Pachuca and other nearby mining towns in Hidalgo, which had been famous as colonial silver-mining centers. In the 1830s a British mining company spent fabulous sums to bring in new machinery and personnel to rehabilitate these mines. In 1849 this company declared bankruptcy, suspended its operations, and turned over its properties to a group of Mexican investors for the ridiculously low price of $30,000. Afterward, the new company—the Real del Monte Mining Company— struck a mother lode of silver and produced huge fortunes for its principal shareholders. In December 1853 Martínez del Río Hermanos acquired 10 of the company's 405 shares from Manuel Escandón. For most of the decade these shares, costing $10,000 each, paid monthly dividends of $2,640.

Apart from filling an empty cash box, the highly prized properties could be used as collateral. To guarantee repayment of a $247,000 loan received from Francisco Yturbé in June 1856, the firm placed its Real del Monte shares (numbered 109 to 112 and 161 to 166) in the custody of the lender and assigned the income from those dividends to pay interest on the loan. Short of cash in 1857, the firm was obliged to cede these shares to Manuel Escandón in exchange for payment of debts owed to Yturbé.[30]

Table 17 lists mining investments made by Martínez del Río Hermanos

Table 17
Selected Mining Investments and Returns, Martínez del Rio Hermanos

Year of Acquisition	Name of Mine	Location	Holdings	Cost (Current Pesos)	Profits[a] (Current Pesos)	Comments
1838/ 1843	Fresnillo	Fresnillo, Zacatecas	1.25 *aviadora* shares; .63 *aviada* shares	13,883[b]	15,000	Productive through 1849
1850	San Rafael	Guanajuato, Guanajuato	4 shares	8,000	—	Total loss
1850(?)	Mineral del Oro	Tlalpujahua, Michoacán	—	—	—	Bankrupt, 1853
1851	Guadalupe	Temascaltepec, México	4.5 *barras aviadoras*	4,500	—	—
1852	San Vicente de Paulo	Guanajuato, Guanajuato	0.5 *barra*	16,000	—	—
1853	Real del Monte	Pachuca, Hidalgo	10 shares	100,000[b]	100,000	Sold shares at cost in 1857
1853	Tlalpujahua	Tlalpujahua, Michoacán	1 share	2,500	—	Total loss
1854	Guadalupe	Guanajuato, Guanajuato	5.49 *barras aviadoras*	—	—	—
1855	Sangre del Cristo y Villariño	Guanajuato, Guanajuato	4.6091 shares	55,309	—	Total loss
1855	Maravillas	State of Guanajuato	8.9867 shares	9,706	—	Total loss
1855	La Arizona	State of Guanajuato	5 shares	8,500	—	Total loss
1855(?)	Placeres del Oro	State of Guerrero	16.5 shares	1,850	—	Total loss
1856	Santa Cruz	Chiltepec, México	6.5 *barras*	4,815	—	Total loss

Table 17 (continued)

Year of Acqui- sition	Name of Mine	Location	Holdings	Cost (Current Pesos)	Profits[a] (Current Pesos)	Comments
1856(?)	San Antonio de Santa Anna	Temascaltepec, México	2 *barras*	615	—	Total loss
1856	San Victoriano	Pachuca, Hidalgo	6 shares	912	—	Total loss
1856	La Soledad	Tepenené, Hidalgo	10 shares	5,000	—	Total loss
1857	El Jacal	Pachuca, Hidalgo	.06 *barra*	4,500	—	—
1858	La Cantabria	State of Guanajuato	2 shares	520	—	—
1860	San Vicente	Unknown	—	60	—	—
	Total 1838-60			236,670	115,000	

Source: CMRFH.

Notes: If investment principal repaid is included with profits, then $236,670 invested returned total of $228,883.

[a] Net returns after all costs paid

[b] Principal of investment recovered (see note)

— means no information

between 1838 and 1860. Although its investments yielded profits totaling $228,883, its cash outlays for mining shares and for assessments on those shares exceeded $236,613. Table 17 does not include all mining investments and their profits and losses, but an overall negative trend is unmistakable. In assessing the poor results of the firm's adventures in mining, several observations can be made.

First, timing seems to have been a crucial factor. The sequence, frequency, and intensity of the firm's investments in mining were more a function of its internal cash flow situation (that is, whether or not it had extra cash to spend) than a response to actual or perceived opportunities. Most investments were initiated in two periods, 1838 to 1840 and 1853 to 1855, when the firm's cash boxes were full. Mining investments were channeled into areas linked with the firm's other activities and were not necessarily put into locations that objectively promised the best prospects.

Second, the firm's financial weakness encouraged investments in a variety of small-scale ventures, which did not require large outlays of capital, but which correspondingly had remote chances of success. At the same time, even successful investments like Real del Monte could be undone by failures in other areas.

Third, the lack of useful social resources cost the partners of Martínez del Río Hermanos dearly. Because they were outsiders, their access to the best opportunities were limited by the circumstances discussed in chapter 3, and the comparative advantages lay with better-equipped investors. Often, the Martínez del Ríos were minority shareholders in enterprises managed to appease private or family interests or, like other foreign investors, they were forced to depend on unreliable third parties, often their commercial correspondents, to look out for their interests. As was the case with their investments in New Orleans and New York, whether because of fraud, indifference, or accident, the end result was costly and unproductive mismanagement.

Fourth, the mining industry was generally too depressed to offer reasonable prospects for profits. The fortunes made at Real del Monte and Fresnillo were the products of simple luck *and* the huge investments made by the defunct foreign companies. But for every Real del Monte there were hundreds of La Arizonas into which thousands of pesos disappeared without visible results. In the early 1850s Mexican investors put more than $200,000 into an ambitious gold-mining operation at Tlalpujahua and El Oro near the boundary between the states of Michoacán and Mexico. The venture (one in which Gregorio José participated) turned out to be a total loss. Profitable mining of gold deposits there had to await the arrival of new technologies and a new, grander scale of investment not available until the beginning of the twentieth century.

In combination, Martínez del Río Hermanos's mining properties worked quietly, almost invisibly, to help undermine the firm's finances. Assessments on each mining share amounted to only a few pesos monthly. But over a twenty-year period, the collective demands of dozens of these speculations weighed heavily on the firm. In the end, a collection of worthless mining shares displaced more substantial forms of capital in the company's portfolio of properties. Some of the partners were not unaware of this creeping menace. Ventura de la Cruz insisted in October 1851 that the firm terminate its mining speculations: "You know that the *avíos* always begin small, then one is committed and it is necessary to continue forward, and then come the obligations and works."[31]

Land

Martínez del Río Hermanos was slow to show an interest in acquiring real property. Its land acquisitions prior to the disamortization law of 1856 were incidental and unplanned. After 1856 the possibility of converting otherwise worthless government debt issues into potentially valuable real properties did encourage a change of attitude, but already the condition of the firm was too unstable to permit full exploitation of the developing opportunities. By 1858 the firm had difficulty putting together even the small amounts of cash needed to acquire land. Also, in these later years the firm's partners increasingly preferred to acquire property in their own names as the bankruptcy of Martínez del Río Hermanos became more probable.

It was in its role as a lender (not as a land speculator) that Martínez del Río Hermanos acquired title to land in Texas: eleven *sitios* located along the Brazos River in the Department of Béxar (near present-day Waco, Texas), which had been granted to Joaquín Moreno in 1830. Moreno had ceded the grant to Emelia Vitalba, the infant daughter of Juan Vitalba. Because his speculations in public debt issues had fared poorly, Juan Vitalba owed Martínez del Río Hermanos $8,719 for loans that were overdue in December 1838. The following year Vitalba borrowed an additional $3,000 to finance a trip to the United States. His attempt to recover his land in Texas failed, and Martínez del Río Hermanos accepted the Moreno grant as a partial payment on his debts.[32] Because the land belonged to his daughter, Vitalba could not legally make the transfer. To protect its rights, Martínez del Río Hermanos subsequently purchased a quitclaim on the land from Vitalba's widow and from Emelia's guardian. This document, which required court approval, noted that the land grant was probably worthless because the land had been illegally occupied by settlers in Texas since 1836.[33] Despite repeated efforts to gain possession of the property, the firm's partners failed to make good on their title.[34] Much later, in the 1880s, José Pablo's children would win partial payment for the land, and in the 1920s his grandchildren, claiming that their property had been illegally usurped by the State of Texas, would file a $2 million claim against the U.S. government.[35]

In June 1850, on the eve of Ewen MacKintosh's declaration of personal bankruptcy, Martínez del Río Hermanos purchased from his wife fifteen *sitios* of land located near San Andrés Tuxtla, Veracruz. The stipulated price for the property, known as the Terrenos del Uvero, was $52,787, payable as $35,662 in shares of Guadalupe y Calvo and the Casa de Moneda de Culiacán and with the balance in cash.[36] The sale was a disguised loan, as MacKintosh reserved the right to repurchase the property before October 1851. The complete collapse of his finances made that impossible, and Martínez del Río Hermanos retained possession.

With the disamortization of corporate lands, Martínez del Río Hermanos moved quietly to share in the opportunities for speculation in urban real estate. In September 1856 the Parcialidades de Santiago Tlaltelolco (a civil corporation) sold José María Marroquí land belonging to Indian communities located on the northwestern outskirts of Mexico City. The price charged for several lots totaling 1.5 caballerías in size was $4,800.[37] The *escritura* registering the sale noted that Marroquí acted on behalf of an unidentified company, which had been formed to develop such properties. Two years later the agent identified Martínez del Río Hermanos and Manuel Campero as sole owners of the company.

Several factors prevented Martínez del Río Hermanos from profiting from its speculation. The buyers could not take immediate possession of the property because in 1858 Benito Juárez, as Supreme Court justice, ruled that Indians living on lands affected by the disamortization law might continue to occupy their houses. More important, the huge volume of properties put on the market because of disamortization depressed real estate prices. Not until the 1880s did land values in Mexico City begin to rise rapidly enough to create favorable conditions for urban land developers. Unable to wait, Martínez del Río Hermanos ceded its interest in the property to Campero in the early 1870s, probably in settlement of a debt.[38]

Other Enterprises

In the twenty-plus years of its active existence as one of the most important banking houses in Mexico, Martínez del Río Hermanos was associated with a number of enterprises that defy easy classification. By far the most interesting of these were the annual games of chance at San Agustín, a full day's ride by horseback from Mexico City. The revelry, which lasted for several days in June, featured cockfights and gaming of all varieties and was attended religiously by *empresarios* and politicians alike. The games provided merchants and politicians an informal setting in which to plan campaigns and to make and break alliances. Ritual conquests (and defeats) took the place of physical combat—the games simulated the erratic, highly politicized Mexican economy. Here too, substantial redistributions of income occurred. All transactions were in onzas de oro (gold pesos) exchangeable with pesos fuertes (silver pesos) at a ratio of 16:1. Firms like Martínez del Río Hermanos shared in the action by backing their favorite players. Profits and losses were divided between players and their backers according to a complex formula. Table 18 lists individuals bankrolled by the firm in the 1838 games. In private games on their own account, Pedro won 139 onzas and Ventura de la Cruz lost 60 onzas in 1838, but by the standards of the day their involvement was modest. Manuel Escandón regularly won large sums. Santa Anna won and lost huge sums. Tomás Morphy, famous for his heavy losses in these games, lost 1,200 onzas in 1839, 1,500 in 1842, and even more in 1844.[39]

Continuing along the lines established by the Spanish Crown in colonial times, economic initiative in early national Mexico was restrained and regulated by the state. The introduction of new economic innovations was discouraged by an irregular system of special licensing, which took the place of the established body of legislation and commercial codes found in Europe and the United States. Consider Martínez del Río Hermanos's experience with artesian wells. In 1849 Colonel Luis Ruiz, who was among other things a cotton planter in Veracruz, sold the firm (for $200) the exclusive right to use machinery to drill artesian wells in Mexico. Ruiz acquired this "right"

Table 18
Investments and Returns in San Agustín Games, Martínez del Río Hermanos, June 1838

Sum Invested	Player	Profit or Loss
250 onzas	J. V. Lubervieille	30 onzas
200 onzas	Antonio Garay	20 onzas
200 onzas	Manuel Escandón	−30 onzas
150 onzas	Domingo Noriega	120 onzas

Source: Pedro Ansoátegui to Gregorio Martínez del Río, Mexico City, 22 June 1838, CMRFH.
Note: Total investment of 800 onzas ($12,800) produced profits of 140 onzas, equivalent to a 17.5 percent return on capital invested.

from his friend Santa Anna in 1843. Making use of its property, Martínez del Río Hermanos hired André Fulton in 1853 to drill wells with his machinery at selected sites near Miraflores. To preserve its monopoly on the drilling of such wells anywhere in Mexico, the firm instructed its attorneys "to proceed against whoever attempts to attack its property in said privilege."[40]

A final example of the curious enterprises that Martínez del Río Hermanos promoted was the Agencia de Créditos de la Frontera.[41] Its purpose in 1854 was not, as its name might suggest, to provide financial services to Northern Mexico. Rather, it was a speculative venture to buy up the claims of individuals who suffered losses from Indian raids staged from U.S. territory before 1853. None of these claims were paid before the 1870s, however, and once again Martínez del Río Hermanos only succeeded in tying up more of its rapidly dwindling store of capital in unproductive assets that could not be easily liquidated.

Collections

Like other businesses in early national Mexico, Martínez del Río Hermanos was plagued by debtors who would not, or more often, could not pay back loans or keep their accounts current. Like other businesses, the firm occasionally was stuck with bad paper—unpaid *libranzas* and other promissory notes. Prior to 1844 Martínez del Río Hermanos did not protest nonpayment (that is, begin a judicially supervised collection process) of a single *libranza*. Aside from unpaid *libranzas* associated with the $1.5 million church loan of 1847, protests for the balance of the 1840s were rare as well. Although the number of protests increased dramatically in the next decade, as more businesses went bankrupt, unpaid *libranzas* and other kinds of debts seem to have played a relatively minor role in reducing the profitability of the firm's operations. Table 19 lists selected instances in which Martínez del Río Hermanos appointed special agents to collect from its debtors. These uncollected debts accounted for only a small proportion of

Table 19
Selected Collection Proceedings Instituted by Martínez del Río Hermanos

Date	Debtor	Location	*Apoderado*
May 1840	Becerra & Company	Tampico	Jolly & Baker
July 1842	Various	New Orleans	Schmidt & Company
July 1849	Lino Carballo	Havana	Various
Apr. 1853	Gamio & Domereq	Mexico City	José María Zaldívar
Aug. 1855	Robert Smith	Oaxaca	Domingo Ansoátegui
Sep. 1855	Various	Puebla	Anselmo Gutiérrez
Oct. 1855	A. Smith & Co.	Oaxaca	José María de León

Source: Pedro Ansoátegui to Gregorio Martínez del Río, Mexico City, 5 May 1840; Domingo Ansoátegui to Gregorio Martínez del Río, Oaxaca, 11 August 1855, CMRFH; AN-169-1842:640-642, 8 July 1842; AN-464-1849:109-110, 12 July 1849; AN-169-1853:373-374, 9 April 1853; AN-169-1855:743-744, 3 September 1855; AN-169-1855:880-881, 30 October 1855.

the firm's unproductive assets before 1860, and the accumulation of these debts was not a plausible explanation for the firm's insolvency after 1861. For the whole period of this study, the most consequential debts owed to the firm were public and deliberate—originating in its speculations in government debt issues as reported in chapters 7 and 8.

Profits

The complex operations of Martínez del Río Hermanos, its curious assortment of properties, and the sometimes bewildering management strategies pursued by its partners can best be understood by reemphasizing that the primary business of the firm was to provide banking services. Exchange operations were important to both Drusina & Martínez, the importer, and Martínez del Río Hermanos, the banker. Though outwardly similar, the nature of these exchanges and their purpose were different. For Drusina & Martínez, exchange worked to move merchandise. Martínez del Río Hermanos wanted to move money, not goods. In theory, Martínez del Río Hermanos invested in activities that would provide it with a steady stream of income upon which its banking operations would float. In practice, the grandiose scheme was unworkable—none of the firm's investments consistently generated sufficient income. Over the long term, neither private nor public loans in Mexico yielded dependable rates of interest. The manufacturing sector was worse, a sinkhole gobbling up enormous quantities of capital. In the great lottery that was mining, the firm was simply unlucky. In short, the downwardly spiraling Mexican economy characteristic of the half century before 1860 hardly encouraged a happy outcome, especially for those short on social and political resources.

From the beginning the firm was doomed. Very quickly the logic of its operations was inverted. It became a borrower instead of a lender. Exchange funds for banking operations were diverted to cover bad investments. The solid foundation of liquid capital upon which the firm was based in 1838 was supplanted over time by a large and flimsy structure composed of unprofitable, even unmarketable, properties. Table 20 lists the firm's assets and liabilities for selected years. Table 21 summarizes its profit and loss accounts for 1839 to 1842. Table 22 presents capital to profit-loss ratios for selected years 1838 to 1857. The developing trend toward declining profits matured into consistent year-end losses after 1842. Not until 1853 and 1854, on the strength of temporary successes in mining and government debt speculations, did the firm make real profits (about 16 percent). Afterward, the old pattern returned and deepened. When the firm declared a profit in 1857, it was already in serious financial trouble. In that context, profit taking was thinly disguised decapitalization aimed at bolstering the partners' individual positions before the company collapsed.

Table 20

Assets and Liabilities, Martínez del Río Hermanos, Selected Years

(Current Pesos)

Assets & Liabilities	1839	1840	1841	1842	1843	1857	1858	1861
Assets								
Cash	14,899	579	15,850	19,374	1,056	7,022	7,214	56
Loans/negotiable paper	200,465	347,977	209,908	100,559	17,056	0	4,457	0
Operating accounts	258,814	201,641	211,450	123,305	83,420	355,444	322,111	145,509
Mining	36,991	33,388	32,013	27,270	31,199	72,181	84,303	94,903
Manufacturing/industrial	—	—	132,937	200,480	291,727	714,477	599,416	559,078
Other nonpublic enterprise	22,380	39,431	70,534	53,121	43,101	45,934	37,060	8,407
Real property	—	—	7,856	7,856	7,856	108,219	99,432	126,533
Mexican public debt issues	26,476	68,268	152,284	206,012	284,731	554,027	421,416	17,136
Non-Mexican public debt	—	—	133,485	115,161	93,761	151,088	151,892	151,892
Total	560,025	691,284	966,317	853,138	853,907	2,008,392	1,727,301	1,103,514
Liabilities								
Operating accounts	38,634	112,609	178,900	174,287	178,253	927,230	424,411	16,346
Finance accounts	0	14,495	30,163	108,927	95,174	426,875	822,161	707,157
Capital accounts	490,000	497,000	568,000	560,000	560,000	550,000	550,000	550,000
Differential balance shortage/surplus*	+31,391	+67,180	+189,254	−9,924	+20,480	+104,287*	−69,271*	−169,989
Total	560,025	691,284	966,317	853,138	853,907	2,008,392	1,727,301	1,103,514*

Source: Various accounts, CMRFH.

*Does not include Dolores A. as creditor for $84,186.78

Table 21
Profit and Loss Accounts, Martínez del Río Hermanos
(Current Pesos)

Income		Expenses	
1838			
Interest account	66,809.14	General costs	27,803.95
Cotton venture	1,199.52	Owed to exchange account	9,471.71
Promissory notes			
(*vales de alcance*)	568.31	Miscellaneous	783.23
Commission account	504.53		
Destination Veracruz	224.81		
Various	143.85		
Total	69,450.16	Total	38,058.89
	Profit 31,391.27		
1839			
Interest account	50,144.75	General costs	27,641.05
Exchange account	4,333.29	Owed to commission	1,788.84
Venture with government	3,642.27	Miscellaneous	2,460.34
Casa de Moneda (Mint)	2,654.25		
17% Fund bonds	2,085.51		
Cochineal venture	1,948.66		
Derechos de consumo	1,151.29		
Destination Veracruz	200.00		
Various	1,518.89		
Total	67,678.91	Total	31,890.23
	Profit 35,788.68		
1840			
Interest account	43,044.29	General costs	28,599.84
17% Fund bonds	36,849.42	Miscellaneous	983.24
Exchange account	2,278.30		
South American bonds	1,428.65		
Commission acount	1,117.73		
Promissory notes	1,030.67		
Casa de Moneda	49.00		
Total	85,798.06	Total	29,583.08
	Profit 56,214.98		

Table 21 (continued)

Income		Expenses	
1841			
Exchange account	17,876.95	General costs	28,599.84
Interest account	16,392.74	Miscellaneous	983.24
Commission account	3,249.22		
17% Fund bonds	1,325.36		
Fresnillo mine	1,045.13		
Various	405.78		
Total	40,295.18	Total	29,583.08
	Profit 10,712.10		
1842			
Chilean bonds	17,313.18	General costs	26,139.98
Commission account	7,015.55	Loss in interest account	9,880.63
Fresnillo mine	6,000.00	Loss in cochineal	6,540.30
Various	225.00	Miscellaneous	2,732.85
Total	30,553.73	Total	45,293.76
	Loss 14,740.03		

Source: CMRFH.

Borrowing

Given the problematic nature of its portfolio of properties, Martínez del Río Hermanos constantly needed to borrow large sums to sustain its operations. If the firm's experience in this regard was at all typical, then it was certainly much easier to borrow money than to make money in early national Mexico. Martínez del Río Hermanos financed its deficits with monies obtained from a variety of sources—from commercial houses in Europe and from depositors and moneylenders in Mexico.

Commercial houses in Europe and the United States assigned the firm moderate amounts of credit.[42] Although this credit was intended to facilitate exchange operations, Martínez del Río Hermanos often used it as a source of short-term financing for its debts in Mexico. For example, in June 1843 the firm wrote £2,000 in drafts drawn on Lemmè & Company in London to pay Dickson, Gordon & Company in Mexico City. In August 1846 the firm drew £3,000 from Lemmè for the same reason. Such operations required that Martínez del Río Hermanos must soon ship funds overseas to cover its accounts, perhaps further aggravating its situation in Mexico. Carelessness in attending to its overseas obligations would create immediate mistrust and might easily cripple the firm's ability to conduct international exchanges.

Table 22
Profit/Loss to Capital Ratios, Martínez del Río Hermanos, Selected Years
(Current Pesos)

	1838	1839	1840	1841	1842	1843	1854	1857
Profit/loss	31,391.27	35,788.68	57,214.98	10,712.10	−14,740.03	−20,000.00	90,000.00	105,000.00
Capital	450,000.00	497,000.00	568,000.00	560,000.00	560,000.00	560,000.00	550,000.00	550,000.00
Profit as % of capital	7.0	7.2	10.1	1.9	−2.7	−3.6	16.4	19.1

Source: CMRFH.

Domingo Ansoátegui commented on one such dilemma in December 1846: "We agree that the best way to inspire confidence is to make frequent and punctual remittances; but I very much fear our present situation will not permit us to make any for now, even though in future we will clearly need to draw on an even larger amount."[43] At this time Martínez del Río Hermanos already owed J. L. Lemmè & Company £8,217. Although these accounts provided financing at lower rates of interest (5 percent to 6 percent annually) than was commonly available in Mexico (18 percent to 24 percent annually), this type of financing was relatively expensive, given the costs of international exchange.

As partners in the family firm and as individuals, the Martínez del Ríos attempted to secure cheap, long-term financing in Europe.[44] In August 1846 Pedro suggested that Gregorio José seek a loan at 5 percent to 6 percent interest using their friend William Sillem's connections in Germany. When that proved impossible, Pedro proposed the following month that his brother-in-law negotiate a £50,000 loan with Lemmè. That did not work either. In June 1847 Ventura de la Cruz approached the Sancho family in Spain with the same object—with the same results. In the early 1850s the Martínez del Ríos tried to use Stephen Williams to arrange a £50,000 loan in London secured with a mortgage on the textile factory in Mexico. As late as 1859, their employee Edward J. Perry attempted to raise a £60,000 loan from the City Bank of London by offering a mortgage on English Convention Bonds issued the Mexican government. Nothing worked. Although the Martínez del Ríos had reasonably good connections in European financial centers, investors there shied away from making loans secured by properties in Mexico. In 1858 Gregorio José obtained an £8,000 loan from Sir Charles Wheatstone, but only after depositing personal collateral (South American bonds) with the lender. As Martínez del Río Hermanos's credit deteriorated in the late 1850s, Gregorio José was obliged to guarantee its account with Lemmè & Company by placing personal property in Lemmè's custody.

By comparison, it was much simpler to borrow in Mexico.[45] Ample commercial loans were available with interests rates averaging 1 percent to 1.5 percent monthly (table 23 itemizes loans contracted by the firm between 1838 and 1858). The implications of borrowing at 15 percent annually to finance unproductive activities should be readily apparent. The situation manifested itself in a snowballing effect as progressively larger and more frequent loans were required to keep the firm solvent. The process began quite early. In June 1838 the company needed to pay out $20,723 in current obligations, but its projected receipts were only $11,014 for that month. As it had no cash reserves, it was obliged to borrow to cover the deficit. In the three months between April and June 1842 the firm anticipated an income of $27,271, but had to pay out $57,220. Again the solution was to borrow.

Table 23
Selected Loans Contracted by Martínez del Rio Hermanos

Date	Amount (Current Pesos)	Lender	Interest	Comments	Due Date
May 1838	10,000	Ycaza	1.5% mo.	1 month	June 1838
1841(?)	30,000	G. Mier y Terán	—	$33,600 repaid	Nov. 1841
1841(?)	12,000	Laurent	—	$13,200 repaid	Dec. 1841
1842	40,000	F. Vallejo	1% mo.	Deposit	Indefinite
Dec. 1843	40,000	S. Galenzowski	1% mo.	Deposit	Indefinite
June 1845	220,500	B. Maqua, J. A. Béistegui, Muriel Herm.	—	For purchase of $496,000 in tobacco bonds	June 1847
Aug. 1846	183,280	J. A. Béistegui	—	For purchase of additional tobacco bonds	Dec. 1847
May 1848	150,000	J. M. Pacheco	—	As extension of previous loan from 1846	Nov. 1849
May 1847	150,000	F. Guate	1% mo.	—	Feb. 1849
June 1847(?)	20,000	T. Bahre	1% mo.	Repaid with $21,200	Jan. 1848
July 1847	32,000	C. Rubio	—	For cotton	Feb. 1848
1847	12,000	Celis	—	For cotton; $12,943 repaid	Dec. 1847
1848(?)	—	Agüero, González y Cía.	—	Large loan	1849
Nov. 1849	150,000	J. M. Pacheco	1% mo.	Security: mortgage on public debt bonds	Sep. 1850
1850(?)	200,000	F. Yturbé	—	Security: mortgage on bonds and *permisos*	—
July 1851	40,000	F. Pérez Gálvez	0.5% mo.	Security: mortgage on Miraflores; repaid in gold	July 1853

Date	Amount	Lender	Interest	Security/Terms	Term
July 1851	12,832	Capellanías	0.5% mo.	Security: mortgage on Miraflores	Indefinite
Nov. 1851	200,000	F. Yturbé	1.25% mo.	Security: mortgage on $1 million in bonds	Mar. 1854
Sep. 1853	34,000	F. Vallejo	1% mo.	Deposit guaranteed by mortgage on Miraflores	Indefinite
June 1856	247,000	F. Yturbé	—	Mortgage on all assets; Real del Monte shares	Apr. 1857; paid off by M. Escandón
July 1856	151,117	B. Maqua	—	For purchase of convention bonds	—
May 1857	354,000	J. A. Béistegui	—	Mortgage on $1.2 million in bonds	Aug. 1858; paid off by H. Viya
May 1857	11,000	J. Macartney	0.5% mo.	Mortgage on La Hormiga	Indefinite
Oct. 1857	140,000	S. Galenzowski	1% mo.	Deposit guaranteed by mortgage on all assets	Indefinite
Jan. 1858	242,901	H. Viya	—	Mortgage on all assets	Aug. 1858
Aug. 1858	504,000	H. Viya	—	As repurchase option for $1.2 million convention bonds	Jan. 1859

Source: CMRFH.
Note: — means no information.

Seven years later it needed to pay out $398,523 to its creditors in the eighteenth-month period between July 1847 and January 1849. In November 1851 the firm was scheduled to repay $342,666 in the eleven months between April 1852 and March 1853. By 1857 Martínez del Río Hermanos had exhausted its borrowing capacity and reluctantly began alienating selected assets in a desperate attempt to reduce its indebtedness to manageable proportions. Yet the properties most desired by creditors were those that were most productive, such as the Real del Monte shares. As those assets were lost, the firm's cash flow problems worsened.

Bankruptcy

On 16 November 1861 an attorney for Martínez del Río Hermanos delivered a petition from the firm to Judge Luis Méndez requesting that he convene a *concurso* of creditors to arrange a settlement of the firm's indebtedness.[46] Four days later the company proposed to its assembled creditors that it be granted a five-year grace period in which to put its financial house back in order, recover its economic equilibrium, and, eventually, be in a position to repay its creditors in full. The firm alleged that if it were forced into immediate liquidation, its creditors would receive only a fraction of the amounts owed. At this time Martínez del Río Hermanos had exactly $56.14 in its strongbox. On paper, the firm owned assets totaling $1,103,514 (see table 20). Of that sum, only $416,469 was convertible to cash to pay debts of $786,619. The partners estimated that Miraflores, which they valued at $559,078, would bring only $315,028. Lands in San Andrés Tuxtla and Mexico City, which cost $55,558, would, if sold under distress conditions, yield only 25 percent of the cost of acquisition. All of its mining properties might produce up to $14,952. Of $29,837 in debts from current accounts, perhaps 33 percent was collectible.

A majority of creditors voted to accept the firm's proposal. Martínez del Río Hermanos was authorized to negotiate a loan to finance the continued operation of Miraflores. All of the firm's annual profits were to be divided among its creditors under the following system of priorities: first, creditors with guarantees; second, the new loan for Miraflores; last, all other creditors, including the firm's depositors. Two commissioners, Cornelio Prado, representing the largest creditor, Hermengildo Viya, and Edward J. Perry, a clerk-turned-creditor, monitored compliance with the pact and approved all contracts for the sale of the firm's properties. María Dolores received consideration as a favored creditor of the firm because Pedro had invested her dowry as his share in the company.

A small group of disgruntled creditors refused to accept the judgment of the *concurso*. Nicanor Béistegui, as the *apoderado* for Juan A. Béistegui, branded the whole procedure illegal and contrary to the Ordenanzas de

Bilbao. After Judge Méndez approved the *concurso*'s action, Béistegui went to another court demanding that the properties of Pedro Ansoátegui be embargoed for $3,559. The attorney for Martínez del Río Hermanos responded by moving the case back to a friendly court, where he secured a favorable decision. Nevertheless, those not in agreement were paid off first to avoid continuing legal harassment.

There *were* several peculiarities about the *concurso*. Just before it delivered its petition to the court, Martínez del Río Hermanos had sold to Viya a large quantity of Miraflores textiles at a 12 percent discount. The firm's formal explanation was that Viya had threatened judicial action to recover past-due loans totaling $240,506. To keep the peace, Martínez del Río Hermanos had been forced to grant him special privileges. There were, however, other less obvious considerations at work. Back in 1859 María Dolores had consented to surrender her status as most-favored creditor in exchange for Viya's extension of a deadline to repay an overdue loan. After receiving the textiles in August 1861, Viya returned favored-creditor status to María Dolores.[47]

Within the *concurso*, the partners of the firm and their relatives appeared as prominent creditors. María Dolores claimed $84,187 from her dowry. José Ansoátegui (Pedro's son) and Juan Fernández de la Vega (Pedro's son-in-law) asked $5,062 for salaries owed to them as employees of the firm. Manuel María's children demanded the return of funds deposited since 1840 with interest—$34,872. Pedro and José Pablo appeared as creditors of their own company for $5,583 owed to personal accounts. All together, family credits accounted for one-fourth ($129,704) of all unsecured debts owed by the company. Among debts owed to the company (and listed as uncollectible) appeared those of Domingo Ansoátegui for $29,659 and Crispiano del Castillo for $4,159. In a private document Domingo alleged that a part of his debt had resulted from the transfer of charges from José Ansoátegui's account.[48] Castillo was the attorney for Martínez del Río Hermanos during the bankruptcy proceedings.

The firm's proposal to its creditors was based on the premise that it could obtain a $150,000 loan to finance the purchase of cotton, repair parts, and labor costs for Miraflores. It promised that with this operating capital the factory would produce an annual net profit of $75,000 (after repaying the $150,000 loan with 8 percent annual interest). Considering the factory's past performance, the claim seemed exaggerated. Certainly, most lenders thought so. The firm failed to interest any moneylender in its plan. Accepting the hopelessness of their position, the partners abandoned their attempt to save Martínez del Río Hermanos. On 31 May 1864 the *concurso* reconvened to approve a final settlement. Ownership of the factory of Miraflores was transferred to the firm's three principal creditors as payment for debts totaling $360,094. Martínez del Río Hermanos was free to make individual arrangements with its other creditors with the understanding that preference would be given to the salaries of the clerks and to María Dolores's dowry.[49]

For this generation of the Martínez del Río family, it was the last act of a painful drama. A half century's stay in Mexico had cost them nearly a half million pesos, by the standards of the day an enormous fortune. The manner in which the bankruptcy was arranged, however, constituted a quiet victory that enabled the family to minimize its losses. Although nearly all of Martínez del Río Hermanos's assets were surrendered to creditors, the personal property of the partners (except that put up as guarantees for their firm) was unaffected. María Dolores, as a favored creditor, was awarded Martínez del Río Hermanos's claims against the governments of Colombia, Venezuela, and Ecuador.

Precisely *how* Martínez del Río Hermanos distributed its assets is worth examining. In the spring of 1864, the manager of Miraflores, Jacob Robertson, purchased the claims of Benito Maqua, Francisco Vallejo, and Hermengildo Viya for $96,347, $24,650, and $239,097, respectively, and formed a new company called J. H. Robertson & Company to take charge of Miraflores. The new enterprise's first act was to draw up contracts whereby Mexico City merchants delivered to the factory raw cotton to be manufactured into yarn and cloth for a set fee. These arrangements helped to reduce the capital required to operate Miraflores. Moreover, as Miraflores was acquired so cheaply, the cost of capitalizing the plant declined sharply in relation to the income it generated and it became a simpler matter to make a profit from its operations. Under new management the factory prospered, at least for the next decade. In 1870 Robertson revealed publicly that his partners in the company since 1864 had been his son, Phillip Robertson, José Ansoátegui y Martínez del Río, and José Antonio Sosa y Ansoátegui. All had contributed equal shares to buy Miraflores. Members of the extended Martínez del Río Hermanos clan had managed to retain 50 percent of the factory even after the bankruptcy of the family firm.[50]

Juan Fernández y Vega, a former employee of Martínez del Río Hermanos, who was married to Ana Ansoátegui y Martínez del Río, purchased the Rancho de Miraflores y Avelar from the bankrupt firm in July 1864 for $16,500. The property included all land not occupied by the factory and all livestock, cultivations, and equipment of the agricultural enterprise that Martínez del Río Hermanos had organized on its lands in Chalco. In the fall of 1861 the firm had assessed the value of this property at $50,516. The income from its sale was assigned to pay part of the debt owed to Dr. Severino Galenzowski. Because Fernández could not keep up payments, he resold the property in February 1870 to J. H. Robertson & Company. In settlement of his debt, Galenzowski received the proceeds from that sale as well as from the sale of the house at No. 2 Factor Street

(Martínez del Río Hermanos's business location) and the Terrenos del Uvero.[51]

Conclusion

Why was Martínez del Río Hermanos such a failure? The partners, in their communications with creditors and the court during the *concurso*, blamed the civil war beginning in 1858, which continued unabated through 1864. Certainly, that episode was the final blow and an immediate cause for failure. Nevertheless, the firm's problems had begun as early as 1842, long before the War of the Reforma would explode across Mexico. A more plausible explanation lies in the nature of the Mexican economy itself. The material conditions for prosperity were simply lacking. Martínez del Río Hermanos, like so many of its contemporaries, was sucked under by the downwardly spiraling currents of the economy. The firm never situated its large reserves of capital so as to provide the prerequisite stable cash flow upon which a functional banking operation would depend. Finance, export trading, mining, land speculation, and overseas investments all failed to yield profits. By default, that left speculation in the public debt and investments in manufacturing as the remaining areas in which worthwhile profits might be encountered.

Unlike Drusina & Martínez, Martínez del Río Hermanos never found for itself a profitable niche in the Mexican economy. Nor did it have the use of Drusina's Mexican kin to look out for its interests. Even so, in relative terms the firm was more successful than many, using its capacity to borrow to postpone the inevitable. It operated under the same name with the same partners for nearly twenty-five years, a rare achievement. During that time, scores of Mexican companies went bankrupt, including Drusina & Company and Manning & MacKintosh.[52]

As for the precise reasons why Martínez del Río Hermanos failed, the social character of the family was a telling factor. As strangers in Mexico, their most consistent trait was a propensity to misunderstand Mexico's complex politicized economy. They surmised correctly that speculation in government debt issues could be a substitute for more substantive economic activities, which simply were not remunerative. But as chapters 7 and 8 will show, Martínez del Río Hermanos's partners lacked the resources to be successful *agiotistas*. They imitated the form, but they lacked the substance. In their other endeavors, they missed the social connections that facilitated access to the best of admittedly few opportunities. At home in neither Latin America nor Europe, Martínez del Río Hermanos's partners depended everywhere on unreliable second-hand advice. All of these shortcomings were manifested in the company's unwise commitment to Miraflores. In purely economic terms, the tendency of textile manufacturing and public debt speculation to absorb progressively larger shares of the firm's operating capital without generating a consistent flow of income was the principal cause of its bankruptcy. Yet one must not forget that it was the dismal performance of the ordinary investments described in this chapter that set the stage for and motivated the actors in those dangerous speculations in more exotic commodities.

6. Textile Manufacturing in Mexico: Miraflores, 1840-1860

The Factory

The adventure began simply enough—an opportunity to invest in an enterprise that promised sure and easy profits, *if* one could get in. Pedro outlined the prospects to Gregorio José in April 1840:

F. N. del Barrio has a speculation in yarn and in an iron foundry on a small hacienda named Miraflores that is 10 leagues from here [Mexico City], situated at the foot of the volcanoes and that one can reach by country coach in 4-1/2 hours; the major part of the 3,500 spindles with which to start have arrived already in Veracruz and will be installed probably in three or four months, as he has everything already prepared; the power for the machinery is water from . . . three streams; I believe we might be able to obtain an interest in this business; I like it very much; Pablo and I have visited it and are enchanted with it. . . . All the factories of this kind that have been established are producing copiously and even though they are increasing every day, I think they are not sufficient to suit the country and for a long time it will be a good speculation. . . . The establishments of this kind are already a guarantee it will protect them, particularly as they owe their origin to the Yorkinos and since their opponents have continued to sustain them.[1]

In the summer of 1840 Martínez del Río Hermanos lent Barrio cash to buy machinery that José Domingo Rascón had brought from the United States.[2] The firm purchased one thousand quintales of cotton to supply the factory and paid the costs of moving the equipment and supplies from Veracruz to Chalco.[3] Afterward, Martínez del Río Hermanos joined the enterprise as Barrio's partner because, as Pedro pointed out in July 1840, "all those who have yarn factories are profiting greatly."[4]

The political economy that made those factories so profitable was the work of diverse interest groups with unequal capacities to make demands on the Mexican state. After enduring ruinous competition from British textiles in the years following independence, artisan cotton spinners and weavers pressured Guerrero's government to approve the Law of 22 May 1829, a measure that banned future imports of cheap cotton cloth. When

Bustamante's government relaxed those constraints on imports the following year, it initially sought to appease that constituency by promising (with the Law of 6 April 1830) to set aside a portion of customs duties collected on formerly prohibited articles to help the ailing (artisan) textile industry in Mexico. Nevertheless, given the greater sensitivity of the Bustamante government to the entreaties of *empresarios*, new legislation in October 1832 authorized the use of that quota of customs duties to fund a development bank, the Banco de Avío, to subsidize the establishment of mechanized cotton textile factories to replace traditional artisan workshops. Before its liquidation in 1842 (it had exhausted its funding by 1836), the Banco de Avío had lent $509,000 for the purchase of machinery and the construction of facilities for textile mills situated in the states of Mexico, Puebla, Veracruz, and Querétaro. Estevan de Antuñano, the principal beneficiary of these low-cost loans, received $146,000 to build La Constancia Mexicana in Puebla. Lucas Alamán, the minister in Bustamante's government who had worked to create the Banco de Avío, borrowed $60,000 for his partnership with Legrand Hermanos in the factory of Cocolapam in Veracruz.[5]

The demands for protection of this new group of industrialists (and the old group of artisans) were answered with the Tariff of 11 March 1837, which banned the import of cheap cotton yarns and cotton cloth (*manta*). This powerful incentive persuaded many more investors to move into the industry, even without the promise of inexpensive loans from the development bank. Through 1840 the attempt to create for manufacturers a closed market—with the use of import prohibitions and the artificial scarcity they induced—helped to push prices high enough to cover profitably the substantial costs of manufacturing textiles in Mexico. From four cotton textile mills in 1837, the industry expanded in less than a decade to more than fifty mills—representing a $10 million investment.

It was with that political economy of textile manufacturing in mind that Martínez del Río Hermanos and Barrio entered into a partnership on 5 December 1840.[6] Because Barrio failed to comply with his contracted obligations, Martínez del Río Hermanos had to finance by itself the expensive works needed to put the factory into full operation. For this reason, it had a free hand in managing the factory, and Barrio remained very much a silent partner. By mutual consent their partnership was terminated prematurely on 31 December 1848 under conditions not provided for in the original contract. Martínez del Río Hermanos secured exclusive ownership of Miraflores by purchasing Barrio's share for $99,900 (payable to the V. a de Echeverría é Hijos mortgage, which had kept Barrio out of bankruptcy in 1843).[7]

The Sinkhole

As early as July 1840 Pedro prepared elaborate calculations to demonstrate to skeptics like Ventura de la Cruz and Gregorio José the profitability of an investment in textile manufacturing.[8] The installation of up to fifteen hundred spindles and the purchase of essential equipment, labor, and raw materials for the first two years of operation would amount to $240,000. The daily manufacture of 2,875 pounds of yarn in a year with 260 working days would provide an annual production of 747,500 pounds of yarn. This yarn, if sold at an average profit of 2 r. per pound, would generate an annual income of $186,875, a 78 percent return on the $120,000 invested each year. Returns from the factory in 1841 and 1842 fell far short of Pedro's projections. Costs for purchasing and installing machinery, for recruiting and training workers, and, especially, for buying raw cotton exceeded expectations. Worst of all, demand and prices for cotton yarn tumbled after 1841.

If expectations failed to meet unrealistic projections, why did the firm make progressively larger investments in the factory over the next two decades (see tables 24 and 25)? In July 1842 Pedro conceded that even though their factory might make a small profit, "it will never compensate for the frights, vexations, and work."[9] José Pablo concluded in December 1843 that it should be sold—if they could find a buyer. Unwilling to accept the heavy losses that would result from selling out under adverse conditions, the

Table 24
Investments in Miraflores Textile Factory, Martínez del Río Hermanos,
Selected Years
(Current Pesos)

Year	Assessed Value of Factory	Value of Inventory and Consignments	Martínez del Río Hermanos Share as % of Total
1841	250,000	7,937	51.5 ($132,937)
1842	324,502	75,480	50.1 ($200,480)
1843	325,462	166,727	79.5 ($291,727)
1848	491,076	—	79.7 ($391,176)
1849	491,076	—	100.0
1853	500,274	—	100.0
1854	512,267	—	100.0
1857	512,267	212,210	100.0
1858	532,525	66,891	100.0
1861	532,525	26,553	100.0

Source: CMRFH.

Table 25
Inventory of Miraflores Textile Factory and Annexes, 1854
(Current Pesos)

Item	Assessed Value
Buildings for factory	220,556.93
Machinery for yarn factory	119,828.01
Machinery for cloth factory	86,331.84
Hydraulic installations	54,117.80
Land occupied by factory	9,000.00
Factory store	11,000.00
Fixtures and utensils	11,432.08
Masonry shop ($248.00)	
Wheel house (*cuarto de torno*) ($6,920.49)	
Furniture ($1,786.98)	
Stores (*caballerizas*) ($1,239.62)	
Tin shop ($62.62)	
Carpenter shop ($570.62)	
Blacksmith ($603.75)	
Total for factory	512,266.66
Buildings for ranches	14,947.76
Irrigation network	4,317.37
Maguey installation	2,057.23
Alfalfa installation	300.02
Miraflores ranch land	9,000.00
Avelar ranch land	6,048.47
Livestock	6,525.94
Total for ranch operation	43,196.79

Source: Martínez del Río Hermanos accounts, CMRFH.

partners preferred to wait for an expected turnabout in the industry. José Pablo predicted the return after 1843 of "another happy era—for those who survive the present crisis."[10] In fact, brief revivals of favorable conditions did occur periodically, but Miraflores's owners responded to the improving market for textiles by making new commitments and investments, putting off for a while longer the sale of the factory. After a good year (1845), José Pablo judged in July 1846 that the time of crisis for the factories had passed. Three months later, raw materials were expensive and scarce, and finished products could hardly be sold at any price.[11]

In a desperate attempt to wring profits from Miraflores, its owners made costly new improvements to the physical plant. The impetus for constructing facilities to weave cloth derived from the need to find an outlet for Miraflores's yarn. In 1846 the factory could not respond fully to market conditions of high demand and high prices for textiles. Because of drought conditions and a water shortage, it lacked sufficient power to keep its machines in motion. The solution was a costly improvement to the hydraulic installations. Faced with the reality of earning only small returns on a huge capital investment, the partners attempted to make better use of their machines by operating them day and night, but the increased overhead costs (for salaries and oil to keep lamps lit) further reduced profit margins. Ventura de la Cruz proposed in 1849 to use the recently invented electric arc light to reduce illumination costs and make night operations at Miraflores more efficient. Although his proposal was never acted on, it does illustrate the manner in which the Martínez del Ríos attempted to deal with their problems. Again in 1855, Pedro recommended the placement of more technology—a steam engine—to increase productivity. With production-side improvements, it was possible to manufacture textiles with small margins of profit over the costs of routine inputs such as cotton—as long as there were no marked disruptions of the marketplace. There is no evidence that Miraflores's owners ever included the depreciation of the physical plant in their accounting methods, and, if the cost of amortizing the capital invested in the plant is added to the routine expenses of manufacturing, profits for Miraflores were nonexistent.[12]

Administration

For bookkeeping purposes, Martínez del Río Hermanos maintained two accounts pertinent to Miraflores. The first consisted of an inventory of the physical plant and the capital required to construct the plant. The second account, the Agencia de Miraflores, encompassed more routine commercial relations. The expense side of this account included purchases of cotton and other supplies, payments for transport costs, and *libranzas* drawn by the management of the factory against Martínez del Río Hermanos. The income side consisted of payments received for consignments arranged by the firm. Little, if any, cash moved directly from the factory to the firm. For its internal operations, the factory maintained a separate set of books, which reported expenses for employee salaries and other routine costs and listed income earned from direct sales of the factory's textiles.

As the resident manager of Miraflores, Jacob H. Robertson's duties included the supervision of normal operations, the management of new installations and constructions, and the verification of accounting procedures.[13] For these services, the firm paid him an annual salary of $2,400 plus a 2.5 percent share of all profits from the factory. The Scot had a free hand in running the factory. The partners had little technical training pertinent to textile manufacturing and, as a matter of principle, they preferred to limit themselves to matters of finance and to stay out of production.

The Work Force

Little is known about the workers who operated the machines at Miraflores that transformed raw cotton into yarn and cloth. Skilled workers of this category were scarce; labor costs were relatively high (by Mexican standards).[14] The problem of retaining workers was such that management was obliged to operate the factory during unprofitable periods, for fear that the workers, if idle, would move elsewhere. Periodic shortages of operators obstructed efforts to increase production, as in September 1844, when no more than forty looms could be operated because of a lack of workers. Other factories reacted to the shortage of trained workers by importing textile workers from Great Britain, but Miraflores's workers were Mexicans who had been trained to operate the imported machinery.

Miraflores was one of the largest factories in Mexico—with a correspondingly large work force. In 1854 it employed 256 employees who earned annual wages totalling $96,000.[15] These included operators and clerks as well as craftsmen such as carpenters and blacksmiths. Wages were paid partially in cash and partially in script or tokens redeemable in the company store. Miraflores traded yarn and cloth to local hacendados in exchange for supplies of wheat, corn, and beans to feed its workers.[16] The factory's employees resided in company-owned housing located adjacent to the factory.

Production

Table 26 shows the expansion of Miraflores's installed capacity to produce yarn and woven cloth (*manta*). Production began in November

Table 26
Installed Capacity and Output, Miraflores, Selected Years

Year	Spindles	Pounds of Yarn	Looms	Pieces of Cotton Cloth
1841	4,080	159,159	0	0
1842	4,080	202,455	0	0
1843	5,030	—	0	0
1844	5,700	—	40	1,456
1845	4,380 (3.8%)	—	160 (7.6%)	16,331
1846	—	500,000	—	—
1850	5,556	—	238	—
1854	—	—	—	67,200

Source: CMRFH.
Note: numbers in parentheses = Miraflores output as % of national production.
— means no information.

1840, when about half of the 3,912 spindles that Barrio had purchased were installed. In January 1841 Martínez del Río Hermanos placed a $10,000 order in New York for additional machinery to increase the factory's yarn output in 1842. To begin production of woven cloth, the factory purchased 120 power looms from Duport & Company in Mexico, which had ordered but never used the looms for another factory. These looms cost Martínez del Río Hermanos $15,500. Their installation cost another $10,000. Because of delays in constructing a building to house the machines and the necessary hydraulic installations to power them, the factory had only 40 looms in operation as late as September 1844. The following year the firm purchased 40 more looms in Mexico for $2,200. Their installation cost $4,000. In 1845 Miraflores's installed capacity rose to 160 looms, and the drive to increase production continued. Good fortune in its other enterprises enabled Martínez del Río Hermanos to increase the tempo of its investments in the factory during the early 1850s. By 1854 the firm had invested $119,828 in machinery for yarn production and $86,332 in that for cloth. In the mid-1850s the factory's installed capacity stabilized with 5,556 spindles and 238 looms.[17] The exhaustion of exploitable hydraulic resources precluded the installation of additional machines.

In January 1841 the factory's daily output was 500 pounds of yarn. By July 1845 weekly output had reached 11,000 to 13,000 pounds. Expressed differently, yarn production for 1840 totaled 3,631 pounds. With more spindles in operation, that figure increased to 159,159 pounds in 1841 and 202,455 pounds in 1842. By 1846 the factory was spinning over 500,000 pounds of yarn annually, doubling its output over the same installed capacity.

A similiar phenomenon occurred with *manta*. Production increased from 1,456 pieces in 1845, to 16,331 in 1846, to 67,200 by 1854.[18] Although the expansion of Miraflores's productive capacity proceeded rapidly after the mid-1840s, it lagged behind the more favorable market trends. For example, prices for *manta* soared in 1843. Established mills such as La Constancia in Puebla easily sold their weekly output of six hundred *mantas* at $7.00 per piece, a handsome profit.[19] Before installations to produce this item at Miraflores had been completed in 1844 and 1845, the market for *manta* collapsed. In 1846 the factory was hard-pressed to sell it at any price.

Miraflores produced many grades, classes, and varieties of textiles. Its line of cotton yarns and threads included the standard sizes No. 10 (coarse) to No. 24 (fine) as well as special lower-price grades spun from waste cotton and remnants. *Manta* production began with an imitation of Ledvar's Baize, a flannel-like English weave. Miraflores's baize, a high-quality and well-made product, compared favorably with the European fabric, but the disadvantage of this weave was that its production required large amounts of cotton. As prices for cloth fell, Miraflores began fabricating an imitation of lightweight Puebla *manta* made with much less cotton. *Mantas* of both types were manufactured in pieces about thirty-two yards long and marketed in 175 pound lots (tercios). The price per tercio of *manta* depended on the class and grade of the product. In December 1859 tercios branded "YT" or "GB" contained twenty pieces, and brand "A" had thirty-two pieces. Other markings included "MF" (twenty-five pieces), "MG" (twenty-two pieces), and "M²" (twenty-eight pieces).[20]

Although they improved the factory's efficiency by raising the volume of production, Miraflores's managers were less successful in lowering production costs on a per unit basis (see table 27 for costs for producing yarn and *manta* for the few years in which reliable data on costs at Miraflores are available). The effects of scarce and high-priced cotton on Miraflores's operations and the attempts by Martínez del Río Hermanos to speculate in cotton are discussed in a separate section.

Marketing

If a single lesson can be drawn from the experience of Miraflores, it is that making textiles was easy; selling textiles at a consistent profit was nearly impossible. Although production costs remained more or less constant, the long-term market trend was toward a pronounced decline in prices. Those economic facts of life help to explain why the textile industry came to be a sinkhole for the capital of unwary investors like the Martínez del Ríos.

Martínez del Río Hermanos did not retail the textiles produced by its factory. The profits from a retail operation were unlikely to make up for the bother and, in any event, an 1843 decree restricted the retail trade to Mexican citizens. The firm did engage in the wholesale trade in textiles,

Table 27
Production Costs, Yarn and Cotton Cloth (*Manta*), Miraflores, Selected Years
(Current Pesos)

Year	Yarn			Cloth		
	Cotton ($/lb.)	Spinning	Total Costs/ Lb.	Yarn	Weaving	Total Costs/ Piece
1840	0.500	0.125	0.625	—	—	—
1844	0.299	0.144	0.443	3.45	1.09	4.54
1845	0.293	0.114	0.407	—	—	—
1846	—	—	0.485	—	—	4.77

Source: CMRFH.
Note: — means no information.

especially in the early 1840s. Guillermo Drusina in Mexico City and Germán F. Pohls in Guanajuato placed orders for Miraflores's yarn as early as January 1841. Most sales were tied to credit terms giving buyers up to six months to pay for purchases. After the mid-1840s, the administrator at Miraflores usually handled direct sales, although Martínez del Río Hermanos negotiated terms for volume deliveries. For example, Gamio & Domereq contracted in January 1853 to receive a weekly allotment of twenty-eight tercios of *manta* at a guaranteed price of $3,028 per lot. Payments were made in *libranzas* drawn by Miraflores against Gamio & Domereq and payable to Martínez del Río Hermanos.[21]

Direct sales carried certain disadvantages. Most were made on credit and repayment was postponed for considerable periods of time. The buyer might go bankrupt or otherwise fail to cover the purchase. For example, in October 1850 Carballeda & Gamio asked Martínez del Río Hermanos for 80 tercios of *manta*, promising to pay for these textiles with weekly installments extending over three months. This sale was risky because the buyer was known to have weak finances. With a large inventory of textiles piling up in warehouses, Pedro ignored the risks and approved the sale. Three weeks after making delivery, he learned that Carballeda & Gamio had declared bankruptcy. Shrewdly, Pedro rushed a notary to the scene to inventory the textiles still stored in the debtor's place of business. These would be seized before a *concurso* could be convened. His foresight paid off, as Carballeda & Gamio allegedly owed $1.8 million in debts against assets of $300,000.[22]

Even with such drawbacks, most businesses preferred direct sales to the alternative arrangement for marketing—consignment. Under the consignment system the seller shouldered all the burdens of finance, transport, commission, and risk. In the 1850s Martínez del Río Hermanos found itself playing a role reminiscent of the relations between the European manufacturers and Drusina & Martínez in the 1830s. In a buyers' market the firm had no choice but to submit to sometimes onerous terms. Its experience in 1849 with 5,935 pieces of *manta* consigned to Olasgarre & Prieto in Guadalajara showed what could happen with consignments. The *manta* sold for an average price of about $5.00 per piece, but deductions for transport, taxes, and other costs reduced the gross receipts from these sales to $24,609. On this sum, Olasgarre & Prieto charged its 2.5 percent commission, reducing the net unit sales price per *manta* to $4.04. Unit manufacturing costs at Miraflores for these textiles were substantially higher, about $5.00 per piece.[23]

The shift from direct to consignment sales is evidence that the terms of trade deteriorated for textile manufacturers in the 1840s. Miraflores experienced, as well, a geographical contraction of its market. Prior to the war with the United States, Martínez del Río Hermanos regularly reported sales of Miraflores's textiles to Zacatecas, Guadalajara, San Luis Potosí, and Guanajuato. As late as July 1847, of $112,595 in bills owed for deliveries of the factory's textiles, $47,273 originated in sales and $32,663 derived from consignments to those areas. After the war, high transport costs, local trade barriers, new textile plant production, and an expanding contraband trade caused the factory to lose its markets in the North.[24]

Outside the crowded and competitive market in the Valley of Mexico, only Guanajuato remained as an important destination for Miraflores's products. As a leading commercial house in Guanajuato, Germán F. Pohls & Company (also Pohls & Goerne) had marketed since the early 1840s the textiles supplied by Martínez del Río Hermanos. Pedro described Pohls's business in October 1846:

P.s G.e [Pohls & Goerne] have never been punctual in their payments, and even though he is paying some interest, and higher than he should, I consider that this results from the disorder in which he carries on his business rather than from necessity; I place him as one of the most respected men in the country; apart from the many investments he has in haciendas, the Luz mine in Guanajuato has rewarded him with hundreds of thousands of pesos each year to replace those lost in Cocolapam.[25]

Pohls invested with Lucas Alamán in the ill-fated textile factory of Cocolapam, which went bankrupt in 1841. Alamán was ruined, but profits from mining helped Pohls to make up for his losses in manufacturing and commerce. Like Pohls, Gregorio Jiménez (also Jiménez & Hijo) sold Miraflores's textiles in this mining center and, like Pohls, Jiménez's commercial relationship with Martínez del Río Hermanos gradually changed during the 1840s from that of a buyer to a new status as consignee. Pohls and Jiménez each charged Martínez del Río Hermanos 2.5 percent commission on sales and a 1.5 percent warehouse or brokerage fee on the total volume of merchandise they handled in Guanajuato.[26]

Beginning in September 1853, Martínez del Río Hermanos introduced an innovation in marketing that the firm hoped would alleviate the worst disadvantages of direct and consignment sales alike. The firm and José María Carballeda formed a company to sell Miraflores's textiles.[27] This arrangement promised not only to reduce marketing costs, but also to produce modest profits. As the *socio capitalista*, Martínez del Río Hermanos put up the venture capital to begin the enterprise and supplied the new company with textiles. Carballeda, the *socio industrial*, managed the new company (José María Carballeda & Company) and assigned to it his rights as the renter of a building located at No. 3 Flamencos Street in Mexico City. The company sold yarn and cloth at both the retail and wholesale levels. In addition, the Miraflores product went into clothing fashioned and marketed in Carballeda's clothing factory and store, El

Cometa, located at the same address. In the beginning, their company worked well and the contract was extended for another five years beginning in 1858. Afterward, with the outbreak of the Three Years' War, sales began to fall, the company's profits declined sharply, and Martínez del Río Hermanos ordered the premature liquidation of the partnership in January 1860. The experiment ended with Carballeda owing Martínez del Río Hermanos $36,000.[28]

Although J. M. Carballeda & Company foundered in the late 1850s, José Antonio Sosa y Ansoátegui did a brisk busines selling Miraflores's textiles on consignment in Cuernavaca. Figure 2 shows his gross sales for September 1859 through October 1860. Sosa charged his supplier (Martínez del Río Hermanos) the customary 2.5 percent on sales plus 0.5 percent for brokerage. Characteristically, the volume of sales was erratic and varied greatly from month to month.

For the whole period of this study, demand for textiles remained volatile. The decade of the 1840s began with heavy demand and high prices. Then in mid-1841 a prolonged political crisis paralyzed commerce. From December 1841 through late 1843, sales of yarn and *manta* were slow. Demand increased after 1844, peaking between the eve of the outbreak of hostilities between Mexico and the United States in 1845 and the actual occupation of Mexico City in 1847. Faced with an avalanche of contraband after 1847, the industry suffered through another period of depressed demand until the early 1850s. Then the market improved briefly, only to turn down sharply as civil war engulfed the country after 1858. The bad times continued unrelieved through the early 1860s, aggravating Martínez del Río Hermanos's cash flow problems and helping to provoke its bankruptcy.

In 1840, when Barrio began finishing the initial construction at Miraflores and when Martínez del Río Hermanos calculated its probable share of profits in the enterprise, No. 16 yarn sold for 7.5 r. per pound. Five years later it brought only 4.5 r. per pound. This increased to 4.88 r. for a short period in 1846, only to fall to 3.5 r. by 1853. The price for No. 16 yarn in 1859 was 3.88 r. per pound (table 28 lists the combined average selling prices for yarn and cloth for selected years, 1840 to 1860). A reasonably accurate measure of Miraflores net receipts from these sales can be computed by subtracting 10 percent from the prices listed in table 28 to cover transport and other overhead costs paid to market these textiles. Comparison of these adjusted prices with actual production costs listed in table 27 reveals only a minute margin between profit and loss. Reliable information on Miraflores's profits is scarce. Table 29 lists the best available data for selected years. Although profits ranging up to 20 percent were sometimes reported, overall returns were generally disappointing, as the owners claimed they spent $1 million on the factory between 1840 and 1861. Table 30 shows these reported profits as a percentage of Miraflores's assessed value for selected years.

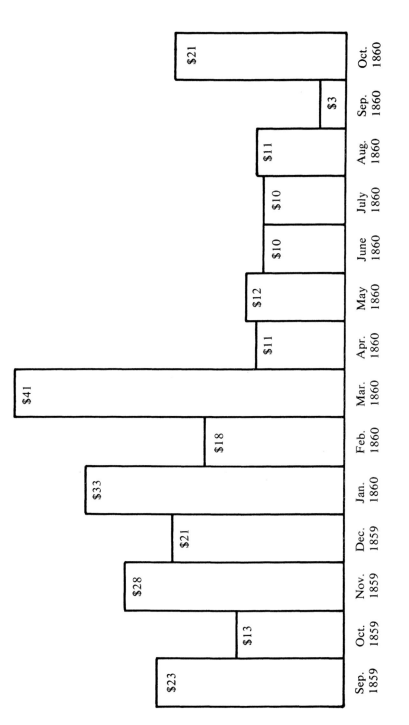

Fig. 2. Monthly sales of Miraflores textiles by José A. Sosa y Ansoátegui (thousands of pesos), September 1859–October 1860

Table 28
Average Selling Price, Miraflores Textiles, Selected Years
(Current Pesos)

Month/Year	Price/Lb. of Yarn	Index of Yarn Prices	Average Price/Piece of Cotton Woven Cloth (*Manta*)
Nov. 1840	0.938	100	—
Nov. 1841	1.072	114	—
May 1844	0.547	58	6.000
Oct. 1845	0.651	69	—
June 1846	0.685	73	—
Feb. 1847	—	—	6.250
Nov. 1849	—	—	4.125
Jan. 1853	0.512	55	4.297
Jan. 1859	0.531	57	4.500
Dec. 1859	0.546	58	—

Source: CMRFH.
Note: — means no information.

The Politics of Profit

Political variables—the degree of a government's commitment to protectionism, its effectiveness in impeding the flow of contraband into Mexico, the imposition of taxes on industry, and the inability of any government to long sustain itself in power—very often influenced, or even determined, market conditions for Miraflores textiles. The owners of Miraflores—the Martínez del Ríos—had only limited resources for dealing with Mexican politics. They were reduced most of the time to a role as passive observers, aware of their interests, impotent to affect political outcomes, and dependent on others to articulate and defend the interests of the textile industry. In this area, the family's genius for persuading the British to protect them could not be employed, as protection for Mexican factory owners (whatever their nationality) was anathema to British policymakers.

Fiscal considerations, pressure from textile-exporting countries like Great Britain, disillusionment with the prospects of ever developing an efficient domestic industry, and sheer political chicanery combined in 1841 to erode Bustamante's commitment to enforcing statutory prohibitions on textile imports. To raise money to finance a promised new offensive against Texas in 1841, the commander of the Army of the North, General Mariano Arista, authorized the sale of special licenses to permit the import of yarn through the port of Tampico. Guillermo Drusina and Cayetano Rubio engineered this circumvention of tariff codes, drawing on themselves and on

Table 29
Estimated Annual Returns as Percentage of Capital Invested in Miraflores

Year	% Profit	Year	% Profit	Year	% Profit
1841	−21.0	1847	+/−1.0	1853	0
1842	+/− 1.0	1848	+/−1.0	1854	9.6
1843	+/− 1.0	1849	+/−1.0	1855	0
1844	10.2	1850	7.4	1856	10.9
1845	19.4	1851	0	1857	− 5.2
1846	8.4	1852	0		

Source: CMRFH.

Table 30
Estimated Production Costs, Cotton Cloth (*Manta*)
(Current Pesos)

Year/Mill	Cost of Cotton (% of Total)	Other Costs (% of Total)	Total Costs	Sale Price	Mark Up (%)
1800—Artisan	$0.50	$8.50	$9.00	$11.00	22
(Puebla)	(5.6)	(94.4)	(100)		
1843—La Constancia	$2.69	$1.01	$3.70	$ 7.00	89
(Puebla)	(72.7)	(27.3)	(100)		
1844—Miraflores	$2.32	$2.12	$4.54	$ 6.00	32
	(51.2)	(48.8)	(100)		

Source: CMRFH; Bazant, "Industria algodonera poblana," p. 138.
Note: Mark up = gross profit/total costs

Bustamante's government the wrath of textile factory owners and other protected groups in Mexico. As neither the president nor his ministers were anxious to confront Arista on this issue, those affected called on Santa Anna to enforce the law. Pedro reported in February 1841 that "*el cojo* [Santa Anna] is in favor of the manufacturers and [cotton planters]; the only thing that worries me about this question is that it may lead to a revolution, which will delay payment of our [government public debt] funds. Aside from that, I am pleased with these developments, as they will reaffirm the rights of the manufacturers."[29]

Enjoying influence with neither Bustamante nor Santa Anna, the many foreigners who had invested in Mexican industry rushed to enlist the aid of their home governments in overturning Arista's action. The French minister supported his nationals' reclamation; the British minister did not. British investors complained in a manifesto to Pakenham dated 11 February 1841 "that in the faith of the inviolability of this law [the Tariff of 1837] we have embarked large capitals in the establishment of works for the manufacture of these articles."[30] By staging a public demonstration outside the minister's residence, a group of angry Britons led by factory owners Andrew Lyall and Archibald Hope planned to pressure the minister into changing his mind. Mexican authorities intervened, however, and outlawed the meeting. Furious with this abridgment of their rights as Englishmen, the demonstrators naïvely asked Pakenham to intervene so that they might meet to protest his arbitrary behavior. The minister declined their invitation.[31]

Pakenham worked quietly, but vigorously, to defeat the prohibitions. On 26 February 1841, he confided gleefully to the British Foreign Office in London that "the licenses to import prohibited goods are illegal, but I am humbly of the opinion that they are quite legal enough to bind the Mexican government."[32] Although Congress probably wished to act otherwise, powerful political pressures persuaded it to decree Arista's licenses illegal. According to a jubilant Pedro, the outcome was entirely predictable: "It could not happen any other way, as there are at present many enterprises and projected factories for making yarn in various parts of the Republic and associated with these can be found persons of consequence for their wealth and connections."[33]

The wave of protest that followed the brazen attempt to evade the prohibitions weakened Bustamante's government and helped to create the climate of political discord that led to Santa Anna's successful revolt in the autumn of 1841. On assuming power in October, one of Santa Anna's first acts was to order that all cotton yarn and cloth brought into the country because of Arista's licenses be burned in the ports or wherever else they might be discovered. Santa Anna further recognized the interests of the textile manufacturers in December 1842 by granting them corporate status as the Junta de Industria.

Despite these demonstrations of sensitivity to the special needs of the industrialists, however, this caudillo was susceptible to the same forces that had shaped economic policy in the government he replaced. Veiled threats and intimidation from the British foreign minister (mixed with promises of rewards), outright bribes from enterprising importers, and the most powerful inducement of all, the bankruptcy of the National Treasury, tempted Santa Anna to forget his commitment to protectionism. As early as March 1842 the influence peddlers were back at work: "Morphy is the secret Minister of his S.E. *El cojo* and is doing enough . . . he is entrusted by Drusina, Rubio, etc., to effect the reinstatement of Arista's licenses that caused such an uproar and was annulled by the Congress . . . in my opinion Pakenham is assisting them greatly, as his interest is in lifting the prohibitions."[34]

Drusina and his associates managed to strike a deal with Santa Anna whereby they were allowed to import up to 700,000 pounds of yarn with duties ranging from 2 r. to 4 r. per pound.[35] It was the first step toward a subtle reordering of the political economy of textile manufacturing and a matter that portended grave consequences for factories such as Miraflores. In July 1842 Pedro assessed the situation:

Last year the revolution and in this year the fear that the new tariff will lower prohibitions, linking them to a scarcity for the manufacturers, made the price for yarn fall at the same time that cotton remained high, now the former did not recover and the latter stays high. If this continues, the outlook for the balance of the year for this establishment will be bleak and if there is any profit it will be miserable.[36]

Implemented late in 1842, the new tariff schedule pleased no one. Mexican manufacturers worried about the relaxation of prohibitions. Pakenham protested that high duties on imports damaged British trade interests and warned that "such an unfriendly line of policy towards England" might have grave consequences at a time when the United States had begun to look hungrily toward Mexican territories.[37] After assessing the political risks a careless attitude toward the prohibitions would carry, Santa Anna's government chose to ignore British threats. It revoked the permissive 1842 Tariff and replaced it with the restrictive Tariff of 14 August 1843.[38] But once again, the ink was hardly dry on this latest decree before the influence peddlers began conspiring to undo it. In October 1843 José Pablo warned,

Mr. Pakenham, with the aid of Ml. Escandón, has tried to secure from the present corrupt administration a treaty whereby Mexico is obligated to admit English goods under certain tariff schedules, and *not to change* these tariffs for a good number of years!! They promised *El cojo* $250,000—and V. assures me . . . that he had already *received* that sum—all was prepared when Rubio succeeded in undoing it—or complicating it with a thousand works, because that was convenient to his own interests [Rubio had acquired an interest in various textile factories in Mexico City and Querétaro]. . . . Rubio himself communicated this to V. in confidence.[39]

As rumors of the proposed treaty leaked out, the manufacturers hastily reminded Santa Anna of the political costs a betrayal would entail. José Pablo described the confrontation in November 1843:

According to the reports that I go about collecting from all parts, it seems that the industrialists of Mexico—of this Republic—are very resolved to confront the government in case it wishes to sacrifice their interests to those of England. I have been told that they have even warned the Saint [Santa Anna] that in case those interests are not maintained, they will make another revolution to overthrow him. By this I can understand that the manufacturers are going to have to pass through a crisis, and that those who survive it will afterward find a more advantageous situation, and even more so, as some of them inevitably will have to shut down their factories for lack of money.[40]

Faced with an ultimatum, Santa Anna stopped dallying with Pakenham. The debate over protectionism lapsed into an uneasy stalemate, but opposition to the privileged status of the textile industry continued to grow. The importers and their political allies in the liberal camp were becoming increasingly strident in their denunciations of protectionism. Pedro attempted to reassure Gregorio José in September 1845: "The disposition that you observe in the importers against the manufacturers and the bondholders is nothing new, as this conflict has always existed and each one works for his interest."[41] After legislation to reform the tariff schedule and to abolish the prohibitions narrowly failed passage in Congress in the autumn of 1849, Domingo Ansoátegui reassessed the political outlook for the textile industry:

About this business it is not likely they will return to deal with it until next year, and then we will have some more defenders among the deputies, even so we will have an increase in the number of enemies among the senators; nevertheless, as here all questions are not seen by the general interest, but by that of party, no one can predict. Among the deputies we have Alamán, Olasgarre, Palomar, and others, some interested and others decided in favor of the industry that will make a good and well-sustained defense. Mr. Pedro Echeverría, who was among those who voted against the industry, was in favor. He is a committed enemy of the monstrous project and will attack it.[42]

Although liberals failed in their efforts to reform the tariffs, opponents of industry began to tax it as a means to compensate the Treasury for revenues lost because of the prohibitions. The 1850 Congress imposed an annual tax of 1.5 r. per loom. This was doubled in 1853. Textile manufacturers were required after 1850 to pay an annual tax of 1.5 percent on the value of their buildings and machinery. As the decade progressed, friends and foes alike taxed whatever property they could find, and textile factories were notoriously difficult to hide. In 1857 the liberal Supreme Court justice Juárez approved a tax reform that lowered the assessment on industry to 0.5 percent, but the following year the conservative General Miramón tacked on an additional 1 percent assessment. These charges were increased to 10 percent in July 1859. Then came new property valuations and requirements that taxes be paid one year in advance.[43]

State and local governments levied a variety of taxes on industrial establishments. Although they were a costly nuisance, property taxes were not as detrimental to a factory's operations as were the *alcabalas*. These were discriminatory taxes that worked to protect local producers from outside competition. States and municipalities with textile factories or artisan workshops charged a tax on each piece of *manta* or pound of yarn that entered their jurisdiction from outside. The *alcabala* for textiles usually was set at about 8 percent of value, although Puebla's was fixed at 12.5 percent.[44] The imposition of such taxes is a plausible explanation for Miraflores's loss of lucrative markets in Zacatecas, Guadalajara, and San Luis Potosí.

Because of vacillations in government policy toward the textile industry and the consequent harm inflicted on their interests, textile manufacturers who were burdened with increasingly unprofitable enterprises attempted to squeeze an indemnity out of the state. The Martínez del Ríos felt that such compensation was perhaps the only way to rid themselves of Miraflores. The first serious discussion of an indemnity surfaced after promulgation of the Tariff of 1842. Manufacturers proposed that the Mexican government should borrow from Great Britain to purchase their factories. As the British were unwilling to lend more money to Mexico, even in exchange for liberal trading concessions, the project was abandoned. In 1846 a new proposal for the same purpose took shape. The more knowledgeable political observers conceded that such an irregular undertaking could be realized "only when Morphy has his padrino in the Candelero [that is, when Santa Anna returned to power]." As the lot of factory owners worsened after the war, the idea of an indemnity surfaced again in 1849 and 1850. Because such an undertaking would require not only the complicity of politicians but also a commitment of financial resources quite beyond the capacity of any Mexican government, the indemnity was doomed to remain a study in fantasy.[45]

The contraband trade is treated here as a political variable because such activity naturally follows a government's attempt to circumvent market forces. The greater the discrepancy between natural conditions of supply and demand and the artificial conditions prescribed by the state, the greater must be the coercive capacities of the state if its policies are to be effective. Mexican textile manufacturers could not produce yarn or cloth at cost levels reasonably close to those of foreign manufacturers. The raw cotton needed to produce a pound of cotton yarn often cost $0.30 a pound or more delivered to Miraflores. The finished Mexican product cost about $0.40 a pound. English yarn could be delivered in Veracruz for $0.21 a pound.[46] Whatever their predisposition toward protectionism, no Mexican government of this period had the power to override market forces of this magnitude. Higher tariffs only encouraged more smuggling. The collapse of each government (there were thirty-three between 1840 and 1860) opened the way for successive escalations in the scale of illegal activity.

It is difficult to measure objectively the impact of contraband textiles on enterprises such as Miraflores. The periods in which contraband traffic was heaviest do seem to coincide with the times in which the factory's management found it most difficult to market textiles—1842 to 1844, 1847 to 1850, and 1857 to 1864. The loss of Texas after 1836 left Northern Mexico exposed to overland trafficking in textiles from the United States. At the same time, the national government's growing weakness facilitated the establishment of large-scale smuggling operations based in the West Mexican ports and mining towns. The declaration of war with the United States in 1845 disrupted the contraband trade, as smugglers were reluctant to move goods that might be caught between advancing armies in Northern Mexico or be intercepted by blockading naval units from the United States.

Nor could complacent Mexican officials continue without grave risks to overlook clandestine movements of men and materials in areas under their jurisdiction. The blockade and invasion of Veracruz early in 1847 isolated the center of the country and created, briefly, the artificial scarcity that Mexican industrialists longed for. Once Mexico City had been taken late in 1847, however, the way was open for a flood of foreign manufactures. The national government disintegrated and for a time no successor could be found to impose any level of control. With the loss of California and New Mexico, it became progressively easier for smugglers based in the United States to penetrate the Mexican market. For a brief period after Santa Anna's return to power, contraband activity seems to have declined because of increased vigilance. After 1858 contraband poured into Mexico as the nation suffered a generalized political breakdown.

Apart from making trade in prohibited articles less difficult, the Civil War and the French intervention damaged Mexican and industrial interests by disrupting communications and by provoking a serious labor shortage (workers were conscripted by both sides). Of all these factors, Martínez del Río Hermanos insisted that unfair competition from foreign products provoked its bankruptcy and the "ruin of manufacturers."[47] What Martínez del Río Hermanos and most other owners of textile factories were reluctant to discuss publicly was *why* their products were so noncompetitive.

The Political Economy of Cotton

Cotton was cultivated in the lowlands of Veracruz long before the Conquest of Mexico. Through the 1850s, this region remained the primary zone of cultivation. Other areas, which produced less cotton and which were disadvantageously located for the manufacturers of Central Mexico, included narrow portions of the Pacific Coast near Acapulco and Tepic and well-watered river valleys in the deserts of Durango and Coahuila in Northern Mexico. New Orleans supplied most of the foreign cotton legally imported through the ports of Tampico and Veracruz, although some cotton from Texas moved overland along with other classes of contraband. Miraflores also occasionally consumed cotton shipped from Guayaquil, Ecuador.

The cost of domestically produced cotton textiles in Mexico was a function of cotton prices, as the raw material accounted for one-half to four-fifths of the cost of the finished articles. To encourage the development of

Mexican agriculture (and to keep the cotton planters appeased), manufacturers were obliged by law to purchase all cotton from domestic sources. Despite the incentive of high prices, Mexican production chronically fell far short of demand. Table 30 shows how the changing cost of raw materials affected overall production costs. Whereas cotton accounted for less than 6 percent of the cost of *manta* woven in Puebla in 1800, it made up 73 percent of the costs of manufacturing *manta* in 1843, undoing many of the savings introduced with mechanization.[48] Raw cotton made up 70 percent to 80 percent of the expenses incurred in the manufacture of cotton yarn and about 50 percent of the costs of manufacturing cotton *manta* at Miraflores in the 1840s. The procurement of cotton required more attention on the part of Martínez del Río Hermanos than any other aspect of the factory's operations. The 800,000 to 900,000 pounds of cotton consumed annually by Miraflores usually cost between $200,000 and $300,000—a sum that exceeded the cost of the machines that spun and wove the raw material into finished products. Ordinarily, cotton purchases were financed with generous credit terms, but large sums of cash in advance were required to make the most advantageous deals. Sometimes no cotton could be obtained at any price, and Miraflores and other mills were obliged to make costly shutdowns.[49]

Whether acquired from Veracruz planters or from Mexico City speculators who had obtained special import licenses, cotton cost manufacturers (and consumers) dearly. Table 31 lists estimated and

Table 31
Reported Market Prices, Mexico City/Miraflores, Puebla, Veracruz,
Selected Years
(Current Pesos/100 Lbs.)

Year	Veracruz	Puebla	Mexico City/Miraflores
1810	6-7	10	12
1840	—	—	40 (Nov.)
1841	—	—	44 (July)
1842	—	—	36 (July)
1843	26 (Sep.)	34-40 (Dec.)	40 (Jan.)-28 (Dec.)
1844	—	—	33 (Sep.)
1845	—	38 (Aug.)	33 (Aug.)-36 (Oct.)
1846	—	29 (June)	27 (June)-31 (Aug.)
1847	—	—	28 (Mar.)-32 (Sep.)
1848	—	—	—
1849	15-21 (Oct.)	22-25 (Nov.)	—

Sources: CMRFH; Bazant, "Industria algodonera poblana," p. 138.
Note: — means no information.

reported prices for one-hundred-pound bales of cotton in Mexico City, Puebla, and Veracruz. By way of comparison, cotton from the United States could be delivered in Veracruz in 1845 for $12.00 per quintal. During October and November 1851, cotton in New Orleans cost $7.50 and $8.00 per quintal. Import licenses and other duties, transport costs, and fees to middlemen might triple the price of cotton as it moved from New Orleans to Mexico City. In November 1851, shippers charged 10 r. ($1.25) per tercio to carry cotton from New Orleans to Veracruz. Moving cotton from the coast as far inland as Puebla might add $4.00 to $7.00 per quintal. The whole trip from Veracruz to Mexico City probably increased costs by $10.00 per quintal (including charges by the *arrieros* and formal and informal duties charged by interior customs houses).[50]

Regardless of how cheaply or efficiently their machines and their work forces performed, the high cost of cotton made it impossible for Mexican factories to manufacture textiles at competitive prices. What accounts for the failure of the factory owners to free the market of the costly prohibitions on cotton imports that made the industry ruinously noncompetitive? First, in ideological terms, the monopolization of any commodity, no matter how expensive and inefficient the results, was consistent with the traditional organization of the Mexican economy.[51] Second, in practical terms, a free trade in cotton would undercut broad support for protectionist policies (that is, the ban on cotton yarn and cloth imports), which gave manufacturers and their enterprises a privileged status. If manufacturers deserved protection from foreign competition, then so did agriculturalists whose enterprises were even more expensive and inefficient when compared to the standards of the world market. Besides cotton, imports of staples like tobacco and cane sugar distillates (aguardiente) were banned because producers could not compete in a free market.

As early as 1821 the Veracruz planters demonstrated their political clout by persuading Iturbide to decree a ban on the import of raw cotton. Well organized, with practical experience doing business with an overtly monopolized commodity like tobacco, the Veracruz planters had the additional advantage of close ties with Santa Anna, the dominant political figure in early national Mexico.[52] Following Santa Anna's conservative coup in 1835, the Law of 18 August 1836 prohibited the import of raw cotton (even before the prohibitions on imports of cotton cloth were reinstated).[53] In the summer of 1842, after his regime had granted licenses to import limited quantities of yarn, many observers expected Santa Anna to lift the prohibition on cotton imports. That was not the case—because "doubts caused by fear of some movement on the coast" obliged Santa Anna to treat planters with deference.[54] There was already the precedent of his own revolt in 1841. Such was the influence of the planters that the ban on raw cotton imports was incorporated as Article 67 of the Bases Orgánicas, the conservative constitution adopted in 1843. Under authority of the Law of 12 April 1843, a few special licenses to import raw cotton were granted, but these were limited to the privileged few who had influence with Santa Anna. The procedure for obtaining these permits remained clandestine and semisecret. Among the firms able to deal with *el cojo* in such a sensitive matter was the politically experienced commercial house, Agüero, González & Company, which imported seventy thousand quintales for a fee of $6.00 per quintal.

Even after Santa Anna was ousted in 1844, the planters obstructed attempts by General Herrera's government to loosen the prohibitions on cotton imports. Not until after January 1846, when Mexico desperately needed funds to finance the war effort, did Congress and the chief executive freely make available an unlimited supply of *permisos de importación de algodón* at a cost of $10.00 per quintal. Generous discounts were advertised as the war progressed.[55] After the war, the prohibitions on raw cotton imports were reinstated (by a liberal government) and no new *permisos* were issued.

Although the cotton growers were a powerful political force, the textile manufacturers included many of Mexico's wealthiest and most influential citizens. But unlike the growers, who worked together to achieve their purpose, the manufacturers were not united by a common purpose. Estevan de Antuñano, who worked tirelessly to promote the textile industry, failed time after time to mobilize the manufacturers in support of proposals to lift the prohibition on raw cotton imports. In 1840 his campaign to persuade the Bustamante government to adopt a more liberal policy was opposed by other manufacturers, who benefited from the scarcity of cotton.[56] The manufacturers as a group did not seek an open market in cotton because individual manufacturers were the principal speculators in this commodity. As early as 1841, Pedro was moved to comment, "Cotton. This article continues to present a vast field of speculation."[57]

Whereas risk aversion initially kept many factory owners from buying large quantities in advance, the practice of buying small shipments to meet current requirements left them at the mercy of speculation-minded suppliers. By necessity, then, manufacturers became speculators as they sought to acquire "comfortable" inventories of cotton for their factories. The costs of these purchases against future cotton prices determined the overall profitability of their manufacturing establishments. For example, the purchase of a large supply of cotton at lower-than-average prices in 1844 helped Miraflores turn a $50,000 profit.[58] Few manufacturers wished for cotton prices to fall quickly. Lower prices would destroy the value of supplies of raw cotton already purchased and inventories of yarn and cloth manufactured from expensive cotton would be transformed into permanent liabilities. These losses might bankrupt any mill owner.

Martínez del Río Hermanos's speculations in cotton between 1846 and 1851 illustrate the practical considerations that enticed manufacturers to enter into progressively larger speculations. Unwilling to risk his firm's shaky finances in a costly speculation with imported cotton, Pedro outlined his scheme for securing the cotton Miraflores needed for the summer of 1846:

I did not wish to obtain any *permisos de algodón*, first, because it is not urgent and we must not make any disbursements for an end so far in the future, and, second, because knowing this country, I was hoping to get them more advantageously than the government was giving them, and that is what happened, as before the suspension [of payments to the public debt] they offered them to me at a 25 percent discount. Besides, I was hoping to trap the Güero [Rubio] in one of his fixes, in order to get enough to last the rest of the year with a comfortable price and terms . . . but all has come undone with the suspension and the blockade . . . but still I am resolved to secure it [the cotton] here, if I can get it reasonably, to avoid having to make drafts on New Orleans for that and for the large advance we would have to make for *permisos*, transport, etc.[59]

Sticking to his plan, Pedro arranged in June 1846 to buy two thousand quintales from Rubio at the "convenient" price of $27.00 per quintal, but within two months Miraflores had consumed that supply and prices for cotton had risen. As a stop-gap measure Martínez del Río Hermanos purchased eight hundred quintales from Manuel Martínez del Campo at $31.00 per quintal. As Miraflores used seven hundred quintales per month, more cotton had to be found quickly and that would be costly. Pedro's conservative approach to the problem of cotton had miscarried.[60] With that experience in mind, Martínez del Río Hermanos and a few well-placed associates were quick to take advantage of the government's plight in September 1847 to purchase a large quantity of *permisos* at very low prices.

Within Mexico, Miraflores's most dangerous rivals were fifteen textile mills in Puebla, which accounted for 40 percent of the industry's output in 1845.[61] Table 31 compares the costs of producing *manta* in Puebla's largest factory, La Constancia, with production costs at Miraflores. Labor and other costs (excluding cotton) per unit were about 50 percent cheaper in the Puebla factories. Although La Constancia employed more workers than Miraflores, the majority of Puebla's factories were small enterprises (ninety to nineteen workers), technologically primitive and labor-intensive, and perhaps better-suited than Miraflores to the conditions of the Mexican market. As an additional advantage, Puebla's manufacturers tended to have cheaper and more reliable access to cotton supplies in Veracruz. By raising raw material supply costs for Puebla's factories, Martínez del Río Hermanos could make Miraflores's products more competitive.

Working in combination with Smith & Duncan of Puebla, Viya

Hermanos of Veracruz, and Guillermo Drusina and Manuel Escandón of Mexico City, Martínez del Río Hermanos began a bold campaign in 1849 to monopolize the supply of cotton in Mexico. As this syndicate owned all remaining prewar import licenses, they could control the inward flow of foreign cotton. As Pedro explained to J. L. Lemmè in November 1849, "The business in which we have entered is not a monopoly conceded now by the government, but incidental from past circumstances."[62] He boasted that the combine had acquired all but one thousand quintales of the Veracruz harvest.

Although his claim was exaggerated, the group did control much of the domestic supply of cotton—enough to interest another group of seasoned speculators. Manuel Lizardi and Cayetano Rubio offered to trade $1 million in government debt issues for the cotton. Martínez del Río Hermanos proposed instead to trade Miraflores, but a factory was not as lucrative as the cotton needed to keep it running, so nothing came of these negotiations.[63] To keep cotton prices high Martínez del Río Hermanos refused to use its import licenses "until the opportune moment."[64] Although it already had stockpiled nine thousand quintales of cotton at Miraflores, the firm ordered its agents in Veracruz and Puebla to purchase all the cotton that came on the market there. Martínez del Río Hermanos also attempted to buy the crops in Acapulco and San Blas. In Mexico City Domingo Ansoátegui gloated, "The cotton speculation is turning out brilliantly."[65] In Veracruz, Gregorio José reported, "Here the people are very alarmed with our purchases . . . the thing looks good."[66] Later, Domingo confirmed, "The Pueblans have been hoping to obtain cotton in Veracruz—but now they have learned it will not be possible, as they have been unable to fill the orders that have gone to this port . . . and soon they will begin to fall in our pockets."[67] That left only one other concern. Gregorio José warned, "I fear the jealous ones will make some cheating deal or intrigue in the Chambers to remove the prohibitions on the articles, or authorize the government to emit new *permisos* since our friend [sic] Otero is working in the Senate to lift the prohibitions."[68] Their fears remained unrealized, perhaps because the liberals were wooing the Veracruz planters. Domingo noted with relief, "They [the Congress] have not been very busy scrutinizing our business with '*permisos*.' "[69]

In September and October of 1851 Martínez del Río Hermanos used its remaining *permisos* to put together a last grand venture with José Velasco, the owner of El Patriotismo Mexicano.[70] Velasco furnished cash to buy 35,000 quintales of cotton in New Orleans and to transport it to Veracruz. Martínez del Río Hermanos provided the *permisos* to make the importation legal. When the shipment arrived in the port, Velasco took 10,000 quintales to use in his factory; Martínez del Río Hermanos took an equal quantity for Miraflores. They marketed the remaining 15,000 quintales in Veracruz, Jalapa, and Mexico City. As Martínez del Río Hermanos already had another 3,000 quintales stored in Veracruz, the firm chose to keep for its factory only 8,000 quintales (a year's supply) of the total 13,000 quintales situated in Veracruz. The firm sold the surplus cotton to pay the costs of transporting the remaining 8,000 quintales to Miraflores.

Pedro calculated that of the 720,000 pounds of yarn spun from 800,000 pounds of raw cotton, 320,000 pounds of yarn would be marketed at $0.45 per pound. *Mantas* would be woven of 400,000 pounds of yarn and would sell at $4.00 per piece. After deducting $70,000 for manufacturing costs from the $344,000 earned from the sales of the finished products, that would leave a clear profit of $274,000.[71] Although this sum would appear on the firm's books as a profit from Miraflores, it was more properly the result of a successful speculation in cotton.

For Velasco these speculations were a routine part of his business. Since the 1840s he had monopolized the supply of cotton in the principal cotton-growing town of Tlacotalpam, Veracruz. Although his mill, El Patriotismo, paid $34.00 per quintal for cotton in 1843, his competitors were forced to pay up to $40.00 per quintal. Velasco could afford to pay higher-than-average wages in Puebla while still enjoying consistent profits from his factory. Antuñano, who did not speculate in cotton, went bankrupt owing $200,000 (equal to his investment in machines and buildings at La Constancia) to cotton suppliers.[72]

By 1854 Martínez del Río Hermanos had lost its enthusiasm for speculative ventures in cotton. Its supply of *permisos* was exhausted. Perhaps it had gambled once too often and lost. Its partners began to insist that the practical solution to the supply problem was not speculation, but cultivation. They urged manufacturers to take charge of growing cotton to assure a cheap and reliable supply of the vital raw materials. The successful Puebla mill owners were those who integrated their factories into vertical enterprises linked directly with cotton estates in Veracruz. José Pablo had long experimented in planting cotton in areas adjacent to Miraflores. Pedro praised his effort in July 1854: "If we succeed in establishing it [cotton] in the valleys neighboring our factories, we will not require more protection."[73] To promote his ideas, José Pablo circulated in Mexico his 1854 translation of a French work on cotton cultivation.[74] Unfortunately, geography and climate conspired to defeat his plans. A century and a quarter later, Mexican cultivators still cannot fully supply the textile industry in Mexico.[75]

Conclusion

The manufacture and sale in Mexico of domestically produced textiles was an activity that was overtly political in nature. The market for these goods was an artifice of the state. The prosperity of manufacturers depended almost exclusively on the willingness *and* the capacity of the state to police the marketplace. As the progeny of an interventionist state, the textile industry that was constructed in early national Mexico had more in common with the monopolistic practices of Spanish colonial commerce than with industrial establishments, physically identical, which were situated in Western Europe or the United States. The latter were more properly genuine expressions of economic liberalism; the former clearly were in keeping with the precepts of the older. Consequently, Mexican manufacturers were more likely to be affiliated with the conservative cause. Conversely, opponents of protectionism and of other programs favoring industry were often liberals.

Ironically, when sizable numbers of investors had been drawn into textile manufacturing, the devotion of Mexican governments to the ideal of protectionism had begun to wane after 1841. Worse still, the state showed visible signs of political degeneration, a trend that continued unrelieved through the next two decades. The absolute decline in the market prices for textiles reflected the slow disintegration of the politicized economy in textile manufacturing. This decline is measured in table 32, which lists prices for *manta* in Mexico City markets from 1800 until 1859. Although *empresarios* like the Martínez del Ríos invested heavily in new technology to make their factories more efficient (and, they hoped more profitable), the increase in productivity hardly compensated for the fall in prices. Mexican manufacturers were never remotely competitive with their overseas competitors.

The high price of native cotton, more than any other factor, priced

Table 32
Index of Wholesale Prices, Cotton Cloth (*Manta*), Selected Years
(Current Pesos)

Year	Price/Piece	Index
1800	11.00	100
1835	9.50	86
1836	10.50	95
1839	8.62	78
1843	7.50	59
1845	5.63	51
1847	6.25	57
1849	4.13	38
1853	4.30	39
1859	4.50	41

Sources: CMRFH; Potash, *Mexican Government and Industrial Development*, p. 163.

Mexican textiles out of a poorly protected market. Because individual manufacturers reaped the rewards of speculations based on the government's protective policy toward the cotton growers, the manufacturers as a group were not a force for liberalization of the marketplace. In sum, the failure of Miraflores and the Mexican textile industry owed principally to the persistence of structural obstacles to economic growth of the sort described by Coatsworth.

The larger implications of this economic failure should be obvious. There was no indigenous "Industrial Revolution" in Mexico. No dynamic entrepreneurial class emerged to transform Mexican society. Rather, as the case of Martínez del Río Hermanos and Miraflores demonstrate, what in other circumstances might have marked the birth of a Mexican bourgeoisie—the formation of a new class of industrial capitalists—here brought only failure. The *empresarios* and their enterprises were caught up and strangled by the contradictions of an enduring superstructure that stubbornly refused to be superseded. In fact, changes in Mexico would not be thwarted, at least not entirely, but these changes would occur in a manner distinct from the European ideal model. That saga is the subject of the next chapter.

7. The Funds and the Conventions, 1838-1848

Public Debt and Private Profit

Why did Martínez del Río Hermanos invest so heavily in Mexican government debt issues? The most plausible explanation for what seems in retrospect to have been foolish, even dangerous, behavior was that the firm responded to the same stimulus that motivated so many others, namely, comparative advantage. As chapters 4 and 5 showed, there were few opportunities elsewhere. Commerce stayed depressed. Business bankruptcies were the rule, not the exception. Mining was unpredictable. Lending to the private sector was problematic. Why make private loans, which more often than not were destined to finance a larger transaction with the government? If the deal was a bust, the lender felt the consequences anyway. If not, then the borrower, not the lender, reaped most of the profits. The state may have been a bad risk, but so were private borrowers. For the *agiotista*, the government's debility was itself an asset. Pedro summed up this argument as his contribution to an ongoing debate within the family between 1838 and 1844: "It is important that you judge this country as best for a merchant who wishes to make large or small fortunes according to the risks. . . . What would become of us if there were a well-established government swimming in money? For us there would remain no recourse except to give up our accounts and become farmers or mortgage our Capital, like the nuns and friars, to live vegetating on our revenue."[1]

Nothing else promised the 15 percent to 20 percent annual returns the family expected from its investments. Foreign investments had given poor results. Along with other investors, the Martínez del Ríos suffered the reverses occasioned by the banking collapse that began in the United States in 1835. The year 1836 witnessed the coronation of Queen Victoria and the beginning of a commercial panic in London. In 1840 a great depression weighed down the economies of all the industrializing nations.

For the Martínez del Ríos the worst part of investing abroad was that, although profit rates (that is, interest and dividends) were low, risks remained high. Conventional wisdom dictated that the family should return to proven, more traditional investment practices—in Latin America—not in Europe or the United States. Pedro reminded Gregorio José, a promoter of investments in the metropolitan countries, that "your father told me once in Panama that having his money in the strongbox on the 31st day of December, he made 6 percent on it before midnight; I will apply that to what we have in New Orleans; if we had it in our box the 31st of December we could get with it 9 percent, which is the most it could make for us in New Orleans [in a year]."[2] And in Mexico, the government was the best of all possible clients:

This government is the best repayer that I know, as, with rogues, fools, and honorable men in the Ministry, one needs only the necessary prudence to not become overextended because of ambition and to enter strictly in those deals that can be sustained without having to pay the interest of the plaza [Mexican money market rates]: The proof that it is a repayer is that the old 15 percent [Fund] is already completed; and that none of the funds today that are being paid have paper [credits] that are less-deserving of payment than those of the 15 percent, as you remember that in it were placed a multitude of orders that cost only 18 percent to 22 percent.[3]

Pedro's assessment of the history of the funds through 1839 was correct, but he had learned a false lesson. Because the government had met its obligations in the past, this did not mean that it would or could do so in the future. Equally fatal, Martínez del Río Hermanos never demonstrated the self-restraint essential to keeping speculation in government debt issues at a manageable level. As was the case with Miraflores, the defense of established investments led to costly new expenditures. Once ensnared, the struggle to escape only sucked the victim deeper into the quagmire.

The Funds, 1838-1842

The first great surge of *agiotaje*, speculation in the public debt of Mexico, began in 1827, when the government used up the last installment of the £6 million borrowed from London banks in 1824. The Law of 27 January 1827 authorized the president to negotiate a new loan of up to $4 million, with repayment guaranteed by setting aside $100,000 monthly in receipts from the maritime customs houses and $35,000 monthly from tobacco monopoly revenues. As Guadalupe Victoria's government already had defaulted on interest owed to the London loan, foreign banks refused new loans. The government's only recourse for deficit financing lay with *agiotistas* at home. So began the orgy of speculation, which was doomed to collapse once the state had mortgaged all its revenues and once it had surrendered all its properties to creditors.

Before that eventuality, there was, momentarily, a Golden Age of *agiotaje*. Incessant political violence, the separatist movement in Texas, and the "war" with France drastically increased the government's need for income in the 1830s. To pay the Treasury's many creditors, the Banco de Amortización, founded to amortize the worthless copper currency, auctioned the properties of the Inquisition and the Jesuits, which the government had inherited from the colonial regime. Acquisition of these properties and access to progressively larger shares of government revenues gave *agiotistas* excellent returns on their speculations.

What made it possible for the government to pay its obligations even in such stressful times was that new investors, hoping to duplicate the recent successes of notorious *agiotistas*, lent the government even more money. An additional factor, rarely considered, which helped to keep the government *and* the *agiotistas* solvent was that the wars themselves provided a pretext for the cynical manipulation of Mexican chauvinism and patriotism. Successive governments from 1836 to 1844 used forced loans and voluntary fund-raising drives to finance new military campaigns to reconquer Texas and to erase the humiliation of San Jacinto. No serious campaign was ever mounted, nor was there an accounting of the large sums received for the campaigns. These monies simply flowed into the National Treasury, where they were used to cover routine government operations—including payments to creditors.

The first of the several public debt funds that proliferated in the late 1830s was created by the Law of 20 January 1836. This law set aside a 15 percent quota of revenue from the maritime customs houses (*aduanas marítimas*) to be used to pay off all existing loans and contracts with the government. Creditors no longer could charge their orders against the customs houses separately, as Drusina & Martínez and other speculators had done in the past. Instead, they were obliged to pool their credits into the 15 Percent Fund. An *apoderado*, chosen from among the creditors, managed the fund and received the *libranzas* from the customs houses. Periodically, when a large sum had been accumulated, the members of the fund received dividends proportional to their shares in the fund. By 1839 the government had managed to pay off all but $360,000 owed to the 15 Percent Fund. The paper credits that speculators had introduced into this fund (as a part of a loan to the government) usually cost them 20 percent or less. Because dividends on the bonds were paid exclusively in silver, the profits earned from the 15 Percent Fund had been exceptional. After it had redeemed the bonds issued against this fund, the government created a new "15 Percent Fund" consisting of about $1 million in credits on government salaries and pensions (*vales de alcance*). With what was to become a favorite device for obliging reluctant creditors to furnish new loans, the government required all creditors of the 15 Percent Fund to pay in 1839 a 15 percent restoration fee (*refacción*) as the price for receiving dividends from the fund.[4]

The Decree of 20 May 1837 created a 17 Percent Fund, similar in purpose to the 15 Percent Fund, with a principal of $2,534,020. Of this sum, credits for $1,735,030 drew no interest, but the balance of $800,000 earned 2.5 percent to 4 percent monthly interest—giving the whole a nominal interest equivalent to about 8 percent annually. The Ministry of Hacienda required the creditors of this fund in 1839 to pay a *refacción* totaling $100,000. Aside from these extortions, the 17 Percent Fund, like the 15 Percent Fund, was a good investment because, even in the difficult years 1838 to 1840, the government faithfully paid dividends of 6 percent to 10 percent several times annually. Speculators might reap additional profits as the market value of bonds issued against this fund increased as it became more certain that the fund would be fully repaid. Bonds from the 17 Percent Fund sold at less than 50 percent of face value in 1838, but by January 1839 they were up to 55 percent, and by June 1839 they brought 65 percent. One had to pay 75 percent for these bonds in August 1840.[5] Two months later, when the principal had been fully amortized, Martínez del Río Hermanos's partners jealously noted the profits their colleagues in commerce had earned with the 17 Percent Fund: "Montgomery & Nicod must have made plenty, as, besides what they had originally, the former made additional purchases, and then at high prices, and calculating today just what can be made on interest, it is a beautiful profit."[6]

Agiotistas looked hungrily at the quota of customs duties that would become available when payment to the 17 Percent Fund was complete. This time Martínez del Río Hermanos was determined to share in the profits. In early July 1840 the firm joined a syndicate that included the broker (*corredor*) Juan Rondero, a second British commercial house (Montgomery Nicod & Company), and Antonio Garay (the *alcalde* of Mexico City), who had been chosen by the group to negotiate an $800,000 loan with the government.[7] By combining their resources with those of a second group of lenders headed by Ignacio Loperena and Francisco Yturbé, the syndicate arranged in November 1840 to provide Bustamante's government with a much larger $2 million loan, repayable with 17 percent of the revenue from the maritime customs houses. Pedro explained the details:

The business of the two million . . . was finished at last by Rondero with 45 percent in cash and 55 percent in paper, with 0.5 percent [monthly] interest on the whole; in it we have taken $250 thousand, of which we ceded $30 thousand to Béistegui, who had asked us for it last year; the balance stayed with Dn. G. M. y Terán [Gregorio Mier y Terán]; to whom he will divide I do not know. The assessments of coin must be made as 100,000 pesos monthly; for the paper there is a six-month term; these I believe we can obtain at 12 percent [of nominal value]. . . . Montgomery Nicod & Company told me confidentially that they were going to give a share to the French Minister as well as to the English, and in virtue of the law that authorized the Government [to make the loan], they [the ministers] had made this deal.[8]

Table 33
Contributions to 1840 Loan Guaranteed by 17 Percent Fund
(Current Pesos)

Contributor	Amount
Gregorio Mier y Terán	400,000
Montgomery Nicod & Company	380,000
Martínez del Río Hermanos	200,000
José M. Sancho	200,000
Juan Rondero	200,000
Benito Maqua	100,000
Antonio Berruecos	100,000
Joaquín Lledías	50,000
Fernando del Valle	50,000
José Joaquín de Rosas	50,000
Francisco M. Yturbé	60,000
Francisco de P. Sayago	25,000
Nicanor Béistegui	30,000
Vicente de la Fuente	25,000
Francisco Miranda	25,000
Cándido Guerra	20,000
Ignacio Lizaluturri	20,000
Javier Echeverría	25,000
Juan Suárez Ybáñez	20,000
Domingo Ansoátegui	9,000
Brígido Martínez	6,000
Vicenta Diez de Landazuri	5,000
Total	2,000,000

Source: Pedro Ansoátegui to Gregorio Martínez del Río, Mexico City, 25 Jan. 1841, CMRFH.

Experience taught foreign merchants to use their legations as insurance against the arbitrary and often illegal acts of the politicians. In a memorable case, a group of British merchants in Mexico City lent the government a large sum to outfit a punitive expedition against Texas in the autumn of 1836. The loan was repayable as advance payments "entered" into the books of the Veracruz customs house as credit against future imports of merchandise. Later, when the merchants' goods began arriving in the port, the government reneged on its agreement, ordered repayment of the loan through the ordinary funds, and forced the merchants to pay their duties on the spot.[9]

The lifting of the French blockade of the Gulf ports early in 1839 brought new opportunities for moneylenders. Pedro described a deal being arranged in March 1839:

Now they are trying to deliver weekly to the Government $50,000 in cash, and various English houses have combined for this purpose, and under the recognition and intervention of Mr. Pakenham [the British minister] they propose a deal for 1,350 thousand; for each $100 in cash delivered, they will deliver also one of these three credits: if in *créditos antiguos* [preindependence credits], $16; in *vales de alcance*, $20; and in orders of the 58 percent and 68 percent, $30; obliging the government to pay 1 percent monthly for the cash and to deliver payment in *libranzas*, which incessantly must arrive from Veracruz. The intervention of Mr. Pakenham in this business makes it very secure and for this reason we have subscribed for $150 thousand. I calculate that our disbursement will not reach the half of that, because the unloading of the ships has already begun in Veracruz and within seventy days the first duties will be paid, so that a great part, and in my opinion at least two-thirds of the cash that we have to pay will come from the same that we are receiving. . . . I have calculated on the capital that we have to disburse, and supposing the half, that will give us 35 percent [profit]. Until now, those involved are Geaves and almost all the English houses, the Echeverrías, and us. Sillem continues doing business in company with Loperena and now is very uncomfortable, because this deal undoes a proposal they had made in league with Carrera, Mier y Terán, Agüero C. [Agüero, González & Company].[10]

Heroism against French marines cost the general his leg, but restored to him the political reputation lost after the Texas debacle. To make their deal, the British merchants and their Mexican associates were obliged to use Francisco Morphy as a conduit to Santa Anna. After this group had begun delivering their weekly supplements to the government, they found themselves outfoxed by rivals who shared a more intimate relationship with *El Cojo*. On 30 April 1839, before "retiring" once more from public office to return (heavily laden) to Manga de Clavo (his hacienda near Jalapa), Santa Anna negotiated with Lorenzo Carrera a $300,000 loan to pay the first installment of the indemnity owed to the French. Carrera and his associates furnished the loan as $200,000 in cash and $100,000 in *pagas corrientes* (orders) on the customs houses. Because this new arrangement jeopardized repayment of their loan, the English merchants retaliated by suspending payments to the government and asking Pakenham to intervene. That the government paid competitors with Veracruz *libranzas* promised to the English merchants was serious enough; that these interlopers had secured twice as much interest was intolerable. With Pakenham's mediation the merchants and the government agreed to compromise. The contract of June 1839 was canceled; the $300,000 already disbursed was to draw 2 percent monthly interest until repaid with 10 percent of the revenue from the maritime customs houses.[11]

When Bustamante's government suspended these payments in September 1839 to force the creditors to pay a *refacción*, the English again sought out their minister. In a note to the Mexican foreign minister on 8 October 1839, Pakenham warned of the serious consequences of breaking this second agreement and he protested the inclusion of other debts in the 10 Percent Fund, which had been promised exclusively to repay the so-called English Loan. What especially annoyed foreign creditors was that these new debts originated from transactions of (more) dubious legality: "In the time of Santa Anna, continuation of Minister Cortina, and afterward Ministers Lombardo & Tornel, were made another series of deals that I will not say were crazy, but infamous, which weighed on 56 percent of the maritime customs houses."[12] After heated discussions, the English merchants agreed to permit the inclusion of those credits in the 10 Percent Fund in exchange for receipt of all the special sales taxes (*derechos de consumo*) collected from English merchants. The following year, in September 1840, the government reneged on its agreements and diluted the 10 Percent Fund by issuing and marketing additional 10 Percent Fund bonds. Although the obligations of this fund were considerable, these bonds remained highly regarded because they were backed by a mortgage against the Fondos de los Californias, an ensemble of valuable estates once owned by the Jesuits. Since trade was brisk for most of 1839, about one-half of the $300,000 in principal owed to the English Loan had been repaid by July 1840. The fund's *apoderado*, Pedro Ansoátegui, predicted that the balance would be paid off before the end of the year if the government abolished the 15 percent special sales tax. To avoid paying the tax, merchants in Veracruz refused to ship their goods to the interior and, instead, kept them under bond in the port's warehouses. The government's heavy-handed attempt to raise revenue by putting the squeeze on merchants had paralyzed commerce and, inadvertently, disrupted its own income sources and those of its creditors in the public debt funds. Even with such setbacks, the government continued to pay dividends, albeit at a slower rate, to the 10 Percent Fund, and the market value of those bonds improved, rising from 35 percent in July 1840 to 55 percent by November 1840.[13]

The 8 Percent Fund originated in credits owed from what observers charged were "*loco*" transactions approved by Santa Anna's minister of hacienda, José Gómez de la Cortina, during the French blockade. To pay off $2.2 million in contracted debts, Santa Anna set aside 12 percent of customs duties and issued bonds earning monthly interest of up to 2 percent. Unlike the 15 Percent and the 17 Percent funds, this 12 percent quota had not been authorized by law. The creditors had collected about 11 percent of the principal when, in September 1839, Bustamante forced them to pay a $40,000 *refacción* and reduced their quota to 8 percent. The *apoderado* and principal creditor of the 12 Percent-turned-8 Percent Fund was Agüero, González & Company. Eight Percent Fund bonds sold at about 35 percent of value in July 1840. By November 1840, 37 percent of the $2.2 million in principal had been amortized.

Congress created a new 12 Percent Fund in the summer of 1841. The nominal purpose of the fund was to amortize the copper currency. Because Bustamante's government was on the verge of collapse, it was obliged to concede generous terms on this debt issue. The bonds for the 12 Percent Fund, earning 0.5 percent monthly interest, were marketed for 46 percent in cash (three-fourths in copper coin; one-fourth in silver coin) and 54 percent in paper credits of any category.

Considerations apart from a simple profit motive encouraged *agiotistas* to enter this venture. Pedro reported that Martínez del Río Hermanos had subscribed for $25,000 in cash because "this I have not considered properly as a business deal, and I have entered it only to help nourish this sick one for seven months and to extract in this time all possible from the other funds."[14] Because they rightly feared what might follow, most Mexico City speculators maintained a high regard for Bustamante's government. Although his government had forced creditors to pay *refacciones* and had reduced the quotas for certain funds, *agiotistas* generally regarded those acts as a legitimate response to the excesses of the previous administration and as essential to the government's survival.[15] Bustamante and his minister of hacienda, Echeverría, were well liked because, under difficult circumstances, they had repaid many credits. Table 34 is a summary of the 8 Percent, 10 Percent, 15 Percent, and 17 Percent funds, showing payments applied to principal as of July 1840. Table 35 lists Martínez del Río Hermanos's holdings in the funds as of July 1840.

In 1840 government debt issues accounted for $68,268 of Martínez del Río Hermanos's combined assets, which totaled $691,284. Although these credits made up only 9.8 percent of the firm's assets, they produced $37,878 (44.9 percent) of the gross profits of $85,798 reported by the firm.[16] It was with these numbers in mind that Martínez del Río Hermanos began a new round of aggressive speculations after 1840. Table 36 lists public debt issues owned by the firm between 1839 and 1843. What the firm's partners failed to appreciate, however, when they began these new investments in public

Table 34
Status of 8 Percent, 10 Percent, 15 Percent, 17 Percent Funds, July 1840

Fund	Principal (millions of current pesos)	% Principal Amortized	Monthly Interest Rate (%)
8 Percent	2.2	34	—
10 Percent	2.0	—	0–2.5
15 Percent	1.6	28 + 12 pending	—
17 Percent (old)	2.5	86	0–4

Source: Pedro Ansoátegui to Gregorio Martínez del Río, Mexico City, 6 July 1841, CMRFH.

Table 35
Mexican Public Debt Issues Held by Martinez del Rio Hermanos, 31 December 1840
(Current Pesos)

Type of Paper	Nominal Representation	Amount Collected	Amount Owing	Cost of Acquisition
10 Percent bonds (1st Class)	107,644	41,981	65,663	42,966
10 Percent bonds (2d Class)	2,483	—	2,483	Included in 10 Percent Fund Certificates
10 Percent bonds (3d Class)	35,830	—	35,830	Included in 10 Percent Fund Certificates
English Loan (in 10 Percent Fund)	80,000	56,000	24,000	Included in 10 Percent Fund Certificates
10 Percent Fund certificates	—	24,310	24,599	48,599
8 Percent bonds	57,882	—	33,572	20,567
8 Percent Fund certificates	—	—	10,057	—
Total	283,839	122,291	103,666	112,132

Source: Martinez del Rio Hermanos accounts, CMRFH.
Note: — means no information.

debt issues, was that the political economy of *agiotaje* might change radically in the years to come.

The problem all *agiotistas* would have to face sooner or later was that government debt after independence had continued to increase more rapidly than income. Estimates of the government's disposable income for 1838 to 1842 are listed in table 37. Revenue from the maritime customs houses constituted the government's primary source of income. When the total amount of duties declined after 1840 and when the government began forcibly after 1841 to expropriate progressively larger shares of mortgaged customs quotas, creditors were obliged to war on one another for control of those dwindling resources. Nor were the *agiotistas* in Mexico City the only group dependent on the state. To pay its creditors the Bustamante government reduced the size of the army and the civil service. These groups waited impatiently, along with out-of-favor power brokers like Morphy, for a chance to recoup their losses.

The Mexico City *empresarios* were the backbone of the Bustamante regime; many of its principal figures, like the Echeverrías, were themselves merchants and moneylenders. Even so, when in the summer of 1841 it was apparent that the old regime could no longer sustain itself, an important faction of the Mexico City group abandoned Bustamante to begin making an accommodation with Santa Anna. The most prominent defectors were the powerful *empresarios* who owned the Empresa del Tabaco and who were desperate to return the monopoly to government administration under favorable terms. In the spring of 1841 their several attempts to persuade Bustamante's government to buy back the monopoly had failed. The devaluation of the copper currency that consumers used to buy tobacco products, the inability of the Bustamante government to implement an effective plan to amortize copper, and the prospect of being bankrupted if they could not cancel their five-year contract with the government encouraged the company's shareholders to betray an administration that had treated them kindly in the past.[17] Observers described the *empresarios'* antics in the summer of 1841:

Our Minister of Hacienda [Manuel Canseco] was placed in the chair by the E. de Tabacos, as it believed he was the most convenient, and in little more than a month he gave it $514,000; such that in the first six weeks of his Ministry he spent nearly a million pesos, with which D. Javier [Echeverría] could have managed four months; Now, the E. is draining the corpse and far from helping is trying to squeeze out the $300 thousand it has left there; our man [Canseco] is now in the worst fix and has not stopped making his blunders. The past week he called the *apoderados* of the funds and asked them for alms and they gave him $100,000, which they divided in fourths between each of the funds and which will come out of the first *libranzas* that arrive; this will retard the dividends a little more. This occasion gave me an opportunity to

Table 36
Mexican Public Debt Issues and Related Paper Owned by Martínez del Rio Hermanos
(Current Pesos)

	1839	1840	1841	1842	1843
17 Percent Fund (old)	7,157	—	—	—	—
Preindependence credits	3,887	3,887	1,214	1,214	1,214
Peaje (toll) credits	13,431	12,001	22,827	19,631	16,891
Loan to government	2,000	—	—	—	—
Current orders (*pagas corrientes*)	—	1,847	3,117	11,288	—
Promissory notes (*vales de alcance*)	—	532	—	—	—
English Loan (10 Percent Fund)	—	50,000	25,058	7,464	5,248
10 Percent Fund	—	—	54,460	41,316	28,154
17 Percent Fund (new)	—	—	22,000	95,117	105,360
8 Percent Fund	—	—	20,567	14,927	13,843
Import credits for yarn	—	—	2,992	15,006	67,371
Certificates of deposit	—	—	49	49	49
12 Percent Fund	—	—	—	—	45,380
Certificate for Casa de Moneda	—	—	—	—	1,220
Total	26,475	68,267	152,284	206,012	284,730

Source: CMRFH.
Note: — means no information.

Table 37

Mexican Public Debt Fund Quotas and Mexican Government Income and Expenditure Patterns

Year	Estimated Customs Revenues (millions of pesos)	%/Customs Duties Pledged to Pay Internal Debt (millions of pesos)	%/Customs Duties Pledged to Pay Foreign Debt (millions of pesos)	%/Customs Duties Free to Mexican Government (millions of pesos)	Estimated Government Expenditures (millions of pesos)
1838	3.5	88/3.1	0	12/0.4	20.0
1839	16.1	56/9.0	16.66/2.7	27.34/4.4	17.6
1840	13.5	50/6.8	16.67/2.2	33.33/4.5	18.9
1841	7.7	62/4.8	16.67/1.3	21.33/1.6	21.8
1842	6.7	62/4.2	16.67/1.1	21.33/1.4	26.6

Source: Calculated from data in Mexico, Ministerio de Hacienda y Crédito Público, *Memoria,* 1869-1870.

deal for the first time with S. E. [Canseco], who seems to me a poor man, very good as a *mayordomo* of a convent, but in no way fit for the position he occupies.[18]

The 25 Percent/26 Percent Fund and the British Conventions, 1842-1848

The reaction that *agiotistas* feared might accompany Santa Anna's return to power was quick to materialize. The strongman from Veracruz assumed the presidency on 10 October 1841. The following day he ordered the suspension of payments to the 8 Percent, 10 Percent, 12 Percent, 15 Percent, and 17 Percent funds. The Decree of 14 October 1841 lifted the suspension temporarily, but reduced the quota of import duties for each fund by one-half. At the same time, Santa Anna began to increase dramatically the size of the army and the bureaucracy.[19]

Apart from the army and established corporate interests such as the church, the dictator's political coalition for the 1841 revolt incorporated other diverse and heterogeneous forces. Staunch supporters of the old order, Veracruz planters wanted protection for sugar, cotton, and tobacco. Import merchants in Gulf ports were liberals and advocates of free trade, but they joined the conservative movement to protest profiteering in the public debt. Normally, the port merchants paid customs duties with *libranzas*. The government endorsed these *libranzas* to the creditors of the funds. Importers viewed the funds as a fradulent device used to enrich rival merchants and *empresarios* in Mexico City.

The last important block in the Santanista movement of 1841 consisted of regional interests committed to changing the pattern of government expenditures to shift the flow of resources away from the center and toward themselves. Once Santa Anna had taken power, the coalition began to dissolve—but not before launching a virulent attack on the public debt speculators.

Before Santa Anna's return, port merchants had been required to write separate *libranzas* for each of the funds according to the prescribed quotas. Afterward, they won a reform of this procedure. Santa Anna's government required the funds to select an *apoderado general* to receive all the *libranzas* from the customs houses. *Apoderados* for each fund accepted their share of *libranzas* from the *apoderado general* and distributed the proceeds among the individual creditors. Because the *apoderados* already charged a 1 percent commission and now the *apoderado general* charged a 0.5 percent commission, the new procedure slowed down the payment process and increased overhead costs for the creditors.[20]

Santa Anna intended to keep his regime solvent by reducing payments to the national debt. Since the 16.67 percent quota for the foreign debt owed to Great Britain could not be set aside except at grave political risk, that left the public debt funds as the only targets of opportunity. Fearing Santa Anna's designs, the *apoderado general*, Gregorio Mier y Terán, and the *apoderados*—Agustín Prado for the 15 Percent, A. J. Atocha for the 12 Percent, and Pedro Ansoátegui for the 10 Percent—published on 9 February 1842 a protest denouncing any scheme to set aside the mortgages on the maritime customs houses or to alter the "method and practice" the government itself had established for the funds.[21]

Ignoring those protests, Santa Anna suspended payments to the funds on 19 February 1842. The suspension continued unrelieved for the next few months. Under such strains, the delicate consensus that united the *agiotistas* began to splinter. Rivalry and petty jealousy always characterized the *agiotistas'* behavior, yet they had in the past manifested a rudimentary collective consciousness, confronting the governemnt as a bloc and benefiting as a whole from the unanimity of purpose. Predictably, the split occurred along lines of nationality. The more powerful native creditors began to make separate deals for themselves. They could bargain efficiently with Santa Anna; family connections, political promises, and appropriate gifts brought favorable resolutions from politicians at the highest levels. The cooperation of the career civil servants who managed routine government affairs was secured through other arrangements. By law, appointees to posts involving fiscal responsibilities had to have a *fiador* guarantee their good behavior in office. *Empresarios* like the Rubios, the Escandóns, and the Fagoagas put up *fianzas* (bonds) for dozens of officials, ranging from the head of the customs house in Tampico to the tax administrator of Tlalpam. In contrast to the proven Mexican model, foreign merchants like the Martínez del Ríos failed to develop useful relations with either the politicians or the bureaucrats, trusting instead that their legations would look after their interests.[22]

Santa Anna announced in July 1842 that payments to the funds would be resumed—under certain conditions. The combined 8 Percent, 10 Percent, 15 Percent, and 17 Percent funds might receive 15 percent of customs duties if each agreed to pay a $40,000 *refacción*. Because the new quota would not provide enough revenue even to pay interest on the principal owed, the creditors listened to the proposal without enthusiasm. Many of them were shocked to learn three days later of a new decree that lifted the suspension of payments to the 15 Percent Fund. Only after this fund had been paid in full, were the other funds to receive payments from that quota, according to the order of their seniority. The special deal for the 15 Percent Fund was the work of Ignacio Loperena and Antonio Garay, *agiotistas* who had intimate associations with Santa Anna and who had invested heavily in that fund.[23] Through the ubiquitous Morphy, Santa Anna made it known to the others that a $300,000 *refacción* would be the price fixed for returning to them a 31 percent share of the maritime customs duties.[24] In late September 1842 Pedro described the inconclusive negotiations being carried on between the creditors and the government:

> Eight days ago, by invitation of the government, the creditors of the funds met in the Lonja; here the *apoderado general* read to them an offer from the Min. of Hacienda, which amounted to a request for a 10 percent *refacción* in exchange for 16 percent of the customs duties to pay the 8, 10, 12, and 17 percent; It was decided to name a commission; that was composed of Mr. Rosas, Yturbé, and Berruecos, authorizing that they offer for the 8, 10, and 12 Percent funds the sum of $100,000 in order that half the quota of Hacienda and made its offer in those terms, but nothing was resolved. Nicod, as representative for the 17 Percent, told the Junta he would give nothing; he has the hope Mr. Pakenham will receive some instructions about this fund.[25]

Unable to reach a collective agreement with the government, the last vestiges of cooperation between creditors vanished, to be replaced by heated confrontations and controversies. In early October 1842 Martínez del Río Hermanos, along with many other foreign firms, called on the British minister for help: "The Prior [senior partner] in our firm having become a naturalized British subject, we have the honor to solicit your protection. . . . A large portion of our capital having been placed in jeopardy by the President's decree . . . which suspends for an indefinite period the payments on the different funds."[26] The company reported that it had paid weekly subscriptions for the $300,000 loan to Bustamante's government (the 17 Percent Fund) until Santa Anna's revolt in the summer of 1841 reduced its share of dividends. When Martínez del Río Hermanos tried to withdraw from this commitment, "the head of the Mexican government obliged us to pay the full amount that we had originally agreed on."[27] Now that same authority refused to pay back the sums owed. Unjustly, "claims of foreign creditors [were] wholly disregarded" while Santa Anna's government made payments to "the Mexican holders of the same bonds and of other paper less formally guaranteed."[28]

At first Pakenham was loath to support such claims and he suggested that creditors like Martínez del Río Hermanos should seek recourse from the courts of Mexico. Although he agreed to seek instructions from the Foreign Office, he insisted that Martínez del Río Hermanos must first provide official evidence of Gregorio José's naturalization.[29]

Put off by Pakenham, the Martínez del Ríos tried their hand at arranging a Mexican solution. Pedro suggested that "by giving Morphy a good share in which he can interest El Cojo, we can get out of everything at once."[30] The newcomers were slow to appreciate that however useful bribes might be, *empresarios* needed other, more indispensable resources to ensure the successful execution of such complex maneuvers. When their overtures to Morphy failed, the Martiínez del Ríos had no alternative except to plead for Pakenham's intervention.

The favored of Mexico needed no legation to intercede for them. Gregorio Mier y Terán paid an $80,000 *refacción* to secure a private 8 percent quota of customs duties to pay off his $800,000 investment in public debt bonds. Rosas and Yturbé also made private arrangements. Although Pakenham declined Pedro's request that he secure a similar arrangement for Martínez del Río Hermanos's bonds, the show of favoritism by the Mexican government did stimulate the British minister to seek a diplomatic solution for the claims of his nationals.[31]

On 15 October 1842 the ministers of hacienda and foreign relations signed an agreement with Pakenham that pledged the Mexican government to pay British citizens' claims that had been pending since the 1830s. The three major claims were those represented by Manning & Marshall (assumed by Manning & MacKintosh), J. P. Penny & Company, and Martínez del Río Hermanos. The claims of J. P. Penny & Company originated with forced loans and the seizure of the company's goods by government troops in Zacatecas in 1836. Martínez del Río Hermanos represented the investors in the English Loan of 1839. The $250,000 principal of the Pakenham Convention was payable with a quota of 2 percent on the Veracruz customs house and 1 percent on the Tampico customs house. The *apoderado* of this fund, the 2 Percent and 1 Percent funds, was Pedro Ansoátegui.[32] After the convention was signed, Martínez del Río Hermanos rushed to buy credits that could be included in the new fund. As late as December 1842 this paper sold at less than 50 percent of face value. Referring to the convention, Pedro exclaimed, "This business is better than ever . . . because this is more secure, signed as it is as a convenant with the Minister of S.M.B. [Great Britain] and as it is between Government and Government. Mr. Pakenham has told me that he will not give protection for the other funds and if he does it now for the 17 Percent, it is only for the past denigration of justice, this will serve as a counsel for me in the future."[33]

With Pakenham's intervention, the Mexican government pledged in a second *convenio* signed on 21 January 1843 to repay the $2.2 million loan of 1840, which formerly had been part of the 17 Percent Fund. To cover the principal, interest, and a 6 percent *refacción*, the government issued new bonds earning 1 percent monthly interest to replace 17 Percent Fund bonds, which had drawn only 0.5 percent monthly interest. The new bonds were repayable with *libranzas* endorsed to Montgomery Nicod & Company against an 8 percent share of the maritime customs house. As of January 1843, Martínez del Río Hermanos's share in the $2.2 million loan and in the 17 Percent Fund and, hence, in the new arrangement was $220,000 in principal and $75,904 in interest. In March 1843 the firm acquired additional 17 Percent bonds by putting up 2 percent of the 6 percent *refacción* owed by Montgomery Nicod & Company. Nicod, who master-minded the original speculation with the 17 Percent Fund, had by this late date lost patience with the constant intrigues that after 1841 were synonymous with operations in the public debt. José Pablo reported from Paris, "According to what Mrs. Lubervieille has told me, Nicod has gone mad as a result of all the disgusts he has had in his dealings with the government: I suppose in other words this means the 17 Percent."[34]

The 25 Percent/26 Percent Fund, 1843-1849

Nicod was not the only one disturbed by the handling of the 17 Percent Fund. Santa Anna had retired to Manga del Clavo in late October 1842, perhaps to escape association with the capitulation to British pressures. In early March 1843 he rushed back to Mexico City and reassumed the presidency, a position that his subordinate, Nicolás Bravo, had occupied. Creditors of the funds reported that "Santa Anna has come back furious with all the acts of his substitute . . . so that the arrangement of the 17 Percent also enters into this . . . he has given a secret order to suspend it."[35]

Santa Anna and his partisans also looked with disfavor on Bravo's decision to lift the suspension of payments to the 8 Percent, 10 Percent, and 15 Percent funds in December 1842. The caudillo had hoped to pry more cash from the creditors as the price for such action. The best the Bravo government had gotten from them was their acquiescence to another 50 percent reduction of the funds' quotas. But because the British government had forced Mexico to increase its quota for the foreign debt from 16.67 percent to 20 percent of maritime customs duties, the surrender of even $456,000 annually from the fund quotas was not enough to cover the government's deficit. In returning to Mexico City, Santa Anna's intention was to consolidate all the internal debt into a single fund and to finance this with a small quota of customs duties. For that purpose, the Law of 11 May 1843 created a 25 Percent Fund (later 26 Percent) and ordered that the 8 Percent, 10 Percent, 12 Percent, 15 Percent, 17 Percent and all other classes of public indebtedness be paid with a 25 Percent quota of customs duties.[36] As the price of admission into the new fund, all credits were required to pay an additional 6 percent *refacción*. The alternative to not entering the 25 Percent Fund was an indefinite suspension of payments. Aggregated to the 25 Percent Fund (but exempt from the *refacción* were $5 million in tobacco debt bonds issued to the Empresa del Tabaco in January 1842. Allegedly, the tobacco *empresarios* had purchased this preferential treatment for the tobacco bonds (and won a separate concession that transferred to the Empresa the government's shares in the Fresnillo mines) by favoring Santa Anna with an $80,000 bribe.[37]

Most creditors had no choice but to go along with the onerous conditions decreed by the Law of 11 May 1843. Santa Anna did not attempt to force the 2 Percent and 1 Percent Fund, protected by the Pakenham Convention, into the 25 Percent Fund, but he did challenge the arrangement of Montgomery Nicod & Company's $2.2 million in the 17 Percent/8 Percent funds. Despite strenuous objections from Pakenham, the suspension of payments to the $2.2 million debt (the 8 Percent Fund) continued until mid-1844, when the government reorganized it as the 5 Percent Fund. Although Martínez del Río Hermanos looked to the British to defend their interests against Santa Anna's schemes, José Pablo clung to the delusion that the family might yet be able to arrange its own deal. He wrote Pedro from Paris in March 1843 to suggest that

if Morphy returns to Mexico could you interest him in [securing] payment of the 17 Percent—The knowledge I have of the people and things of that place make me believe that it would not be so difficult to obtain the payment of this fund under some pretext, singing the mandarins a lullaby, that is to say, giving them a share of the dividends. Santa Anna knows how to squeeze blood from stones and he who knows how to manage Santa Anna will always be able to do business.[38]

Corruption was commonplace. To arrange the consolidation of Mexico's foreign debt in London, the Lizardis bribed Santa Anna with $125,000 and Morphy with $60,000 in October 1843. When his collusion with the Lizardis was detected, Morphy was forced to give half his share to the minister of war, José María Tornel, and to pay lesser amounts to the British consuls in Great Britain.[39] In April 1844 the minister of hacienda, Ignacio Trigüeros, ordered the payment of $214,000 in *pagas corrientes* at full face value. This class of government debt issues was nearly worthless (selling in the market for less than 7 percent of nominal value), so this transaction gave privileged speculators (and their political patrons) a minimum 93 percent return.

How were Santa Anna and his group spending the profits of public office? José Pablo described their antics: "Los Santos just had another round of gaming and cockfights at the Hacienda del Encero and it is said that the Gang won some $80 D [thousand]!! Morphy was losing an equal sum and finally succeeded in dropping everything; Escandón left winning with 30 to 40,000 [gold ounces]."[40]

Meanwhile, the lot of many *agiotistas* was grim. The combined principal of the 25 Percent Fund in 1843 was about $13.5 million. This extraordinary dilution of the historical ratio between credits and quotas was reflected in the market price for its paper. Early sales of 25 Percent Fund bonds yielded up to 37 percent of face value. By August 1843, no buyer could be found at 35 percent. That stood in sharp contrast to the 60 percent to 65 percent prices for various classes of bonds in 1841. And the situation only worsened. In August 1844 the 25 Percent bonds dropped to 23 percent. In 1846 and 1847 they sold at 18 percent. Declining further in the next decade, their value fell to 7 percent by 1856.[41]

British protection enabled Martínez del Río Hermanos and other creditors with foreign connections to escape total submersion in the 25 Percent Fund. For their holdings in the 8 Percent, 10 Percent, and 12 Percent funds there was no alternative but to convert them. Table 38 lists the principal and interest owed the firm in May 1843 for bonds nominally valued at $228,534 (representing a real investment of $94,200). The performance of bonds backed by a British guarantee (the 2 Percent and 1 Percent, and 5 Percent funds) contrasted vividly with the 25 Percent bonds: higher interest rates (12 percent annual versus 6 percent annual), higher market value (80 percent versus 18 percent), and regular dividends large enough to pay principal and interest.

The reaction of Martínez del Río Hermanos to these circumstances was predictable. It made new investments in the 2 Percent and 1 Percent, and 5 Percent funds, and it tried to get rid of its 25 Percent bonds. José Pablo explained these operations to Gregorio José in 1844:

I am confident that this business [the 5 Percent Fund] will continue very good and that the results will be satisfactory to you . . . because the English Legation does not lose sight of it. For the same reasons I am not in accord with your idea of buying in preference the credits of this government that are less expensive [that is, 25 Percent bonds]: these today are trash and the trash heap is growing every day, in contrast the English guarantee is very well sustained so that John Bull will make of it an exceptional and privileged fund.[42]

The Laws of 2 March 1845 and 1 May 1845 rechristened the 25 Percent Fund as the 26 Percent Fund, but set aside only a 6 percent quota of the maritime customs duties to amortize the fund. Pedro was outraged at this development:

I do not believe that the government had the right to make the law that created the 26 Percent Fund. . . . Certainly, I was opposed to the majority of those who attended, as they were *compinches* [sic] of Dn. Francisco [Yturbé, the minister of hacienda] and such hypocrites . . . his way [Yturbé's] is to work concealed . . . all the rest that concurred were not working for more than their own special interests and in no way for the well-being, or peace, or community of creditors.[43]

The following year the government issued more bonds on the 26 Percent Fund, depressing its value still further. In March 1846 Martínez del Río Hermanos tried to sell $100,000 in 26 Percent bonds, but it could find no buyer even at 18 percent.[44]

Prominent native *agiotistas* like Yturbé were not powerless to defend their interests, but given the government's lack of resources it was unrealistic to expect the state to liquidate the public debt—no matter who controlled the government. Therefore, the strategy native creditors adopted was to maximize their share of whatever payments the state did make. Necessarily,

Table 38

Principal and Interest Paid and Pending on Mexican Public Debt Funds Held by Martinez del Rio Hermanos, May 1843
(Current Pesos)

Fund	Principal	Principal Paid	Principal Owed	Interest Owed	Total Owed
8 Percent	47,075	24,914	22,161	17,647	39,808
10 Percent	87,032	47,232	39,800	29,405	69,205
12 Percent	112,992	4,418	108,574	10,858	119,432
Total			170,535	57,910	228,445*

Source: Martinez del Rio Accounts, CMRFH.
* Converted into 25 Percent Fund bonds.

that entailed a sustained attack on the privileged status of foreign creditors. José Pablo complained:

Having entered recently as Minister of Hacienda, Yturbé . . . enemy of the 5 Percent, the first measure he took was to decree the suspension of *monthly payments*; this has been sustained until now with the greatest obstinacy; there is no doubt that in doing so his principal object has been to harm that fund and all that is foreign. That is, also suspended are the payments, corresponding to the old English debt!!—that of the 1 Percent & 2 Percent, etc., in a word all—all payments . . . as also the Minister of War, Tornel, has found his powder contract suspended, etc., it will not be strange if he [Tornel] makes some mischief to rid himself of so vexatious a colleague . . . in spite of [Yturbé's] having said to his friends that he would hang before abandoning the post. The extra-avaricious genius of Yturbé is recognized, and his judaism [*sic*] is so notorious that naturally the whole world believes he will care for his own interests before the public good; and as he has a large sum ($800,000) in the 26 Percent, it is probable that his measures in regard to this fund will not harm that in the least.[45]

As the United States army marched toward Mexico City in the summer of 1847, well-placed *agiotistas* took advantage of the confusion to cut their losses in public debt speculation. While Santa Anna was instructing his army to retreat, the minister of war, Ignacio Gutiérrez (described by José Pablo as "a cursed and vile creature of Santa Anna"), the minister of foreign relations, Manuel Baranda, and the minister of hacienda, Juan Rondero, were using the $1.5 million church loan of 1847 as a vehicle to rid themselves of the useless 26 Percent Fund bonds. This loan consisted entirely of *libranzas* drawn against agencies of the church. Rondero, Mier y Terán, Rosas, Yturbé, and other officials skimmed off the choicest of these *libranzas*, paying 50 percent in cash and 50 percent in 26 Percent bonds. Less-privileged persons paid 67 percent in cash and 33 percent in 26 Percent bonds, without being able to choose their *libranzas*. Selection was an advantage because *libranzas* drawn on the poorer church agencies were virtually worthless.[46]

Xenophobes and Xenophiles

With the government's credit rating with the *agiotistas* impossibly low after 1841, forced loans became a universal solution to the problem of deficit financing. Like other foreign merchants, the Martínez del Ríos used their nationality to win exemptions from the forced loans. When Mexican officials threatened to embargo Miraflores after Martínez del Río Hermanos refused in April 1843 to pay its share of a new forced loan, the British Legation interceded, the matter was conveniently forgotten, and the company was left unmolested for a time.[47]

With the coming of war, a new urgency was added to the state's relentless search for revenue sources. The Decree of 17 June 1847, which announced the imposition of another forced loan, assigned Martínez del Río Hermanos a quota of $2,250—a sum presumably based on the amount of capital that the firm employed in Mexico. Edward Thornton, representing the British Foreign Office, wrote the Mexican foreign minister, José María Pacheco, on 7 July 1847 to suggest that this assessment was too high. He pointed out that most of the firm's capital was invested in Miraflores, where it had produced few profits. The remainder of its capital was tied up in government debt issues. Since payments to the public debt had been suspended, those assets could not be counted as capital in circulation.

Despite Thornton's intervention, a detachment of soldiers appeared at the firm's doors two weeks later and announced that Martínez del Río Hermanos had been embargoed and that its properties would be seized and sold. In a panic, Pedro rushed back to see Thornton, who ordered the Mexican foreign minister and the military commander of Mexico City to suspend those proceedings. Pedro gleefully confided in November 1847 that, according to the instructions of the British foreign minister, Lord Palmerston, the firm would be exempt from any forced loan. For Pedro it was a personal triumph: "I am very happy, as much for the savings of money as for the blow dealt to Yturbé and his friends, who were very vainly boasting of having won the principle that the foreigners should not escape."[48]

Given the institutional context of these desperate times, neither the strategies of Yturbé and other native creditors to use personal influence and public office to promote their private interests nor the plans of the Martínez del Ríos to protect their investments with British power were unusual or immoral. To stay in business everyone needed insurance against the arbitrary, capricious, and frequently illegal exactions of the government. What was new and dangerous was that public debt speculation had become a zero-sum game. If native creditors prevailed, then foreign merchants who had invested heavily in public debt issues wuld be ruined, and vice-versa. Initially, creditors with foreign connections were the more successful group, as demonstrated by the higher returns of the conventions in the 1840s. But the battle was far from over. Foreign merchants became favored targets for political harassment by nationalist interests. Decrees in 1842 and 1843 imposed a 4.5 percent tax on foreign capital employed in Mexico, outlawed foreign participation in the retail trade, and restricted the use of public debt issues to pay import duties.[49] There were other proposals to expel foreigners from the interior and to restrict them from the coast. These reprisals were visible evidence that a "community of creditors" no longer existed in Mexico. Inevitably, as the rift dividing the monied class widened, native creditors would join other interest groups in a general offensive to realign Mexico's politicized economy.

8. The Tobacco Debt Bonds and the Conventions, 1845-1861

The Tobacco Debt Bonds

All in all, the experience of Martínez del Río Hermanos in government debt speculations through 1845 suggested to the family that this activity was more profitable and more secure than mundane commercial operations. The lesson, as Pedro and José Pablo interpreted it, was that it was a simple task to harness the might of the British Empire and to put its energy to work for the family in Mexico. Only Ventura de la Cruz, who had no influence on decision making within the family, seemed to grasp the dangers of the developing situation. From Rome in March 1845, he warned his brothers, "The protection of John Bull, I think is a thing on which we must count but little, because when it is convenient to this gentleman he gives and when not he does not."[1]

His words went unheeded. When its projects in Mexico failed, the family continued to explain those setbacks as the work of aberrant political personalities or moral corruption. Political corruption was pervasive, but more generally Martínez del Río Hermanos's strategy to employ Great Britain as its debt collector in Mexico failed because the interests of the firm and the interests of Great Britain were too different. In particular, the tobacco debt operation brought disaster to the firm because its partners ignored their own dictum that borrowed money should never be used in such speculations and that no single speculation should entail unacceptable losses.

In marked contrast to many of its other ventures, Martínez del Río Hermanos's speculations with the tobacco debt bonds did not develop incrementally nor was the original plan of operation modest in any way. From the beginning it was a scheme cleverly calculated, daring in the risks it involved, and demanding of the firm's and the family's resources. The plan was based on intelligence gleaned from contacts in Mexico, Great Britain, and France; but as beautifully conceived as it was, it was hopelessly flawed.

In 1845 Ewen MacKintosh (the British consul in Mexico and the managing partner of Manning & MacKintosh) began a project to consolidate Mexico's foreign debt.[2] After Santa Anna's government was overthrown in December 1844, the Lizardis had been fired as Mexico's representative to the London bondholders and they lost their exclusive access to the funds that the Mexican government assigned to the foreign debt. Santa Anna's government had defaulted on this debt in 1843. The overt hostility of the United States toward Mexico in 1845 gave a new urgency to the attempts by General Herrera's government to consolidate the foreign debt. Working with its agents in London, Manning & MacKintosh began negotiations for a conversion that would placate British owners of the London debt and make Great Britain a more responsive ally. Advised of these developments by Morphy, Gregorio José rushed to London in 1845 to buy London debt bonds, now greatly devalued because they were so far in arrears for principal and interest. In Mexico his brothers maneuvered to share in the opportunities developing there.

Under the terms of a contract that had never been bilaterally abrogated, the assets of the national tobacco monopoly were mortgaged to guarantee the payment of the bonds issued to pay for the $5 million inventory delivered by the Empresa del Tabaco to Santa Anna's government in January 1842.[3] Violating its contract with the *empresarios*, the government combined the tobacco bonds with the 25 Percent Fund in May 1843, retarding repayment and lowering the market value of the tobacco bonds. Santa Anna appropriated for his own use the mortgaged revenues of the tobacco monopoly. Thus, the tobacco bonds had two differing values—one, a low market value based on the diluted internal debt fund, and a second, potentially higher, value based on the presumed legal obligations of the Mexican government. What was relevant in 1845 was that any conversion of the foreign debt might be linked to the tobacco monopoly, believed by many to be the only productive revenue source left to the government of Mexico. Whoever controlled the tobacco bonds might control the monopoly. Without the monopoly there could be no conversion.

Manning & MacKintosh had been the agent for the tobacco bonds since 1842. As a partner in this firm, MacKintosh acquired $300,000 in tobacco bonds. Only about $2 million in bonds remained in circulation in 1845. To secure a majority control of the tobacco debt MacKintosh needed to buy only $700,000 in bonds. Although he enlisted Escandón in his scheme, MacKintosh's relations with the other tobacco bondholders were troubled. Disagreements with Rubio in 1844 led to the forced arbitration of a disagreement over the firm's accounting methods. Working quietly to exploit those differences, Martínez del Río Hermanos used Morphy to deliver a secret proposal to the bondholders that they replace Manning & MacKintosh as their agent. In a general meeting of the bondholders in late May 1845, the consul surprised everyone by presenting a final accounting and surrendering his powers as representative. He announced that he would buy the group's bonds, but only at 25 percent of face value. Rubio "turned colored" and did not utter a single word. The other principal bondholders, Benito Maqua and Nicanor Béistegui, excused themselves and the meeting broke up without a resolution. Pedro chortled, "When I learned this I knew that soon they would come back to us."[4]

Refusing MacKintosh's offers (through intermediaries) to buy Rubio's bonds at 35 percent, the bondholders sold $496,000 in tobacco bonds to Martínez del Río Hermanos at 44 percent. Of these bonds, $300,000 came from Rubio, $116,000 from Maqua, and $80,000 from Béistegui and Muriel Hermanos.[5] The sale was kept confidential under the terms of a secret *convenio* in which the bondholders and Martínez del Río Hermanos formed a company to manage the bondholders' remaining shares.[6] With the advantage of hindsight, it is easy to see that the firm paid too high a price for the tobacco bonds ($220,500), as the current price for the 25 Percent Fund obligations from which tobacco bonds were paid was only about 25 percent and falling in mid-1845.

The firm's second blunder was to suppose that if it controlled the tobacco bonds it could use them as well as MacKintosh. Secretly, Martínez del Río Hermanos had obtained from the British Legation's archive copies of correspondence between MacKintosh (as agent for the tobacco debt), Charles Bankhead (as the British minister), the British Foreign Office in London, and the Mexican government. These documents revealed that General Herrera's government considered the tobacco debt to be a British property and that the British government had committed itself to securing a settlement. To gauge British willingness to help *their* firm collect the debt, Pedro and José Pablo visited Bankhead at his home in late June 1845. They found him supportive and sympathetic, if somewhat suspicious. Before making a decision to consult the Foreign Office for instructions, the minister insisted on speaking first with MacKintosh, who he suggested might wish to be included in any collection proceedings. To that point, Pedro replied that MacKintosh "would not have as much interest as us in activating this matter because it might be that he had other plans for getting payment."[7]

Two days later when Pedro encountered Bankhead in the Lonja, the minister's attitude had changed radically. He told Pedro there was no way the business could be considered English; he insisted he was at a loss to understand why the firm had entered into it. Pedro responded that the business was now more British than when managed by Manning & MacKintosh, because Martínez del Río Hermanos was not simply a representative, but a "true proprietor," and he reminded the minister of the official communications on this subject. Unmoved, Bankhead answered only that he would write Lord Aberdeen, the British foreign minister, for instructions. Afterward, Pedro bitterly observed, "It seems that S.E.

[Bankhead] was sent here to care for the businesses of British subjects only when convenient to the interests of MacKintosh."[8]

To get around the consul and his puppet, Pedro and José Pablo urged Gregorio José to present their case personally to the British Foreign Office. As they believed the Mexican government was eager to please Great Britain, just a "slight insinuation" that the Foreign Office wanted to see the mortgaged revenues returned to the tobacco bonds would be enough. What worried the family more was not the attitude of the Mexican government, but the intrigues of the British consul, who they feared would begin, with covert aid from Bankhead, to wage a clandestine war against their firm.[9]

To reach a profitable understanding with the Mexican government, the Martínez del Ríos counted heavily (too heavily) on Morphy, whose talents as a broker they had long admired. Crushing their expectations, Morphy lent them little help after the sale of the bonds had been arranged.[10] Acting for the Lizardis (who entertained their own plans for consolidating the Mexican foreign debt), Morphy used his naïve friends as pawns to obstruct MacKintosh's scheme and then abandoned them to their own devices.

To replace Morphy and to handle negotiations with the government of General Joaquín Herrera, Martínez del Río Hermanos contracted the services of Mariano Otero. Their agent's principal qualifications for the job were his close relations with the minister of hacienda, Luis de la Rosa, and other Cabinet members. His object was to persuade the government to resume monthly payments of $35,000 from the tobacco monopoly and to provide, additionally, an indemnity to replace the silver export duties from the Pacific ports, which also had been promised to pay off the tobacco bonds. An arrangement seemed imminent in December 1845. Pedro formally delivered to the government a proposal that Martínez del Río Hermanos would pay a $50,000 *refacción* to receive $25,000 monthly from tobacco revenues.[11]

Before a deal could be struck, General Paredes's revolt drove Herrera from power. Six months of behind-the-scenes groundwork went for naught and Martínez del Río Hermanos was forced to seek relief in the Mexican courts. If, afterward, the government did not pay up, José Pablo boasted, "Victoria will take charge to make it comply."[12] For the court test, the firm contracted an attorney, Miguel Barriero, who claimed to have unusually good relations with the judges, public employees, and ministers handling the case. Barriero advised his clients that the case would be costly to prosecute because, even though the judges were honest, an attorney needed "to make little gifts . . . to conquer hearts."[13]

As their case moved "with Tortoise steps" through the courts in 1846, the Martínez del Ríos had the perverse satisfaction of knowing that MacKintosh too had fallen awry of Mexican politics. The abrupt change in government disrupted ratification of the planned conversion. Undiscouraged, the consul worked out a new, scaled-down operation, and on 5 March 1846 Manning & MacKintosh signed a contract with the minister of hacienda whereby the firm pledged to market in Europe £4,650,000 in the new bonds issued by the Mexican government to pay the costs of consolidating the London debt.[14] Revenue from the tobacco monopoly was pledged to cover amortization and to pay 5 percent annual interest on the new bonds.

On learning from Gregorio José that such a proposal might be accepted by the London bondholders in August 1846, the Martínez del Ríos committed their third fatal error in this business. Convinced that the conversion was imminent and that the value of tobacco bonds must rise, they purchased additional tobacco bonds—$447,000 in face value—costing $178,800.[15] Again, they paid too much for the bonds (40 percent), as the tobacco bonds were useless if tobacco revenues were not pledged as part of the consolidation plan. Table 39 lists the approximate distribution of tobacco bonds owned or managed by Martínez del Río Hermanos in June 1845 and August 1846. The first installments to repay the $339,000 borrowed to finance these purchases were due beginning in June 1847. Except for the still-undecided Supreme Court case, there was little evidence to support the Martínez del Ríos' conviction that they could soon dispose of these bonds with a profit. After another coup in August 1846, Paredes was replaced by Santa Anna and Gómez Farías. The new government repudiated the agreements for consolidating the foreign debt and appointed a commission to study the matter. Pedro explained, "The business of the Conversion has now been submitted to a commission (very heterogenous) and for the same reason I expect it will be a long thing: the more so because the new Minister of Hacienda (Haro) seems to have an [interest] in annulling that accord, and to arrange to make a new one, but *by the Lizardis*."[16] The politicians and their patrons and clients were still squabbling over who should handle the

Table 39
Ownership of Tobacco Debt Bonds Represented by
Martínez del Río Hermanos
(Current Pesos)

Bondholder	June 1845	August 1846
Cayetano Rubio	832,000	—
Benito Maqua	330,000	330,000
José Antonio Béistegui	157,000	542,000
Muriel Hermanos	124,000	124,000
Martínez del Río Hermanos	490,000	937,000
Total	1,933,000	1,933,000

Source: Pedro Ansoátegui to Gregorio Martínez del Río, Mexico City, 6 August 1846, CMRFH.

foreign debt and under which terms when American troops marched into Mexico City one year later.

After many delays, on 20 October 1846 the Supreme Court of Mexico handed down a decision on Martínez del Río Hermanos's suit to force the government to respect its original compromises concerning the tobacco bonds. At best, it was now only a partial victory for the plaintiffs. Pedro lamented,

The lack of dignity of the little old men of the Supreme Court, or more than anything the immorality of this country, has obliged us to make new sacrifices to obtain a sentence for our business . . . in the end we had to agree to pass the case back to the Government through the offices of the Minister of Hacienda; that is, it was necessary that he arrange it; and at the end of last week he returned it with a memorandum [for the terms of settlement]. Yesterday, the Chamber met and according to our attorney they dictated a verdict that should be signed today. In substance, they will pay us $35,000 monthly, and for the part in arrears the government will make arrangements as circumstances permit, declaring that after the costs of administration and payments to the planters, our mortgage will have preference.[17]

In formal compliance with the Supreme Court decision, the minister of hacienda, Antonio Haro y Tamariz, informed the Guadalajara and Zacatecas administrations of the tobacco monopoly that they should begin paying to Martínez del Río Hermanos the stipulated amount. When the firm went to collect the first month's installment, they discovered that the minister had included with those instructions secret orders *not* to pay them.[18] Even worse, the tobacco monopoly was on the verge of collapse. Pedro reported in December 1846 that "Santa Anna is destroying the tobacco monopoly, because under the pretext of war he is taking all the products from whichever administration he can reach, without leaving enough for payments to the planters."[19] Although the Supreme Court ordered that Martínez del Río Hermanos should receive additional supplements from the 26 Percent Fund, this also was meaningless, as all payments to the fund were suspended.

The partners in Martínez del Río Hermanos began the new year of 1847 secure in the unhappy knowledge that their grand scheme had gone completely awry. Without the conversion, the bonds that Gregorio José bought in London were worthless. Faced with the prospect of having to begin payments for the tobacco bonds in June 1847, the Martínez del Ríos feared that their speculative adventure in Mexico also might fail. José Pablo concluded in December 1846,

Even though Pedro seems to me very adept at the management of ordinary business, I figure he is not right for these tricks, and if God wants to extract us properly from this enterprise, it is essential to appreciate the lesson so that we not return to meddle in another of similar class; because to my view these deals are not for us. Neither do I believe it is prudent on our part to let all our interests be exposed to the allures of this disgraceful country; in accordance with your principal project, we must try to divide risks. . . . I hope to God that the Bonds there rise with the payment of a dividend, and that you make use of the opportunity to sell, as the happenings at this moment make me fear that each day they will fall more.[20]

The Martínez del Ríos' hope for material salvation lay not with God, but with British intervention. Because of their past experiences, however, they were pessimistic about aid from that quarter:

It happens that the Legation is against us and . . . the Consul is really the Minister. I have been told by a good source that all the secrets of the Legation are in the pockets of the same Consul and Escandón; by another source, less reliable, I have heard it said that Mr. Bankhead filled his money bag with the Convention deal. For some time it was supposed that Doyle was sold out to Escandón, and if the English Government knew what went on here no doubt it would fire this Mr. Minister.[21]

Stymied in Mexico, Martínez del Río Hermanos turned its attention to the British Foreign Office in London. The object now was to convert the tobacco debt into something analogous to the 5 Percent Fund—to cloak the tobacco bonds with diplomatic status—transforming an internal public debt into an international obligation. As José Pablo explained, "it would be more advantageous to depend on the customs instead of the tobacco funds that the military is constantly usurping, etc., and whose own existence is somewhat precarious, as in the interior there always have been and continue to be many plots for the freedom of tobacco."[22]

It must have seemed that their prayers had been answered in the spring of 1847 when the Martínez del Ríos learned from Thornton that Great Britain would aid them because the Mexican government had illegally disregarded the Supreme Court decision. For added insurance, the family in Mexico sent Gregorio José detailed instructions about the tactics he should pursue in London. Domingo Ansoátegui suggested, "This is a new motive for you to take care to speak with Mr. Addington; even though if for that you must sacrifice your intellect, comfort, and money if it is necessary to give, as in all the world the latter is the soul of business, with the difference that in some parts, as here [Mexico], one gives in coin, and in others in ice cream, punch, or Turkeys."[23]

Following instructions from the Foreign Office, Bankhead sent a note to the Mexican foreign minister, Manuel Baranda, in May 1847, conveying his government's concern that the government of Mexico abide by the Supreme Court decision.[24] But already the American army was approaching the capital from the east, and what government as still existed in Mexico lacked the resources to pay the debt. The occupation forces abolished the tobacco monopoly in areas under their control, flooding Mexico with cheap Virginia tobacco and ruining prospects that the monopoly could soon produce income.[25] The British government replied to Martínez del Río Hermanos's request that the United States pay an indemnity for damages to the tobacco monopoly with the observation that "the persons who have had such a monopoly pledged to them will have their remedy against Mexico."[26] Although Martínez del Río Hermanos was obliged to await the outcome of the war before its claims could be resolved, the demands of its own creditors could not be postponed. To help cover the cost of tobacco bonds purchased in June 1845, the firm borrowed $150,000 from Francisco Guati in May 1847. Another payment of $183,200 was owed to Béistegui in December 1847 for bonds acquired in August 1846.[27]

The suspension of hostilities in 1848 brought no relief. Before the first installment of the promised $15 million indemnity from the United States reached Mexico, the *agiotistas*, politicians, and other interested parties began lining up for their share of the windfall. To keep Martínez del Río Hermanos from sharing in the bounty, the Law of 14 June 1848 expressly forbade the government to pay the creditors of the tobacco debt with indemnity monies. As the principal creditor and agent for the tobacco bonds, Martínez del Río Hermanos was the target of vicious political attacks. Ironically, since purchasing its share of the bonds, Martínez del Río Hermanos had not yet collected even one peso toward payment of the tobacco debt. At the firm's insistence, in November 1848 the British Legation began to press the Mexican government for a settlement when it became apparent that otherwise the firm would be left out entirely.[28]

A new scheme hatched by MacKintosh and Escandón helped as much as British intervention to bring about the long-awaited resolution of the tobacco debt. In March 1847 José Pablo reported, "It is said that MacKintosh has his eyes on renting the tobacco monopoly; it seems he wants to follow the same route of a certain friend of ours [Barrio] who was ruined by meddling in that business."[29] MacKintosh passed a note to Béistegui proposing that past differences be set aside—that Rubio should draw up plans for a company formed by the tobacco planters in Veracruz and the tobacco debt bondholders in Mexico City. After paying rent to the government for the use of the monopoly, all profits would be divided between the planters, the bondholders, and the partners in the company. A fixed share would be set aside to finance conversion of the foreign debt. From Paris, Escandón wrote Gregorio José in August 1847, extolling the proposed enterprise as a "brilliant business" and urging the Martínez del Ríos to forgive past misunderstandings. On 18 August 1848 the new company signed a contract to rent the tobacco monopoly from the government.[30]

Pedro and Domingo Ansoátegui were eager to join the venture; José Pablo, remembering Barrio's experience and fearing Escandon's treachery, vetoed the idea. Martínez del Río Hermanos looked favorably on any measure that might revive the defunct monopoly, but it would not participate as an investor. Neither would Rubio, because of his dislike for MacKintosh. As José Pablo predicted, MacKintosh's investment in the Tobacco Company of 1848 proved to be the consul's undoing. Investors in the tobacco monopoly needed large financial reserves, as profits in these ventures would be forthcoming only after four or five years of patient waiting. Overextended in other speculations, caught without cash, and with his credit exhausted, MacKintosh was forced to begin selling off his assets (including his share in the tobacco company) in 1850 as a prelude to personal bankruptcy.[31]

As had been the case with the Empresa del Tabaco in the previous decade, the Tobacco Company of 1848 provided a medium in which empresarios might pool their financial and political resources to promote large-scale banking and speculative operations. On 4 July 1849, in a transaction unrelated to the tobacco monopoly, the Tobacco Company purchased for $30,000 the properties of a bankrupt English enterprise that had worked the Real del Monte mines. Less than two years later, a new deposit of rich silver ores was uncovered. The partners of the Tobacco Company of 1848, Escandón, Béistegui, and Miguel Bringas, became the wealthiest empresarios of the era—forever free from the specter of the liquidity crisis that haunted their contemporaries. Not in their company was MacKintosh, who went bankrupt a moment too soon, nor were the Martínez del Ríos and Rubio, who, fatefully, declined the opportunity.[32]

The 6 Percent Fund, 1849-1851

Although the Martínez del Ríos failed to share in the bonanza promised by the Tobacco Company, there was the consolation that their long-hoped-for goal of converting the tobacco debt into a convention watched over by a great foreign power had been realized. On 26 January 1849 General Herrera (as the president of Mexico), Martínez del Río Hermanos (as the agent for the tobacco bondholders), and Percy Doyle (as the representative of the British government) jointly signed a convenio whereby the government of Mexico pledged to repay the debts owed to the tobacco bonds.[33] The Tobacco Company of 1848 was to deliver $16,000 monthly to Martínez del Río Hermanos. In addition, a 6 percent quota was detached from the 26 Percent Fund to create two separate public debt funds—the 6 Percent Fund and the 20 Percent Fund. The former was capitalized at $3,462,000. New 6 Percent Fund bonds in that amount were issued and exchanged for an equal amount of tobacco debt bonds and other internal debt issues. The convention obliged Mexican customs houses to remit separate *libranzas* to Martínez del Río Hermanos as the *apoderado* of the 6 Percent Fund. Table 40 lists creditors of the 6 Percent Fund in June 1851.

Table 40
Creditors of 6 Percent Fund, June 1851
(Current Pesos)

Creditor (Nationality)	Principal and Interest Owed	% of Total
Martínez del Río Hermanos (British)	$1,003,348.97	32.6
Juan Antonio Béistegui (Spanish)	841,122.61	27.3
Benito Maqua (Spanish)	354,053.55	11.5
Muriel Hermanos (Spanish)	155,974.87	5.1
Edward J. Perry (British)	31,837.33	1.0
John S. Bengough (British)	251,899.03	8.2
Rafael Beraza (Mexican?)	18,621.85	0.6
Manuel Escandón (Mexican?) (Spanish?)	156,749.65	5.1
Viuda de Echeverría e Hijos (Mexican)	138,158.25	4.5
Francisco Fagoaga (Mexican)	74,627.32	2.4
Agüero González & Company (Mexican)	43,004.47	1.4
Juan Rodríguez de San Miguel (Mexican)	8,601.10	0.3
Total	3,077,999.00	100.0

Source: Martínez del Río Hermanos to Percy Doyle, Mexico City, 20 June 1851, FO-204-107:240.

With the 6 Percent Fund, Martínez del Río Hermanos enjoyed a ratio of 1 percent shares in customs duties per 100,000 pesos of government indebtedness of better than 1:6. Creditors of the 20 Percent Fund faced a ratio worse than 1:146. Whereas the principal of the 6 Percent Fund was about $3.5 million, that of the 20 Percent Fund was $88 million (if all internal public debts were consolidated there).[34] Each fund had a 6 percent quota of customs duties. An international treaty protected the 6 Percent Fund; Mexico governed the 20 Percent Fund. When the $15 million indemnity had been squandered and the Mexican government needed revenues from customs duties to sustain itself, it chose to evade its obligations to the 20 Percent Fund and its national creditors rather than to jeopardize relations with Great Britain. In 1849 and 1850 General Arista's government paid into the 6 Percent Fund a total of $299,811. In contrast, the 20 Percent Fund received only $147,721 to cover a debt nearly thirty times larger.[35] For national creditors, prejudicial treatment of the 6 Percent Fund was less threatening than the proliferation of such quotas assigned to creditors with foreign connections. For the British, there was the 20 percent quota for the London debt, the 2 Percent and 1 Percent Fund, the 5 Percent Fund, and now the 6 Percent Fund—altogether 33 percent of Mexico's maritime customs duties. The Spanish and the French had their own conventions and their own quotas. Although the London debt was generally recognized as a legitimate national obligation, native creditors who were justly terrified that nothing would be left over to pay their debts were quick to complain that many of the credits protected by the foreign conventions were no different from their own. For these reasons, the creation of the 6 Percent Fund provoked a profound political reaction among creditors who lacked foreign connections.

The *apoderados* of the 26 Percent fund campaigned against the partition of the fund on two fronts—in the courts and in the Congress. Although their appeal to the Supreme Court failed to produce conclusive results, the *apoderados* were more successful in Congress. Many of the *agiotistas* prejudiced by the creation of the 6 Percent Fund were deputies and senators sitting on congressional finance committees. Their indignation took the shape of a proposed law to consolidate the public debt. The 6 Percent bonds would be penalized with a 17 percent discount before being forcibly included in a new consolidated debt fund. The legislation easily passed through the Chamber of Deputies, but failed to make it through the Senate.[36]

This setback was the result of two unresolved problems. First, the nationalist *agiotistas* were a minority faction within the Congress. They had only begun to coalesce around the newly formed Liberal party and they had not yet reached political understandings with other interest groups.[37] Yet, as was clear from Domingo Ansoátegui's sardonic account of Francisco Yturbé's political misfortunes in November 1849, the Mexico City speculators-turned-politicians and liberal-minded import merchants on the coast might, after all, share some common interests:

Dn. Francisco Yturbé entered for the second time the Ministry of Hacienda, and the deeds of his ministerial life, reduced to ten days, are the following. Initiative that he be conceded authority to dispose of and to negotiate with the $3,540,000 that must be received from the United States—received in the Chamber of Deputies . . . with disapproval . . . various visits to the Senate Chamber, beginning the first one by giving them a scolding; that was answered by another, Pedraza telling him he was an Ignoramus, etc.; afterward there was more maiming, but S.E. [Yturbé] proposed as a means of Salvation, that they would convert the customs duties into a river of gold, that the prohibitions would be lifted, as that would not prejudice industry and besides too much protection had been given—his proposal was not received with cries of approval—In conclusion, S.E. [Yturbé] ceased to exist [as Minister of Hacienda] the tenth of the present month—his death, like his life, was abrupt.[38]

The second factor that helped to determine the outcome in 1849 was the vocal opposition of the foreign diplomatic community to any attempt to set aside the conventions. Percy Doyle sent a sharp note to the Mexican foreign minister on 8 November 1849, giving notice that the proposed law was contrary to the spirit and letter of signed protocols between Mexico and Great Britain.[39]

The following year nationalist sentiments could not be shunted aside. A broader Liberal coalition had enough clout to push the Ley de Crédito Público through Congress.[40] Effective 30 November 1850, this law created a $25.7 million fund into which most categories of the internal debt, including the conventions, were to be consolidated. To create public support for this legislation, proponents published stinging attacks on the conventions, especially on the 6 Percent Fund and its *apoderado*, Martínez del Río Hermanos. The pages of Liberal newspapers like the *Monitor Republicano* were crowded with these denunciations in 1850.[41] Manuel Payno, an influential Liberal deputy who helped to draft the law, conceded that it was aimed "particularly at the foreigners who acquired Mexican credits at ruinous prices to afterward make them valuable with the support and force of their Ministers."[42] The new law suspended payments to the public debt funds and conventions. Credits not incorporated into the consolidated fund within a specified period faced the threat of being deferred for ten years. To make the consolidated fund more attractive to creditors, the law promised to set aside $2.5 million from the war indemnity to amortize a portion of the principal placed in the fund. It promised to convert bonds such as those of the 6 Percent Fund by paying 40 percent of the face value in cash with the balance payable in the new 3 percent bonds of the consolidated fund. As most creditors must have known, $6 million would have been required to process all credits in the prescribed manner. In the end, even the promised $2.5 million was diverted to other uses, as the government struggled to stay solvent amidst unrelenting deficits.

Martínez del Río Hermanos's reaction to the new and threatening political offensive was immediate—and predictable. It delivered successive notes to Doyle in December 1850 and January 1851 asking that Great Britain intervene to undo the Law of 30 November 1850. For the firm, the purpose and implications of the legislation were obvious: "A total want of principle and complete disregard of all former engagements are rendered so glaring by that iniquitous law."[43] Again the British representative and the other foreign ministers applied pressure, but this time the executive and the Congress were determined to test the commitment of foreign governments to their conventions.

The Junta of Public Credit (a body, created by the public credit law, which consisted of the *apoderados* and principal creditors of the 26 Percent Fund) in January 1851 began to exercise its authority under the new law to receive and disburse all revenue from the maritime customs houses. On 14 February 1851, when Martínez del Río Hermanos's representative attempted to pick up the firm's share of *libranzas* for duties, he was informed by officials that they had "express orders from His Excellency the

President" not to deliver these because the firm had not "hitherto entered into any kind of compromise." On learning of the incident, Doyle intervened: "I spoke to the President . . . and orders were given to make over to Messrs. Martínez del Río the drafts they claimed."[44]

Despite his assurances to Doyle, Arista did not lift the suspension of payments. Because the indemnity had been gobbled up, attacking the quota of foreign creditors was the only means left to the government for increasing its income. Faced with official intransigence, Doyle sent more threatening notes to Arista's government in April and May of 1851, suggesting the likely consequences of violating the diplomatic agreements of 1842, 1843, and 1849.[45] Functionaries answered Doyle's protests with legalistic and pragmatic defenses of the government's behavior. They pointed out that the executive was constitutionally powerless to act because the suspension was mandated by a law of Congress. The acting minister of foreign relations, José María Ortiz Monasterio, defended the law as an essential measure "to oblige the national creditors to come forward and assist the government in its present state of near bankruptcy."[46] President Arista voiced his fear to Doyle that if he supported the conventions he would be ruined politically. His enemies in Congress would charge that he had sacrificed Mexico to foreign creditors. The British representative reminded him there was more to fear than Congress if payments were not resumed.[47]

After new delays, Doyle interviewed Arista again on the morning of 4 June 1851. He lectured the president on the dangers of intransigence at a time when Mexico needed the support of friendly European governments to counterbalance the aggressive designs of its hostile northern neighbor. Doyle boasted to the Foreign Office that the interview ended with "H.E. [Arista] begging me to assure Y.L. [Lord Palmerston, minister of foreign relations] that he would not under any circumstances break through force any diplomatic agreement" and that Arista "promised the amount due to Mssrs. Martínez del Río, either from the contributions or in such a manner as would be considered satisfactory." Doyle added that he had not formally withdrawn his protest because "in a country like Mexico where the most solemn engagements are so lightly broken through, too much faith cannot be placed on simple promises." Doyle warned that conflict between Great Britain and Mexico might be unavoidable because Arista was surrounded by advisers whose "dominant feeling is hatred to Foreigners."[48]

Skeptical of Doyle's earnestness in looking out for their interests, the Martínez del Ríos began making plans to lobby British policymakers directly. They wanted their English trading associates and acquaintances to join them in a Memorial addressed to Lord Palmerston, which would argue the need for a more forceful British posture toward a malingering Mexican government. Representatives of the Mexican government were no less active in London. Manuel Payno attempted to persuade Palmerston that the new law for public credit was just and necessary and that British interests had not been prejudiced by the Mexican government's position on this matter. He pointed out that in the three years since the end of the war with the United States his government had paid British creditors a total of $6.4 million.[49]

Meanwhile, Mexican officials attempted to measure the British commitment to the conventions. In a private interview requested by the minister of hacienda, Manuel Piña y Cuevas, in June 1851, Doyle answered a query about possible British reactions to a continued suspension of payments: "Perhaps the best answer I can give you is to recall to your mind the measures the conduct of the Greek government at length forced H.M. government to take, as well as what has lately taken place at San Salvador, and you cannot forget the speech made by Lord Palmerston in Parliament and the references made in it to other Spanish American Governments."[50]

In spite of the blunt language and a barrage of protests, nothing was resolved.[51] As the war of words escalated, Lord Palmerston instructed Doyle in July 1851 to warn Arista's government of "the serious consequences which must inevitably result from a violation of the engagements formally entered into with the British government."[52] Even with the world's strongest military power pressing hard, the stalemate continued into August and September. The Mexican Congress remained adamant in its intention to break the conventions and Arista refused to act without congressional approval. The leader of the intransigent faction in Congress was Martínez del Río Hermanos's old nemesis, Francisco Yturbé. Doyle explained to Palmerston that individuals like Yturbé had bought up widows' pensions and other credits and feared their claims would be set aside if those of foreigners were settled first.[53]

In the autumn of 1851 the finances of Martínez del Río Hermanos reached a critical stage. The firm depended wholly on loans for its solvency.[54] Its $1 million in 6 Percent Fund bonds were mortgaged to creditors. Its valuable licenses to import cotton remained in Yturbé's custody to guarantee the $200,000 loan the firm had received from its worst enemy in Congress. José Pablo complained of the injustice that weighed so heavily on the family's business: "Up till now these thieves had not given in; tomorrow the Junta of governors will convene even though they have not yet all arrived.—We must expect nothing from this, or from any other Junta.— They are resolved to throw down the Conventions, and I am glad, because that way the English Govt. will be obliged to show its teeth; That is our only hope."[55]

It did appear by late September 1851 that Great Britain's patience had been exhausted—that the conflict soon might enter a more violent stage. In a new interview, Doyle confided to Arista that, although the British government normally looked to "the Executive in Power . . . for redress," these irregular circumstances "will force H.M. Government to look for redress to the Nation at large." Doyle pointed out that the law on public credit was no excuse for inaction, as the government had disregarded these restrictions on more than one occasion. If the Congress could evade the law to pay its own salaries, then it could pay its debts. Not yet ready to surrender on the issue, Arista pleaded, "If all the quotas are returned, you will take from us the means of carrying on the government, for literally we have not a dollar in the Treasury."[56] In a second interview with Doyle, on 4 October 1851, Arista pledged secretly that if Congress refused to act he would evade the public credit law and set aside on his own authority 10 percent of the maritime customs duties to pay the British conventions. This same day the Congress convened a secret session to decide how the government should respond to the dangerous situation that had developed. At 9:00 P.M. the Chamber of Deputies approved a measure giving the executive authority to make a special arrangement for the conventions. Doyle warned that his government would wait no longer for a remedy and, in a show of theatrics, he delayed departure of the British mail packet from Veracruz for twenty-four hours to allow time for the Senate to approve the legislation. It did so, grudgingly, and the Law of 30 November 1850 was undone.[57]

There remained only the questions of how and under what terms the problems of the conventions would be resolved. The Mexican government insisted obstinately that the interest rate on the convention debts should be lowered to a level matching that offered to the consolidated public debt fund. The creditors themselves preferred armed British intervention to the surrender of the 1 percent to 2 percent monthly interest rates that their claims enjoyed. Doyle complained to his superiors that his clients "seem to conceive that no hesitation can be felt by H.M. Govt. in sending vessels of War to blockade the Ports of the Republic to ensure payment of their claims." In urging moderation, the British representative reminded the creditors that "there were other interests than theirs, other capital invested in mining and other speculations to be attended to." British commerce might be permanently prejudiced by a blockade because Mexico would be inundated with goods brought overland from the United States. For the creditors, as well, a blockade would be counterproductive: "One of the first results would be a revolution throughout the country, and a state of anarchy created, which would probably end in the separation of several States from the Union, an event which might prove fatal to your interests."[58] With his brusque manner, Doyle forced the creditors to see the restraints that governed the application of British foreign policy and he gave them an ultimatum: "You have seen that H.M. Government have afforded you every possible support, even to menacing this government; therefore the question to be answered now is, whether or not you will accept the terms proposed. If you do the question is settled. If you do not . . ."[59]

Despite their tough posturing, creditors like Martínez del Río Hermanos lacked the means to hold out long. The firm's depositors had begun to withdraw their funds under various pretexts, aggravating a serious cash flow problem. Those withdrawals reflected the firm's particular problems and the general lack of confidence that was sweeping the business community in 1851. As Doyle analyzed the situation, business and politics had been inseparably intertwined in Mexico, but now the government was hopelessly bankrupt:

> In other times, when there was a vast quantity of national property to be sold, some of the leading commercial houses came to the assistance of the Government in moments like the present by making with it more or less ruinous contracts, but now the Government has not that resource left, and as the Houses in question were more or less supported by such operations, the Government has become . . . momentarily bankrupt for want of support of those houses, while some of them from entering into wild speculations, forgetful that they no longer had the Government to fall back upon, have in like manner shared the same fate.[60]

Manning & MacKintosh and Guillermo Drusina & Company were among the casualties; if it could not soon secure refinancing of its indebtedness, Martínez del Río Hermanos might join them. Although his plans in Congress went awry, Francisco Yturbé (already a major creditor of the company) remained willing to lend the firm an additional $200,000. This loan kept the firm solvent through March 1853. For his services, Yturbé charged 1.25 percent monthly interest and took for collateral a mortgage on government debt issues nominally worth $1 million and an assignment for $60,000 in accounts owing from the sale of Miraflores's textiles.[61]

The Convention of 1851

Unhappy with the prospect of earning low interest on a debt it financed with high-interest loans, Martínez del Río Hermanos had to be content with victory on another front—incorporating formerly unprotected government debt issues into the new convention. The firm hoped to place $500,000 in 20 percent bonds into the new fund. That would give the banking house nearly $2 million in paper guaranteed by the British Empire. Pedro gloated, "If we obtain that as I expect, our friends in the 20 Percent, who have waged such a war on us, will be furiously angry in spite of the favor that we have done them."[62] As the probability increased that the firm would win for itself a new convention, its associates in the tobacco debt and the 6 Percent Fund became anxious they might be left out. Béistegui, Maqua, and Muriel Hermanos called on the Spanish minister in Mexico to ensure that their bonds would be included in the new arrangement.[63]

After a delay to allow all parties to jockey for position, Percy Doyle and José Ramírez, the Mexican foreign minister, signed on 4 December a diplomatic convention for the settlement of all British claims in Mexico.[64] The pact combined the conventions of 1842, 1843, and 1849 with other reclamations to create a new public debt fund capitalized at $4,984,214. On this sum, the Mexican government was obliged to pay 5 percent annual interest on the principal and 3 percent annual interest on past due interest. After four years these rates would be increased to 6 percent and 4 percent, respectively. The fund was granted a 12 percent quota of maritime customs duties, but because of a continuing deficit in payments, this was increased to 15 percent in November 1852 and to 16 percent in 1854. Named as the *apoderado* for the Convention of 1851, Martínez del Río Hermanos received the quota of *libranzas* directly from the customs houses. With this arrangement, the creditors of the convention had won for their private use more than half of the revenues available to the Mexican government in 1851.

For his efforts in arranging this settlement, the Foreign Office commended Doyle, and Queen Victoria promoted him to minister plenipotentiary to Mexico. Her instructions to the ambassador included the usual remonstrances to look out for British commercial interests, but they also contained secret provisions that ordered Doyle to procure intelligence relating to troop movements and military fortifications. If an armed intervention were required, Great Britain would be prepared.[65]

With all its income pledged to third parties, Arista's bankrupt government easily succumbed to a conservative coup in 1853. It was succeeded by a new government headed by Santa Anna, who was occupying the presidential chair for the eleventh time since 1833. Although the demise of Arista's liberal government removed the threat of ideologically inspired attacks on the conventions, Santa Anna was tempted to menace the quota for practical reasons—the need for income, any kind of income, to keep his regime afloat.

After a prolonged period of depression, there was a large increase in shipping in the autumn of 1853, and the customs houses in the ports began receiving considerable revenues. Ignoring warnings from Doyle that schemes to reduce the convention's quota "would probably lead to such disorders throughout the Republic as might be disastrous to the present administration," Santa Anna diverted funds from the quota to his own uses.[66] By March 1854 the convention was $188,000 in arrears. Applying pressure from another direction, Addington, the undersecretary of state for Great Britain, called on the Mexican minister in London, J. M. Castillo y Lanzas, to express his government's dismay with Mexico's failure to comply with sacred obligations. After listening to the now familiar liturgy of veiled threats from the British government, Castillo apologetically informed Lord Clarendon, the British foreign minister, that although dire necessity—the need for funds to combat revolts in Baja California and Southern Mexico—had forced this temporary measure on his government, Mexico remained deferential to the convention and its agents.[67]

To raise cash, Santa Anna's regime was prepared to sell off national properties, but none were left. The church owned valuable properties, but the defense of corporate privileges and properties was the cornerstone of the Conservative movement and an open attack on that quarter was out of the question. Instead, Santa Anna preferred to sell national territory. Under the terms of the Treaty of Mesilla, which was signed in December 1853 and ratified in March 1854, the United States paid Santa Anna $10 million for a small tract of land in Northern Mexico. When news of the sale leaked out, the commerical houses of Mexico rushed to lend money to his government. Like the others, Martínez del Río Hermanos counted on winning a part of this prize for itself. In March 1854 the firm sent Doyle a persuasive note asking that a portion of the Mesilla revenues be applied to bring the convention account up to date.[68]

In an interview with Santa Anna in May 1854, Doyle secured the promise of a share of Mesilla monies for the convention.[69] In London Addington proposed the same project to the Mexican minister and no objections were voiced. These proved to be empty gestures, a foretaste of a new and devastating tactic for dealing with the British—promise them everything and do nothing, a variation of the colonial formula, "Obedezco pero no cumplo." El Santo avoided the surrender of a single peso from the Mesilla revenues and he continued to siphon from the convention's quota of customs revenues.

By October 1854 the convention was $466,000 in arrears. Again the Foreign Office showed its teeth, instructing Doyle to convey the following message: "If the Mexican Govt. desires to maintain friendly relations with England and prefers our alliance to our hostility, Her Majesty's Governt. trust that no further complaints such as those which the above mentioned Convention has given rise to will be preferred against the Mexican Govt."[70] Santa Anna responded to this tangible threat by surrendering to Martínez del Río Hermanos another state resource—the right to administer and collect the *derechos de muelles* charged to ships using the port of Veracruz.[71]

In June 1854 Pedro visited the Mexican consul in New York, General Juan Almonte, who had just received the first installment of the Mesilla indemnity. Pedro exclaimed, "I had in my hand the drafts for $7,000,000 and in that moment I admired the confidence of Sta. Anna in placing this sum in the hands of one man."[72] Since the consul was fired because of much-publicized irregularities in the handling of those funds, that trust may have been misplaced. From Philadelphia in July 1854, Pedro instructed his partners in Mexico City, "Do not miss the opportunity of the stay of O.e [Manuel Olasgarre] in the Ministry [of Hacienda]!"[73] In late July Olasgarre approved a contract awarding Martínez del Río Hermanos a 2 percent commission for transferring $1 million from New York to the National Treasury in Mexico City. Apart from this gesture (worth $20,000), the Martínez del Ríos were never able to use their friend's influence to capture a share of Mesilla monies for the convention debt.[74]

When the last dollar from the Mesilla sale had been spent, Santa Anna suspended payments to the convention in the spring of 1855. The British talked loudly, but they were occupied with the Russians in the Crimea and they would not do more than talk. Impatient, and fearing what seemed to be in store for the family, José Pablo began to promote an unlikely scheme to transfer the convention to the United States, trading bonds for land. Writing from Georgetown, Pedro warned José Pablo not to try to do business with Santa Anna: "Take much care with El Santo del Día. We are little angels for him. Do not be precipitous in undoing our convention, as I have the hope that for us it has returned to a more tranquil life. What one has to study is the way of escaping the storm that we have on the horizon, and that is so intense I can read the barometer from here, but there is no way to avoid it."[75] Remembering his experience with Texas lands, Gregorio José also opposed the project. Powerless to extract themselves from their speculations in the public debt, the Martínez del Ríos waited passively in the summer of 1855 to see what new surprises would emerge from the Mexican political landscape.[76]

Out of money and out of ideas, Santa Anna's regime was swept away by a profound nationalist reaction. Guiding this blossoming liberal political movement was the premise that to survive as a nation Mexico would have to put its financial house in order. According to the rumors of the day, Santa Anna and the Conservatives were prepared to sell Yucatan and Tehuantepec to the United States. Sonora might go to the French. Where would the process stop? The self-interest of speculator-politicians like Yturbé gave the Liberal party a socioeconomic base and a political relevancy that previously was absent in the Liberal movement. In common with the few genuinely disinterested elements in the Liberal party, native creditors had come to share a practical enthusiasm for fiscal responsibility and autonomy. They viewed with apprehension the fact that private firms (especially foreign firms) could capture a large share of tax revenues without the state being able to exercise any control. They opposed any arrangement that jeopardized the integrity of a state they had all come to depend on. The painful experience of the first quarter century of national life had begun to transform the attitudes of Mexico's dominant class. To sustain themselves and the state, Liberals would reclaim traditional sources of government revenues—breaking the conventions—and they would tap new income sources—dismembering the church and the civil corporations and selling their properties.[77] Almost in spite of themselves, state and society in Mexico would begin to drag one another into the modern age.

After expelling Santa Anna, Juan Alvarez's government lifted the suspension of payments to the public debt in November 1855. For Martínez del Río Hermanos, this good news was just a brief interlude to a prolonged nightmare—a replay of the drama of 1850 and 1851, with old and new characters and a different ending. For the overture, in November 1855 Manuel Payno published an exposé of the English Convention, casting the Martínez del Ríos as conniving foreigners whose vile speculations helped to ruin the fortunes of loyal national creditors and to bankrupt the National Treasury.[78] Payno's accounting of the history of the public debt was colored to suit political convenience and many charges were grossly untrue.[79] As before, the bombastic press campaign against the conventions signaled the promulgation on 1 January 1856 of a new law on public credit. This law named a Commission on Public Credit to receive and distribute all customs revenues.[80] Concurrently, the government repealed decrees that allowed up to 15 percent of customs duties to be paid in public debt bonds. Following a well-worn script, the British minister in Mexico, George Lettson, was invited by Martínez del Río Hermanos in February 1856 to deliver the first of many notes protesting this law and its violations of the Convention of 1851.[81]

After giving verbal pledges that the convention would be respected, Payno ordered the maritime customs houses to cease giving up revenues to the agents of Martínez del Río Hermanos in the ports and to deliver such revenues only to the Commission on Public Credit. Again, the Mexican government adopted the clever policy of verbally complying with every request of the British government while doing exactly the opposite. A standard scenario was for Martínez del Río Hermanos to protest the continuing suspension of payments. The British minister would demand that payments be restored. A Mexican official replied that orders had been given and that the agent for the convention would be paid. The firm would produce evidence that the government had lied and that it was using convention revenues to pay other creditors. Then the cycle would begin again.[82]

In its many years of dealing with government intrigues, Martínez del Río Hermanos developed an extensive and sometimes effective intelligence system.[83] After the Mexican minister of foreign relations assured Lettson that orders had been issued to pay the firm's agent in Tabasco, the firm retrieved a copy of the government's order to the Tabasco customs house directing it to remit all duties to the Committee on Public Credit. To answer allegations that payments had been resumed in Mazatlán, the firm offered as proof to the contrary correspondence that identified the ships, cargoes, consignees, and customs duties paid in that port. Its agent reported that in July 1856 the consignee of the cargo from the *Dancer* had paid duties totaling $59,000. Of this, $9,440 belonged to Martínez del Río Hermanos and should have been delivered to its agent by customs officials. Instead, a Mr. Afuría received all the duties under a separate agreement with the government. The same Mr. Afuría arranged to take all the duties from ships that had not yet arrived, the *Auguste*, the *Antilla*, and the *Fairy*. Indignant because these abuses were commonplace, the firm complained in November 1856 "that whilst we are led to believe by such orders that our assignment is properly attended to, the portions of duties belonging to it, and which strictly speaking can only be considered as our private property, is constantly taken to pay more favored creditors, particularly in Veracruz."[84] In Veracruz alone more than $240,000 had been diverted illegally from the convention between January and October 1856.

The response of Martínez del Río Hermanos to such abuses was despair over the reluctance of the British government to use force, but this was coupled with a determination to cultivate closer and more direct relationships with the policymakers in London. The firm protested to Lettson in June 1856 that it had been betrayed by complacent British officials in Mexico:

In vain did we submit to accept 3 p. cent. ann. interest for our money, instead of 6, 12, 18, and even 24 p. cent. ann. to which various claims were previously entitled ... thus depriving ourselves of our money for a number of years and consequently losing all the opportunity . . . of turning that money to advantage . . . on his part Mr. Doyle distinctly assured us that if we submitted to such sacrifices we should have the constant and strenuous support of the Mission to ensure the fulfillment of those hard conditions.[85]

The firm made certain that the British foreign minister in London, Lord Clarendon, was properly tutored about the unhappy developments in Mexico. It composed and delivered to him a lengthy reply to Payno's published attacks on the convention and it commissioned Thomas Worrall to give Clarendon a personal account of the attack on the convention and to explain the menace to British interests that this represented. The Martínez del Ríos' impressive network of English friends worked for the same purposes. The results of the lobbying campaign were mixed. Worrall announced in June 1856 that Clarendon was convinced a forceful approach was needed if the convention were to be saved. Soon afterward, he was obliged to amend his report. Agents of the Mexican government persuaded him that Mexico had changed its policy and would respect the convention.[86]

In fact, despite Martínez del Río Hermanos's insistence to the contrary, there had been a shift in the Liberal government's attitude toward the conventions. Internal conflicts over the functioning of the Commission on Public Credit led to Payno's dismissal as minister of hacienda in June 1856. He was replaced by the more temperate Miguel Lerdo de Tejada, who consigned the commission to oblivion.[87] The Mexican government was moving away from a deliberate confrontation with foreign creditors as it acted to resolve the problem of corporate privileges and properties. Faced with the prospect of paying a high cost (perhaps political dismemberment by the Great Powers) if it tried to break by force the British, Spanish, and French conventions, the alternative of a showdown with the church seemed to promise a more attractive mixture of risks and profits. The government of Ignacio Comonfort continued periodically to divert funds from the conventions for its own uses, but for purely pragmatic reasons. To minimize these losses for the convention, British words, and not deeds, were all that was required. For this, Martínez del Río Hermanos could count on the goodwill of the British minister in Mexico, George Lettson, who promised his friends in November 1856, "You may rely gentlemen upon my best endeavors being directed to obtain justices for the wrongs so frequently, I may say, so constantly, inflicted upon you."[88]

That the firm perceived this change in policy is suggested by its behavior in August 1856, when it deepened its interests in the convention and began a new public debt speculation. Nearing bankruptcy, Benito Maqua sold the remainder of his convention bonds to Martínez del Río Hermanos for $159,900 (payable in monthly installments ending in January 1860 and secured with a mortgage on Miraflores).[89] Such a commitment would seem mad, except for the prospect that the government now would respect the convention and that these convention bonds might rise in value because public debt issues could be used to buy the corporate properties being disamortized by the Liberal regime. What the firm failed to appreciate was that the disamortization might have a neutral or even opposite effect on the value of the convention bonds.

Before 1856, the 3 Percent bonds of the consolidated internal public debt fund were almost worthless, costing 6 percent to 7 percent of face value. Convention bonds, because of the foreign guarantee, were preferred by investors and could be marketed at higher prices, 40 percent to 50 percent of face value. Decrees allowing the use of public debt bonds as partial payment for disamortized property changed all that. Demand for the 3 Percent bonds increased; demand for the convention bonds decreased. Because of the large quantity of 3 Percent bonds in circulation, their cost did not rise significantly, but any decline in demand for the convention bonds was felt because of the compactness of the market. As the Martínez del Ríos surmised, convention bonds could be used to purchase property. But why use convention bonds when it was six or seven times cheaper to use 3 Percent bonds? In this manner, the quirk of comparative advantage precluded Martínez del Río Hermanos's joining other speculators in the rush to acquire the properties of the corporations.

The Gran Colombia Debt

The near-bankruptcy of Comonfort's government in the summer of 1856 gave the Martínez del Ríos an opportunity to buy the rights to a £63,000 debt owed Mexico by Gran Colombia. In 1826 the Mexican representative in London advanced Gran Colombia a portion of Mexico's English loan with the understanding that Gran Colombia was soon to receive its own loan and would reimburse Mexico. English bankers refused Gran Colombia's application and the country was unable to repay the advance. After it fragmented in the 1830s into New Granada, Venezuela, and Ecuador, each of the new nations assumed a proportional share of the debt to Mexico. Repeated attempts to recover the £63,000 produced nothing, as Mexico lacked the means to compel these nations to pay their foreign debts.[90]

In contrast, the Martínez del Ríos had impressive connections in the region. Born in Panama, they were citizens of New Granada. Pedro and Domingo Ansoátegui were New Granada's consuls in Mexico City. Through the Mosquera family, the Martínez del Ríos enjoyed access to impressive centers of power in New Granada. When in the autumn of 1839, at Gregorio José's urging, Pedro first proposed that Mexico cede the Gran Colombia debt to Martínez del Río Hermanos in exchange for internal debt issues in an equivalent amount, he was answered with a counterproposal from the Bustamante government that the firm pay $100,000 in cash. To this, Pedro replied "that in cash I would not give a real [$0.125], and that I considered it as an ancient debt of the country and because of pure patriotism I was going to exchange it."[91] Motives other than patriotism prompted the firm to make a second offer in February 1840: $40,000 in cash and $275,000 in preindependence credits and *pagas corrientes*.[92] Assuming this paper could be acquired at 10 percent of nominal value, the actual cost of the debt would be $67,500. Again, nothing came of the offer. Mexico expected that its representative in Bogotá might arrange a settlement.

Pedro complained in 1846 that the price asked by the government was still too high, even though the deal could be made in 26 Percent bonds if one worked through the minister of hacienda, Antonio Haro y Tamariz. The problem was one of "incidental" costs: "Even though I believe that while Dn. Ant.o [Haro] is in power it could be done with these [26 Percent bonds] or with paper costing less, this would cost good pesos for the reasons that you are not ignorant of, as to these people the good of the country means nothing, but they do look out for their own purse, and Dn. Ant.o is just the same."[93] There were more opportunities in 1847 to secure the debt cheaply, except that Martínez del Río Hermanos—like the government—had little cash to spare.[94]

Comonfort's government needed money desperately in the summer of

1856. It had been unable to float bonds on a $1 million forced loan from the Diocese of Puebla. With that in mind, Martínez del Río Hermanos announced on 5 August 1856 that it would be pleased to aid the government by purchasing from it the Gran Colombia debt for $400,000 in 3 Percent bonds and $30,000 in cash. Eleven days later Comonfort accepted an amended proposal to purchase the debt for $30,000 in cash and $800,000 in 3 Percent bonds. Assuming $50,000 was a reasonable value (6.25 percent) for these bonds, the formal cost of the operation was $80,000, which is the price the French minister cited in his report of the transaction to his government. As the face value of the Gran Colombia debt in 1856 was about $800,000, counting principal and interest, the real cost to the firm was only about 10 percent, leaving plenty of room for profit in the future. There were, however, hidden costs of the sort Pedro had warned about in 1846. The French minister alleged that to get its contract Martínez del Río Hermanos lent Comonfort $100,000. Although this transaction is not recorded in the firm's accounts, there are indirect indications of hidden costs. The firm listed the value of the debt in its books as $151,087. Usually, such valuations reflected the costs of acquiring a particular asset, not its market value.[95]

Two days after acquiring the debt from the Mexican government, Martínez del Río Hermanos began its effort to collect from the government of New Granada. It named Dr. Justo Arosemena, a native of Panama and a New Granadan senator, as its agent. Arosemena orchestrated a rigorous lobbying effort in Bogotá, but there was a considerable residue of opposition to be overcome. He secured a prompt settlement, though with more sacrifices than his clients would have wished. New Granada agreed to pay its share (50 percent) of the principal and interest owed since 6 October 1827. Repayment was made in New Granadan internal debt bonds, themselves of little value, so it is unlikely that in cash values the transaction yielded more than 25 percent of the nominal value of the debt. As the cost of acquiring the debt from Mexico was about 20 percent, that left only a marginal profit. Ecuador and Venezuela refused to make any payments on the debt. With this complex speculation in an international public debt, the firm tied up capital in an asset that, however valuable it might be in the future, was neither productive nor readily convertible to cash.[96]

Prelude to Ruin

Through most of 1857 it appeared that Martínez del Río Hermanos's wild gamble with the convention might pay off. The 16 percent quota of import duties continued to produce a large amount of income. Though it spared the convention, the Comonfort regime's attacks on corporate interests provoked an unexpectedly savage reaction from the church and the army. During the bloody three-year civil war lasting from December 1857 through December 1860, both sides seized and used all the revenue sources within their reach. With commerce paralyzed and payments to the convention interdicted after 1857, Martínez del Río Hermanos had no income to service the enormous private debt it had accumulated in two decades of doing business in Mexico. In other times the firm weathered periods of crisis by mortgaging more of its belongings or by using the friendly persuasion of its partners to induce depositors to increase their investments. In 1858 there was nothing left that lenders would accept for security. To Béistegui alone the firm owed $366,409. To prevent seizure of its mortgaged properties, Martínez del Río Hermanos was obliged to sell its convention bonds to Hermengildo Viya on 5 August 1858. In exchange for commercial credits worth $509,000, the firm ceded to its Veracruz friend sixty-nine bonds issued in denominations of $5,000, $10,000, and $20,000, with a combined face value of $1.2 million. Viya paid off Béistegui; the balance was credited against the large debt Martínez del Río Hermanos owed Viya. Martínez del Río Hermanos was granted an option until 31 December 1858 to repurchase the bonds.[97]

At the same time it was making this pact with Viya, Martínez del Río Hermanos actively participated in the discussions preliminary to British recognition of General Félix Zuloaga's conservative regime. In these meetings the firm's partners registered verbal complaints and introduced documentary evidence of the losses and injuries caused by Mexico's failure to abide by the terms of the Convention of 1851. Under the provisions of the Otway Convention, signed 10 August 1858, Zuloaga's government was recognized in exchange for its pledges to deliver 16 percent of the maritime customs duties to Martínez del Río Hermanos.[98] This covenant was rendered meaningless when the Liberals occupied Veracruz.

Needing funds to buy more arms to fight the Conservatives, the Liberals refused to separate any portion of customs revenues for the use of foreign creditors. To punish the Liberals, a British naval force commanded by Captain Dunlop took up station outside the port of Veracruz on 24 January 1859. Its purpose was "to remove the just indignation with which Her Majesty's Government has viewed the frequent infringement of the rights of British subjects in Mexico."[99] In a new agreement concluded on 8 February 1859, the Liberals pledged to pay 24 percent of customs duties to Martínez del Río Hermanos. When the British lifted the blockade, the Liberals ignored the Dunlop Convention and suspended payments to the public debt. The following year Captain Aldam and the British fleet persuaded the Liberals once more to increase the size of the quota. The Aldam Convention also bound the Liberal government to dismiss any official "who shall again attempt to infringe the present agreement,"[100] but like the previous interventions it failed in practice to guarantee a sustained flow of government revenues into Martínez del Río Hermanos's cash boxes.

Three times in three years Great Britain energetically intervened to defend the Convention of 1851, but for Martínez del Río Hermanos the show of force was ineffective and far too late. Unable to pay its debt, the firm was obliged to surrender its bonds to Viya on 15 January 1859.[101] Later, after learning that Viya had resold a portion of the bonds to an unfriendly business rival, José Pablo vented his frustration:

Very badly I have learned of the last operation on the Convention by Dn. Hermengildo [Viya], because concretely I see no escape from the clutches of the tiger to whom we have been delivered; certainly our sad experience has made me know how hard can be the hearts of certain persons; that, combined with their great avarice, makes them capable of ruining a whole generation to increase their treasure a little more.[102]

What earned Viya such a hearty condemnation was his sale of convention bonds to the Lizardis, who were attempting to wrest representation of the convention away from the Martínez del Ríos. Since losing their bonds in January 1859, the family had been obsessed with the need to maintain their status as the *apoderado* for the convention. José Pablo insisted that this position belonged to the family "as a specie of property acquired with so many years of struggle and commitment."[103] It was crucial to their firm's survival for several reasons.[104] First, there was the sense of power it conveyed—the ability to call down the wrath of the British Empire—or so Martínez del Río Hermanos wished the public to believe. Second, the convention linked the firm to economic and political resources in both Mexico and Great Britain. Third, when payments resumed, the cash flow would give the firm liquidity, and the commission it earned as an agent would be a significant source of income. The family still owned a small amount of bonds (about $40,000), which it might be able to put to good use if it were agent. As late as the autumn of 1859 the Martínez del Ríos hoped to use the convention to launch one last spectacular business deal. In the end, none of their plans bore fruit, and by December 1859 they had become reconciled to failure. Although they managed to stave off the indignity of formal bankruptcy proceedings for one more year, their spirit had been broken. José Pablo summed up their feelings: "The state of our House, each day more critical and precarious, is naturally a nightmare that incessantly torments me, and being already tired of a struggle so painful, there are times that I would like to bring it to an end, shutting down the machine . . . until at last the day of resurrection arrives."[105]

Conclusion

Speculation in government debt issues, based as it was on the prerogatives of British nationality, contributed in no small way to the bankruptcy of Martínez del Río Hermanos and, as José Pablo so poignantly noted, to the ruin of a whole generation. Under certain conditions, however, this activity was more rewarding than other kinds of business endeavors in early national Mexico. Precisely what were the profits and losses and who were the beneficiaries of Martínez del Río Hermanos's speculations in government debt issues? A reexamination of the firm's most important operations yields suggestive conclusions.

Only after 1840 did Martínez del Río Hermanos begin to make large investments in this area. That was a result of the comparative advantages these speculations had demonstrated in 1838, 1839, and 1840. Unfortunately, the political economy of debt speculation changed drastically after 1841 (the outcome of the firm's speculations from 1842 through 1858 is summarized in table 41). Public debt issues protected by the British Conventions of 1842 and 1843 produced good returns if a 50 percent value is assigned to the unpaid portions consolidated in the Convention of 1851. Operations in other funds, placed without British protection in the 25 Percent/26 Percent Fund, caused heavy losses. To simulate the actual costs of employing the firm's capital for these speculations, an arbitrarily chosen finance charge (12 percent annual interest on the principal for three years) is applied in column 5 of table 41. The costs and income for the 1849 Convention are included (to simplify computations) with the 1851 Convention.

The buying and selling prices of Martínez del Río Hermanos's shares in the 1851 Convention were about equal (roughly 40 to 45 percent). Moreover, its share of government payments to the conventions between 1842 and 1858 was a large sum, equal in magnitude to the simple cost of buying the shares. What, then, explains how and why this speculation ruined the firm? When the costs of financing the acquisition of the tobacco bonds (beginning in June 1847) and the costs of continuing to finance this debt over the next ten years at money market rates (15 percent annually) are considered, the firm's problems with its speculations can be appreciated. Altogether, the firm recovered from its quotas of customs duties and from the sale of its debt issues about 50 percent of the nominal $2 million in bonds it had acquired. Simple costs for those bonds were about 33 percent, leaving room for a profit. But for whom? If reasonable (by the standards of the day) finance charges are included, the costs for these bonds zoom to 70 percent. This calculation is consistent with Pedro's observation in 1856 that the firm would need 75 percent from the bonds to make even a modest profit. The real winners in the firm's speculations in the public debt were moneylenders like José Pacheco, Francisco Yturbé, and José Antonio Béistegui, who took all the income received from the government *and* a goodly portion of Martínez del Río Hermanos's capital. If the firm's debt speculations

Table 41
Speculations in Government Debt Issues, Martinez del Rio Hermanos, 1842-1858
(Current Pesos)

	A. 25 Percent	B. 2 Percent & 1 Percent	Debt Fund C. 5 Percent	D. 6 Percent	E. 16 Percent
Principal	NA	250,000	2,120,000	3,462,000	4,984,214[a]
Firm's nominal share/ % of whole	228,534/NA	32,602/13	295,804/15	1,142,460/33	2,291,046/46
Cost of firm's nominal share	87,377	5,248	105,360[a]	399,300	747,554
Other costs	31,456	1,889[b]	37,930[b]	NA[c]	855,000[d]
Government payments to whole	NA	250,000[e]	1,813,837[e]	NA	1,706,937[f]
Firm's share of government payments	NA	32,500	271,953	NA	644,982
Income to firm from sale or conversion	87,377	14,618[g]	95,242[g]	399,300[g]	504,000[h]
Total income from share to firm	87,377	47,118	367,195	399,300	1,148,982
Total costs to firm for share	118,833	7,137	143,930	399,300	1,602,554
Profit/loss	− 31,456	39,981	223,265	NA	− 453,472

Table 41 (continued)

Sources: Various CMRFH; Martínez del Río Hermanos to Percy Doyle, Mexico City, 20 June 1851, F0-204-107-240; AN-426-1856:441-443, 25 August 1856; AN-529-1859:2-15, 15 January 1859; Mexico, Ministerio de Hacienda y Crédito Público, *Memoria,* 1869-1870, pp. 376-378.

Notes: A. 25 Percent/26 Percent Fund; B. 1842 Convention; C. 1843 Convention; D. 1849 Convention; E. 1851 Convention. NA means not available or not applicable.

[a]Computed as A ($411,502) + B ($224, 889) + C ($1,269,892) + D ($3,077,931).

[b]Cost of financing principal for three years at 12 percent annual interest.

[c]Cost of financing included with 1851 Convention.

[d]Estimated finance costs, 1848-1858.

[e]Minimum; actual figure would be larger.

[f]Computed as 1848-51 ($803,837) + 1852-55 ($506,502) + 1856 ($211,828) + 1857 ($46,962) + 1858 ($137,808).

[g]As 50 percent of presumed value of portion included in 1851 Convention.

[h]Product of sale of $1.2 million of 1851 Convention.

between 1842 and 1858 are considered as a whole, then Martínez del Río Hermanos's partners lost through these operations $221,782, about two-fifths of their capital shares in the firm.

Because it overextended itself and because it used other people's expensive money to finance its speculations, Martínez del Río Hermanos was a loser. Harder to assess is the question of whether the firm maximized its income from these speculations by employing foreign nationality as a protective device. Before 1842 its commitments took place independent of such a strategy, but the successes of the 1842 and 1843 conventions showed how useful the British could be. With that experience in mind and with an unrealistic faith in the efficacy of British interventionism, the firm rushed into the fatal tobacco bonds speculation. To its surprise, it learned that such protection was neither effective nor unconditional. It was never able to force the Mexican government to pay its claims with the large amounts of cash secured in the war indemnity or with the sale of national territory. Those monies went into the pockets of favored creditors, avaricious politicians, and special interest groups. Armed intervention by Great Britain was counter-productive, as Doyle pointed out in 1851, or simply ineffective, as proven by events after 1857.

An alternative strategy would have been to cultivate good relations with all parties in the domestic political arena to ensure that governments of every political (and personalist) tendency would be receptive to the firm's input. An extraordinarily successful *empresario*, Manuel Escandón, did business with Liberals and Conservatives alike. Other businessmen-politicians, like Francisco Yturbé, invested their resources in the victorious Liberal party and were rewarded with rich profits. Because they counted exclusively on Great Britain, the Martínez del Ríos allowed the tentative Mexican connections they had developed in the early 1840s to atrophy. A call to the British minister became a conditioned response to whatever problem was on the agenda. This exaggerated reliance on foreign protection made the firm an easy target for political attacks and entangled it in a cataclysmic political confrontation after 1856. Although intellectually more at home with Liberals, the Martínez del Ríos were pushed by economic and political forces into an ill-fated fling with the Conservatives.

Why did the Martínez del Ríos fail to choose a more propitious strategy— emphasizing domestic instead of foreign political resources? As chapter 3 showed, the family lacked the *social* resources to make the strategy work. Socially, and so politically, they remained outsiders and, as such, they were at the mercy of a capricious political system. Forced loans, seizures, and other arbitrary acts by the state made up the political parameters of a hostile economic environment. Even for the initiated the perils were great. As this book has shown, public debt speculation was part of a great engine of income distribution, making and breaking fortunes according to the state's propensity to pay or not to pay its more favored creditors. The politically strong flourished; the weak and the indifferent perished. British protection did not permit the Martínez del Ríos to escape ruin, but it enabled them to delay it. Until the Liberals and their partisans overwhelmed and defeated speculative strategies based on plausible threats of foreign intervention, it was the best insurance the family could devise against the hard times when government revenue was scarce and there were more creditors than resources.

9. Kinship, Business, and Politics: A Historical Perspective

I have looked at selected problems of economic and political development through the perspective of family history. Using the case study method and a narrative style, I have tested general propositions about state and society against the unembellished, real-life experience of a single family over the course of a half century's residence in Mexico. An examination of the family economy and the microeconomies of family enterprises showed how commerce functioned (or failed to function) in early national Mexico. Taken as a body, the statistics on profitability and productivity and the reconstructions of investment portfolios and entrepreneurial strategies indicate the need for a revision of an admittedly limited historiography. The findings reported here are not definitive and they are subject to the methodological limitations listed in the introduction, but they do suggest the kinds of problems that future studies should deal with. The substantive content of this study corroborates the following arguments.

An interventionist state and a highly politicized economy, superstructural survivals of the colonial experience in New Spain, continued to be familiar fixtures in early national Mexico. Hence most economic activity—even that which mimicked modern forms of industrial capitalism—took place in intimate physical and spiritual proximity to the state. Besides relying on the state to define and to police the marketplace, Mexican *empresarios* manipulated the public debt to reapportion existing wealth within Mexican society. Unwitting prisoners of their own intrigues, they were incapable of producing new wealth with their many enterprises; much less could they begin to tear down the institutional barriers that restrained Mexican productivity. An attempt at industrialization based on import substitution of domestically produced cotton textiles was not frustrated by the free-trade imperialism practiced by the already industrialized nations like Great Britain. Instead, *empresarios* fell victim to the machinations of a political economy that they helped to build and to sustain in Mexico. There could be no other plausible outcome, as the *empresarios*' relationship to the state and to the Mexican institutional structure was opposite to that of their entrepreneurial counterparts in Western Europe and the United States. It should be emphasized that the economic failure did not result from the absence of a spirit of enterprise. Mexican *empresarios* were well educated, attuned to the latest philosophical currents of Western thought, and intimately acquainted with life in Europe and the United States. Guided by the profit motive, they manifested no psychological predilection for traditional modes of production. Their enterprises showed evidence of innovation, especially in regards to the introduction of new technology from abroad. Unfortunately, the installation of modern machines in Mexico did not, by itself, provoke a modernization of the social structure.

Because there was so little institutional support for a free marketplace based on individual initiative, comparative advantage, and the impersonal laws of supply and demand, and because no disinterested state apparatus ensured that all economic actors abided by formally established rules, family functioned as a nearly reliable surrogate for those absent institutions. The example of the Martínez del Río family suggests that the economy and polity of early national Mexico were structured to suit the needs of multifamily alliances and patron-client networks. These family-based groups monitored political and economic activity and restricted access to optimal opportunities to their membership. Entry into these clans was a function of marriage and required the investment of substantial social resources. The Martínez del Ríos misread or ignored the social cues and they paid a heavy price in economic and political setbacks.

Surface appearances notwithstanding, Mexican society always has been dynamic. Since the Conquest of Mexico in the sixteenth century, and continuing throughout the colonial era in New Spain, there was a constant circulation of elites based on social and political criteria rather than on purely objective economic considerations.[1] The dramatic upheaval of independence accelerated and intensified the process. New actors came and went, but the system itself defied change because of its enormous capacity to absorb new elements and to limit elite conflict through the mediation of family politics. The greatest drawback of this type of societal accommodation was that, although it managed conflict avoidance well, it eliminated salutary challenges to an antiquated economic system. Once integrated, economic actors had more to lose than to gain from making modifications to the system. Because profit continued to be a function of political resourcefulness, there were few incentives for increasing economic productivity.

By trading economic growth for social stability, society in New Spain remained remarkably tranquil for nearly three centuries. The shock of independence brought on by outside forces destroyed this fine balance. The system no longer guaranteed political peace and the cost of maintaining it was staggering. Yet the same forces that gave stability and integrity made change nearly impossible. Mexico's problem in the first half of the nineteenth century was not that it was socially disarticulated; rather, the intertwining of family economies and clientelistic politics had retarded social and economic differentiation.

Because Mexico lacked a bourgeoisie and a feudal aristocracy, its way out of the dilemma was different from the Western European model for the transition to capitalism. As the Mexican economy continued its resolute, downward plunge after independence, the dominant class sustained itself by borrowing, converting, or otherwise expropriating state resources for private gain. With increasing demands on its income and the loss of its revenue sources, the state suffered chronic fiscal strangulation. The diversion of its resource base progressively debilitated the state, and it became less and less capable of fulfilling its ordained role as mediator of society and director of the economy. Bereft of guidance and awash in a sea of political turmoil, the Mexican economy became increasingly disarticulated, mismanaged, and unproductive. As the private sector shrank, speculation in the poorly financed public sector swelled. Finally, the exhaustion by 1842 of a supply of national properties that could be assigned to creditors of the state without jeopardizing the vested interests of traditional sectors of society set off a chain reaction of controversy beginning with a bitter political contest for control of the public debt and ending in a bloody civil war and foreign intervention.

Conflict and change in Mexico became possible, and inevitable, because persistent economic reversals undermined the homogeneity and integrity of the monied class. The precipitating factor that destroyed class consensus was the debate over public finance. The Liberal party, a coalition of native creditors, import merchants of mixed nationalities, and disgruntled regional concerns, sought to redeem the national debt from foreign control by destroying the conventions. At the same time it hoped to rationalize the economic system by terminating the privileges of the corporations and forcing them to place their coveted properties on the market. Since the Liberals would use the state and a political process to enrich themselves, their actions were altogether consistent with the Mexican historical experience. Mexican liberalism was not propelled forward by the weight of foreign ideology, but by the inertia of the politicized Mexican economy.

Although the Liberal coalition was united by the hope that structural reforms could salvage partisan economic interests, the grander Liberal ideal and ideological underpinning that gave the movement its strength was pragmatic nationalism—the imperative need to preserve and protect the state essential to the survival and prosperity of Mexican society. Freeing the marketplace from precapitalist obstacles to economic growth and promoting economic liberalism were simply instrumental means to an end. Liberals did not attempt to redefine the relationship between polity and economy to cater to the whims of an entrepreneurial-minded constituency. Most *empresarios* were either apolitical opportunists or pragmatic conservatives. Although Mexican Liberals borrowed heavily from European liberalism to rationalize and legitimize their program, the substance of their movement was altogether different.

Even more poorly defined in a progammatic sense was the Conservative party in Mexico. In political terms it was less a coalition than an agglomeration. It had no platform, no generally recognized leadership, and no systematic doctrine other than the preservation and protection of established practices and privileges. Circumstance brough together soldier and priest, villager and bureaucrat, and artisan and *empresario*. Their only bonds were structural ties to the past and a shared anxiety, economically reinforced, about real or imagined reforms and social change. Embedded in the Conservative movement was a fateful alliance of convenience with Mexico's foreign creditors. Obliged to defend a system so moribund that it could no longer sustain even a shadowy semblance of the vital interventionist state that was the cornerstone of traditional social organization, the Conservatives could not mobilize a national consensus for their hopeless cause.

A political crisis and recurrent business failure, not indigenous economic development, induced a badly needed restructuring of Mexican institutional life. For modern Mexico, the significance of the economic and political misadventures that have been chronicled in this study is found in the Reform—the response of Mexican society to an impossible situation—and in the configuration of economic and political organization beget by Liberal reform. Consistent with Mexico's larger historical experience and with the priorities of Mexican liberalism, the dominant class in Mexico today is married first to the state and, afterward to the productive apparatus. A (functional) interventionist state and a politicized (mixed) economy are prominent features of the institutional landscape. Not surprisingly, family-based enterprises and extraordinarily complex clientelistic networks continue to flourish in that environment.[2]

10. Epilogue: The Martínez del Río Family, 1864-1984

The imperative to defend the claims of their nationals against Mexico provided a pretext for the Allied Occupation of Veracruz in 1861. Great Britain and Spain soon withdrew, but France did not. Having been decisively beaten by Liberals in the Three Years' War, Conservatives encouraged the pretensions of Napoleon III in a desperate attempt to undo La Reforma. For the Martínez del Ríos the French Intervention seemed to promise an escape from the disaster that had befallen them in Mexico. José Pablo explained how he came to be involved with the Conservatives: "After our house was ruined because the Government did not fulfill the pacts in which it had been involved for so many years the [the Convention of 1851], I was seduced by the single hope of salvaging that catastrophe."[1]

José Pablo joined the Mexican delegation that formally presented the crown of Mexico to Maximillian in April 1864. Because of his fine manners, comportment, and command of European languages, José Pablo was a logical choice as official spokesman for the delegation. The anomaly of his nationality was rectified after the coronation. The former Austrian prince naturalized as a Mexican citizen the Panamanian doctor who longed to be British. As a reward for his collaboration with the empire, José Pablo was inducted into the ranks of a new Mexican nobility, the Order of Guadalupe, and was appointed imperial emissary to the king of Greece and the sultan of Turkey.[2] The doctor accepted his commission eagerly:

I will remember constantly that through my mouth speaks the insignia of the Hapsburgs that God has conceded to us as a sign of his clemency . . . even though the actual state of my health is delicate, and though I am here involved in great projects that not only concern the fortune of my family, but that are also connected with the progress and prosperity of Mexico, I will not hesitate in putting aside everything.[3]

Accompanying the appointment was a £5,000 allowance that, given the collapse of personal and family fortunes, was sorely appreciated.

The new ambassador enjoyed a glorious tour of Greece and Turkey. He left London in early September 1864 bound for Constantinople. Proceeding by way of Paris, he was delayed in the French capital for several days while tailors outfitted him in a new wardrobe. From Paris he continued through Milan to Vienna and then down the Danube to Turkey. He brought along as a private secretary his nephew Pablo Doré y Martínez del Río, Manuel María's oldest son. The envoy pointed out in his report to the Mexican minister of foreign relations that, "in view of the Sumptuous Embassies that the other sovereigns have here, it would have been very sad and unattractive if I had been presented alone." José Pablo judged that because of "the great importance Orientals have in matters of form," his silk suits from Paris were not worthy of an appearance before the sultan. He ordered a new wardrobe. He described his favorite as "a coat of carmine velvet with very rich tassels and a border of gold equally rich with the Crown and the initials of our August Sovereign." In a splendid reception to honor the envoy, the sultan of Turkey decorated José Pablo with the Order of Mejidie, First Class. His nephew received the same decoration, Fourth Class. After a luxurious farewell party organized by the grand vizier, the doctor journeyed to Greece to see the king. There he received another commendation, the Royal Order of the Saviour. Deciding against an optional visit to deliver his credentials to the emperor of Persia, José Pablo began his return to Western Europe via Messina and Milan. Except for a violent argument with customs officials at Trieste who refused to recognize his diplomatic status, the trip ended splendidly.[4]

What José Pablo never imagined was that Maximillian's regime might soon collapse and that his light-hearted collaboration would prove costly. Ironically, his cooperation with the empire did not bring any material benefits to the family in Mexico. José Pablo had been working on a scheme to colonize Encinillas with Frenchmen, but nothing came of that. Given the large numbers of past and present creditors of the Mexican Treasury who joined Maximillian's entourage, it was not surprising that the emperor refused to return the church properties that had been purchased with public debt issues. But as Martínez del Río Hermanos had not been able to buy many of those properties, that policy brought few benefits to the family. In 1865 Gregorio José was obliged to pay a large sum to Maximillian's government after it audited the accounts for the house he purchased in 1856. That his brother was an imperial envoy counted for nothing in Mexico.[5]

In contrast to Conservative indifference, the Liberals took offense at José Pablo's activities on behalf of what it considered an illegal government. On 13 February 1865, Juárez decreed the confiscation of all the doctor's properties in Mexico. Twenty-two months later the Liberal government sold Encinillas to José Pablo's former tenants for $8,000. That ruined a colonization project José Pablo had pending with Baron Von Gerolt and Senator Aspinwall in Washington.[6] In December 1866, José Pablo, now a widower, wished to return with his children to join the family in Mexico, but he feared the reception he might receive: "I am in doubt about the risks I might run of being molested or even persecuted because of my political opinions and antecedents; the party that is now triumphant [the Liberal party] has been relentless and unsparing in its revenge."[7]

The following month Gregorio José felt compelled to warn his brother to postpone his return.[8] The French were withdrawing, Mexicans who had cooperated with Maximillian's regime were fleeing with them, and Maximillian's cause was lost. But in Milan, José Pablo was running out of money—he needed to go back to Mexico to recover his properties. Now he was a man without a country. According to the government of New Granada, the doctor lost his citizenship when he accepted the diplomatic post. His naturalization in Mexico was of dubious value because the Liberals had declared all acts of the imperial government illegal. José Pablo's attempts to win British or American citizenship ended in failure. His only recourse was to secure permission to return to Mexico and to obtain from Juárez a pardon for his political sins. José Pablo put his case before the Mexican consul in Paris. Pleading personal hardship and poverty—"The only thing I have left is a large family to maintain"—the doctor asked that he be allowed to return to resume his medical practice.[9] He pledged not to engage in political activity. Juárez refused to accept the consul's recommendation that José Pablo be granted amnesty.

Through the intervention of Schyler Hamilton, Gregorio José obtained a letter of recommendation to General Rosencrans, who arrived in Mexico City in December 1868 as the head of a U.S. military mission. At the family's behest, Rosencrans interviewed Vice-President Lerdo, but Juárez again refused to permit the doctor's return. Nor did requests by the U.S. minister yield positive results. Other individuals who were more compromised than José Pablo had already returned with pardons. What kept José Pablo out were not matters of state, but the intrigues of the new owners of Encinillas, Henrique Müller and Luis Terrazas, and the realization that the Martínez del Ríos were no longer a wealthy family. Not until January 1870 did José Pablo receive a license to return.[10]

For the Martínez del Ríos the order of the day after 1867 was to recover their lost properties and rightful status. The Law of 10 October 1870 opened the way. It granted a general amnesty and ordered that confiscated properties not already sold be returned to their owners. In January 1871 José Pablo asked Juárez to require the return of those portions of Encinillas that had not been included in the sale of lands to Muller and Terrazas in 1866. As a physician to the wife of the minister of hacienda, Matías Romero, José Pablo was well placed to lobby on his own behalf. In November 1871 the Ministry of Hacienda dispatched a special order to Chihuahua supporting José Pablo's claim. Muller and Terrazas continued to occupy the disputed lands, however, and despite a Herculean effort José Pablo failed to regain personal possession of his property in Northern Mexico before his death in 1882. He was more successful with his rustic estate, La Hormiga, which he had sold to Maximillian's government in 1865 for $25,000. Only half of the purchase price had been paid before the imperial government collapsed. In a transaction authorized by the minister of hacienda in September 1872, José Pablo reacquired La Hormiga by paying only $3,190 in cash and $5,143 in credits.[11]

José Pablo stayed far removed from politics. He devoted himself to Mexico, built up a respectable practice, and, in recognition of his advances in medicine, was named vice-president of the National Academy of Medicine. Internationally recognized for his competence as a surgeon, he published numerous articles on medical subjects, especially gynecology and obstetrics. His great hobby was scientific agriculture. As a member of the Mexican Agricultural Society, he published *Curso de agricultura. Cultivo de algodón*, a work that proposed the development of hybridized cotton to supply Mexico's textile industry.

La Hormiga, portions of Encinillas, certain houses and lands in Mexico City and Tlalpam, the Gran Colombia debt, and certain debts owed to Martínez del Río Hermanos still belonged to the family in the 1870s, despite the bankruptcy and the confiscations. Although potentially valuable, none of these properties produced income, and the family's financial situation was grim. The family-owned mining company, San Nicolás de Nauchititla, was a total loss in 1868, and $35,000 invested there was wasted. Creditors forced Gregorio José to sell his shares in the New York Bank of Commerce in 1867. In 1870 he lost his remaining government bonds to London creditors. With no other source of income, he tried to get a license as a broker (*corredor*), but his applications were refused by both imperial and Liberal governments. These harsh circumstances forced him to sell his furniture to raise money to live on. In November 1874 he mortgaged his home to Antonio Escandón for $16,000 cash. The following year he sold the house, becoming a tenant instead of a property owner. Even before this latest setback Gregorio José had been psychologically crushed by the family's misfortune. Suffering from a great depression, he cried, "My desperation is already so great, that I feel physically and morally useless for anything, and with the single desire of resting in the grave."[12]

Pedro fared no better. After 1864 he depended until his death in 1867 on loans from José Pablo and allowances from his son. As a broker and a partner in Miraflores, José Ansoátegui y Martínez del Río prospered, although on a scale far inferior to that of his father and uncles in the previous decades. Evidence of his marginality included the mortgage of the Ansoátegui residence at No. 3 Tiburcio Street in Mexico City to secure a much-needed $16,000 loan from Francisco Yturbé in 1874. Four years later the house was sold to Miguel Bringas & Company for $24,000.

Within the family pecking order, José Pablo remained absolutely the wealthiest. Before leaving Europe he had managed to borrow a sizable sum and in Mexico he owned several properties and earned a respectable income from his medical practice. His situation was such that both Gregorio José and Pedro owed him money. Though wealthier, he had more expenses—six dependent children to look after.[13]

The tremendous external stresses exacerbated conflict that always had been present within the family. Gregorio José complained in 1868 that the Ansoáteguis had been able to maintain a façade of respectability—a luxurious home, a coach and horse—while his own living room was bare and his clothing was ragged. Because the Ansoáteguis lived so well, the family's friends in Europe who were owed large debts had become embittered, believing the bankruptcy a sham. Gregorio José concluded, "It would not be strange that they think that under the name of Pepito [José Ansoátegui y Martínez del Río] we have an interest in Miraflores."[14] Pedro's estate was valued at $41,275 in 1868, but his heirs refused to repay the $15,000 owed to José Pablo. The disagreement wound up in the courts in 1876. Four years later, after many harsh words had been spoken, the matter was settled with a court-supervised compromise. José Pablo ceded the $15,000 debt to the Ansoáteguis in exchange for their rights in all assets owned by Martínez del Río Hermanos, including the Gran Colombia debt.[15]

The shrewdest investment made by the family in this difficult period of decline was in human resources—education. At a great sacrifice, José Pablo enrolled his sons Nicolás and Pablo Santiago in Stonyhurst College, a prestigious grammar school in England. Pablo Santiago excelled in his studies and continued his education at the Jesuit School of Feldkirch in Austria. He grew up in the company of classmates who were the next generation of Europe's elite. Even portions of the Mexican upper-crust were there. Two Escandóns were enrolled at Stonyhurst and their mother was president of one of the school's auxiliary societies. The boarding school experience insulated Pablo Santiago from the worst aspects of the tragedy in Mexico, but it nurtured an almost obsessive concern for matters of family prestige. He asked his older brother, Nicolás, in 1874, "I would also like you to send me a minute description of our coat of arms and to tell me whether we really have the right to a crown of count around the helmet, and also the date of our nobility, is it really [A.D.] 1250?"[16] When he arrived in Mexico as a young man he would be driven to restore the family to its rightful prominence. In 1880 Pablo Santiago completed his education with a degree from the National Law School of Mexico and began to practice law in Mexico City. Although he was the youngest of José Pablo's sons, he quickly asserted his leadership over the family.

The key to the second generation's renaissance lay in the combination of

Pablo Santiago's talents as a lawyer and the collection of potentially valuable properties left over from the fiasco in the 1860s. Again, the family economy dominated and had precedence over individual economies. José Pablo, who died in 1882, purposely created a family corporation by ordering in his will that the goods of his estate (in which nearly all the properties of the first generation had been concentrated) not be partitioned. He instructed his children to jointly administer his estate and to share equally the income it produced. This arrangement, he believed, was "the way to conserve the good harmony that always should reign between brothers."[17]

For José Pablo's heirs the immediate task was the recovery of Encinillas. As Pablo Santiago reminded Nicolás in August 1884, "It [Encinillas] is not, as you say, a *considerable part* of our patrimony, but it is our patrimony, at least for now . . . as on it depends all our other affairs."[18] Using carefully cultivated contacts in the Ministry of Development, Pablo Santiago obtained a title to or compensation for a large portion of Encinillas's lands. Most of this land was resold to raise cash, but one large section, Ojo Caliente, was developed into a cattle ranch. After a lengthy and costly struggle, Pablo Santiago beat Terrazas and Muller in courtroom battles lasting until 1886. Porfirio Díaz intervened and forced both sides to accept a compromise in 1888. Muller and Terrazas were obliged to buy the lands they had illegally occupied and to pay an indemnity for damages. These monies, and the income from the sale of other portions of Encinillas, financed the family's dramatic recovery in Porfirian Mexico.

To make good on Encinillas, Pablo Santiago used purely Mexican political inputs. He contracted the services of the minister of development, General Pacheco, and hired a crafty influence peddler, Telésforo Garcia, promising them both a share of the proceeds. He placated or neutralized important decision-makers like Matías Romero. Pablo Santiago needed as well the support of friends like José Yves Limantour who had begun to make a name for themselves in the Díaz administration. These acquaintances formed a compact group—labeled by their political enemies the *científicos*. To guarantee his victory, Pablo Santiago successfully pleaded his case before Díaz, who was the final arbiter.

The young attorney used these same skills to promote the interests of foreign entrepreneurs and corporations who hoped to do business in Mexico. His first important client, Read & Campbell, was one of a dozen public works contractors seeking a government contract for the Desagüe of Mexico. When, after a fierce competition, Read & Campbell won the contract, Pablo Santiago's reputation was made and he was invited to represent the largest railroad and mining companies in Mexico. Owing to his European education, his preparation for that task had been ideal, but to excel he needed the cooperation of Díaz. As a politician whose political control of the country was consolidated through a complex clientelistic network, Díaz needed always to please his friends. One way was with employment and other favors from the large foreign enterprises doing business in Mexico. For that, he could rely on Pablo Santiago's services. In return, the president, who seems to have been personally an honest man, was considerate of the interests of Pablo Santiago and his clients. Based on that reciprocal working relationship, Pablo Santiago's law firm became the most successful practice in Porfirian Mexico.

Under those auspices, Pablo Santiago's personal fortune was built and the family's patrimony recovered. With Díaz's support, the Martínez del Ríos included themselves as Venezuela's creditors when the United States and the European powers intervened in 1903 to force Venezuela to pay its foreign debt. For its share of the Gran Colombia debt, Venezuela was compelled to pay the family £102,000 in gold. As a manifestation of this economic resurrection and of the closeness of the family corporation, the Martínez del Ríos constructed for themselves a set of handsome houses, placed side-by-side on the Bucareli lands that Gregorio José acquired in the 1850s.

The new political and economic strategies the family adopted to cope with the Mexican reality were reflected in a social alignment that contrasted sharply with that of the first generation. José Pablo's oldest son, Manuel, married Amelia Zamacona, the daughter of Manuel Zamacona, Díaz's political ally since the 1860s. José Pablo's oldest daughter, Dolores, married into a wealthy and noble Italian family. Angela, his second-oldest daughter, married Manuel Thomas y Terán, an individual with excellent connections to the old families and to Díaz. José Pablo's youngest daughter, Julia, married Manuel González y Pavón. Julia's twin brother, Ventura, married Rosa Bermejillo, the daughter of Eustaquio Bermejillo, a Spanish merchant whose family had long been known in Mexico for its successes in mining. Together, these marriages tied the Martínez del Ríos to the most prominent and powerful elements of Porfirian society.

By 1910 the Martínez del Ríos had attained economic and political power on a scale only dreamed about by the first generation. The family's resurrection was scarcely completed, however, before the onset of the Mexican Revolution in 1910. The thirteen years of political madness that followed nearly ruined the family. Pablo Santiago had died in 1907 leaving a large estate in the care of his widow, Bárbara Vinent. As was customary, his assets were liquidated and converted into presumably secure mortgages on urban real estate. Throughout the nineteenth century this was a common and effective means to pass wealth from one generation to the next. In her own name and in that of her minor children, Bárbara lent $2 million secured with mortgages between 1908 and 1911. These mortgage contracts specified only that the loans were repayable in national currency (and not in gold or silver as was the more common practice). When the loans came due between

1914 and 1917, they were repaid in worthless paper script forcibly circulated by the many revolutionary factions. Currency devaluation put the family on the road to ruin. Had it not lost its political resources, and many of its social resources, in the destruction of the Porfirian regime, this might not have mattered so much—the family always could have made a new fortune, somehow. As it was, only the survival of a portion of its social resources saved the family from total devastation in the 1920s. Old family friends like the Panís and the Robles, who occupied high offices in the Obregón and Calles administrations, helped the Martínez del Ríos make special arrangements, which cushioned the shock of the Revolution.

By 1940 the Martínez del Ríos' economic resources were nearly exhausted. Pablo Santiago's branch of the family, the wealthiest during the Porfiriato, was particularly troubled. His oldest son, Pablo Francisco, was on his way to becoming a distinguished anthropologist and historian, but in no way was his branch of the family situated to share in the economic boom of the 1940s and 1950s. In contrast, Ventura's branch of the family, less well-off in the Porfiriato, blossomed in the 1950s. Starting out with modest assets, his grandson Eustaquio Martínez del Río y Icaza, developed a prosperous business enterprise that rehabilitated and refurbished the fortunes of that branch of the family. Within the politics of the extended family, Eustaquio today occupies a role analogous to that played in past generations by José Pablo and Pablo Santiago. If the Mexican economy prospers—and barring political uncertainties—the Martínez del Río family may yet win for itself a secure place within the ranks of Mexico's elite.

Abbreviations

AGN	Archivo General de la Nación
AHR	*American Historical Review*
AJ	Archivo Judicial del Tribunal Superior de Justicia del D.F.
AN	Archivo General de Notarías
AN (PH)	Archivo General de Notarías (Protocolo de Hacienda)
CMRFH	Archive of Carlos Martínez del Río y Fernández de Henestrosa
FO	Great Britain. Foreign Office Correspondence
HAHR	*Hispanic American Historical Review*
HM	*Historia Mexicana*
JFH	*Journal of Family History*
JLAS	*Journal of Latin American Studies*
LARR	*Latin American Research Review*
SRE(A)	Archivo Histórico de la Secretaría de Relaciones Exteriores
SRE(S)	Archivo de la Secretaría de Relaciones Exteriores
TAm	*The Americas*

Notes

1. Introduction

1. A useful survey of the Mexican independence era is John Lynch, *The Spanish American Revolutions, 1808-1826* (New York: Norton, 1973), chap. 9, pp. 294-334.

2. For the Hidalgo and Morelos revolts, see Hugh M. Hamill, *The Hidalgo Revolt: Prelude to Mexican Independence* (Gainesville: University of Florida Press, 1966); and Wilbert A. Timmons, *Morelos: Priest, Soldier, Statesman of Mexico* (El Paso: Texas Western College Press, 1963).

3. Useful surveys of political and economic life in early national Mexico include
. Charles C. Cumberland, *Mexico: The Struggle for Modernity* (New York: Oxford University Press,1968), pp. 141-189; Jan Bazant, *A Concise History of Mexico from Hidalgo to Cárdenas* (Cambridge: At the University Press, 1977), pp. 30-94; Michael C. Meyer and William L. Sherman, *The Course of Mexican History*, 2d ed. New York: Oxford University Press, 1983), pp. 313-430. The discussion that follows draws heavily on Cumberland's insights.

4. For church-state relations in this period, see Wilfred H. Calcott, *Church and State in Mexico, 1822-1857* (Durham, N.C.: Duke University Press, 1926); and Michael P. Costeloe, *Church and State in Independent Mexico: A Study of the Patronage Debate, 1821-1857* (London: Royal Historical Society, 1978).

5. For Mexican-Spanish relations, see Harold Sims, *La explusión de los españoles de México, 1821-1828* (Mexico City: Fondo de Cultura Económica, 1974).

6. For Mexican-French relations, see Nancy Barker, *The French Experience in Mexico, 1821-1861: A History of Constant Misunderstandings* (Chapel Hill: University of North Carolina Press, 1979).

7. For Texas-Mexican and North American–Mexican relations, see David M. Pletcher, *The Diplomacy of Annexation: Texas, Oregon, and the Mexican War* (Columbia: University of Missouri Press, 1972).

8. Nelson Reed, *The Caste War of the Yucatan* (Stanford, Cal.: Stanford University Press, 1964).

9. Stuart Voss, *On the Periphery of Nineteenth-Century Mexico: Sonora and Sinoloa, 1810-1877* (Tucson: University of Arizona Press, 1982); Evelyn Hu-DeHart, *Missionaries, Miners, and Indians: Spanish Contact with the Yaqui Nation of Northwestern New Spain, 1533-1820* (Tucson: University of Arizona

Press, 1981); and idem, "Development and Rural Rebellion: Pacification of the Yaquis in the Late Porfiriato," *HAHR* 54:1:72-93 (Feb. 1974).

10. Jean Meyer, *Problemas campesinos y revueltas agrarias, 1821-1910* (Mexico City: Secretaría de Educación Pública, 1973).

11. For a case study of a British mining fiasco, see Robert Randall, *Real del Monte: A British Mining Venture in Mexico,* Latin American Monographs, no. 26 (Austin: University of Texas Press, 1972).

12. For Mexican government assistance to the textile industry, see Dawn Keremitsis, *La industria textil mexicana en el siglo xix* (Mexico City: Secretaría de Educación Pública, 1973); and Robert A. Potash, *Mexican Government and Industrial Development in the Early Republic: The Banco de Avío* (Amherst: University of Massachusetts Press, 1983).

13. John H. Coatsworth, "Obstacles to Economic Growth in Nineteenth Century Mexico," *AHR* 83:1:80-100 (Feb. 1978).

14. For example, Charles Cumberland in his influential survey of Mexican history (*Mexico: The Struggle for Modernity*) titled his chapter on the early national period "Marking Time."

15. Examples of these approaches to early national Mexican political history include William S. Robertson, *Iturbide of Mexico* (Durham, N.C.: Duke University Press, 1952); Wilfred H. Calcott, *Santa Anna: The Story of an Enigma Who Once Was Mexico* (Norman: University of Oklahoma Press, 1936); Michael P. Costeloe, *La primera república federal de México, 1824-1835* (Mexico City: Fondo de Cultura Económica, 1975); and Charles A. Hale, *Mexican Liberalism in the Age of Mora, 1821-1853* (New Haven, Conn.: Yale University Press, 1968).

16. Richard N. Sinkin, *The Mexican Reform, 1855-1876: A Study in Liberal Nation-Building*, Latin American Monographs, no. 49 (Austin, Tex.: Institute of Latin American Studies, 1979).

17. André Gunder Frank, *Capitalism and Underdevelopment in Latin America* (New York: Monthly Review Press, 1967).

18. The classic work that attempts to link value systems to economic development is Max Weber, *The Protestant Ethic and the Spirit of Capitalism*, trans. Talcott Parsons (New York: C. Scribner, 1958).

19. An entrepreneurial theory of economic development was first systematically postulated in Joseph A. Schumpeter, *Theorie der wirtschaftlichen entwicklung* (Leipzig: Dunker & Humblot, 1912).

20. Karl Marx, *Capital: A Critique of Political Economy* (New York: Charles H. Kerr, 1906). For the European transition to capitalism, see also Ernest Mandel, *Long Waves of Capitalist Development: The Marxist Interpretation* (New York: Cambridge University Press, 1978); Paul M. Sweezy, *The Theory of Capitalist Development: Principles of Marxian Political Economy* (New York: Oxford University Press, 1942); Immanuel M. Wallerstein, *The Modern World-System*, 2 vols. (New York: Academic Press, 1976, 1980).

21. For the application of structuralist theory to Latin America, see William P. Glade, *The Latin American Economies: A Study of Their Institutional Evolution* (New York: Van Nostrand, 1969).

22. Barbara A. Tenenbaum, "Merchants, Money, and Mischief: The British in

Mexico, 1821-1862," *TAm* 35:1:317-340 (Jan. 1979); Margarita Urías H. et al., *Formación y desarrollo de la burguesía en México: siglo xix*, intro. Ciro F. S. Cardoso (Mexico City: Siglo Veintiuno, 1978); John H. Coatsworth, *From Backwardness to Underdevelopment: The Mexican Economy, 1810-1910* (New York: Columbia University Press, forthcoming).

23. Tenenbaum, "British in Mexico," p. 40.

24. Note that during this same period, foreign and native merchants responded to the broader opportunities offered in the Argentine economy by investing in a wide variety of enterprises—meat packing, transportation, land, as well as mining and finance: see Vera B. Reber, *British Mercantile Houses in Buenos Aires, 1810-1880* (Cambridge: Harvard University Press, 1979), pp. 110-136.

25. David W. Walker, "Las ubérrimas ubres del estado," *Nexos* (Mexico City) 2:2:15-18 (Feb. 1979).

26. Coatsworth, "Obstacles."

27. For a general introduction to family history, see Theodore K. Rabb and Robert I. Rotberg, eds., *The Family in History: Interdisciplinary Essays* (New York: Harper & Row, 1973); a frequently cited standard in the field is William J. Goode, *World Revolution and Family Patterns* (New York: Free Press of Glencoe, 1963).

28. Francesca M. Cancian, Louis Wolf Goodman, and Peter H. Smith, "Capitalism, Industrialization, and Kinship in Latin America: Major Issues," *JFH* 3 (Winter 1978):323.

29. Stephanie Blank, "Patrons, Clients, and Kin in Seventeenth-Century Caracas: A Methodological Essay in Colonial Spanish American Social History," *HAHR* 54:2:260-283 (May 1974).

30. Peter Marzahl, "Creoles in Government: The Cabildo of Popayán," *HAHR* 54:4:636-656 (Nov. 1974).

31. Mary L. Felstiner, "Kinship Politics in the Chilean Independence Movement," *HAHR* 56:1:58-80 (Feb. 1976).

32. Important associations between kinship and commerce in preindustrial British North America are described in Bernard Bailyn, "Kinship and Trade in Seventeenth Century New England," in Hugh G. J. Aitken, ed., *Explorations in Enterprise* (Cambridge: Harvard University Press, 1965); and Kenneth Wiggins Porter, *The Jacksons and the Lees: Two Generations of Massachusetts Merchants, 1765-1884*, vol. 1 (Cambridge: Harvard University Press, 1937), pp. 98-110.

33. Susan M. Socolow, *The Merchants of Buenos Aires, 1778-1810: Family and Commerce* (Cambridge: At the University Press, 1978); and John E. Kicza, *Colonial Entrepreneurs: Families and Business in Bourbon Mexico City* (Albuquerque: University of New Mexico Press, 1983).

34. Charles H. Harris III, *A Mexican Family Empire: The Latifundia of the Sánchez Navarro Family, 1765-1867* (Austin: University of Texas Press, 1975).

35. Enrique Semo, *Historia del capitalismo en México* (Mexico City: Ediciones Era, 1973).

36. Coatsworth, "Obstacles," p. 97.

37. Doris M. Ladd, *The Mexican Nobility at Independence, 1780-1826*, Latin American Monographs, no. 40 (Austin, Tex.: Institute of Latin American Studies, 1976).

38. John M. Tutino, "Hacienda Social Relations in Mexico: The Chalco Region in the Era of Independence," *HAHR* 55:3:496-528 (Aug. 1975); idem, "Creole Mexico: Spanish Elites, Haciendas, and Indian Towns, 1750-1810" (Ph.D. diss., University of Texas at Austin, 1976).

39. Richard B. Lindley, "Kinship and Credit in the Structure of Guadalajara's Oligarchy, 1800-1830" (Ph.D. diss., University of Texas at Austin, 1976).

40. Levi D. Erville, "The Prados of São Paulo: An Elite Brazilian Family in a Changing Society, 1840-1930" (Ph.D. diss., Yale University, 1974).

41. Cancián, Goodman, Smith, "Capitalism," p. 319; in this regard, see also Manuel L. Carlos and Lois Sellers, "Family, Kinship Structure, and Modernization in Latin America," *LARR* 7 (Summer 1972):95-124.

42. Raymond T. Smith, "The Family and the Modern World System: Some Observations from the Caribbean," *JFH* 3 (Winter 1978):338.

43. For a discussion of the economic and political costs associated with the tobacco monopoly, see David W. Walker, "Business as Usual: The Empresa del Tabaco in Mexico, 1837-1844," *HAHR* 64:4:675-705 (Nov. 1984).

2. Family Life, 1792-1860

1. For the genealogy of the Martínez de Retes–Martínez del Río family from 768 to circa 1850, see David W. Walker, "Kinship, Business, and Politics: The Martínez del Río Family in Mexico, 1824-1864" (Ph.D. diss., University of Chicago, 1981), 392-395.

2. Protocol of 13 May 1835, Notary no. 531, 70-85 ff., Archivo General de Notarías (AN), Mexico City, hereafter cited as AN-531-1835:70-85 (13 May 1835). Socolow reports that certain merchants in late colonial Buenos Aires increased their fortunes fifty-one and forty-four times over (*Merchants of Buenos Aires*, pp. 30-31).

3. For Martínez's dealings with O'Ryan, see the evidence and depositions introduced in Ventura Martínez v. Daniel O'Ryan, 1829-1837, Archivo Judicial del Tribunal Superior de Justicia del D.F. (AJ), Mexico City, Historical Section, File: Ventura Martínez, hereafter cited as Ventura Martínez v. Daniel O'Ryan, AJ, Ventura Martínez. For Martínez's dealings with Olasgarre, see the series of letters introduced as evidence in Ventura Martínez v. Manuela Azcárate, 1830-1835, AJ, Ventura Martínez.

4. Ventura Martínez v. Manuela Azcárate, 1830-1835, AJ, Ventura Martínez.

5. Ventura Martínez v. Guillermo Dollar, 1828-1833, AJ, Ventura Martínez.

6. Ibid.

7. Ibid.

8. AN-529-128:121-122 (8 Nov. 1828).

9. V. Martínez v. E. Grothe, 1829-1834, Archivo de la Secretaría de Relaciones Exteriores (SRE), File: 3-2-3820, hereafter cited as SRE(S)-3-2-3820.

10. Martínez's agents included the following: José Estrada (Guadalajara), AN-529-1830:112-113 (23 Nov. 1830); José Mariano Ximénez (Aguas Calientes), AN-529-1831:145-146 (29 Aug. 1831); José María Cuevas (Mexico City), AN-529-1831:191-192 (11 Nov. 1831); Julián Sosa, Gregorio Gómez, Manuel Quesada, Ramón Díaz (Panama), AN-529-1833:19-20 (7 Feb. 1833); Frederick Huth (Lima), AN-529-1833:54-55 (12 Mar. 1833); Justo Ruperti (Hamburg), AN-

529-1833:116-117 (7 June 1833). Overall, only about 50 percent of the old debts owed to Martínez in Peru, Mexico, and Europe were recoverable: see Edward P. Wilson to Ventura Martínez, Mexico City, 21 Nov. 1833, Ventura Martínez v. Manuela Azcárate, 1830-1835, AJ, Ventura Martínez.

11. José Pablo Martínez del Río to Ventura Martínez, Paris, 12 Oct. 1835, Archive of Carlos Martínez del Rio y Fernández de Henestrosa (CMRFH), Mexico City.

12. AN-169-1852:747-750 (21 Aug. 1852).

13. Pedro Ansoátegui to Gregorio José Martínez del Río, Geneva, 19 Jan. 1829, CMRFH.

14. José Pablo Martínez del Río to Ventura Martínez, Paris, 24 July, 21 Aug., 24 Sep. 1833; 24 Feb., 3 Apr. 1834, CMRFH.

15. Ibid., 26 Nov. 1834, CMRFH.

16. José Pablo Martínez del Río to Gregorio José Martínez del Río, Paris, 28 Mar. 1843, CMRFH.

17. Ventura de la Cruz Martínez del Río to José Pablo Martínez del Río, Aix-les-Bains, France, 23 Sep. 1844, CMRFH. For correspondence pertinent to Ventura de la Cruz's adventures in Europe, see Pedro Ansoátegui to Gregorio José Martínez del Río, Mexico City, 10 Nov. 1845; Ventura de la Cruz Martínez del Río to José Pablo Martínez del Río, Veracruz, 30 Apr. 1844; Ventura de la Cruz Martínez del Río to José Pablo Martínez del Río, Rome, 17 Jan. 1845, CMRFH.

18. José Ansoátegui y Martínez del Río to Gregorio José Martínez del Río, Paris, 10 Jan. 1852, CMRFH.

19. AN-531-1835:70-85 (13 May 1835).

20. Pedro Ansoátegui to Ventura Martínez, Mexico City, 16 Nov. 1831, CMRFH.

21. Ibid., 11 Feb. 1831, CMRFH.

22. Ibid.

23. Ibid.

24. AN-529-1833:85-89 (4 May 1833).

25. Pedro Ansoátegui to José Pablo Martínez del Río, Georgetown, U.S., 4 Dec. 1855, CMRFH. For correspondence pertaining to Pedro's travels, see Pedro Ansoátegui to Gregorio José Martínez del Río, New Orleans, 24 June 1837; Pedro Ansoátegui to José Pablo Martínez del Río, Berryville, U.S., 22 Sep. 1854; Pedro Ansoátegui to José Pablo Martínez del Río, Georgetown, 3 Jan., 20 Feb. 1855; Pedro Ansoátegui to José Pablo Martínez del Río, Veracruz, 4 Dec. 1856, CMRFH.

26. Pedro Ansoátegui to Gregorio José Martínez del Río, Mexico City, 30 Aug. 1845, CMRFH.

27. When Martínez del Río Hermanos was short of cash in 1841, it was a simple matter to transfer Gregorio José's deposits in two other Mexico City commercial houses to his account with Martínez del Río Hermanos: see Pedro Ansoátegui to Gregorio José Martínez del Río, Mexico City, 30 Aug. 1845, CMRFH.

28. Account books (1833, 1845), Gregorio José Martínez del Río, CMRFH.

29. Gregorio José Martínez del Río to José Pablo Martínez del Río, Brighton, Eng., 27 Oct. 1840, CMRFH.

30. José Pablo Martínez del Río to Gregorio José Martínez del Río, Mexico City, 19 Dec. 1843, CMRFH.

31. For Gregorio José's bond speculations, see Account books, "borrador de 1841, 1843," and "Rough Ledger, 1856- ," CMRFH.

32. Mexico, Ministro de Hacienda y Crédito Público, *Memoria* (1883-84), doc. no. 29, "Registro Público de la Capital," pp. 99, 112; 1858 Register (13 Mar. 1858), Great Britain, Public Record Office, Foreign Office Correspondence, Group 207, Vol. 32, No. 16, hereafter cited as FO-207-32:16; Gregorio José Martínez del Río to Consejo de Estado, Mexico City, 11 Mar. 1865, CMRFH.

33. AN-721-1853:30-35 (22 Feb. 1853); AN-721-1853:58-63 (18 Apr. 1853); AN-169-1860:554-555 (19 Nov. 1860).

34. Gregorio José Martínez del Río to José Pablo Martínez del Río, London, 26 June 1840, CMRFH.

35. Ibid., Brighton, Eng., 27 Oct. 1840, CMRFH.

36. Chaumeil to Ventura Martínez, Paris, 14 Apr. 1835, CMRFH.

37. José Pablo Martínez del Río to Ventura Martínez, Stanford Hill, Eng., 10 May 1835, CMRFH.

38. Ibid.

39. José Pablo Martínez del Río to Gregorio José Martínez del Río, Mexico City, 27 July 1839, CMRFH.

40. Ibid.

41. Ibid., 29 Dec. 1839, CMRFH.

42. Ibid., 27 July 1839, CMRFH.

43. José Pablo Martínez del Río to Ventura de la Cruz Martínez del Río, Madrid, 30 Dec. 1841, CMRFH.

44. José Pablo Martínez del Río to Gregorio José Martínez del Río, Mexico City, 27 Oct. 1847, CMRFH.

45. Convenio de Sociedad . . . Luis Flores, J. P. Martínez del Río para la Hacienda de Apapaxco, . . . " Mexico City, 29 May 1850, CMRFH.

46. For correspondence relating to the administration of Apapasco, see Juan Medina to Luis Flores, Apapasco, Mex., 2 July 1850; Juan Medina to Pablo Martínez del Río, Apapasco, Mex., 15 July 1850; Luis Flores to José Pablo Martínez del Río, Mexico City, 23, 30 July, 7, 12 Aug. 1850; Luis Flores to José Pablo Martínez del Río, Apapasco, Mex., 25 Jan., 15 May 1841, 25 Jan. 1855, CMRFH.

47. Luis Flores to José Pablo Martínez del Río, Mexico City, 12 Aug. 1850, CMRFH.

48. El señor Dn. J. P. Martínez del Río, su c/part.r con Martínez del Río Hermanos (1855), Martínez del Río Hermanos Accounts, 1838-1880, CMRFH.

49. AN-658-1855:811-813 (16 Oct. 1855); AN-658-1856:54-56 (31 Jan. 1856); AN-169-1856:245-247 (10 Apr. 1856).

50. José Pablo Martínez del Río to Gregorio José Martínez del Río, Paris, 18 Apr. 1843, CMRFH.

51. José Pablo Martínez del Río to Ventura de la Cruz Martínez del Río, Paris, 23 Oct. 1842, CMRFH.

52. José Pablo Martínez del Río to Gregorio José Martínez del Río, Mexico City, 18 May 1844, CMRFH.

53. José Pablo Martínez del Río to Gregorio José Martínez del Río, Mexico City, 28 June, 18 Aug. 1847; Pedro Ansoátegui to Gregorio José Martínez del Río, Mexico City, 22 July 1847, CMRFH.

54. AN-169-1848:278-303 (28 May 1848).

55. For transactions relating to the Bethlemitas house, see AN-426-1850:1131-1136

(23 Dec. 1850); AN-426-1850:843-850 (18 Oct. 1850); and Manuel Escandón to José Pablo Martínez del Río, Mexico City, 11 Feb. 1857, CMRFH.

56. For transactions relating to the Arazam house, see AN-169-1853:628-633 (30 June 1853); AN-169-1856:823-824 (4 Oct. 1856); AN-169-1857:694 (28 July 1857).

57. For transactions relating to La Hormiga, see AN-169-1853:31-39 (15 Jan. 1853); AN-169-1855:212-213 (10 Mar. 1855); AN-658-1856:53-54 (26 Jan. 1856); AN-658-1856:859-863 (20 Nov. 1856); AN-658-1857:354 (18 May 1857); AN-658-1859:289-297 (19 Apr. 1859).

58. José Pablo Martínez del Río to Gregorio José Martínez del Río, Mexico City, 22 Nov. 1846, CMRFH.

59. AN-658-1854:565-570 (28 Aug. 1854); AN-658-1854:711-713 (9 Nov. 1854).

60. AN-169-1855:612-618 (21 June 1855).

61. General Angel Frías to Crispiano del Castillo [José Pablo's attorney], Chihuahua, Mex., 26 Aug. 1854, CMRFH.

62. AN-658-1857:53-55 (19 Jan. 1857).

63. José J. Durán to José Pablo Martínez del Río, Chihuahua, Mex., 15 Sep. 1857, CMRFH.

64. José Pablo Martínez del Río to Gregorio José Martínez del Río, Milan, 5 Sep. 1859, CMRFH.

65. For examples of intrafamily exchanges of goods and services, see AN-592-1838:86-87 (27 Apr. 1838); Gregorio José Martínez del Río to José Pablo Martínez del Río, London, 15 Feb. 1840, 9 Jan. 1843; José Pablo Martínez del Río to Ventura de la Cruz Martínez del Río, Bordeaux, 7 Nov. 1841; José Pablo Martínez del Río to Gregorio José Martínez del Río, Paris, 28 Mar. 1843; José Pablo Martínez del Río to Gregorio José Martínez del Río, Mexico City, 29 July 1843, 24 June 1847; Ventura de la Cruz Martínez del Río to José Pablo Martínez del Río, Seville, 16 Nov. 1848, CMRFH; AN-529-1837:119-120 (3 June 1837); AN-169-1841:70-71 (11 Feb. 1841); AN-169-1844:272-274 (19 Apr. 1844). For other examples of the subordination of individual interests to the needs of larger family economies, see John E. Kicza, "The Pulque Trade of Late Colonial Mexico City," *TAm* 37:2:193-221 (Oct. 1980); and Ida Altman, "A Family and Region in the Northern Fringe Lands: The Marqueses de Aguayo of Nuevo León and Coahuila," in Ida Altman and James Lockhart, eds., *Provinces of Mexico: Variants of Spanish American Regional Evolution* (Los Angeles: University of California Press, 1976), pp. 253-277.

66. For other family-based enterprises in early national Mexico, see Margarita Urías H. et al., *Formación y desarrollo de la burguesía en México:Siglo xix* (Mexico City: Siglo Veintiuno, 1978).

67. Pedro Ansoátegui to Gregorio José Martínez del Río, New Orleans, 24 June 1837, CMRFH.

68. Ibid., Mexico City, 27 July 1843, CMRFH.

69. Ventura de la Cruz Martínez del Río to José Pablo Martínez del Río, London, 31 Jan. 1850, CMRFH.

70. José Pablo Martínez del Río to Gregorio José Martínez del Río, Mexico City, 19 May 1841, CMRFH.

71. Pedro Ansoátegui to José Pablo Martínez del Río, Georgetown, U.S., 4 Dec. 1854, CMRFH.

3. The Martínez del Río Family in Mexico, 1830-1860

1. For Creole-peninsular intermarriages in colonial Guadalajara, see Richard B. Lindley, "Kinship and Credit." For marriage and commerce in colonial Spanish America, see Susan M. Socolow, *Merchants of Buenos Aires*, pp. 35-53; and John E. Kicza, *Colonial Entrepreneurs*, pp. 25, 156-179, 235-276.

2. O'Ryan's marriage is reported in Ventura Martínez v. Daniel O'Ryan, AJ, Ventura Martínez; Wilson's spouse is noted in AN-425-1836:7-8 (8 Feb. 1836); MacKintosh's wife is in AN-169-1850:668-674 (14 June 1850); Drusina's spouse is listed in AN-426-1830:595-596 (26 November 1830). A papal dispensation for a non-Catholic marriage is discussed in Guillermo Drusina to Ventura Martínez, Mexico City, 10 June 1829, CMRFH. For marriages of the Mexican nobility, see Ladd, *Mexican Nobility*, appendix F, pp. 187-228. British merchants in nineteenth-century Buenos Aires frequently contracted matrimony with the daughers of the local elite: see Reber, *British Mercantile Houses*, pp. 47-48.

3. For clans in colonial New Spain, see Kicza, *Colonial Entrepreneurs*, pp. 155-165, 235-236; and Ida Altman and James Lockhart, eds., *Provinces of Mexico: Variants of Spanish American Regional Evolution* (Berkeley & Los Angeles: University of California Press, 1976), p. 12. The Texas land companies and the Rosario mining company are discussed in greater detail in chapters 4 and 5.

4. Pedro Ansoátegui to Gregorio José Martínez del Río, Mexico City, 6 July 1841, CMRFH.

5. For a more general discussion of the family's place in Mexican society, see Silvia M. Arrom, "Women and the Family in Mexico City, 1800-1857" (Ph.D. diss., Stanford University, 1978).

6. Guillermo Drusina to Ventura Martínez, Mexico City, 8 July 1829, CMRFH.

7. AN-426-1830:34-35 (26 Jan. 1830). Technically, what Martínez was pledged to pay was an *arras*: see Kicza, *Colonial Entrepreneurs*, p. 162.

8. For the divorce and the litigation that followed, see Martínez v. Azcárate, AJ; AN-426-1830:580-581 (24 Nov. 1830); AN-529-1830:134-135 (20 Dec. 1830); AN-426-1831:73-74 (8 Oct. 1831); AN-529-1833:157-158 (9 Aug. 1833); AN-529-1833:274-275 (9 Nov. 1833); AN-169-1835:30-31 (4 Mar. 1835). For an analysis of ecclesiastical divorce in Mexico, see Silvia M. Arrom, *La mujer mexicana ante el divorcio eclesiástico (1800-1857)* (Mexico City: Secretaría de Educación Pública, 1976).

9. AN-426-1835:34-35 (3 Dec. 1835); AN-361-1840:72-73 (26 Mar. 1840).

10. Gregorio José Martínez del Río to José Pablo Martínez del Río, London, 15 Feb. 1840, CMRFH.

11. José Pablo Martínez del Río to Ventura de la Cruz Martínez del Río, Bordeaux, 7 Nov. 1841, CMRFH.

12. Documents related to José Pablo Martínez del Río's marriage are registered in AN-169-1852:770-775 (6 Sep. 1852).

13. Gregorio José Martínez del Río to José Pablo Martínez del Río, London, 26 Jan. 1840, CMRFH.

14. Documents related to Gregorio José Martínez del Río's marriage are registered in AN-4-1912:81-82 (14 Oct. 1912).

15. AN-529-1830:125-126 (11 Dec. 1830); AN-426-1831:279-380 (14 June 1831); Pedro Ansoátegui to Gregorio José Martínez del Río, Mexico City, 9 Apr. 1840, CMRFH.

16. José Pablo Martínez del Río to Ventura de la Cruz Martínez del Río, Málaga, 12 Mar. 1842, CMRFH.

17. For Domingo Ansoátegui's role in Martínez del Río Hermanos, see AN-169-1841:1 (2 Jan. 1841); AN-169-1842:963-967 (22 Nov. 1842); AN-169-1845:271-273 (24 May 1845); AN-169-1851:374-375 (24 Apr. 1851); Pedro Ansoátegui to Gregorio José Martínez de Río, Mexico City, 21 Dec. 1839; Domingo Ansoátegui to Gregorio José Martínez del Río, Mexico City, 31 Mar. 1841, 25 Jan., 24 Sep. 1844; Domingo Ansoátegui to José Pablo Martínez del Río, Mexico City, 2 June 1843, CMRFH.

18. Pedro Ansoátegui to José Pablo Martínez del Río, Georgetown, U.S., 21 Sep. 1855, CMRFH; AN-169-1855:968-970 (19 Dec. 1855); AN-169-1858:27-28 (4 Feb. 1858).

19. Pedro Ansoátegui to José Pablo Martínez del Río, Berryville, U.S., 22 Sep. 1854, CMRFH.

20. José Pablo Martínez del Río to Gregorio José Martínez del Río, Mexico City, 29 July 1844, CMRFH.

21. Ibid., Bordeaux, 7 Nov. 1841, CMRFH.

22. Ibid., Mexico City, 22 Nov. 1846, CMRFH.

23. Gregorio José Martínez del Río to José Pablo Martínez del Río, London, 26 June 1840, CMRFH.

24. José Pablo Martínez del Río to Gregorio José Martínez del Río, Mexico City, 30 Dec. 1841, CMRFH.

25. Ventura de la Cruz Martínez del Río to Gregorio José Martínez del Río, Mexico City, 23 June 1843, CMRFH.

26. José Pablo Martínez del Río to Gregorio José Martínez del Río, Mexico City, 18 May 1844, CMRFH.

27. Ibid.

28. For example, see the problems that resulted from Barrio's failure to cover other short-term debt obligations to Martínez del Río Hermanos in 1846: José Pablo Martínez del Río to Gregorio José Martínez del Río, Mexico City, 22 Nov. 1846, CMRFH.

29. Pedro Ansoátegui to Gregorio José Martínez del Río, Cuautla, Mex., 24 Feb. 1846, CMRFH.

30. José Pablo Martínez del Río to Gregorio José Martínez del Río, Mexico City, 22 Nov. 1846, CMRFH.

31. Ventura de la Cruz Martínez del Río to José Pablo Martínez del Río, London, 31 Oct. 1851, CMRFH.

32. For the compadrazgo system, see George M. Foster, "Cofradía and Compadrazgo in Spain and Spanish America," *Southwest Journal of Anthropology* 9:(Spring 1953):1-21; Donn Vorhis Hart, *Compadrinazgo: Ritual Kinship in the Philippines* (DeKalb: Northern Illinois University Press, 1977); Eric R. Wolf, "Kinship, Friendship, and Patron-Client Relations in Complex Societies," in Michael Banton, ed., *The Social Anthropology of Complex Societies* (New York: Houghton Mifflin, 1966), pp. 1-32.

33. José Pablo Martínez del Río to Gregorio José Martínez del Río, Paris, 20 Oct. 1842, CMRFH.

34. Ibid., Mexico City, 21 Mar. 1846, CMRFH.

35. Ibid., San Angel, Mex., 18 Apr. 1847, CMRFH.

36. Pedro Ansoátegui to Gregorio José Martínez del Río, London, 9 July 1856, CMRFH.

37. For a report on the Magdalena mill, see Pedro Ansoátegui to Gregorio José Martínez del Río, Mexico City, 5 Feb. 1841. For example of Olasgarre's dealings with Martínez del Río Hermanos, see AN-169-1854:667-670 (31 July 1854); José Pablo Martínez del Río's *fianza* for Olasgarre is registered in AN-169-1855:809 (10 Oct. 1855).

38. Gregorio José Martínez del Río to José Pablo Martínez del Río, London, 26 June 1840, CMRFH.

39. José Pablo Martínez del Río to Gregorio José Martínez del Río, Paris, 28 Mar. 1843, CMRFH.

40. Pedro Ansoátegui to José Pablo Martínez del Río, Berryville, U.S., 22 Sep. 1854, CMRFH.

41. José Pablo Martínez del Río to Gregorio José Martínez del Río, San Angel, Mex., 24 Mar. 1847, CMRFH.

42. Pedro Ansoátegui to Gregorio José Martínez del Río, Mexico City, 22 July 1839, CMRFH; Martínez del Río Hermanos to George Lettson, Mexico City, 29 Mar. 1856, FO-204-131:206; Thomas Morphy to Count Malmesbury, London, 12 Jan. 1859, Archivo Histórico de la Secretaría de Relaciones Exteriores (SRE), File: L-E-1655, hereafter cited as SRE(A)-L-E-1655.

43. José Pablo Martínez del Río to Ventura Martínez, Rome, 3 Apr. 1833; 1857 Register (27 Mar. 1857), FO-207-32:10; AN-169-1856:823-824 (4 Oct. 1856).

44. See note 44 in chapter 2.

45. For Hamilton's contacts, see José Pablo Martínez del Río to Gregorio José Martínez del Río, Mexico City, 14 Nov. 1849; Pedro Ansoátegui to José Pablo Martínez del Río, Georgetown, U.S., 3 Jan. 1855; José Pablo Martínez del Río to Gregorio José Martínez del Río, Florence, 4 Dec. 1859, CMRFH.

46. For the Mosqueras' European education and other aspects of Colombian political life in the nineteenth century, see Frank Safford, *Aspectos del siglo XIX en Colombia* (Medellín, Colombia: Ediciones Hombre Nuevo, 1977).

47. Pedro Ansoátegui to Gregorio José Martínez del Río, Mexico City, 6 Nov. 1841; Ventura de la Cruz Martínez del Río to José Pablo Martínez del Río, Madrid, 20 Dec. 1845; José Pablo Martínez del Río to Gregorio José Martínez del Río, Mexico City, 28 June 1847; Domingo Ansoátegui to Gregorio José Martínez del Río, Mexico City, 31 Mar. 1851; José Pablo Martínez del Río to Gregorio José Martínez del Río, San Angel, Mex., 21 May 1847; José Pablo Martínez del Río to Gregorio José Martínez del Río, Florence, 20 Oct. 1849, CMRFH; AN-169-1842:574-576 (25 July 1842); AN-529-1857:120 (8 Oct. 1857).

48. For examples of gossip overheard in the Lonja, see Pedro Ansoátegui to Gregorio José Martínez del Río, Mexico City, 28 Sep., 8 Oct. 1842, 10 Jan. 1846, CMRFH. Similar institutions were organized by British merchants resident in nineteenth-century Buenos Aires: see Reber, *British Mercantile Houses*, p. 45.

49. José Pablo Martínez del Río to Gregorio José Martínez del Río, Paris, 28 Mar. 1843, CMRFH.

50. Ventura de la Cruz Martínez del Río to Gregorio José Martínez del Río, Mexico City, 23 June 1843, CMRFH.

51. Ibid., Aix-les-Bains, France, 23 June 1847, CMRFH.

52. José Pablo Martínez del Río to Ventura de la Cruz Martínez del Río, Paris, 10 Sep. 1841, CMRFH.

53. José Pablo Martínez del Río to Gregorio José Martínez del Río, Mexico City, 28 Jan. 1844, CMRFH.

54. Ibid., Havana, Nov. 1843, CMRFH.

55. British Residents to Richard Pakenham, Mexico City, 1838, FO-204-64:47; AN-169-1855:612-618 (21 June 1855).

56. José Pablo Martínez del Río to Gregorio José Martínez del Río, Milan, 3 July 1859, CMRFH.

4. Commerce in Mexico: Drusina & Martínez, 1828-1837

1. Justo Ruperti to Ventura Martínez and Guillermo Drusina, Hamburg, 10 July 1829; Guillermo Drusina to Ventura Martínez, Mexico City, 8 Apr., 10, 11 June 1829, CMRFH.

2. Guillermo Drusina to Ventura Martínez, Mexico City, 23 May 1829, CMRFH.

3. Ibid., 22 Aug. 1829, CMRFH.

4. Ibid., 8 Apr. 1829, CMRFH.

5. Ibid., 30 Sep. 1829, CMRFH.

6. Ventura Martínez to Guillermo Drusina, 7 Nov. 1829, CMRFH.

7. AN-426-1830:1-4 (4 Jan. 1830).

8. AN-426-1833:452-455 (27 Nov. 1833). The basis for this unlimited liability partnership was the *sociedad colectiva* prescribed in the Ordenanzas de Comercio de Bilbao. This had been the most common form of business organization in colonial Spanish America.

9. For description of several business deals involving dry goods, see Guillermo Drusina to Ventura Martínez, Mexico City, 25 Mar., 11, 25, 29 Apr., 27 May, 29 July 1829, CMRFH.

10. Guillermo Drusina to Ventura Martínez, 11 Apr. 1829, CMRFH. For a political history of this period, consult Michael P. Costeloe, *La primera república federal de México, 1824-1835* (Mexico City: Fondo de Cultura Económica, 1975).

11. For an account of Ruperti's labors in Europe for Drusina & Martínez, see Guillermo Drusina to Ventura Martínez, 27 May, 19 Aug. 1829; Justo Ruperti to Ventura Martínez and Guillermo Drusina, Hamburg, 10 July 1829.

12. In the late colonial period certain companies had begun to specialize in the shipment of silver: see Kicza, *Colonial Entrepreneurs*, pp. 73-74.

13. For commercial exchanges of this paper in New Spain, see ibid., pp. 84-85. *Libranzas* were used extensively all over nineteenth-century Spanish America. For their commercial utility in Argentina, see Reber, *British Mercantile Houses*, p. 60.

14. Guillermo Drusina to Ventura Martínez, Mexico City, 25, 28 Mar., 6 June 1829, CMRFH.

15. Ibid., 11 July 1829, CMRFH.

16. Ibid., 29 July 1829, CMRFH.

17. Ibid., 24 Oct. 1829, CMRFH.

18. British Merchants to Richard Pakenham, Mexico City, 24 June 1836, SRE(A)-L-E-1364; Ewen MacKintosh to José María Ortiz Monasterio, Mexico

City, 9 Nov. 1840, SRE(S)-25-14-2.

19. Guillermo Drusina to Ventura Martínez, Mexico City, 23 May 1829, CMRFH.

20. AN-426-1833:651-653 (30 July 1833).

21. AN-426-1833:813-814 (15 Oct. 1833).

22. For Drusina & Martínez's adventures in the tobacco company, see Guillermo Drusina to Ventura Martínez, Mexico City, 27 June, 8 July, 19 Aug., 2, 9, 12, 15 Sep. 1829, CMRFH.

23. Guillermo Drusina to Ventura Martínez, Mexico City, 8 July 1829, CMRFH.

24. Ibid., 9, 15 Sep. 1829, CMRFH.

25. AN-426-1832:126 (30 Jan. 1832).

26. AN-426-1832:791-794 (21 Aug. 1832).

27. AN-426-1833:926-931 (18 Nov. 1833).

28. Account of the State of the Affairs of the Adventure in Lands in Texas with J. C. Beales & Others, 25 Apr. 1836, CMRFH.

29. AN-215-1836:6-8 (10 Mar. 1836).

30. AN-425-1837:94-95 (22 Aug. 1837); AN-715-1837:82-83 (12 Oct. 1837).

31. Gregorio José Martínez del Río to Ventura de la Cruz Martínez del Río, Havana, 22 Nov. 1836, CMRFH.

32. Ventura de la Cruz Martínez del Río to Gregorio José Martínez del Río, Mexico City, 20 Dec. 1836, CMRFH; AN-170-1837:283-285 (15 July 1837).

5. Banking on Mexico: Martínez del Río Hermanos, 1838-1864

1. AN-529-1857:122-126 (24 Oct. 1857).

2. Pedro Ansoátegui to Gregorio José Martínez del Río, Mexico City, 25 Jan. 1839, CMRFH.

3. Domingo Ansoátegui to Gregorio José Martínez del Río, Mexico City, 28 June 1846, CMRFH.

4. Ibid., 13 Oct. 1849, CMRFH.

5. Pedro Ansoátegui to Gregorio José Martínez del Río, Mexico City, 14 Nov. 1838, 23 Feb. 1843, CMRFH.

6. Ibid., 15 Sep. 1838, CMRFH.

7. Ibid., 21 Dec. 1838, CMRFH.

8. Ibid., 15 Nov. 1838, CMRFH.

9. Ibid., 30 Mar. 1839, CMRFH.

10. Ibid., New Orleans, 21, 26 June, 5, 12 July 1837, CMRFH.

11. For a discussion of the firm's problems with finding suitable exchange mediums, see ibid., Mexico City, 29 Mar. 1840, 27 Aug. 1845, CMRFH.

12. Gregorio José Martínez del Río to Ventura de la Cruz Martínez del Río, Havana, 14 Dec. 1836, CMRFH.

13. Pedro Ansoátegui to Gregorio José Martínez del Río, Mexico City, 20 Feb. 1840, CMRFH.

14. Ibid., 5 May 1840, CMRFH.

15. For examples of the problems with this borrower, see ibid., Mexico City, 22 Jan. 1839, 1 Oct. 1840, 6 July, 6 Nov. 1841, 28 Sep. 1842, 23 Feb. 1843, CMRFH.

16. Ibid., 28 Sep. 1842, CMRFH.

17. Ibid., 23 Feb. 1843, CMRFH.

18. See chapter 3 for a discussion of the social considerations that conditioned the decision to assume an interest in Miraflores; Pedro Ansoátegui to Gregrio José Martínez del Río, Mexico City, 20 Feb. 1840, CMRFH.

19. Pedro Ansoátegui to Gregorio José Martínez del Río, Mexico City, 22 June, 15 Nov., 3 Dec. 1838; 22 Jan., 23 Feb., 30 Mar., 2, 15 June, 22 July, 11 Sep., 4 Oct. 1839; 24 Apr. 1842; 25 June 1845, CMRFH.

20. Ibid., 6 July 1841; Gregorio José Martínez del Río to José Pablo Martínez del Río, Liverpool, 4 Nov. 1842, CMRFH. By way of contrast, although merchants in mid-nineteenth-century Argentina did not have silver or cochineal to export, they were blessed with an unlimited supply of tallow, hides, and jerked meat, which found markets in the Caribbean and in Europe: see Reber, *British Mercantile Houses*, pp. 98-103.

21. Pedro Ansoátegui to Gregorio José Martínez del Río, New Orleans, 21 June, 22 July 1837; Pedro Ansoátegui to Gregorio José Martínez del Río, Mexico City, 15 Sept. 1838; 22 Jan., 18 June 1839; 6 Apr. 1842; 28 Oct. 1845; 10 Jan., 27 July 1846, CMRFH.

22. Pedro Ansoátegui to Gregorio José Martínez del Río, Mexico City, 5 Jan., 1 Mar. 1841; 6, 28 Apr. 1842; 28 Oct. 1845; 26 Feb., 29 Mar. 1846, CMRFH.

23. Ibid., 1 Apr. 1841, CMRFH. The company sold these bank shares to Gregorio José Martínez del Río to raise money in Mexico in 1845.

24. Ibid., 15 Feb. 9 Sep. 1841; José Pablo Martínez del Río to Gregorio José Martínez del Río, Paris, 9 Mar. 1843, CMRFH.

25. Pedro Ansoátegui to Gregorio José Martínez del Río, Mexico City, 27 Oct. 1842, CMRFH.

26. For a general discussion of finance for mines in colonial Mexico, see David A. Brading, *Miners and Merchants in Bourbon Mexico, 1763-1810* (Cambridge: At the University Press, 1971).

27. For the company's investment in silver mints, see AN-169-1836:194-195 (20 July 1836); Pedro Ansoátegui to Gregorio José Martínez del Río, Mexico City, 27 Oct. 1842; 23 Feb. 1843; Domingo Ansoátegui to Gregorio José Martínez del Río, Mexico City, 31 Mar. 1847; Convenio, Socios de la compañía de Guadalupe y Calvo, Mexico City, 25 Feb. 1843; CMRFH. These shares in the mints were sold to Ewen MacKintosh in 1850: see note 37.

28. Pedro Ansoátegui to Gregorio José Martínez del Río, Mexico City, 15 Sep. 1838; 23 Feb., 24 Mar. 1839; 6 Nov. 1841; 8, 23 July 1843; Domingo Ansoátegui to Gregorio José Martínez del Río, Mexico City, 29 Oct. 1846, CMRFH. For the Fresnillo mines in the colonial period, see Peter J. Bakewell, *Silver Mining and Society in Colonial Mexico: Zacatecas, 1546-1700* (Cambridge: At the University Press, 1971).

29. Martínez del Río Hermanos appointed textile consignees like Gregorio Jiménez & Co. and Germán F. Pohls to act as its representatives in Guanajuato mining companies. For example, see AN-169-1852:23-24 (9 Jan. 1852).

30. For an account of the British experience with the Real del Monte mines, see Randall, *Real del Monte*. For Béistegui's participation in the Mexican mining company, see Rosa María Meyer, "Los Béistegui, especuladores y mineros, 1830-1869," in Urías H. et al., *Formación y desarrollo*, pp. 108-139; Pedro Ansoátegui to

José Pablo Martínez del Río, Berryville, U.S., 22 Sep. 1854, CMRFH; AN-169-1856:415-417 (13 June 1856).

31. Ventura de la Cruz Martínez del Río to José Pablo Martínez del Río, Paris, 31 Oct. 1851, CMRFH.

32. Pedro Ansoátegui to Gregorio José Martínez del Río, Mexico City, 15 Nov., 15 Dec. 1838; 30 Mar., 27 Apr., 16 Nov. 1839; 28 Mar, 1840, CMRFH; AN-169-1839:215-219 (4 May 1839); AN-215-1840:3-4 (2 Apr. 1840).

33. Domingo Ansoátegui to Gregorio José Martínez del Río, Mexico City, 26 Feb. 1846, CMRFH; AN-169-1849:1005-1008 (6 Nov. 1849).

34. For the firm's attempt to recover the Moreno land grant, see Ventura de la Cruz Martínez del Río to Gregorio José Martínez del Río, Mexico City, 24 Nov., 22 Dec. 1849; Pedro Ansoátegui to José Pablo Martínez del Río, Georgetown, U.S., 4 Dec. 1854; José Pablo Martínez del Río to Gregorio José Martínez del Río, Mexico City, 20 Nov. 1849, CMRFH.

35. SRE(A)-VI-73(G)-451.

36. AN-169-1850:668-674 (14 June 1850).

37. AN-719-1856:177-190 (25 Sep. 1856).

38. For an account of the experiences of a Mexico City land developer, Francisco Somera, see María Dolores Morales, "Francisco Somera y el primer fraccionamiento de la ciudad de México, 1840-1889," in Urías H. et al., *Formación y desarrollo*, pp. 188-230. For a more general view of the process of urbanization in nineteenth-century Mexico, the following are useful studies: Richard E. Boyer, "Las ciudades mexicanas: perspectivas de estudio en el siglo XIX," *HM* 22 (Oct.-Dec. 1972):142-159; Alejandra Moreno Toscano, "Cambios en los patrones de urbanización en México, 1810-1910," *HM* 22:2(Oct.-Dec. 1972):160-187. For the disamortization law and its consequences for Mexican society, see Robert J. Knowlton, *Church Property and the Mexican Reform, 1856-1910* (DeKalb: Northern Illinois University Press, 1976).

39. For anecdotal accounts of personal adventures at the games, see Pedro Ansoátegui to Gregorio José Martínez del Río, Mexico City, 22 June 1838; 2 June 1839; 1 June 1842, CMRFH.

40. AN-169-1849:881-886 (26 Sep. 1849); Contract, Jacob H. Robertson and André Fulton, Mexico City, 20 Mar. 1852, CMRFH; AN-169-1853:481-482 (3 May 1853).

41. AN-169-1854:1043-1044 (14 Dec. 1854).

42. For examples, see Pedro Ansoátegui to Gregorio José Martínez del Río, Mexico City, 8 July 1843, 29 July 1846, CMRFH.

43. Domingo Ansoátegui to Gregorio José Martínez del Río, Mexico City, 29 Dec. 1846, CMRFH.

44. For examples, see Pedro Ansoátegui to Gregorio José Martínez del Río, Mexico city, 29 Aug. 1840; 21 Mar. 1842; 23 Sep. 1846; 13 Sep. 1851; Ventura de la Cruz Martínez del Río to José Pablo Martínez de Río, Aix-les-Bains, France, 23 June 1847; Ventura de la Cruz Martínez del Río to Gregorio José Martínez del Río, London, 13 July 1851; E. J. Perry to José Pablo Martínez del Río, London, 17 Nov. 1859, CMRFH.

45. For loans in Mexico, see Pedro Ansoátegui to Gregorio José Martínez del Río, Mexico City, 5 May 1838; 21 Mar. 1842; 22 July 1847; 2 Nov. 1851, CMRFH.

46. The proceedings of the *concurso* are documented in Martínez del Río Hermanos v. Junta de Acreedores, 1861-1865, AJ, Concursos.

47. AN-725-1861:286-288 (23 Aug. 1861).

48. Memorandum de Dom.o Ansoátegui sobre su cuenta . . . [1865?], [Mexico City], CMRFH.

49. Martínez del Río Hermanos v. Junta de Acreedores, 1861-1865 AJ, Concursos.

50. AN-726-1864:255-257 (25 May 1864); AN-726-1864:274-277 (3 June 1864); AN-726-1864:381-383 (27 July 1864); AN-726-1864:421-424 (16 Aug. 1864); AN-726-1864:726-728 (21 Dec. 1864); AN-726-1865:537-540 (21 Aug. 1865); AN-726-1869:110-112 (21 Aug. 1869); AN-726-1870:147-149 (31 Jan. 1870); AN-726-1870:327-334 (18 Mar. 1870).

51. AN-169-1864:359-365 (11 July 1864); AN-169-1866:4-7 (15 May 1866); AN-362-1867:15-16 (12 Feb. 1867).

52. Files for several hundred bankruptcies in Mexico City are preserved in AJ, Concursos. A rough estimate for the frequency of business bankruptcies in the Mexico City area in the mid-nineteenth century would probably be in the 80 percent to 90 percent range. By way of comparison, the bankruptcy rate for British commercial houses in Buenos Aires for the period of 1842 to 1850 was about 25 percent, a figure not appreciably higher than the business failure rate in Great Britain and the United States: see Reber, *British Mercantile Houses*, pp. 106-109.

6. Textile Manufacturing in Mexico: Miraflores, 1840-1860

1. Pedro Ansoátegui to Gregorio José Martínez del Río, Mexico City, 9 Apr. 1840, CMRFH.

2. For machinery sales by New England manufacturers to textile mills in Mexico, see George S. Gibb, *The Saco-Lowell Shops: Textile Machinery Building in New England, 1813-1949* (Cambridge: Harvard University Press, 1950), pp. 160-161; and Thomas R. Navin. *The Whitin Machine Works since 1830: A Textile Machinery Company in an Industrial Village* (Cambridge: Harvard University Press, 1950), p. 40.

3. AN-169-1840:899-901 (30 Nov. 1840); Pedro Ansoátegui to Gregorio José Martínez del Río, Mexico City, 30 Nov. 1840, CMRFH.

4. Pedro Ansoátegui to Gregorio José Martínez del Río, Mexico City, 20 July 1840, CMRFH.

5. Potash, *Mexican Government*, pp. 43-51, 56, 67-83, 94, 121. For a general history of the Mexican textile industry, see Keremitsis, *La industria textil*.

6. AN-169-1841:322-324 (10 July 1841).

7. AN-169-1849:200-206 (3 Mar. 1849); Felipe Nerí del Barrio to José Pablo Martínez del Río, Temisco, Mex., 5 Jan. 1849, CMRFH.

8. Cálculo sobre Miraflores, encl. from Pedro Ansoátegui to Gregorio José Martínez del Río, Mexico City, 20 July 1840, CMRFH.

9. Pedro Ansoátegui to Gregorio José Martínez del Río, Mexico City, 20 July 1842, CMRFH.

10. José Pablo Martínez del Río to Gregorio José Martínez del Río, Mexico City, 25 Dec. 1843, CMRFH.

11. Ibid., 27 July 1845; 23 July 1846; 9 Feb. 1847.

12. Pedro Ansoátegui to Gregorio José Martínez del Río, Mexico City, 23 Dec. 1841; 15 June, 23 Nov. 1842; 25 Mar. 1843; 23 June 1846; Ventura de la Cruz Martínez del Río to Gregorio José Martínez del Río, Seville, 16 Apr. 1849; Pedro Ansoátegui to Gregorio José Martínez del Río, Georgetown, U.S., 20 Feb. 1855, CMRFH. By way of comparison, Cayetano Rubio's factory, Hércules (Querétaro), was capitalized at $800,000 in 1844; Antonio Garay's factory, Magdalena (Mexico City), was capitalized at $1,000,000 in 1846 (Potash, *Mexican Government and Industrial Development*, p. 152).

13. Contract, Jacob H. Robertson and Martínez del Río Hermanos, Mexico City, 24 Nov. 1842, CMRFH.

14. For example, factory operatives in factories in Puebla earned daily wages ($0.62-$1.00) three to four times higher than those commonly paid to agricultural workers ($0.25). For wages in Puebla, see Jan Bazant, "La industria algodonera poblana de 1803-1843 en números," *HM* 14:1:131-144 (July-Sep. 1964).

15. By way of comparison, La Constancia in Puebla employed 367 workers in 1843; El Patriotismo employed 204; thirteen other mills each employed from 95 to 19 workers: see Bazant, "Industria algodonera poblana," pp. 140-141.

16. Pedro Ansoátegui to Gregorio José Martínez del Río, Mexico City, 20 July 1842; 28 Sep. 1844, CMRFH; Mexico, Ministerio de Fomento, *Estado de las fábricas de hilados y tejidos existentes en la república mexicana* (Mexico City, 1854). For an exchange of textiles for foodstuffs, see AN-169-1849:809-810 (11 Sep. 1849).

17. Pedro Ansoátegui to Gregorio José Martínez del Río, Mexico City, 30 Nov. 1840, 24 Jan., 15 Feb. 1841; 24 May 1843; 28 Sep. 1844; 29 Sep. 1845, CMRFH.

18. Ibid., 19 Jan. 1841; 29 May 1844; 29 July, 27 Aug. 1845; 24 Feb. 1846, CMRFH; Mexico, Ministerio de Fomento, *Estado*.

19. Bazant, "Industria algodonera poblana," p. 137.

20. Pedro Ansoátegui to Gregorio José Martínez del Río, Mexico City, 5 Jan. 1841; 9 Feb. 1847; Extracto de c/v de José Ant.o Sosa por mantas, [Mexico City], Dec. 1859, CMRFH; AN-169-1853:64-65 (21 Jan. 1853).

21. Pedro Ansoátegui to Gregorio José Martínez del Río, Mexico City, 19 Jan., 6 Nov. 1841; 21 Mar. 1842; 24 May 1843; 29 July 1845; 10 Jan., 24 Apr. 1846; 22 July 1847, CMRFH; AN-169-1853:64-65 (21 Jan. 1853).

22. Pedro Ansoátegui to Gregorio José Martínez del Río, Mexico City, 3, 22 Oct. 1851, CMRFH.

23. Domingo Ansoátegui to Gregorio José Martínez del Río, Mexico City, 14 Nov. 1849, CMRFH.

24. Pedro Ansoátegui to Gregorio José Martínez del Río, Mexico City, 22 July 1847, CMRFH.

25. Ibid., 29 Oct. 1846, CMRFH.

26. Ibid., 19 Jan., 6 Nov. 1841; 21 Mar. 1842; 10 Jan. 1846; Account, Cuenta de venta de 8 tros. manta de Miraflores recib. de Arr.o Raf.l Borja y vendidos de órden y por cuenta y riesgo de los señores Martínez del Río Hermanos, Germán F. Pohls, Guanajuato, 20 Mar. 1860, CMRFH.

27. AN-169-1853:892-893 (19 Sep. 1853); Gregorio Martínez v. José Carballeda, 1869-1870, AJ, Gregorio José Martínez del Río.

28. Domingo Ansoátegui to Gregorio José Martínez del Río, Mexico City, 28

Nov. 1846, CMRFH; Gregorio Martínez v. José Carballeda, 1869-1870, AJ, Gregorio José Martínez del Río.

29. Pedro Ansoátegui to Gregorio José Martínez del Río, Mexico City, 15 Feb. 1841, CMRFH.

30. Various to Richard Pakenham, Mexico City, 11 Feb. 1841, FO-204-76:117.

31. William Barlow to Richard Pakenham, Mexico City, 21 Feb. 1841, FO-204-76:150-151.

32. Richard Pakenham to Lord Palmerston, Mexico City, 26 Feb. 1841, FO-204-72:204.

33. Pedro Ansoátegui to Gregorio José Martínez del Río, Mexico City, 30 Apr. 1841, CMRFH.

34. Ibid., 21 Mar. 1842, CMRFH.

35. Ibid., 15 June 1842, CMRFH.

36. Ibid., 20 July 1842, CMRFH. The tariff Pedro refers to is that of 20 Apr. 1842, which lowered duties and relaxed prohibitions: see Potash, *Mexican Government and Industrial Development*, pp. 139-140.

37. Richard Pakenham to J. M. de Bocanegra, Mexico City, 3 Dec. 1842, FO-204-78:726.

38. Potash, *Mexican Goverment and Industrial Development*, p. 140.

39. José Pablo Martínez del Río to Gregorio José Martínez del Río, Kingston, 18 Oct. 1843, CMRFH.

40. Ibid., Puebla, 25 Nov. 1843, CMRFH.

41. Pedro Ansoátegui to Gregorio José Martínez del Río, Mexico City, 23 Sep. 1854, CMRFH. The debate over protectionism and state interventionism in the economy of Mexico was already old in 1845. Typically, the most vocal opponents of these policies were not Mexican citizens. Examples of works related to this controversy include Alexander von Humboldt, *Political Essay on the Kingdom of New Spain*, 4 vols., trans. John Black (London: Longman, Hurst, Rees, Orme, and Brown, 1811); and Robert C. Willie [Wylie], *México: noticia sobre su hacienda pública bajo el gobierno colonial y después de la independencia* (Mexico City: I. Cumplido, 1845). Humboldt concentrated his criticism on the deleterious effects of the tobacco monopoly; Wylie placed the blame for the sad state of the Mexican Treasury on the government's unwise commitment to promoting an inefficient textile industry.

42. Domingo Ansoátegui to Gregorio José Martínez del Río, Mexico City, 14 Nov. 1849, CMRFH.

43. Keremitsis, *La industria textil*, pp. 46-49.

44. Ibid., 49-50.

45. Pedro Ansoátegui to Gregorio José Martínez del Río, Mexico City, 21 Mar. 1842; Domingo Ansoátegui to Gregorio José Martínez del Río, Mexico City, 26 Feb. 1846; Ventura de la Cruz Martínez del Río to José Pablo Martínez del Río London, 4 July 1850, CMRFH.

46. Keremitsis, *La industria textil*, p. 37.

47. Martínez del Río Hermanos v. Junta de Acreedores, 1861-1865, AJ, Concursos.

48. Calculated from price data reported in Bazant, "Industria algodonera poblana," pp. 134-139.

49. Cotton consumption data are reported in Domingo Ansoátegui to Gregorio

José Martínez del Río, Mexico City, 29 May 1844; 29 May 1846; Pedro Ansoátegui to Gregorio José Martínez del Río, Mexico City, 3 Oct. 1841. Aggregate consumption data for Mexican textile factories are reported in Mexico, Ministerio de Fomento, *Estado*. For problems in finding cotton at reasonable prices, see Pedro Ansoátegui to Gregorio José Martínez del Río, Mexico City, 1 June 1842; 19 Dec. 1843; Pedro Ansoátegui to Gregorio José Martínez del Río, Miraflores, 26 Aug. 1847, CMRFH; and Keremitsis, *La industria textil*, pp. 24-26.

50. For costs associated with buying and transporting cotton from New Orleans to Veracruz in 1851, see Pedro Ansoátegui to Gregorio José Martínez del Río, Mexico City, 3 Aug., 10 Nov. 1851, CMRFH.

51. Coatsworth, "Obstacles."

52. For the role of the Veracruz planters in the tobacco monopoly, see Walker, "Business as Usual."

53. Manuel Dublán and José María Lozano, *Legislación mexicana ó colección de las disposiciones legislativas expendidas desde la independencia de la república,* 34 vols. (Mexico City: Imprenta del Comercio, 1876-1904), p. 3:191

54. Pedro Ansoátegui to Gregorio José Martínez del Río, Mexico City, 15 June, 20 July 1844, CMRFH.

55. Ibid., Tacubaya, Mex., 14 Apr. 1843, Mexico City; 10, 14 Jan. 1846, Mexico City, CMRFH; Potash, *Mexican Government and Industrial Development,* pp. 129, 143.

56. Estevan de Antuñano, *Economía política. Refutación que el que subscribe hace, por notas, del artículo del Monitor de Veracruz de fecha 24 de agosto, sobre importación de algodones extranjeros en rama* (Puebla, 1840). For a discussion of the controversy among manufacturers, see Potash, Mexican Government and Industrial Development, , pp. 141-144. Puebla mill owners like José Velasco especially opposed Antuñano's program.

57. Pedro Ansoátegui to Gregorio José Martínez del Río, Mexico City, 6 July 1841, CMRFH.

58. For early problems with cotton purchases, see ibid., 22 Nov. 1842; José Pablo Martínez del Río to Gregorio José Martínez del Río, Mexico City, 24 Aug. 1844, CMRFH.

59. Pedro Ansoátegui to Gregorio José Martínez del Río, Mexico City, 29 May 1846, CMRFH.

60. Ibid., 28 June, 27 Aug. 1846.

61. For the textile industry in Puebla, see Bazant, "Industria algodonera poblana," and Guy P. C. Thompson, "The Cotton Textile Industry in Puebla during the 18th and 19th Centuries," paper presented at Bielefeld, W. Germany, September 1982.

62. Pedro Ansoátegui to Gregorio José Martínez del Río, Mexico City, 12 Nov. 1849.

63. Domingo Ansoátegui to Gregorio José Martínez del Río, Mexico City, 13 Oct., 14 Nov. 1849; Pedro Ansoátegui to Gregorio José Martínez del Río, Mexico City, 20 Nov. 1849, CMRFH.

64. Pedro Ansoátegui to Gregorio José Martínez del Río, Mexico City, 20 Nov. 1849, CMRFH.

65. Domingo Ansoátegui to Gregorio José Martínez del Río, Mexico City, 13 Oct. 1849, CMRFH.

66. Gregorio José Martínez del Río to José Pablo Martínez del Río, Veracruz, 18 Oct. 1849, CMRFH.

67. Domingo Ansoátegui to Gregorio José Martínez del Río, Mexico City, 14 Nov. 1849, CMRFH.

68. Gregorio José Martínez del Río to José Pablo Martínez del Río, Veracruz, 18 Oct. 1849, CMRFH.

69. Domingo Ansoátegui to Gregorio José Martínez del Río, Mexico City, 14 Nov. 1849, CMRFH.

70. Pedro Ansoátegui to Gregorio José Martínez del Río, Mexico City, 3 Aug., 13 Sep., 3 Oct., 10 Nov. 1851, CMRFH.

71. Ibid., 22 Oct. 1851.

72. Bazant, "Industria algodonera poblana," pp. 138-140; Guy P. C. Thompson, "Traditional and Modern Manufacturing in Mexico, 1821-50," p. 19, paper presented at Berlin, September 1983.

73. Pedro Ansoátegui to Gregorio José Martínez del Río, Philadelphia, 23 July 1854, CMRFH.

74. [José] Pablo Martínez del Río, *Curso de agricultura. Cultivo de algodón* (Mexico City: G. A. Esteva, 1882).

75. For the trials and tribulations of the Mexican textile industry in the twentieth century, see Keremitsis, *La industria textil.*

7. The Funds and the Conventions, 1838-1848

1. Pedro Ansoátegui to Gregorio José Martínez del Río, Mexico City, 15 June 1839, CMRFH.

2. Ibid., 22 July 1839.

3. Ibid., 9 Apr. 1840.

4. Mexico, Ministerio de Hacienda y Crédito Público, *Memoria* (1869-1870) (Mexico City: Imprenta del Gobierno, 1870), p. 154; Pedro Ansoátegui to Gregorio José Martínez del Río, Mexico City, 11 Sep. 1839, CMRFH. Apart from debts inherited from the colonial regime, Mexico's foreign debt originated with the London loan of 1824. Unlike the internal debt, which so far has escaped the attention of researchers, the foreign debt is the subject of several studies. The best of these is Jan Bazant, *Historia de la deuda exterior de México (1823-1946)* (Mexico City: El Colegio de México, 1968).

5. Mexico, Ministerio de Hacienda y Crédito Público, *Memoria* (1869-1870), p. 171; Pedro Ansoátegui to Gregorio José Martínez del Río, Mexico City, 23 May 1838; 25 Jan., 15 June, 22 July, 10 Aug., 11 Sep. 1839; 28 Mar., 4, 20 July, 15 Aug., 30 Nov. 1840; 24 Jan., 19 May, 6 July 1841; 31 Jan. 1842, CMRFH.

6. Pedro Ansoátegui to Gregorio José Martínez del Río, Mexico City, 4 July 1840, CMRFH.

7. Ibid., 30 Nov. 1840.

8. Ibid., 4, 20 July 1840; 30 Apr. 1841; 20 July 1842.

9. Richard Pakenham to J. M. Ortiz Monasterio, Mexico City, 18 Apr. 1837, SRE(A)-L-E-1366.

10. Pedro Ansoátegui to Gregorio José Martínez del Río, Mexico City, 24 Mar. 1839, CMRFH.

11. Ibid., 7 May 1839; Copy of agreement between Ministry of Hacienda and

Creditors, [no signature], [Mexico City], 8 June 1839, CMRFH; Merchants to Richard Pakenham, Mexico City, 30 Apr. 1839, FO-204-66:250.

12. Pedro Ansoátegui to Gregorio José Martínez del Río, Mexico City, 11 Sep. 1839, CMRFH.

13. Richard Pakenham to Juan de Dios Cañedo, Mexico City, 8, 10 Oct. 1839, SRE(A)-L-E-1372; Pedro Ansoátegui to Gregorio José Martínez del Río, Mexico City, 11 Sep. 1839; 4, 20 July, 30 Nov. 1840; 25 Jan., 15 Feb., 19 May, 12 Oct. 1841, CMRFH; AN-717-1839:s.p. (19 Nov. 1839).

14. Pedro Ansoátegui to Gregorio José Martínez del Río, Mexico City, 6 July 1841, CMRFH.

15. For the Martínez del Ríos' attitudes toward Bustamante's reforms, see ibid., 15 Aug., 30 Nov. 1840.

16. Computed from data reported in Martínez del Río Hermanos's sundry accounts, CMRFH.

17. For the tobacco empresarios' relations with Bustamante and Santa Anna, see Walker, "Business as Usual," pp. 698-704.

18. Pedro Ansoátegui to Gregorio José Martínez del Río, Mexico City, 5 July 1841, CMRFH.

19. For example, see the list of new military units created by Santa Anna's decrees between 15 October 1841 and 1 February 1842 in Mexico, Ministerio de Hacienda y Crédito Público, Memoria (1869-1870), p. 218.

20. Ventura de la Cruz Martínez del Río to José Pablo Martínez del Río, Mexico City, 9 Feb. 1842, CMRFH.

21. Gregorio Mier y Terán et al., Representación dirigida al sr. presidente de la república por los apoderados de los acreedores que tienen hipotecas sobre las aduanas marítimas (Mexico City: I. Cumplido, 1842). For an 1842 listing of creditors of the funds, see Walker, "Kinship, Business, and Politics," appendix F.

22. For examples of these transactions, see the Protocolos de Hacienda (AN). These are the unnumbered volumes of the notaries Cabrera, Negrieros, Vigueras, J. M. Ramírez, R. Villalobos, A. Vera y Sánchez, Orihuela, A. Pérez de Lara, Miguel Diez de Bonilla, and Joaquín Abadiano. For the years 1835 to 1855, fianzas make up the single largest category of registered instruments.

23. Pedro Ansoátegui to Gregorio José Martínez del Río, Mexico City, 20 July 1842, CMRFH.

24. Ibid.

25. Ibid., 28 Sep. 1842, CMRFH.

26. Martínez del Río Hermanos to Richard Pakenham, Mexico City, 21 Feb. 1842, FO-204-79:666.

27. Ibid.

28. Ibid., 6 Oct. 1842, FO-204-79:288.

29. Richard Pakenham to Martínez del Río Hermanos, Mexico City, 7 Oct. 1842, FO-204-79:289.

30. Pedro Ansoátegui to Gregorio José Martínez del Río, Mexico City, 21 Mar. 1842, CMRFH.

31. Pedro Ansoátegui to Gregorio José Martínez del Río, Mexico City, 8, 27 Oct. 1842, CMRFH.

32. Richard Pakenham to Ewen C. MacKintosh, Mexico City, 24 Nov. 1842,

FO-204-79:336; Percy W. Doyle to J. M. de Bocanegra, Mexico City, 19 July 1843, SRE(S)-25-14-36; Pedro Ansoátegui to Gregorio José Martínez del Río, Mexico City, 24 Dec. 1842; 28 Aug. 1843, CMRFH.

33. Pedro Ansoátegui to Gregorio José Martínez del Río, Mexico City, 24 Dec. 1842, CMRFH.

34. Convenio por el arreglo del fondo de 17%, Montgomery Nicod & Co., Mexico City, 20 Jan. 1843; Pedro Ansoátegui to José Pablo Martínez del Río, Mexico City, 24 Mar. 1843; José Pablo Martínez del Río to Gregorio José Martínez del Río, Paris, 9 Mar. 1843, CMRFH; Document, Interés del Martínez del Río Herm. en el 17%, [no signature], [Mexico City], [1843], FO-204-83:1010.

35. Pedro Ansoátegui to Gregorio José Martínez del Río, Mexico City, 24 Mar. 1843, CMRFH.

36. Mexico, Ministerio de Hacienda y Crédito Público, *Memoria* (1869-1870), pp. 232-250.

37. José Pablo Martínez del Río to Gregorio José Martínez del Río, Kingston, Jamaica, 18 Oct. 1843, CMRFH. José Pablo reported that after presenting the $80,000 bribe, Escandón tricked Santa Anna out of all but $20,000.

38. José Pablo Martínez del Río to Gregorio José Martínez del Río, Paris, 9 Mar. 1843, CMRFH.

39. Pedro Ansoátegui to Gregorio José Martínez del Río, Mexico City, 29 Oct. 1843, CMRFH.

40. José Pablo Martínez del Río to Gregorio José Martínez del Río, Mexico City, 13 Apr. 1844, CMRFH.

41. Pedro Ansoátegui to Gregorio José Martínez del Río, Mexico City, 28 Aug. 1843; 28 Oct. 1845; 24 Apr. 1846; José Pablo Martínez del Río to Gregorio José Martínez del Río, Mexico City, 4 Aug. 1844; Domingo Ansoátegui to Gregorio José Martínez del Río, Mexico City, 29 Mar. 1846, CMRFH.

42. José Pablo Martínez del Río to Gregorio José Martínez del Río, Mexico City, 19 Sep. 1844, CMRFH.

43. Pedro Ansoátegui to Gregorio José Martínez del Río, Mexico City, 23 Sep. 1846, CMRFH. For controversies involving forced loans and foreigners in the 1830s (including Drusina & Martínez), see British Merchants to Richard Pakenham, Mexico City, 24 June 1836, SRE(A)-L-E-1364. For the 1840s, see Ewen C. MacKintosh to J. M. Ortiz Monasterio, Mexico City, 9 Nov. 1840, SRE(S)-25-14-2; Martínez del Río Hermanos to Ministerio de Hacienda, Mexico City, 27 Apr. 1843, FO-204-83:219; Martínez del Río Hermanos to Richard Pakenham, Mexico City, 27 Apr. 1843, FO-204-83:217; Edward Thornton to J. A. Pacheco, Mexico City, 7 July 1847, SRE(S)-12-30-5; Domingo Ansoátegui to Gregorio José Martínez del Río, Mexico City, 27 Nov. 1847; Pedro Ansoátegui to Gregorio José Martínez del Río, Mexico City, 22 July 1847, CMRFH.

44. Pedro Ansoátegui to Gregorio José Martínez del Río, Mexico City, 23 June 1843, 27 July, 28 Aug. 1846; 28 Jan. 1847; Domingo Ansoátegui to Gregorio José Martínez del Río, Mexico City, 29 Mar. 1846, CMRFH.

45. José Pablo Martínez del Río to Gregorio José Martínez del Río, Miraflores, Mexico, 14 May 1846, CMRFH. For the British minister's unsuccessful attempts to persuade Yturbé to lift the suspensions, see Charles Bankhead to J. Castillo Lanzas, Mexico City, 5 June 1846, SRE(S)-25-14-36.

46. José Pablo Martínez del Río to Gregorio José Martínez del Río, San Angel, Mex., 25 Mar. 1847; Pedro Ansoátegui to Gregorio José Martínez del Río, Mexico City, 24 Sep. 1847, CMRFH.

47. Martínez del Río Hermanos to Ministry of Hacienda, Mexico City, 27 Apr. 1843, FO-204-83:219; Martínez del Río Hermanos to Pakenham, 27 Apr. 1843, FO-204-83:217.

48. Pedro Ansoátegui to Gregorio José Martínez del Río, Mexico City, 27 Nov. 1847, CMRFH.

49. British Merchants to Richard Pakenham, Mexico City, 17 Mar. 1843, FO-204-83:158; Pedro Ansoátegui to Gregorio José Martínez del Río, Mexico City, 23 Sep. 1845, CMRFH.

8. The Tobacco Debt Bonds and the Conventions, 1845-1861

1. Ventura de la Cruz Martínez del Río to José Pablo Martínez del Río, Rome, 17 Mar. 1845, CMRFH.

2. Mexico, Ministerio de Hacienda y Crédito Público, *Memoria* (1869-1870), pp. 262-263, 272-275.

3. For the Empresa del Tabaco and the return of the monopoly to government administration, see Walker, "Business as Usual."

4. Pedro Ansoátegui to Gregorio José Martínez del Río, Mexico City, 29 May 1845; see also Pedro Ansoátegui to Gregorio José Martínez del Río, Cuautla, Mex., 24 Feb. 1846, CMRFH.

5. Pedro Ansoátegui to Gregorio José Martínez del Río, Mexico City, 27 Aug. 1845, CMRFH.

6. B. Maqua, J. A. Béistegui, Muriel Hermanos to J. A. Zayas, Mexico City, 15 Oct. 1851, SRE(A)-1157-12.

7. Pedro Ansoátegui to Gregorio José Martínez del Río, Mexico City, 25 June 1845, CMRFH.

8. Ibid.

9. Ibid.

10. Ibid.

11. Ibid., 29 Dec. 1845, CMRFH.

12. Ibid., 20 Jan. 1846, CMRFH.

13. Domingo Ansoátegui to Gregorio José Martínez del Río, Mexico City, 27 Aug. 1846, CMRFH.

14. Mexico, Ministerio de Hacienda y Crédito Público, *Memoria* (1869-1870), p. 272.

15. Pedro Ansoátegui to Gregorio José Martínez del Río, Mexico City, 27 Aug. 1846, CMRFH.

16. José Pablo Martínez del Río to Gregorio José Martínez del Río, Mexico City, 27 Sep. 1846, CMRFH.

17. Pedro Ansoátegui to Gregorio José Martínez del Río, Mexico City, 29 Oct. 1846, CMRFH.

18. Mexico, Secretaría de Relaciones Interiores y Exteriores, *Documento no. 4 de la memoria que el secretario de relaciones interiores y esteriores presentó á las cámaras, en que se da cuenta de los arreglos hechos para el pago de la deuda garantizada por convenciones diplomáticas* (Mexico City, 1852); Pedro Ansoátegui to

Gregorio José Martínez del Río, Mexico City, 27 Nov. 1846, CMRFH.

19. Pedro Ansoátegui to Gregorio José Martínez del Río, Mexico City, 28 Dec. 1846, CMRFH.

20. José Pablo Martínez del Río to Gregorio José Martínez del Río, Mexico City, 25 Dec. 1846, CMRFH.

21. Ibid., 27 Aug. 1846, CMRFH.

22. Ibid., 5 Dec. 1846; see also José Pablo Martínez del Río to Gregorio José Martínez del Río, San Angel, Mex., 25 Mar. 1847, CMRFH.

23. Domingo Ansoátegui to Gregorio José Martínez del Río, Mexico City, 9 Jan. 1847, CMRFH.

24. Charles Bankhead to Manuel Baranda, Mexico City, 19 May 1847, SRE(S)-27-21-2. Escandón was one of the first to learn of the British decision to aid the firm: Manuel Escandón to Gregorio José Martínez del Río, Paris, 28 Apr. 1847, CMRFH.

25. Pedro Ansoátegui to Gregorio José Martínez del Río, Mexico City, 28 May 1847, CMRFH.

26. Charles Bankhead to Martínez del Río Hermanos, Mexico City, 1 Sep. 1847, as copy incl. in Domingo Ansoátegui to Gregorio José Martínez del Río, Mexico City, 27 Sep. 1847, CMRFH.

27. Pedro Ansoátegui to Gregorio José Martínez del Río, 28 May 1847, CMRFH.

28. Mexico, Ministerio de Hacienda y Crédito Público, *Memoria* (1869-1870), pp. 288-308; Percy Doyle to M. Otero, Mexico City, 1 Nov. 1848, SRE(S)-27-21-2.

29. José Pablo Martínez del Río to Gregorio José Martínez del Río, San Angel, Mex., 25 Mar. 1847, CMRFH.

30. Pedro Ansoátegui to Gregorio José Martínez del Río, Mexico City, 22 July 1847; Manuel Escandón to Gregorio José Martínez del Río, Paris, 12 Aug. 1847, CMRFH; AN-169-1850:283-289 (21 Mar. 1850); Mexico, Ministerio de Hacienda y Crédito Público, *Contrato de compañía celebrado por el supremo gobierno, para la administración y giro de la renta del tabaco y exposición con que lo remitió á las cámaras el secretario del despacho de hacienda* (Mexico City: Imprenta de la Calle de Medinas, 1848).

31. For MacKintosh's bankruptcy, see Tenenbaum, "Merchants," pp. 334-338.

32. The purchase of the Real del Monte mining properties is registered in AN-169-1849:583-587 (4 July 1849). The sale of MacKintosh's shares in the tobacco company is registered in AN-169-1850:52-55 (25 Jan. 1850).

33. Manuel Piña y Cuevas to Ministry of Interior and Exterior Relations, Mexico City, 26 Jan. 1849, SRE(S)-27-21-2.

34. Computed from data reported for the Mexican foreign debt in 1848. At this time the whole public debt was about $144 million: Mexico, Ministerio de Hacienda y Crédito Público, *Memoria* (1869-1870), pp. 304-305.

35. Ibid., p. 330.

36. Manuel Payno, "Memoria sobre la convención inglesa; créditos de Martínez del Río herm.," *La Patria* (Mexico City), 11 Nov. 1855; An-169-1849:402-403 (15 May 1849); Pedro Ansoátegui to Gregorio José Martínez del Río, Mexico City, 9 Oct. 1849; Domingo Ansoátegui to Gregorio José Martínez del Río, Mexico City, 13 Oct., 14 Nov. 1849, CMRFH.

37. For a noneconometric analysis of the evolution of Liberal thought and the Liberal political movement in Mexico, see Hale, *Mexican Liberalism*.

38. Domingo Ansoátegui to Gregorio José Martínez del Río, Mexico City, 14 Nov. 1849, CMRFH.

39. Percy Doyle to J. M. Lacurza, Mexico City, 8 Nov. 1849, SRE(S)-27-21-2; Domingo Ansoátegui to Gregorio José Martínez del Río, Mexico City, 14 Nov. 1849; Gregorio José Martínez del Río to José Pablo Martínez del Río, Veracruz, 18 Oct. 1849, CMRFH.

40. For a discussion of this law and related matters, see Mexico, Ministerio de Hacienda y Crédito Público, *Memoria* (1869-1870), pp. 340-347.

41. For an example of these attacks, see *El Monitor Republicano* (Mexico City), 9 Oct. 1850.

42. Payno, "Memoria."

43. Martínez del Río Hermanos to Percy Doyle, Mexico City, 4 Dec. 1850, FO-204-105:643.

44. For related correspondence, see Percy Doyle to Lord Palmerston, Mexico City, 4 Jan. 1851, FO-204-106:695; Martínez del Río Hermanos to Percy Doyle, Mexico City, 25 Jan. 1851, FO-204-131:51; Martínez del Río Hermanos to Percy Doyle, Mexico City, 14 Feb. 1851, FO-204-107:124; Martínez del Río Hermanos to Percy Doyle, Mexico City, 19 Apr. 1851, FO-204-107:158; Martínez del Río Hermanos to British Legation, Mexico City, 28 Jan. 1851, FO-204-131:52; Martínez del Río Hermanos to Junta de Crédito Público, Mexico City, 3 Mar. 1851, SRE(S)-27-21-9.

45. Percy Doyle to Martínez del Río Hermanos, Mexico City, 22 Apr. 1851, FO-204-109:20; J. M. Ortiz Monasterio to Percy Doyle, Mexico City, 2 May 1851, FO-204-108:59.

46. Percy Doyle to Lord Palmerston, Mexico City, 5 May 1851, FO-204-106:579.

47. Ibid.

48. Ibid., 4 June 1851, FO-204-106:604; see also Pedro Ansoátegui to Percy Doyle, Mexico City, 9 May 1851, FO-204-109:185; Percy Doyle to Pedro Ansoátegui, Mexico City, 13 May 1851, FO-204-109:27; J. M. Ortiz Monasterio to Percy Doyle, Mexico City, 20 May 1851, FO-204-108:91.

49. Ventura de la Cruz Martínez del Río to Gregorio José Martínez del Río, London, 31 July 1851, CMRFH; Manuel Payno to Lord Palmerston, London, 16 June 1851, FO-204-106:241.

50. Percy Doyle to Lord Palmerston (confidential), Mexico City, 5 July 1851, FO-204-106:614. See also Manuel Macedo to Percy Doyle, Mexico City, 17 June 1851, FO-204-108:129; Manuel Macedo to Percy Doyle, Mexico City, 28 June 1851, FO-204-108:132; Percy Doyle to Lord Palmerston, Mexico City, 5 July 1851, FO-204-106:609.

51. For examples, see Percy Doyle to Manuel Macedo, Mexico City, 28 July 1851, FO-204-108:396; and Percy Doyle to José F. Ramírez, Mexico City, 13 Sep. 1851, FO-204-108:411.

52. Lord Palmerston to Percy Doyle, London, 31 July 1841, FO-204-106:35; see also Lord Palmerston to Percy Doyle, London, 30 Aug. 1851, FO-204-105:38.

53. José F. Ramírez to Percy Doyle, Mexico City, 2 Oct. 1851, FO-204-108:221; Percy Doyle to Lord Palmerston, Mexico City, 4 Aug. 1851, FO-204-106:627.

54. Pedro Ansoátegui to Gregorio José Martínez del Río, Mexico City, 3 Aug. 1851, CMRFH.

55. José Pablo Martínez del Río to Gregorio José Martínez del Río, Mexico City, 16 Aug. 1851, CMRFH.

56. Percy Doyle to Lord Palmerston, Mexico City, 5 Oct. 1851, FO-204-106:651.

57. Ibid., and 6 Oct. 1851, FO-204-106:661; José F. Ramírez to Percy Doyle (secret), Mexico City, 4 Oct. 1851, FO-204-109:204.

58. Percy Doyle to Lord Palmerston, Mexico City, 5 Oct. 1851, FO-204-106:651. ·

59. Ibid., 5 Dec. 1851, FO-204-106:878.

60. Ibid.

61. Pedro Ansoátegui to Gregorio José Martínez del Río, Mexico City, 22 Oct. 1851, CMRFH.

62. Ibid.

63. B. Maqua, J. A. Béistegui, Muriel Hermanos to J. A. Zayas, Mexico City, 15 Oct. 1851; J. A. Zayas to J. Ramírez, Mexico City, 19 Oct. 1851, SRE(S)-1557-12.

64. For the text of the 1851 Convention, see Great Britain, Foreign Office, *A Complete Collection of the Treaties and Conventions and Reciprocal Regulations at Present Subsiding between Great Britain and Foreign Powers*, vol. 12 (London, 1871), pp. 642-646.

65. Queen Victoria to Percy Doyle (secret), London, 24 Dec. 1851, FO-204-106:346.

66. Percy Doyle to Foreign Office, Mexico City, 2 Nov. 1853, FO-50-261:109.

67. Pedro Ansoátegui to Gregorio José Martínez del Río, Veracruz, 17 Mar. 1854, CMRFH; J. M. de Castillo y Lanzas to Lord Clarendon, London, 22 July 1854, SRE(A)-L-E-1655. Addington was one of the Martínez del Ríos' social assets in England. The acquaintance had developed through José Pablo's physician friend, Dr. Hegewich (his brother-in-law) in Mexico.

68. Pedro Ansoátegui to Gregorio José Martínez del Río, Veracruz, 17 Mar. 1854, CMRFH.

69. Percy Doyle to Foreign Office, Mexico City, 3 May 1854, FO-50-267:200.

70. Foreign Office to Percy Doyle, London, 9 Oct. 1854, FO-50-264:211.

71. J. M. Castillo y Lanzas to Lord Clarendon, London, 9 Oct. 1854, SRE(A)-L-E-1655.

72. Pedro Ansoátegui to José Pablo Martínez del Río, New York, 18 June 1854, CMRFH.

73. Ibid., Philadelphia, 23 July 1854, CMRFH.

74. AN-169-1854:667-670 (31 July 1854).

75. Pedro Ansoátegui to José Pablo Martínez del Río, Georgetown, U.S., 20 Feb. 1855, CMRFH.

76. Pedro Ansoátegui to José Pablo Martínez del Río, Washington, D. C., 20 May 1855; Pedro Ansoátegui to José Pablo Martínez del Río, Georgetown, 29 May 1855; M. Escandón to José Pablo Martínez del Río, London, 5 July 1855, CMRFH.

77. For the family's attitude toward the church, see Pedro Ansoátegui to José Pablo Martínez del Río, London, 9 July 1855, CMRFH. For the background to church-state relations in nineteenth-century Mexico, see Calcott, *Church and State*

in Mexico; and Michael P. Costeloe, *Church Wealth in Mexico: A Study of the Juzgado de Capellanías in the Archbishopric of Mexico, 1800-1856* (Cambridge: At the University Press, 1971).

78. Payno, "Memoria."

79. For an example of the polemics generated by the controversy, see [Martínez del Río Hermanos], *Contestación de los agentes de la convención inglesa á la memoria del señor Payno* (Mexico City: J. M. Fernández de Lara, 1855).

80. For the Law of 1 January 1856, see Mexico, Ministerio de Hacienda y Crédito Público, *Memoria* (1869-1870), p. 445.

81. George Lettson to Luis de la Rosa, Mexico City, 8, 11 Feb. 1856, FO-204-130:409-410.

82. Luis de la Rosa to George Lettson, Mexico City, 14, 17 Mar., 9, 18, 24 Apr., 3 May, 29 June 1856, FO-204-130:114, 122, 138, 152, 162, 202; George Lettson to Luis de la Rosa, Mexico City, 15 May, 2 June, 15 July, 9 Aug. 1856, FO-204-130:483, 491, 533, 542; George Lettson to Martínez del Río Hermanos, Mexico City, 9 Apr., 6 May 1856, FO-204-131:542, 546; Martínez del Río Hermanos to George Lettson, Mexico City, 24 Apr., 30 Oct. 1856, FO-204-131:254, 461.

83. For examples, see Martínez del Río Hermanos to George Lettson, Mexico City, 9 Apr. 1856, FO-204-131:206; and Torre, Knight & Company to Martínez del Río Hermanos, Mazatlán, Mexico, 19 July 1856, FO-204-131:770.

84. Martínez del Río Hermanos to George Lettson, Mexico City, 17 Nov. 1856, FO-204-131:487.

85. Ibid., 25 June 1856, FO-204-131:317.

86. George Lettson to Martínez del Río Hermanos, Mexico City, 11, 29 Mar. 1856, FO-204-131:538, 206; Pedro Ansoátegui to José Pablo Martínez del Río, London, 9 July 1856, CMRFH.

87. Mexico, Ministerio de Hacienda y Crédito Público, *Memoria* (1869-1870), p. 445. For Payno's report of his term in office, see ibid. (Dec. 1855-May 1856).

88. George Lettson to Martínez del Río Hermanos, Mexico City, 18 Nov. 1856, FO-204-131:576.

89. AN-426-1856:441-443 (25 Aug. 1856).

90. Mexico, Ministerio de Hacienda y Crédito Público, *Memoria* (1869-1870), pp. 92, 441-443; [Carlos Martínez del Río y Fernández de Henestrosa], "Memorandum. Los derechos que los señores Martínez del Río tienen en contra de la república del Ecuador por el parte que a dicho país corresponde pagar a consecuencia del emprestito hecho por México á Colombia en 1826," Mexico City, July 1971 (typescript), CMRFH.

91. Pedro Ansoátegui to Gregorio José Martínez del Río, Mexico City, 21 Dec. 1839, CMRFH.

92. Proposición al Supremo Gobierno, Mexico City, 3 Feb. 1840, as incl. to Pedro Ansoátegui to Gregorio José Martínez del Río, Mexico City, 20 Feb. 1840, CMRFH.

93. Pedro Ansoátegui to Gregorio José Martínez del Río, Mexico City, 29 Oct. 1846, CMRFH.

94. During this same time, Escandón wrote to the Martínez del Ríos from Paris to report that Mosquera had stated that Colombia would pay its share of the debt: Manuel Escandón to Gregorio José Martínez del Río, Paris, 2 Mar. 1847, CMRFH.

95. For a detailed list of the firm's assets and liabilities, consult Walker, "Kinship, Business, and Politics," appendix E; AN-169-1856:529-607 (16 Aug. 1856); A copy of the terms of sale translated by M. Lerdo de Tejada is located in SRE(A)-L-E-1046. For the statements of the French minister, see Lilia Díaz, *Versión francesa de México, informes diplomáticos. 1853-1864*, vol. 1 (Mexico City: El Colegio de México, 1963), p. 320.

96. AN-169-1856:607-608 (18 Aug. 1856); Manuel and Pablo (II) Martínez del Río to Secretaría de Relaciones Exteriores, Mexico City, 31 Jan. 1903, SRE(A)-L-E-1047; Justo Arosemena, *Apelación al buen sentido i a la consciencia pública en la cuestión "acreencia mejicana"* (Bogotá: Echeverría Hermanos, 1857).

97. AN-529-1859:2-15 (25 Jan. 1859).

98. Great Britain, Foreign Office, *Treaties and Conventions*, pp. 12:646-648.

99. Ibid., pp. 648-650.

100. Ibid., pp. 650-653.

101. AN-529-1859:2-15 (25 Jan. 1859).

102. José Pablo Martínez del Río to Gregorio José Martínez del Río, Milan, 20 Oct. 1859, CMRFH.

103. Ibid., 3 July 1859, CMRFH.

104. For reasons, see José Pablo Martínez del Río to Gregorio José Martínez del Río, Paris, 23 June, 1859; José Pablo Martínez del Río to Gregorio José Martínez del Río, Milan, 13 Sep. 1859; E. J. Perry to José Pablo Martínez del Río, London, 17 Nov. 1859; José Pablo Martínez del Río to Gregorio José Martínez del Río, Florence, 25 Nov., 27 Dec. 1859, CMRFH.

105. José Pablo Martínez del Río to Gregorio José Martínez del Río, Milan, 20 Oct. 1859, CMRFH.

9. Kinship, Business, and Politics: A Historical Perspective

1. For an analysis of this subject, see Magnus Mörner, "Economic Factors and Stratification in Colonial Spanish America with Special Reference to Elites," *HAHR* 63:2:335-370 (May 1983).

2. For the significance of family in post-Reform Mexico, see Alan Wells, "Family Elites in a Boom-and-Bust Economy: The Molinas and Peóns of Porfirian Mexico," *HAHR* 62:2:224-253 (May 1982); and Larissa Adler Lomnitz and Marisol Pérez Lizaur, "The History of a Mexican Urban Family," *JFH* 3:(Winter 1978):392-409.

10. Epilogue: The Martínez del Río Family, 1864-1984

1. José Pablo Martínez del Río to Armand Montluc, Paris, 27 May 1868, in Jorge L. Tamayo, ed., *Benito Juárez: documentos, discursos, y correspondencia* (Mexico City: Editorial Diana, 1967), pp. 13:347-348.

2. Tamayo, *Juárez*, p. 13:792. For a biography of Maximillian, consult Joan Haslip, *The Crown of Mexico: Maximilian and His Empress Carlota* (New York: Holt, Rinehart & Winston, 1971).

3. José Pablo Martínez del Río to J. Ramírez, London, 28 Aug. 1864, SRE(A)-L-E-1172.

4. Ibid., Cherapia, Turkey, 21 Oct. 1864; José Pablo Martínez del Río to J. Ramírez, Messina, Italy, 22 Nov. 1864, SRE(A)-L-E-1172.

5. Gregorio José Martínez del Río v. Francisco Schiafino, AJ, Gregorio José

Martínez del Río.

6. Francisco R. Almada, *Juárez y Terrazas: aclaraciones históricas* (Mexico City: Libros Mexicanos, 1958), p. 323; Gregorio José Martínez del Río to José Pablo Martínez del Río, Mexico City, 24 Dec. 1866; José Pablo Martínez del Río to Gregorio José Martínez del Río, Milan, 29 Dec. 1866, CMRFH.

7. José Pablo Martínez del Río to Gregorio José Martínez del Río, Milan, 29 Dec. 1866, CMRFH.

8. Gregorio José Martínez del Río to José Pablo Martínez del Río, Mexico City, 28 May 1868, CMRFH.

9. José Pablo Martínez del Río to Armand Montluc, Paris, 27 May 1868, in Tamayo, *Juárez*, pp. 13:347-348.

10. Gregorio José Martínez del Río to José Pablo Martínez del Río, Mexico City, 10, 27 Dec. 1868; 21 Jan., 10, 28 Feb., 10, 28 June, 10 Oct., 28 Dec. 1869; 28 Jan. 1870, CMRFH.

11. Dublán and Lozano, *Legislación mexicana*, vol. 10; *Diaro Oficial* (Mexico City), 2 Jan. 1875; José Pablo Martínez del Río to B. Juárez, Mexico City, Dec. 1870 (draft copy), CMRFH; José Pablo Martínez del Río to M. Romero, Mexico City, 11 Nov. 1871, Archivo Matías Romero, INAH, Mexico City, hereafter cited as AMR; Gregorio José Martínez del Río to José Pablo Martínez del Río, Mexico City, 9 Dec. 1867, CMRFH; AN(PH)-598-1872:836-843 (30 Sep. 1872).

12. Gregorio José Martínez del Río to José Martínez del Río, Mexico City, 10 May 1868, CMRFH.

13. For Gregorio José's problems with his stocks and bonds, see Gregorio José Martínez del Río to José Pablo Martínez del Río, Mexico City, 28 Nov. 1867; 10 May 1868; 21 Jan., 10, 28 Feb., 10 Nov. 1869; and Gregorio José Martínez del Río to S. Williams, Mexico City, 2 July 1870, CMRFH. For the Nauchitila Mining Company, see AN-726-1870:206-211 (27 Aug. 1870). For the sale of Gregorio José's home, see AN-292-1874:529-533 (9 Nov. 1874). For Gregorio José's attempts to become a broker, see Gregorio José Martínez del Río to M. de Castillo, Mexico City, 17 Feb. 1868; and Gregorio José Martínez del Río to José Pablo Martínez del Río, Mexico City, 2 Apr. 1869, CMRFH. For the division of Pedro Ansoátegui's estate, see AN-292-1867:109-110 (1 Dec. 1867). For the mortgage and sale of the Ansoátegui residence, see AN-292-1874:110-114 (2 July 1874); AN-292-1878:385-389 (4 Nov. 1878).

14. Gregorio José Martínez del Río to José Pablo Martínez del Río, Mexico City, 27 Feb. 1868, CMRFH.

15. Gregorio José Martínez del Río v. María Dolores Martínez del Río de Ansoátegui, AJ, Gregorio José Martínez del Río.

16. Pablo Santiago Martínez del Río to Nicolás Martínez del Río, Mexico City, 28 June 1869; José Pablo Martínez del Río to Gregorio José Martínez del Río, Paris, 15 Aug. 1868; Pablo Santiago Martínez del Río to Nicolás Martínez del Río, Stonyhurst College, Eng., 21 June 1872; Pablo Santiago Martínez del Río to Nicolás Martínez del Río, Chihuahua, Mex., 23 July 1884, CMRFH.

17. José Pablo Martínez del Río's will is registered in AN-294-1879:46-49 (25 July 1879); Pablo Santiago Martínez del Rio to Nicolás Martínez del Río, Mexico City, 19 Apr. 1885, CMRFH.

18. Pablo Santiago Martínez del Río to Nicolás Martínez del Río, Chihuahua, Mex., 9 Aug. 1884, CMRFH.

Bibliography

Primary Sources

Archival Materials

Archive of Carlos Martínez del Río y Fernández de Henestrosa. Mexico City (CMRFH)
Archivo General de la Nación. Mexico City
    Cartas de Seguridad
    Pasaportes
    Tabaco
Archivo General de Notarías. Mexico City (AN)
    Protocolos
Archivo Judicial del Tribunal Superior de Justicia del D.F. Mexico City (AJ)
    Manuela Azcárate
    Concursos
    Gregorio Martínez
    Ventura Martínez
    Pablo Martínez del Río
Archivo Matías Romero, INAH, Mexico City (AMR)
Archivo de la Secretaría de Relaciones Exteriores. Mexico City (SRE)
    Archivo (S)
    Archivo Histórico (A)
Public Record Office. London
    Foreign Office Correspondence 50, 204, 207

Secondary Sources

Published Materials

Alamán, Lucas. *Historia de Méjico desde los primeros movimientos que preparon su independencia en el año de 1808, hasta la época presente.* 5 vols. Mexico City: J .M. Lara, 1849-1852.
Almada, Francisco R. *Juárez y Terrazas: aclaraciones históricas.* Mexico City: Libros Mexicanos, 1958.

Altman, Ida. "A Family and Region in the Northern Fringe Lands: The Marqueses de Aguayo of Nuevo León and Coahuila." In *Provinces of Mexico: Variants of Spanish American Regional Evolution*, edited by Ida Altman and James Lockhart, pp. 253-277. Berkeley & Los Angeles: University of California Press, 1976.

Altman, Ida, and James Lockhart, eds. *Provinces of Mexico: Variants of Spanish American Regional Evolution*. Berkeley & Los Angeles: University of California Press, 1976.

Anon. *Representación al supremo gobierno de los empresarios de fábricas nacionales de hilados y tejidos de algodón*. Mexico City, 1840.

Antuñano, Estevan de. *Economía política. Refutación que el que subscribe hace, por notas, del artículo del Monitor de Veracruz de fecha 24 de agosto, sobre importación de algodones extranjeros en rama*. Puebla, 1840.

Arnold, Linda. "Social, Economic, and Political Status in the Mexico City Bureaucracy, 1808-1822." In *Labor and Laborers through Mexican History*, edited by Elsa Cecilia Frost, Michael C. Meyer, and Josefina Zoraida Vásquez, pp. 281-310. Tucson: University of Arizona Press, 1979.

Arosemena, Justo. *Apelación al buen sentido i a la consciencia pública en la cuestión "acreencia mejicana."* Bogotá: Echeverría Hermanos, 1857.

Arrom, Silvia M. *La mujer mexicana ante el divorcio eclesiástico (1800-1857)*. Mexico City: Secretaría de Educación Pública, 1976.

———. "Women and the Family in Mexico City, 1800-1857." Ph.D. diss., Stanford University, 1978.

Bailyn, Bernard. "Kinship and Trade in Seventeenth Century New England." In *Explorations in Enterprise*, edited by Hugh G. J. Aitken, pp. 296-308. Cambridge: Harvard University Press, 1965.

———. *The New England Merchants in the Seventeenth Century*. New York: Harper & Row, 1965.

Bakewell, Peter J. *Silver Mining and Society in Colonial Mexico: Zacatecas, 1546-1700*. Cambridge: At the University Press, 1971.

Balmori, Diana, and Robert Oppenheimer. "Family Clusters: Generational Nucleation in Nineteenth-Century Argentina and Chile." *Comparative Studies in Society and History* 2:2:231-261 (1979).

Barker, Nancy M. *The French Experience in Mexico, 1821-1861: A History of Constant Misunderstanding*. Chapel Hill: University of North Carolina Press, 1979.

Barrett, Ward J. *The Sugar Hacienda of the Marqueses del Valle*. Minneapolis: University of Minnesota Press, 1970.

Barth, Frederick. *The Role of the Entrepreneur in Social Change in Northern Norway*. Oslo: Universitetsforlaget, 1967.

Bazant, Jan. *A Concise History of Mexico from Hidalgo to Cárdenas*. Cambridge: At the University Press, 1977.

———. "Estudio sobre la productividad de la industria algodonera mexicana en 1843-1845." In *La industria nacional y el comercio exterior (1842-1851)*, pp. 29-85. Mexico City: Banco Nacional del Comercio Exterior, 1962.

———. "Evolución de la industria textil poblana (1554-1845)." *HM* 13:4:473-516 (Apr.-June 1964).

_____. *Historia de la deuda exterior de Mexico (1823-1946)*. Mexico City: El Colegio de México, 1968.

_____. "Industria algodonera poblana de 1803-1843 en números." *HM* 14:1:131-143 (July-Sep. 1964).

Beato, Guillermo. "La casa Martínez del Río: del comercio colonial a la industria fabril. 1829-1864." In *Formación y desarrollo de la burguesía de México. siglo xix*, edited by Margarita Urías Hermosillo et al., pp. 57-107. Mexico City: Siglo Veintiuno, 1978.

_____. "La tercera generación de los Martínez del Río." Mexico 1979 (typescript).

Blank, Stephanie. "Patrons, Clients, and Kin in Seventeenth-Century Caracas: A Methodological Essay in Colonial Spanish American Social History." *HAHR* 54:2:260-283 (May 1974).

Bock, Carl H. *Prelude to Tragedy: Negotiation and Breakdown of the Tripartite Convention of London, October 31, 1861*. Philadelphia: University of Pennsylvania Press, 1960.

Boyer, Richard E. "Las ciudades mexicanas: perspectivas de estudio en el siglo XIX." *HM* 22:2:142-159 (Oct.-Dec. 1972).

Brading, David A. *Miners and Merchants in Bourbon Mexico, 1763-1810*. Cambridge: At the University Press, 1971.

Brown, Jonathan C. *A Socio-Economic History of Argentina, 1776-1860*. Cambridge: At the University Press, 1979.

Bustamante, Carlos María de. *Apuntes para la historia del gobierno del general D. Antonio López del Santa-Anna, desde principios de octobre de 1841 hasta 6 de diciembre de 1844, en que fué despuesto del mando por uniforme voluntad de la nación*. Mexico City: J. M. Lara, 1845.

Calcott, Wilfred H. *Church and State in Mexico, 1822-1857*. Durham, N.C.: Duke University Press, 1926.

_____. *Santa Anna: The Story of an Enigma Who Once Was Mexico*. Norman: University of Oklahoma Press, 1936.

Cancian, Francesa M., Louis Wolf Goodman, and Peter H. Smith. "Capitalism, Industrialization, and Kinship in Latin America: Major Issues." *JFH* 3 (Winter 1978):319-338.

Carlos, Manuel L., and Lois Sellers. "Family, Kinship Structure, and Modernization in Latin America." *LARR* 7 (Summer 1972):95-124.

Chandler, Billy J. *The Feitosas and Sertão dos Inhamuns: The History of a Family and a Community in Northeast Brazil, 1700-1930*. Gainesville: University of Florida Press, 1972.

Coatsworth, John H. *From Backwardness to Underdevelopment: The Mexican Economy, 1810-1910*. New York: Columbia University Press, forthcoming.

_____. "The Impact of Railroads on the Economic Development of Mexico, 1877-1910." Ph.D. diss., University of Wisconsin, 1972.

_____. "Obstacles to Economic Growth in Nineteenth-Century Mexico." *AHR* 83:1:80-100 (Feb. 1978).

Costeloe, Michael P. *Church and State in Independent Mexico: A Study of the Patronage Debate, 1821-1857*. London: Royal Historical Society, 1978.

_____. *Church Wealth in Mexico: A Study of the Juzgado de Capellanías in the Archbishopric of Mexico, 1800-1856*. Cambridge: At the University Press,1971.

_____. *La primera república federal de México, 1824-1835.* Mexico City: Fondo de Cultura Económica, 1975.

Cumberland, Charles C. *Mexico: The Struggle for Modernity.* New York: Oxford University Press, 1968.

Díaz, Lilia. *Versión francesa de México. Informes diplomáticos. 1853-1864.* 3 vols. Mexico City: El Colegio de México, 1963-1965.

Di Tella, Torcuato S. "The Dangerous Classes in Early Nineteenth Century Mexico." *JLAS* 5:79-105 (May 1973).

Dublán, Manuel, and José María Lozano. *Legislación mexicana ó colección de las disposiciones legislativas expendidas desde la independencia de la república.* 34 vols. Mexico City: Imprenta del Comercio, 1876-1904.

Erville, Levi D. "The Prados of São Paulo: An Elite Brazilian Family in a Changing Society, 1840-1930." Ph.D. diss., Yale University, 1974.

Felstiner, Mary L. "Kinship Politics in the Chilean Independence Movement." *HAHR* 56:1:58-80 (Feb. 1976).

Fonseca, Fabián de, and Carlos de Urrutia. *Historia general del real hacienda.* Mexico City: Vicente García Torres, 1845-1853.

Fortes, Meyer. *Time and Social Structure and Other Essays.* London: Atlone Press, 1970.

Foster, George M. "Cofradía and Compadrazgo in Spain and Spanish America." *Southwest Journal of Anthropology* 9:1-21 (Spring 1953).

Frank, André Gunder. *Capitalism and Underdevelopment in Latin America.* New York: Monthly Review Press, 1967.

Gibb, George S. *The Saco-Lowell Shops: Textile Machinery Building in New England, 1813-1949.* Cambridge: Harvard University Press, 1950.

Gibson, Charles. *The Aztecs under Spanish Rule: A History of the Indians of the Valley of Mexico.* Stanford, Cal.: Stanford University Press, 1964.

Glade, William P. *The Latin American Economies: A Study of Their Institutional Evolution.* New York: Van Nostrand, 1969.

Goode, William J. *World Revolution and Family Patterns.* New York: Free Press of Glencoe, 1963.

Great Britain. Foreign Office. *A Complete Collection of the Treaties and Conventions and Reciprocal Regulations at Present Subsiding between Great Britain and Foreign Powers.* Vol. 12. London, 1871.

Greenfield, Sidney M., Arnold Strickon, and Robert T. Aubey, eds. *Entrepreneurs in Cultural Context.* Albuquerque: University of New Mexico Press, 1979.

Greenow, Linda. *Credit and Socio-economic Change in Colonial Mexico: Loans and Mortgages in Guadalajara, 1720-1820.* Boulder: Westview Press, 1983.

Hale, Charles A. *Mexican Liberalism in the Age of Mora, 1821-1853.* New Haven, Conn.: Yale University Press, 1968.

Hamill, Hugh M. *The Hidalgo Revolt: Prelude to Mexican Independence.* Gainesville: University of Florida Press.

Hareven, Tamara K. "Modernization and Family History: Perspectives in Social Change." *Signs. Journal of Women in Culture and Society* 2:190-206 (Autumn 1976).

Harris, Charles H., III. *A Mexican Family Empire: The Latifundia of the Sánchez*

Navarro Family, 1767-1867. Austin: University of Texas Press, 1975.

Hart, Donn Vorhis. *Compadrinazgo: Ritual Kinship in the Philippines.* DeKalb: Northern Illinois University Press, 1977.

Haslip, Joan. *The Crown of Mexico: Maximilian and His Empress Carlota.* New York: Holt, Rinehart & Winston, 1971.

Henry, Robert S. *The Story of the Mexican War.* Indianapolis: Bobbs-Merrill, 1950.

Hoberman, Louisa Schell. "Merchants in Seventeenth-Century Mexico: A Preliminary Portrait." *HAHR* 57:3:479-503 (Aug. 1977).

Hu-DeHart, Evelyn. "Development and Rural Rebellion: Pacification of the Yaquis in the Late Porfiriato." *HAHR* 54:1:72-93 (Feb. 1974).

_____. *Missionaries, Miners, and Indians: Spanish Contact with the Yaqui Nation of Northwestern New Spain, 1533-1820.* Tucson: University of Arizona Press, 1981.

Humboldt, Alexander von. *Political Essay on the Kingdom of New Spain.* 4 vols. Translated by John Black. London: Longman, Hurst, Rees, Orme, & Brown, 1811.

Ianni, Francis A. J. *A Family Business: Kinship and Social Control in Organized Crime.* New York: Russell Sage Foundation, 1972.

Keesing, Roger M. *Kin Groups and Social Structure.* New York: Holt, Rinehart & Winston, 1975.

Kennedy, John N. "Bahian Elites, 1750-1822." *HAHR* 53:3:415-439 (Aug. 1973).

Keremitsis, Dawn. *La industria textil mexicana en el siglo xix.* Mexico City: Secretaría de Educación Pública, 1973.

Kicza, John E. *Colonial Entrepreneurs: Families and Business in Bourbon Mexico City.* Albuquerque: University of New Mexico Press, 1983.

_____. "The Pulque Trade of Late Colonial Mexico City." *TAm* 37:2:193-221 (Oct. 1980).

Knowlton, Robert J. *Church Property and the Mexican Reform, 1856-1910.* DeKalb: Northern Illinois University Press, 1976.

Kriesberg, Louis. "Entrepreneurs in Latin America and the Role of Culture and Situational Processes." *International Social Science Journal* 15:581-596 (Autumn 1963).

Kuznesof, Elizabeth A. "The Role of Merchants in the Economic Development of São Paulo, 1765-1836." *HAHR* 60:4:571-593 (Nov. 1980).

Ladd, Doris M. *The Mexican Nobility at Independence, 1780-1826.* Latin American Monographs, no. 40. Austin, Tex.: Institute of Latin American Studies, 1976.

Lindley, Richard B. *Haciendas and Economic Development: Guadalajara, Mexico, at Independence.* Latin American Monographs, no. 58. Austin, Tex.: University of Texas Press, 1983.

_____. "Kinship and Credit in the Structure of Guadalajara's Oligarchy, 1807-1830." Ph.D. diss., University of Texas at Austin, 1976.

Lomnitz Adler, Larissa, and Marisol Pérez Lizaur. "The History of a Mexican Urban Family." *JFH* 3 (Winter 1978):392-409.

López Rosado, Diego G. *Historia y pensamiento económico de México.* 5 vols. Mexico City: Universidad Nacional Autónoma de México, 1969.

Lynch, John. *The Spanish American Revolutions, 1808-1826.* New York: Norton, 1973.

Mandel, Ernest. *Long Waves of Capitalist Development: The Marxist Interpretation.* New York: Cambridge University Press, 1978.

Martínez del Río, [José] Pablo. *Curso de agricultura. Cultivo de algodón.* Mexico City: G. A. Esteva, 1882.

[Martínez del Río Hermanos]. *Contestación de los agentes de la convención inglesa á la memoria del señor Payno.* Mexioc City: J. M. Fernández de Lara, 1855.

Martínez del Río y Fernández de Henestrosa, Carlos. "Memorandum. Los derechos que los señores Martínez del Río tienen en contra de la república del Ecuador por el parte que a dicho país corresponde pagar a consecuencia del emprestito hecho por México á Colombia en 1826." Mexico City, July 1971 (typescript).

Marx, Karl. *Capital: A Critique of Political Economy.* New York: Charles H. Kerr, 1906.

Marzahl, Peter. "Creoles in Government: The Cabildo of Popayán." *HAHR* 54:4:636-656 (Nov. 1974).

————. *Town in the Empire: Government, Politics, and Society in Seventeenth-Century Popayán.* Latin American Monographs, no. 45. Austin, Tex.: Institute of Latin American Studies, 1978.

Meyer, Jean. *Problemas campesinos y revueltas agrarias, 1821-1910.* Mexico City: Secretaría de Educación Pública, 1973.

Meyer, Michael C., and William L. Sherman. *The Course of Mexican History.* 2d ed. New York: Oxford University Press, 1983.

Meyer, Rosa María. "Los Béistegui, especuladores y mineros: 1830-1869." In *Formación y desarrollo de la burguesía en México: Siglo xix*, edited by Margarita Urías Hermosillo et al., pp. 108-139. Mexico City: Siglo Veintiuno, 1978.

Mexico. Ministerio de Fomento. *Estado de las fábricas de hilados y tejidos existentes en la república mexicana.* Mexico City: Imprenta del Gobierno, 1854.

Mexico. Ministerio de Hacienda y Crédito Público. *Contrato de compañía celebrado por el supremo gobierno, para la administración y giro de la renta del tabaco y exposición con que lo remitió á las cámaras el secretario del despacho de hacienda.* Mexico City: Imprenta de la Calle de Medinas, 1848.

————. *Memoria* (Dec. 1855-May 1856). Mexico City: I. Cumplido, 1857.

————. *Memoria* (1869-1870). Mexico City: Imprenta del Gobierno, 1870.

————. *Memoria* (1883-1884). Mexico City: Imprenta del Gobierno, 1884.

Mexico. Secretaría de Relaciones Interiores y Exteriores. *Documento no. 4 de la memoria que el secretario de relaciones interiores y esteriores presentó á las cámaras, en que se da cuenta de los arreglos hechos para el pago de la deuda garantizada por convenciones diplomáticas.* Mexico City, 1852.

Mier y Terán, Gregorio, et al. *Representación dirigida al sr. presidente de la república por los apoderados de los acreedores que tienen hipotecas sobre las aduanas marítimas.* Mexico City: I. Cumplido, 1842.

Monroy Huitrón, Guadalupe, ed. *Archivo histórico de Matías Romero; catálago descriptivo: correspondencia recibida.* Vol. 1. Mexico City: Banco de México, 1965.

Morales, María Dolores. "Francisco Somera y el primer fraccionamiento de la ciudad de México. 1840-1889." In *Formación y desarrollo de la burguesía en México: Siglo xix*, edited by Margarita Urías Hermosillo et al., pp. 188-230. Mexico City: Siglo Veintiuno, 1978.

Moreno Toscano, Alejandra. "Cambios en los patrones de urbanización en México, 1810-1910." *HM* 22:2:160-187 (Oct.-Dec. 1972).

Mörner, Magnus. "Economic Factors and Stratification in Colonial Spanish America with Special Reference to Elites." *HAHR* 63:2:335-3570 (May 1983).

Navin, Thomas R. *The Whitin Machine Works since 1830: A Textile Machinery Company in an Industrial Village*. Cambridge: Harvard University Press, 1950.

Nunn, Charles F. *Foreign Immigrants in Early Bourbon Mexico: 1700-1760*. Cambridge: At the University Press, 1979.

Nutini, Hugo G., Pedro Carrasco, and James M. Taggart. *Essays on Mexican Kinship*. Pittsburgh: University of Pittsburgh Press, 1976.

Payno, Manuel. "Memoria sobre la convención inglesa: créditos de Martínez del Río Hermanos." *La Patria* (Mexico City), 11 Nov. 1855.

Pletcher, David M. *The Diplomacy of Annexation: Texas, Oregon, and the Mexican War*. Columbia: University of Missouri Press, 1972.

Porter, Kenneth Wiggins. *The Jacksons and the Lees: Two Generations of Massachusetts Merchants, 1765-1884*. 2 vols. Cambridge: Harvard University Press, 1937.

Portilla, Anselmo de la. *Méjico en 1856 y 1857. Gobierno del general Comonfort*. New York: S. Hallet, 1858.

Potash, Robert A. *El banco de avío de México*. Mexico City: Fondo de Cultura Económica, 1957.

————. *Mexican Government and Industrial Development in the Early Republic: The Banco de Avío*. Amherst: University of Massachusetts Press, 1983.

Rabb, Theodore K., and Robert I. Rotberg, eds. *The Family in History: Interdisciplinary Essays*. New York: Harper & Row, 1973.

Randall, Robert W. *Real del Monte: A British Mining Venture in Mexico*. Latin American Monographs, no. 26. Austin, Tex.: University of Texas Press, 1972.

Reber, Vera B. *British Mercantile Houses in Buenos Aires, 1810-1880*. Cambridge: Harvard University Press, 1979.

Reed, Nelson. *The Caste War of the Yucatan*. Stanford, Cal.: Stanford University Press, 1964.

Robertson, William S. *Iturbide of Mexico*. Durham, N.C.: Duke University Press, 1952.

Safford, Frank. *Aspectos del siglo XIX en Colombia*. Medellín, Colombia: Ediciones Hombre Nuevo, 1977.

————. "Merchants in Nineteenth-Century Colombia." Paper presented to the Economic History Seminar, University of Chicago, 1978 (typescript).

Scharrer, Beatriz. "Un empresario agrícola alemán en el siglo XIX." Mexico City, 1979 (typescript).

Schumpeter, Joseph A. *Theorie der wirtschaftlichen entwicklung*. Leipzig: Dunker & Humblot, 1912.

Semo, Enrique. *Historia del capitalismo en México*. Mexico City: Ediciones Era, 1973.

Shafer, Robert. *Economic Societies in the Spanish World*. Syracuse: University of

Syracuse Press, 1958.

Sims, Harold. *La expulsión de los españoles de México, 1821-1828.* Mexico City: Fondo de Cultura Económica, 1974.

Sinkin, Richard N. *The Mexican Reform, 1855-1876: A Study in Liberal Nation-Building.* Latin American Monographs, no. 49. Austin, Tex.: Institute of Latin American Studies, 1979.

Smelser, Neil J., ed. *Karl Marx on Society and Social Change.* Chicago: University of Chicago Press, 1973.

————. *The Sociology of Economic Life.* 2d ed. Englewood Cliffs, N.J.: Prentice-Hall, 1976.

Smith, Raymond T. "The Family and the Modern World System: Some Observations from the Caribbean." *JFH* 3:337-360 (Winter 1978).

Socolow, Susan M. "The Economic Activities of the Porteño Merchants: The Viceregal Period." *HAHR* 55:1:1-24 (Feb. 1975).

————. "Marriage, Birth, and Inheritance: The Merchants of Eighteenth Century Buenos Aires." *HAHR* 60:3:387-406 (Aug. 1980).

————. *The Merchants of Buenos Aires, 1778-1810: Family and Commerce.* Cambridge: At the University Press, 1978.

Stein, Stanley J. "Bureaucracy and Business in the Spanish Empire, 1759-1804." *HAHR* 61:1:2-28 (Feb. 1981).

Sweezy, Paul M. *The Theory of Capitalist Development: Principles of Marxian Political Economy.* New York: Oxford University Press, 1942.

Tamayo, Jorge L., ed. *Benito Juárez: documentos, discursos, y correspondencia.* 13 vols. Mexico City: Editorial Diana, 1963-1968.

Tenenbaum, Barbara A. "Merchants, Money, and Mischief: The British in Mexico, 1821-1862." *TAm* 35:1:317-340.

Thompson, Guy P. C. "The Cotton Textile Industry in Puebla during the 18th and 19th Centuries." Paper presented at Bielefeld, W. Germany, September 1982.

————. "Traditional and Modern Manufacturing in Mexico, 1821-50." Paper presented at Berlin, September 1983.

Timmons, Wilbert A. *Morelos: Priest, Soldier, Statesman of Mexico.* El Paso, Tex.: Western College Press, 1963.

Tutino, John M. "Creole Mexico: Spanish Elites, Haciendas, and Indian Towns, 1750-1810." Ph.D. diss., University of Texas at Austin, 1976.

————. "Hacienda Social Relations in Mexico: The Chalco Region in the Era of Independence." *HAHR* 55:3:496-528 (Aug. 1975).

————. "Power, Class, and Family: Men and Women in the Mexican Elite, 1750-1810." *TAm* 39:3:359-381 (Jan. 1983).

Twinam, Ann. *Miners, Merchants, and Farmers in Colonial Colombia.* Latin American Monographs, no. 57. Austin: University of Texas Press, 1982.

Urías Hermosillo, Margarita, et al. *Formación y desarrollo de la burguesía en México: siglo xix.* Introduction by Ciro F. S. Cardoso. Mexico City: Siglo Veintiuno, 1978.

————. "Militares y comerciantes en México, 1830-1846: las mercancías de la nacionalidad." Paper presented to the V Simposio de Historia Económica de CLACSO, Lima, Peru, April 1978.

Van Young, Eric. *Hacienda and Market in Eighteenth-Century Mexico: The*

Rural Economy of the Guadalajara Region, 1675-1820. Berkeley & Los Angeles: University of California Press, 1981.

Voss, Stuart. *On the Periphery of Nineteenth-Century Mexico: Sonora and Sinaloa 1810-1877.* Tucson: University of Arizona Press, 1982.

Walker, David W. "Business as Usual: The Empresa del Tabaco in Mexico, 1837-1844." *HAHR* 64:4:675-705 (Nov. 1984).

_____. "Kinship, Business, and Politics: The Martínez del Río Family in Mexico, 1824-1864." Ph.D. diss., University of Chicago, 1981.

_____. "Las ubérrimas ubres del estado."*Nexos* 2:2:15-18 (Feb. 1979).

Wallerstein, Immanuel M. *The Modern World-System.* 2 vols. New York: Academic Press, 1976, 1980.

Wasserman, Mark. *Capitalists, Caciques, and Revolution: The Native Elite and Foreign Enterprise in Chihuahua, 1854-1911.* Chapel Hill: University of North Carolina Press, 1984.

Weber, Max. *The Protestant Ethic and the Spirit of Capitalism.* Translated by Talcott Parsons. New York: C. Scribner, 1958.

Wells, Alan. "Family Elites in a Boom-and-Bust Economy: The Molinas and Peóns of Porfirian Mexico." *HAHR* 62:2:224-253 (May 1982).

Willie [Wylie], Robert C. *México. Noticia sobre su hacienda pública bajo el gobierno colonial y después de la independencia.* Mexico City: I. Cumplido, 1845.

Wolf, Eric R. "Kinship, Friendship, and Patron-Client Relations in Complex Societies." In *The Social Anthropology of Complex Societies*, edited by Michael Banton, pp. 1-32. New York: Houghton Mifflin, 1966.

Woodward, Ralph L. "The Merchants and Economic Development in the Americas, 1750-1850." *JLAS* 10:1968:134-153.

Zeitlin, Maurice, and Richard E. Radcliff. "Research Methods for the Analysis of the Internal Structure of Dominant Classes: The Case of Landlords and Capitalists in Chile." *LARR* 10:3:5-61 (1975).

Newspapers

El Monitor Republicano (Mexico City), 1850-1856.
La Patria (Mexico City), 1855-1856.

Index

Lightning Source UK Ltd.
Milton Keynes UK
UKOW02f0859010916

281972UK00001B/37/P

9 781477 306499